MW01193174

# The
# BAREFOOT
# ARCHITECT

## A Handbook for Green Building

## by Johan van Lengen

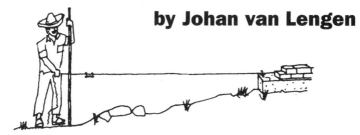

Shelter Publications
Bolinas, California, U.S.A.

This English edition is published by Shelter Publications, Inc., Bolinas, California, USA and is the result of revisions and additions to the following publications: .

Distributed in the United States by Publishers Group West and in Canada by Publishers Group Canada

1: *Manual del Arquitecto Descalzo,* published for Secretaria de Assentamientos Humanos y Obras Públicas do México, 1981; 2: *Manual del Arquitecto Descalzo,* Editorial Concepto, México, 1982; 3: *Cantos del Arquitecto Descalzo,* published for Secretaria de Educación Pública do México, 1991; 4: *Manual do Arquiteto Descalço,* published for Papéis e Cópias de Botafogo e TIBÁ - Instituto de Tecnologia Intuitiva e Bio-Arquitetura, Brasil, 1997; 5: *Manual do Arquiteto Descalço,* published for Casa do Sonho, Brasil, 2002; 6: *Manual do Arquiteto Descalço,* published by Livraria do Arquiteto e TIBÁ, Brasil, 2004.

**Library of Congress Cataloging in Publication Data**
Lengen, Johan van.
   [Manual del arquitecto descalzo. English]
     Handbook for the barefoot architect / Johan van Lengen.
       p.  cm.
   Includes bibliographical references and index.
   ISBN-13: 978-0-936070-42-1 (alk. paper)
   ISBN-10: 0-936070-42-0 (alk. paper)
   1. Sustainable buildings—Design and construction.   2. Sustainable architecture.   I. Title.
TH4860.L46 2008
720'.47—dc22
                                      2007035835

12 11 10 − 17 16 15
(Lowest digits indicate number and year of latest printing.)

Printed in the United States of America on acid-free Glatfelter Natures Book B-05 recycled paper, 50% post-consumer waste, ECF, and GPI-approved


Shelter Publications, Inc., P.O. Box 279, Bolinas, California 94924 USA
Phone: 415-868-0280    Orders, toll-free: 1-800-307-0131
Email: shelter@shelterpub.com

Visit our website
**SHELTER ONLINE**
http://www.shelterpub.com

I dedicate this book to the memory of Rose.

# TABLE OF CONTENTS

# PREFACE

Johan van Lengen is much more than just an architect. He is a builder of communities. In 1987, van Lengen and his wife Rose created the Brazilian community of Centro de Tecnologia Intuitiva e Bio-Arquitetura (TIBÁ), a school for building devoted to teaching the harmonious integration of the human being with the environment.

What is different about van Lengen's approach is that he puts humans at the center of the discussion, pointing out that it is we who are responsible for building the future.

We cannot escape the fact that we are responsible for the health of our planet. As we are painfully aware these days, unchecked progress is leading to environmental devastation. If this destructive growth in cities and the surrounding countryside does not correspond to global human aspirations, wouldn't it be wise to somehow reduce its pace? This is a question for reflection, and van Lengen's work is a great inspiration in this ongoing debate.

Implicit in van Lengen's method is his clear desire for simplicity. This is one of his qualities that I most admire, and an attribute that I fervently believe in, both in my personal and professional life. I have always made simplicity the foundation of my future.

Unfortunately, this attitude sometimes creates difficulties because many people seek solutions that give them material benefits, or have the illusion that it is more glamorous to accumulate grandiose and expensive possessions.

The world today is full of people who promote the idea that everything in life must be complex; but these salesmen of complexities don't realize that by starting from simple, easy-to-implement elements, we shall have a more advanced, sustainable system in the future.

Van Lengen teaches us the essence of building, reminding us of the validity of each of the basic elements: design, materials, doors and windows, water, climate, site layout, heat, sanitary facilities, and even stoves.

The great value of this book lies in the way the author explains his concepts. Using vital, basic language and clear, simple drawings, van Lengen prepares his readers for the building process. Thus, this apparently technical book becomes seductive, making the reader savor every aspect of construction, giving value to each step of the project: space layout, what materials to use, and the site preparation. The author's unique idea here is that building will be in harmony only when it is done in a responsible and compassionate manner.

Johan van Lengen did not write this book to seduce the reader with suave poetry. Rather, his book gives us a very strong message — that when you build a house, you are at the same time making a home, and that a grouping of homes, each with its own harmony, will comprise a harmonious community, a productive and healthy settlement of human beings.

Jaime Lerner, Architect
Curitiba, Brazil

# INTRODUCTION

This manual is for those of you who dream of building a home. I will describe the relationship between a house and its environment: the limitations, and the possibilities. I hope that consulting this book will help you find solutions in realizing your dream.

The information presented in this book is mainly graphic. I believe that simple perspective drawings such as these convey information better than page after page of words. *The Barefoot Architect* is meant not only for individual owner-builders, but also for governmental "sweat equity" programs that require the participation of owner/builders in the community.

I do not necessarily mean to persuade you to build your home in a vernacular manner. The world has changed much; often there are not suitable materials or the skills necessary for vernacular building. In many cases, adhering resolutely to traditional building methods will prove frustrating. The manual is meant to answer the realistic challenges in present-day construction, and to suggest practical solutions by combining traditional and modern techniques. At the same time, I do not mean to imply that these proposed alternative methods will automatically produce a miraculous shelter; rather that a combination of these techniques will guide you in providing a harmonious living environment.

The phrase "barefoot architect" was inspired by the first architects, living in the distant past, who mixed adobe by treading mud with their bare feet. Barefoot architects produced the most incredible buildings of antiquity, such as the Hanging Gardens of Babylon.

## HOW TO USE THIS BOOK

This manual does not propose rigid rules for building, but instead shows many ways of building a house while using a wide range of materials, thus giving you a great variety of choices in its construction.

Where you do not do all the building yourself, understanding the concepts and examples in this manual and how these ideas are used during construction will enable you to have a more productive dialogue with the builder in charge.

When using alternative, non-conventional building techniques, you should employ quality-control testing, especially when fabricating critical structural elements. The author is not responsible for any procedure that is not in accordance with accepted structural building safety practices.

Local climate is important to consider when choosing materials and techniques, in order to achieve the greatest environmental harmony with minimum cost.

This book shows a bit of everything. Read all the chapters first before deciding on the most appropriate materials and techniques.

## ACKNOWLEDGMENTS

The people who most inspired me to gather and share this building knowledge were those in rural areas and "low-rent" neighborhoods in the big cities. Their faith in the possibility of improving their living conditions, in spite of the difficulties of their daily lives, became the inspiration for this book.

Obviously, I did not invent all the techniques cited in this book. Quite a few people shared their experiences, and among them I'd like to thank these marvellous people: Álvaro Ortega, Claudio Favier, Gabriel Camara, Gernot Minke, John Turner, Sjoerd Nienhuys, and Yves Cabannes.

The first Spanish edition, produced in Mexico, would not have been at all possible without the loving help of my Carioca wife, Rose.

I am grateful to Carina Rose, an architect from Canada, who translated and prepared the English version from the original Brazilian edition. Also, Aga Probala for her careful revision of the new layout, Veronica Flores for taking care of the legal matters, and my sons, Marc and Peter, who gave their total support in testing the realities of new concepts in the book. Thanks to all of you!

Johan van Lengen
Rio de Janeiro
September, 2007

**Making plans for one year,
we plant rice.**

**Making plans for ten years,
we plant trees.**

**Making plans for one hundred years,
we prepare people.**

—old Chinese saying

# DESIGN

1

# DRAWINGS

A set of drawings is not always needed to build a house. However, drawings are useful to discuss and explain layouts or our ideas to others. Sometimes they are required to apply for financing, to obtain technical advice from a city building department, or to build public buildings such as schools. Therefore for several reasons it may be necessary to put our ideas on paper.

## THE PLAN OF A HOUSE OR BUILDING

There are three basic ways to represent a building design in drawings:

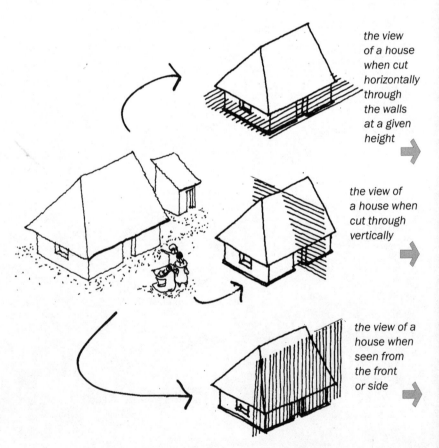

*the view of a house when cut horizontally through the walls at a given height*

*the view of a house when cut through vertically*

*the view of a house when seen from the front or side*

These drawings must show sufficient details to know exactly which steps to follow during construction. The sizes and dimensions of each space and building part must be clearly indicated. On the elevation drawings and the sections, show the heights and dimensions for the floors, roofs, windows and stairs, and provide descriptions of the construction materials.

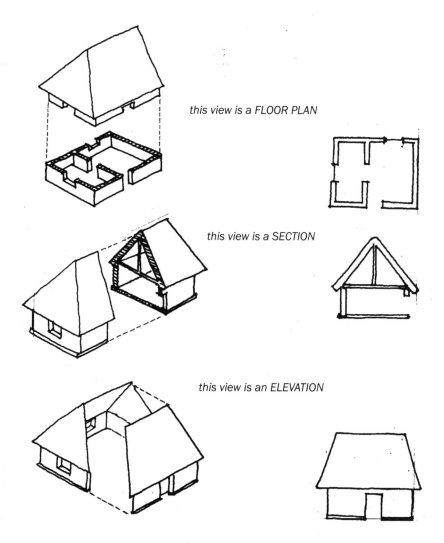

this view is a FLOOR PLAN

this view is a SECTION

this view is an ELEVATION

The locations of doors and windows are indicated on the floor plans:

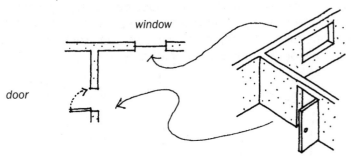

It is necessary to indicate the function of each space as well as sizes from wall to wall:

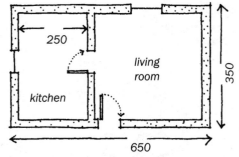

More detailed drawings are required for the builder. These are called working drawings. They contain the location and description of the water and piping distribution system with its fixtures (sinks, showers, taps) and the electrical and wiring system with its components (switches, light outlets).

 The sizes of the shower stalls, toilet bowls and lavatories are drawn to verify that they fit adequately in the bathrooms and kitchens:

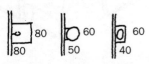

The drawings of a house are drawn at a reduced size and have a scale. A scale is used to create a relationship between the drawing and the real building where the proportions stay the same. For example, if the real window size is one meter high, it is drawn on paper as one centimeter. This scale is one to a hundred (1:100). In other words, when using this size scale, every centimeter on the drawing is equal to one meter of the building.

 The section below shows the heights of the walls and the roof structure:

The types of building materials are also described on the drawings.

 The elevations show the locations of doors and windows and all other project constructions and components that are seen from the exterior.

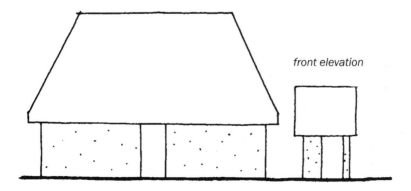

*front elevation*

# 6                                                  DESIGN

## SITE PLAN

A site plan is another type of drawing. It shows the buildings and houses of an area, and the location of the surrounding elements including streets, streams and parks.

The site plan uses symbols to indicate the manmade structures and the natural elements on the property or in the town, such as the ones below.

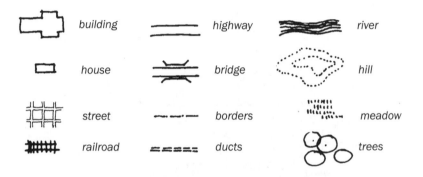

Identify the symbols on this plan...

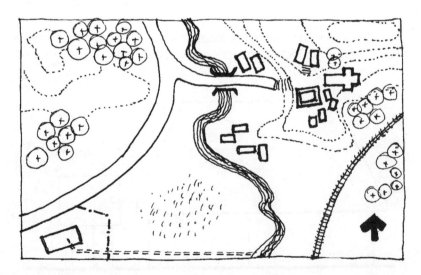

Now compare the previous page with the following perspective drawing of a field with roads, rivers, houses and other elements of the natural environment...

*path of the sun*

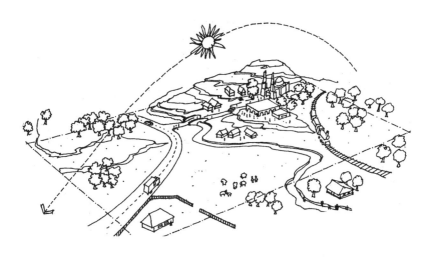

NORTH*

*This applies to the Southern Hemisphere; do the opposite in the Northern Hemisphere.

# HOUSE FORM

In rural zones with hot climates where people spend most of their time outdoors, the roof often covers only two areas of the house: the kitchen area and the bedrooms. The bathroom is sometimes located outside.

The interior walls are usually made with the same materials as the exterior walls, but are thinner and lighter. Built-in floor-to-ceiling cabinets or closets are sometimes used as room dividers.

The entrance doors face the street or, in hotter climates, they are orientated towards the prevailing wind direction to cool the interior spaces when they are open.

## HOW TO DESIGN A HOUSE

The following pages explain how to make a plan of a house and to combine all the necessary spaces.

 There are three basic layouts:

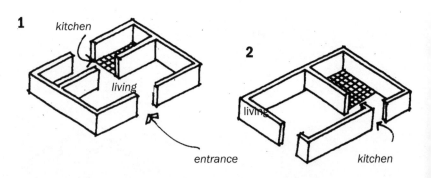

**1** kitchen

living

entrance

living room with a kitchen at the back

**2**

living

kitchen

or with kitchen on the side

Note: These drawings only show the walls at half the full height, as if the house were under construction, in order to better understand the location of the door openings.

**3**

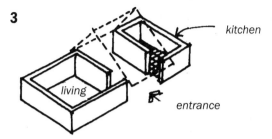

*living room and kitchen separated*

The third layout shows a roof covering the central area between the kitchen and living room. This open room can be used as an area to have meals and as shelter in the long periods of rain.

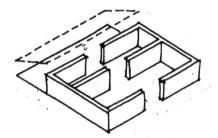

Using the first layout (1), extend the roof towards the back, to create a covered area protected from sun and rain.

Using the second layout (2), there are two ways of providing more sheltered space:

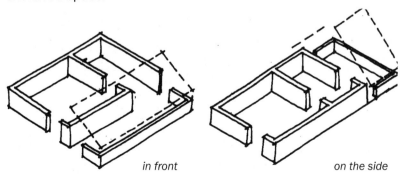

*in front*        *on the side*

Using the same basic layout, add a bathroom:

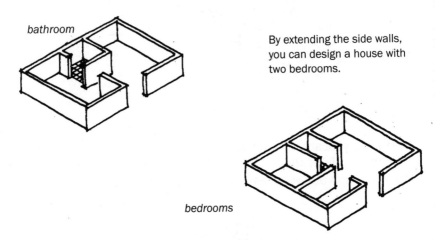

bathroom

By extending the side walls,
you can design a house with
two bedrooms.

bedrooms

A further step would be to provide a separate kitchen by dividing
the cooking area from the living room.

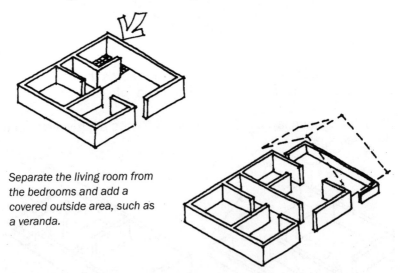

Separate the living room from
the bedrooms and add a
covered outside area, such as
a veranda.

Note: The windows are not shown on these drawings. Their locations depend on the orientation of the rooms to sunlight and wind
direction. See the sections on lighting and ventilation.

The house layout below is often used in the humid tropics on flat sites which have a prevailing lateral breeze:

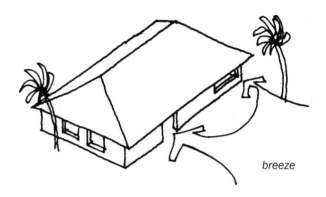

*breeze*

The same type of house has a different layout in a dry tropical zone as shown below – all the rooms are arranged around an interior courtyard:

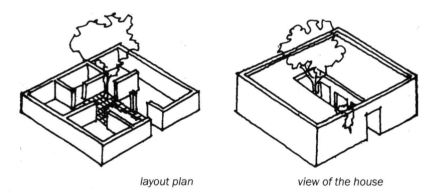

*layout plan*                    *view of the house*

These examples are a few types of layouts, and should not be seen as the only models. Actually every successful space layout should be different, since every design is based on a set of unique conditions, including climate, landscape, vegetation, size of family and their lifestyle, available construction materials and regional construction techniques.

Rectangularly shaped rooms are easy to build and furnish. On the other hand, irregularly shaped areas can provide pleasant surprises when moving from one room to another.

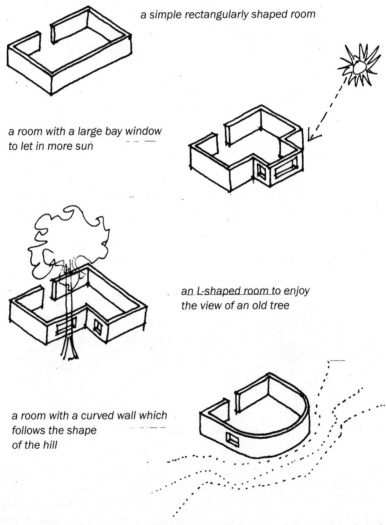

*a simple rectangularly shaped room*

*a room with a large bay window to let in more sun*

*an L-shaped room to enjoy the view of an old tree*

*a room with a curved wall which follows the shape of the hill*

As seen above, the shape of a house is influenced by the land and vegetation of the site.

If the land is on a slope, place the rooms on different levels, and connect these levels with stairs:

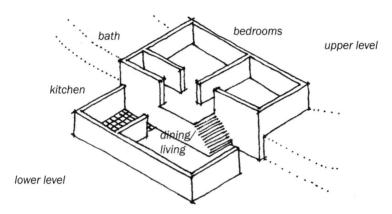

Related spaces should be placed on the same level. The example above shows the kitchen next to the dining area, and the bedrooms near the bathroom.

On a flat site create differently shaped spaces by changing the heights of the ceilings. This improves the airflow through the house, an important consideration in humid tropical zones:

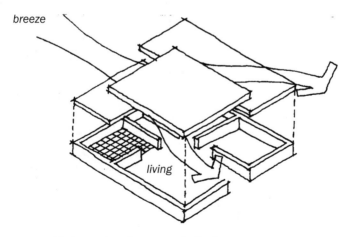

*Breezes are able to reach various areas in the house.*

In an urban setting, where the sizes of the lots are much smaller, a house layout is often distributed on two or several storeys:

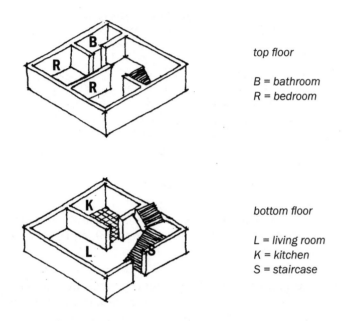

*top floor*

*B = bathroom*
*R = bedroom*

*bottom floor*

*L = living room*
*K = kitchen*
*S = staircase*

*basic layout of a city dwelling*

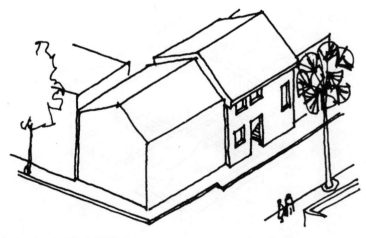

*a house in an urban setting*

The characteristics of the spaces in a house are determined by the lifestyles of the occupants. For those who enjoy preparing meals, a good-sized kitchen is very important. Other people might like the cool night air, so their bedrooms should have a deck or terrace towards a garden, or a large balcony on an upper floor.

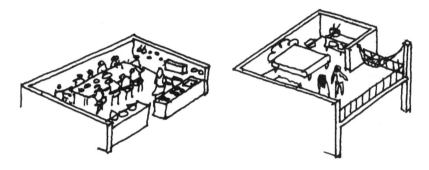

*dining room – kitchen*                         *bedroom – balcony*

When working on the space layout, imagine the way of life of the future inhabitants, and consider the kind of furniture and equipment they may use in their rooms.

The most important outcome of a design is that the occupants enjoy being in their spaces.There is no need to imitate houses from the area, other regions, or cities. The home must be built to satisfy the occupants' own requirements and tastes, without necessarily seeking admiration from the neighbors.

A good layout can save space. For example, well-positioned corridors can take up less space and facilitate access to many rooms. With this saved space there is more area left to make other rooms larger, while still maintaining the overall dimensions of the house.

Compare the two layouts of the house below. Its dimensions are 8m x 7m or 56 square meters.

design A

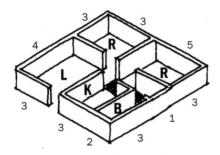

L = living room
K = kitchen
B = bathroom
R = bedroom

corridor: 5 m²
living: 12 m²

design B

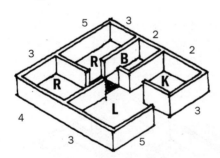

corridor: 2 m²
living: 15 m²

The areas for the bedrooms, bathrooms and kitchens in both designs are the same; however, in design B, the living room is larger by three square meters.

Below are layouts for one-storey houses:

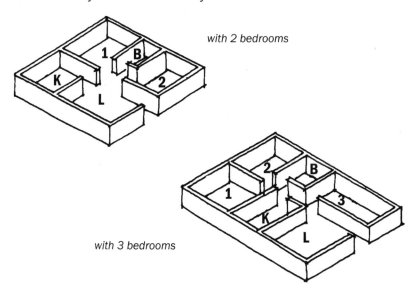

*with 2 bedrooms*

*with 3 bedrooms*

Two-storey houses could be divided like this:

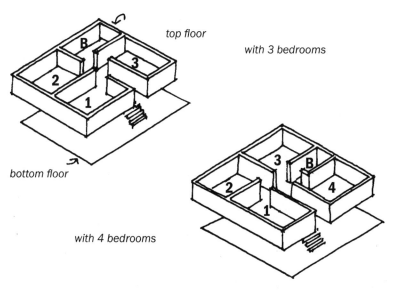

*top floor*

*with 3 bedrooms*

*bottom floor*

*with 4 bedrooms*

The living room and the kitchen are located on the bottom floor.

# HOW TO DESIGN A HOUSE DESIGN

To understand further the design process and how to lay out spaces, follow the example below for a small house, 6m x 9m, with two bedrooms, a living room, one bathroom and a kitchen.

## LAYOUT OF THE SPACES

**1**    Start with the kitchen and bathroom.

**2**    Add the living room

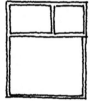

**3**    and then the two bedrooms.

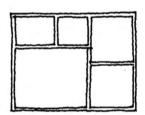

This is a basic layout.

**4**    Now locate doors and windows.

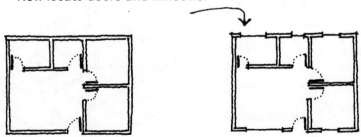

When the land is sloped, rooms can be on different levels and connected by stairs.

*The lined part in this drawing indicates a different level of the house.*

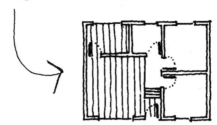

## APPEARANCE

To avoid a house with a box-like appearance, displace or shift some rooms to give the layout an irregular shape. This also makes the form more interesting from the outside.

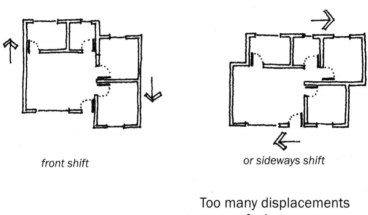

*front shift*                               *or sideways shift*

Too many displacements
are confusing.

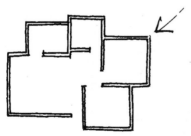

Rounding the corners also gives a
"non-box-like" appearance.

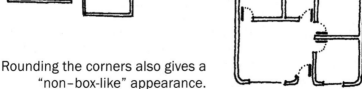

## SITE

The orientation of the house depends firstly on the lot's relationship with street access:

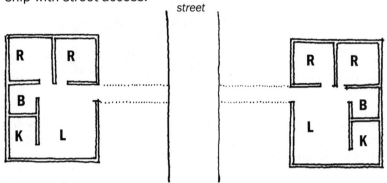

and the path of the sun:

*rising sun*

In dry climates, the rooms are placed around a courtyard:

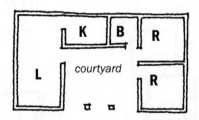

In the example above, the shape of the living room has changed from a square to a rectangle. Being flexible allows for adjustments and the discovery of new possibilities or alternatives during the design and drawing process.

## EXPANSION

The drawing below shows a three-bedroom house instead of the two-bedroom house from previous examples.

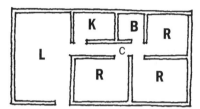

The plan of this house is enlarged to accomodate the additional bedroom. To improve the communication between rooms, a corridor (c) is added. The living room is enlarged, but the extra space could also be used for an entrance porch. In the humid tropics, the upper part of the corridor walls, near the ceiling, is opened to create a cross-ventilation between the rooms.

Another way to enlarge the plan is to project a space outwards from the main rectangle. With this move an additional bedroom is created.

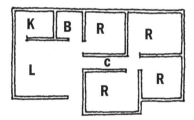

In this layout, the living room and bedrooms are larger. The corridor is L-shaped to provide access to all the rooms.

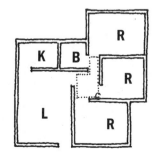

If the previous plan was a little too complicated, move the spaces around slightly, as shown below, to create a clearer plan:

The bedrooms are accessed through the living room and a short corridor (c).

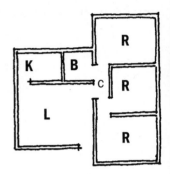

This type of ground-level plan can create diverse and interesting spaces. The same plan can be used on a sloped site with a staircase connecting the upper level to the lower level.

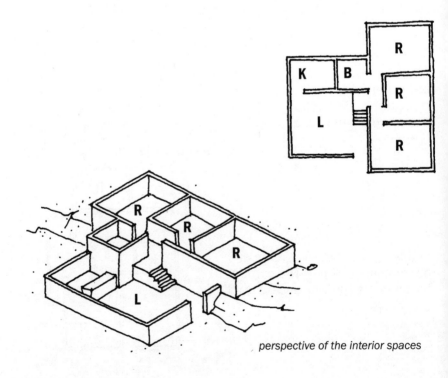

*perspective of the interior spaces*

Our intuition often provides us with an initial good idea. Sometimes it is better to continue to improve on this first idea until it is a satisfactory design instead of trying different solutions. Of course if a plan is not working out, it is preferable to move on to other ideas.

It is difficult to reduce space layouts once they are designed, so start with smaller spaces, and if they need to be larger, increase their size later on.

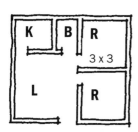
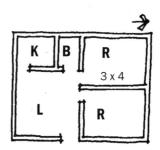

Workshops and stores which are part of a house should be located near the living room area so that their activities do not disturb the privacy of the rest of the house.

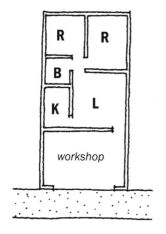
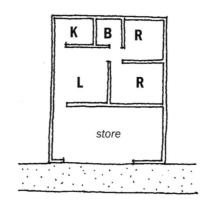

On narrow lots, create interior courtyards between the living spaces and bedrooms to naturally light and ventilate the spaces.

## MODIFYING LAYOUTS

Do not hesitate to move elements around and modify a layout. For example if the windows or doors cannot be located where they are first planned,

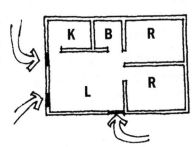

consider placing the kitchen-bathroom on the other side of the living room:

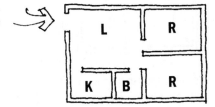

It is important to locate the bedrooms more or less towards the east side so that the occupants wake up with the rising sun. Bedrooms placed on the west side are very warm in the evening when it is time to sleep.

## UPPER FLOOR

On small sites some rooms can be situated on a second storey:

Use the initial plan as a starting point. Place the two bedrooms on the upper storey. The staircase can be against the kitchen-bathroom wall.

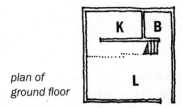

*plan of ground floor*

Use this same wall as a support with handrail to climb the stair. Access to the bedrooms is through a short corridor.

*plan of upper floor*

With one roof over the whole space, the living room can have a high ceiling, and the upper floor can be a mezzanine level. This layout creates a small and comfortable house.

When the site is narrow and sloped, the rooms are laid out one after the other.

To make room for the staircase, the size of the bedrooms is modified from 3m x 3m to 4m x 2.5m.

For a larger three-bedroom house, as seen below, the roof is higher to locate windows in the kitchen and one of the bedrooms.

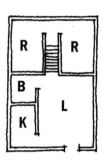

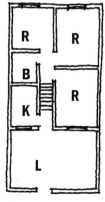

*plan*

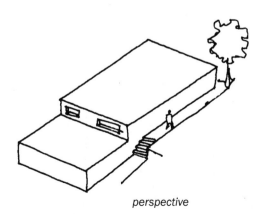

*perspective*

## CLOSETS

The best place for built-in closets is near the entrance of each room, along the partition walls.

*corridor*

The right plan shows a third closet in the corridor.

## DESIGNING A COMFORTABLE HOUSE

It is often believed that a comfortable house is achieved by using expensive materials or with a lot of time and effort. However, the luxury and comfort of a house has no relationship with its size or the type of construction materials. Real luxury means living in a house which perfectly suits your habits and way of life.

The next pages explain how to design your ideal house by realizing your dream spaces. For example, here are:

six spaces to rest, eat, sleep,
work...

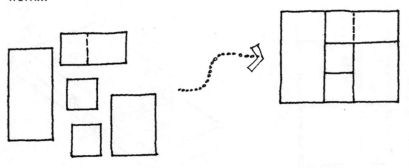

Joined together they make a house.

A plan in perspective:

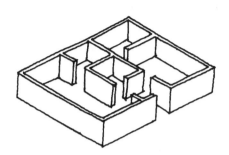

This design does not have any features that draw our attention.

But if the spaces are moved in or out, such as the three rooms below, the shape of the house is slightly changed. This design may be a little more labor intensive, but it is more interesting.

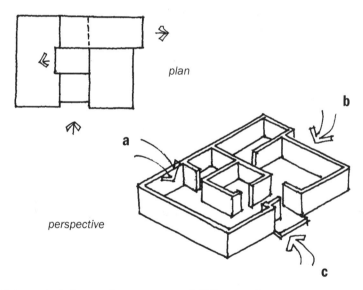

*plan*

*perspective*

This movement generates new possibilities such as:

a. a place for bookcases
b. a wide bench or a veranda
c. a pleasant entrance

## THE LOCAL CLIMATE

In a hot, dry climate where roofs should be flat, the walls can be moved or the ceiling heights varied to create a more attractive facade:

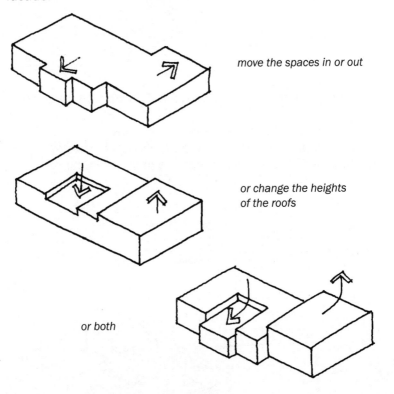

*move the spaces in or out*

*or change the heights of the roofs*

*or both*

In the humid tropics or temperate climates, the roofs are sloped

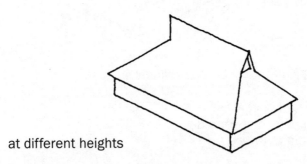

at different heights

with different pitches

or with various types of roofs.

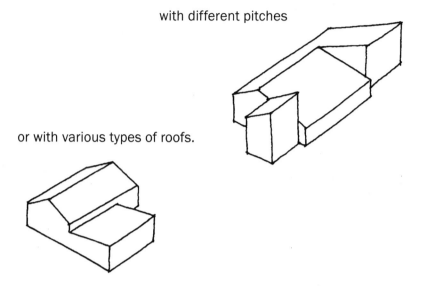

In all climates, beautifully designed house facades can also provide some interesting features. Try integrating:

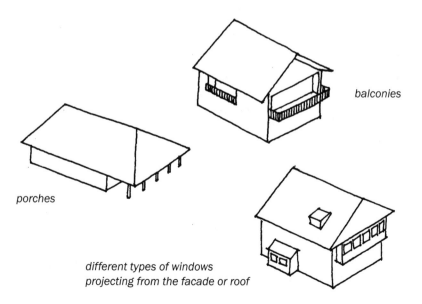

*balconies*

*porches*

*different types of windows
projecting from the facade or roof*

# MODELS

## DESIGNING WITH MODELS

It is sometimes difficult to imagine the outcome of a design in the plans, sections and elevation drawings. A model can help to understand and verify the size of the spaces and the appearance of the house. A good model can be made from cardboard or heavy paper. Below are instructions for making a model at a scale of 1:50.

**1**    Cut 5cm-wide cardboard strips. These represent 2.5-meter-high walls.

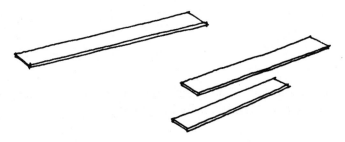

**2**    Draw a sketch of the plan on a sheet of paper. Each meter equals 2cm in the drawing. Leave spaces to show open doors and windows:

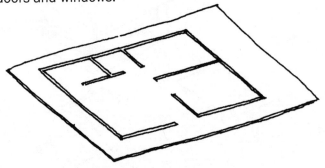

The example above is a typical plan of a house with a living room, two bedrooms, a kitchen and a bathroom.

**3** Cut the strips the same length as the lines of walls on the plan, and glue them onto the lines.

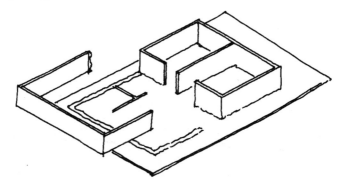

**4** Check if this plan expresses the original idea. It may be necessary to modify or reposition some of the elements of the model, such as doors and walls.

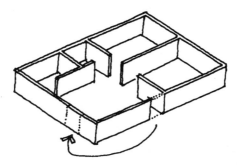

**5** When all the elements are in the right position, cut out or draw in the windows.

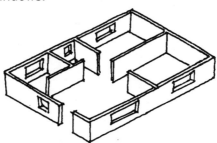

**6**   On the model draw the plumbing lines for the water supply
       and drain pipes, as well as the position for the lighting.

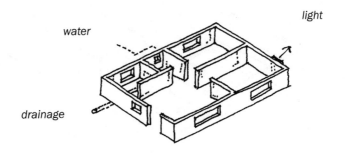

**7**   Decide on the most adequate type of roof shape depending
       on the climate and the construction materials.

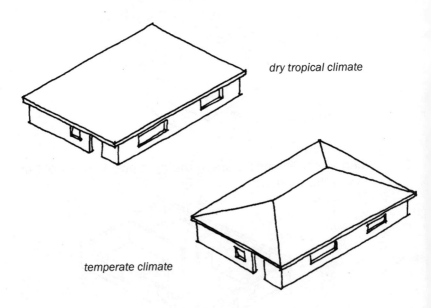

If the whole family agrees with the design, then the work begins!

Below is an example of a simple low-budget house located on a difficult site.

The bedroom and bathroom are on the upper level.

The living room and kitchen are on the lower level.

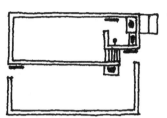

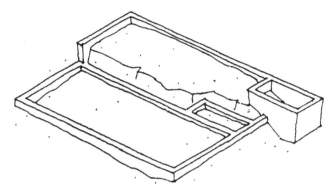

The foundations are also at different heights.

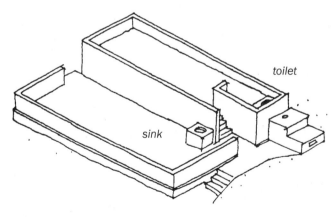

*toilet*

*sink*

Make the walls of the model half the full height in order to see the interior spaces.

This type of plan can be used for beach or mountain sites.

# DIMENSIONS

To have an idea of the size of the house when designing, use as a reference the dimensions of the room you are presently occupying. For example, suppose the room you are sitting in is 3m x 3m.

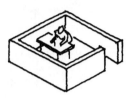

A quick way to start drawing the design is to use grided paper. Assume 1 centimeter equals 1 meter.

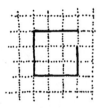

If you want a living room that is double the size of the space you are presently in, draw twice the 3m x 3m square, or a space that equals approximately an area of 18 square meters. Be flexible with the design in order to select the most adequate shape.

3m x 6m
or
4m x 5m

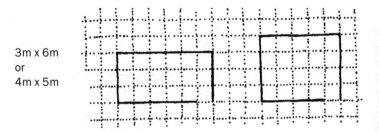

When adding on more spaces, verify how they all fit together.

## DIMENSIONING

After deciding, in a simple drawing, the size of the spaces and their relationship to each other, make another type of floor plan for the builder or contractor.

Here is an example. To the right is a simple drawing for the design of the final layout.

In the new drawing for the builder, represent all the walls with double lines, and indicate the position of the doors and windows.

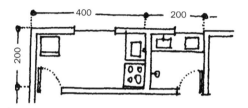

To position the walls, draw their dimensions using corners as references, and then measure the spaces from these points. During construction, the walls are located on the ground using these dimensions:

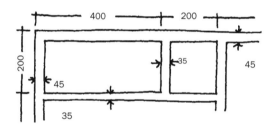

The trenches for the foundations are measured and traced from point to point and marked using stakes.

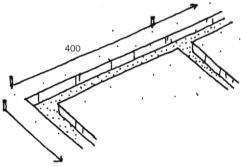

The drawing above shows the excavated trenches...

Below are typical dimensions for house spaces, in square meters:

| living room 5 4 | m² | bedroom 4 3 | m² |
|---|---|---|---|
| | 20 | | 12 |
| kitchen 3 2 | | bathroom 1.5 2 | |
| | 6 | | 3 |

## THE STRUCTURE

To prevent structural problems in earthquake, high wind or flood zones, consider the following principles:

- the thicker the wall, the stronger it is

- the longer the wall, the more easily it bends

- the higher the wall, the more easily it falls

- a heavier roof puts more weight onto the walls

- square corners are easily damaged

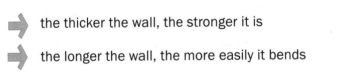
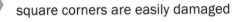

Below is a table demonstrating the resistance of a wall supporting a slab roof. The strength factor varies with the size of the wall.
Assume the higher the factor, the more resistant the wall is to
collapsing.

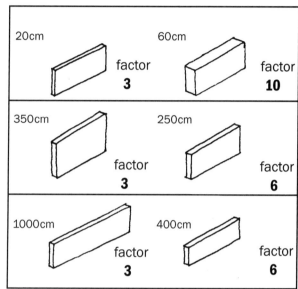

| | | |
|---|---|---|
| modify the width | 20cm factor **3** | 60cm factor **10** |
| modify the height | 350cm factor **3** | 250cm factor **6** |
| modify the length | 1000cm factor **3** | 400cm factor **6** |

The weight of different roof types affects the resistance factor:

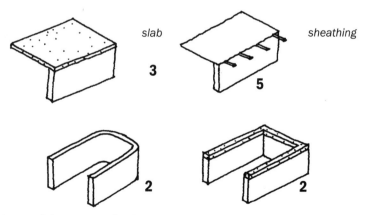

slab **3**

sheathing **5**

**2**

**2**

The shape of the corners is also important. A semicircular wall has the
same strength as a square wall strengthened with reinforcing rods.

A house shelters us from all types of climatic conditions, whether it be the heat, rain, cold, or humidity. It is therefore important to first carefully observe the local climate before designing or building a house.

There are three basic climates:

 The humid tropical climate with very warm temperatures which vary little between day and night, heavy precipitation and rich vegetation

 The dry tropical climate which is also hot, but has large temperature differences between day and night, little precipitation and therefore scarce vegetation

 The temperate climate with a very cold season and cold nights

Immigrants often build in their new homeland the same type of house they had before. This is a common mistake, and can make their houses inadequate for the local conditions, by either being very warm or too cold.

Before designing observe how the local people build their homes. This will help prevent importing designs and materials that do not suit local conditions. The house must adapt to the climate.

Chapters 2, 3 and 4 describe how the characteristics of the three basic types of climates affect the entire design and construction.

## HUMID TROPICAL CLIMATE

➡ Build houses close to hills or elevated sites where there is more air circulation.

➡ Build thin walls so humidity does not accumulate.

➡ Build sloped roofs to evacuate rainwater.

➡ Use materials such as wood, bamboo and reeds.

➡ Install large windows to improve ventilation.

➡ Separate houses to allow cool breezes to circulate.

➡ Build verandas around the house to protect it from rain.

➡ Elevate the ground floor to avoid the earth's humidity.

## DRY TROPICAL CLIMATE

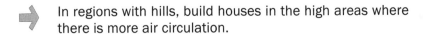 In regions with hills, build houses in the high areas where there is more air circulation.

Use thick walls to decrease the penetration of the heat during the day and the cold at night.

Use materials such as stones, adobe, bricks and blocks.

Install small windows to prevent the entry of dust and sun.

Join houses to expose as few walls as possible to the sun. The houses then shade each other.

Build interior courtyards to ventilate the rooms.

Build the ground floor on the earth's surface to take advantage of the cool ground temperature.

## TEMPERATE CLIMATE

 Build houses in areas with exposure to the sun.

 Build thick walls that prevent heat from escaping.

 Build roofs with an average pitch.

 Use materials such as wood, adobe, bricks and blocks.

 Install small windows on the south side and large ones on the north side. This applies to the Southern Hemisphere; do the opposite in the Northern Hemisphere.

 Protect the house from winds with vegetation and earth berms.

 Use the sunlight to heat rooms. Insulate the floor from the cold ground.

The environmental conditions where you build are not always clearly defined by the basic three climates. In some humid tropical regions forest resources have been destroyed causing a scarcity of wood for building. There are also dry tropical regions with green valleys and abundant palm groves, where the houses are built all in wood.

It is therefore recommended to build only houses that are most ecologically sound and in harmony with the local environment.

Today there are many opportunities to build with new types of materials or imported materials; however it is always preferable to use materials that blend in with traditional building types. Designing a house that is different from the local ones, by modifying all materials, the shape of house, the interior layout, and the use of spaces, eventually causes uncomfortable conditions.

For example: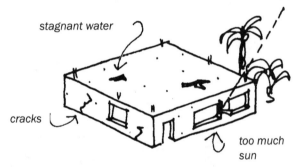

## A HOUSE AND ITS ELEMENTS

A house shelters in three ways:

    1       protection from the sun and rain
    2       protection from ground humidity
    3       protection from wind

A house should withstand winds and the vibrations of heavy vehicles.

A house is composed of these three elements:

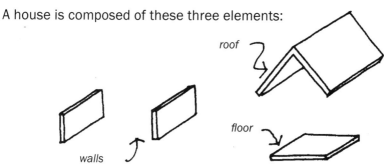

roof

floor

walls

Problems such as water infiltration, insects, excessive heat or cold are first located in the joints or connections of these elements: roof, floor and walls.

here

and here

After exposure to wind, rain or earthquakes, any construction defects often appear first in these joint areas.

## USING THE ENVIRONMENT TO IMPROVE HOUSES

Environmental conditions are often misunderstood and not taken advantage of. By taking a closer look at the environment we can use it to improve housing and house systems.

It is not appropriate to imitate elements or construction styles from other regions with different environmental conditions. For example, a window in a cold climate allows the sun to enter and warm up the room, but the same window in a dry tropical climate overheats the room and makes it unbearable to live in.

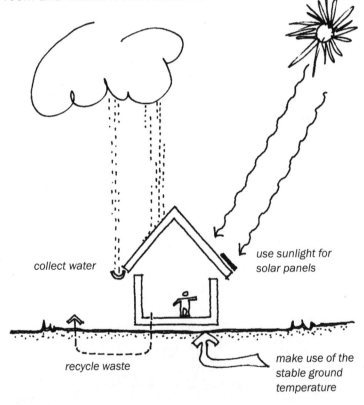

collect water

use sunlight for solar panels

recycle waste

make use of the stable ground temperature

The roof, floor and walls should integrate into the natural environment and climate, and use it in a favorable way. In the later chapters there are detailed descriptions of ways to do this.

# DESIGN

## BUILDING ON SLOPED SITES

Often houses on sloped sites are built identically to ones on flat sites. The result is an overspending on the construction of the foundation and the walls, and the destruction of the environment. When a site is extremely sloped some earth should be moved, but the plan should always suit the shape of the site.

*an expensive construction...*

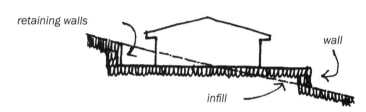

*retaining walls*    *wall*    *infill*

A much more efficient house can be built on the same type of site by placing the spaces on several levels:

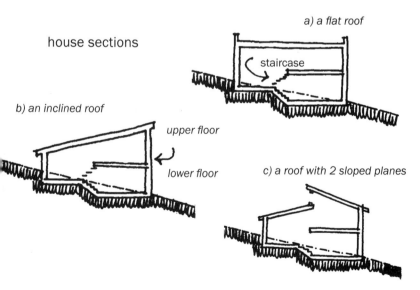

*a) a flat roof*

house sections

*staircase*

*b) an inclined roof*

*upper floor*

*lower floor*    *c) a roof with 2 sloped planes*

The money spent building retaining walls and infill can instead be used for improving other areas or parts of the house.

## SUN AND WIND CONDITIONS

To prevent overheating the interior of the house, follow the principles below:

**1**      Prevent sun rays from hitting the walls

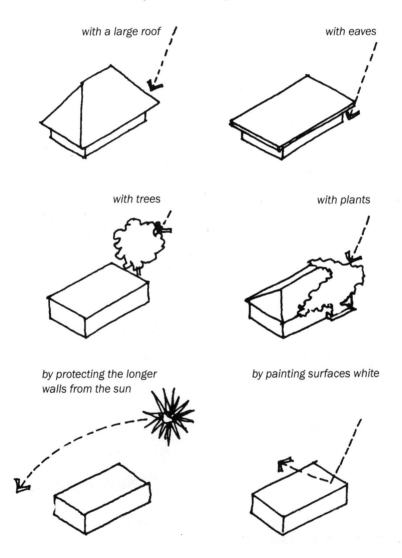

*with a large roof*                                          *with eaves*

*with trees*                                                *with plants*

*by protecting the longer walls from the sun*               *by painting surfaces white*

When the sun's rays hit an outside wall, they heat it up and eventually the heat penetrates into the interior spaces and the temperature inside the house rises.

**2**    Prevent sun reflections from other surfaces:

If a house has many glass windows, the sun's rays can reflect off them and hit the neighboring house on the other side of the street:

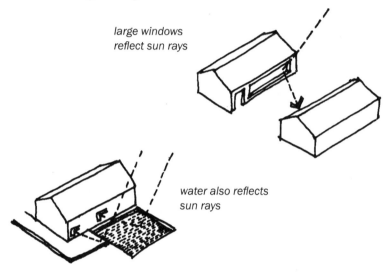

*large windows
reflect sun rays*

*water also reflects
sun rays*

Dark pavement or asphalt absorbs the heat and radiates it onto surrounding buildings.

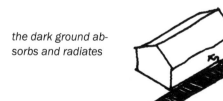

*the dark ground ab-
sorbs and radiates*

The best protection from this outside heat gain are plants and trees, which store cool air between their branches.

**3**   To well ventilate the interior spaces and keep the hot air
circulating and non-stagnant, locate the doors and windows
in relation to the prevailing winds.

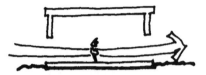

*upper windows:*
*the hot air flows*
*above the head*

*lower windows:*
*the cool breeze is felt*

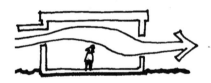

*wind entering under*
*canopy*

*percola or canopy sepa-*
*rate from the wall*

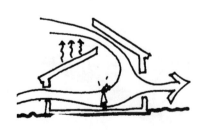

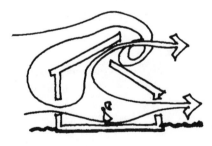

*the heat enters*
*through the roof*

*the heats exits*
*the room*

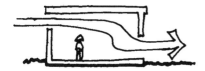

*air circulating from above to below is not very efficient*

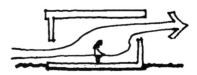

*air circulating from below to above is much more effective*

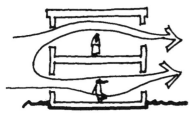

*the closer hot air is to the head, the warmer you feel*

*a cross-circulation is more effective with openings in the lower part of doors*

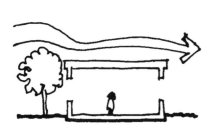

*low trees: the breeze rises and does not enter*

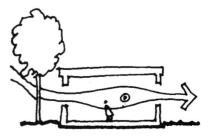

*high trees: the breeze descends and cools*

The distance between plants or trees and the house is also important, for example:

*when a hedge plant is 3 meters from a house, a breeze enters*

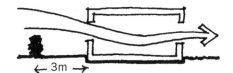

*when a hedge plant is 6 meters from a house, a stronger breeze enters*

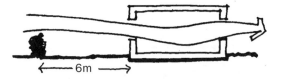

A tree is more effective for cooling when it is planted close to a building:

*when a tree is 6 meters from a house, there is little breeze*

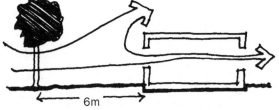

*when a tree is 3 meters from a house, more cool air enters*

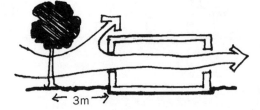

Planting hedges around a house can also change the circulation of prevailing winds:

*without plants the breeze circulates around and away from a house*

*prevailing wind*

*with a front hedge plant the breeze circulates further away from a house*

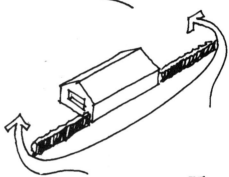

*with a back hedge plant the breeze enters and cools a house*

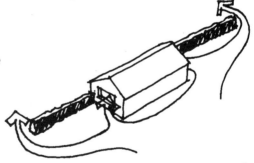

*with one back and one front hedge, a stronger breeze enters*

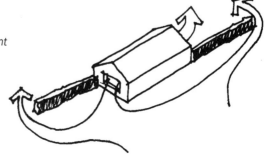

## ROOF VENTILATION OPENINGS

One way to prevent the house interior from heating up is to build openings in the upper part of the walls or in the roof. Since hot air always rises, these openings provide exits for the heat.

There are three ways to ventilate:

**A**    Allow interior hot air to exit:

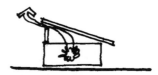

*to let in cool outside air, the interior air must be evacuated*

Examples of method A:

*the hot air exits through openings in the upper walls*

*the hot air exits through roof openings*

**B**    Prevent hot air from entering the rooms:

*the hot air flows into the eaves and exits through openings near the ridge*

Example of method B:

*another type of opening near the ridge*

**C**    Draw hot air between the roof and the top of wall:

*with a flat roof the breeze lifts the air that is stagnant beneath the eaves*

Example of method C:

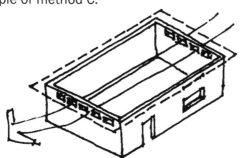

*the breeze enters through holed tiles in the upper part of the walls*

# LIGHTING

## LIGHTING A HOUSE

In the previous pages, there were examples for positioning windows to effectively ventilate with breezes, thereby improving the house's comfort. Another element to consider when locating windows is how they are used to light the house, since sunlight is the best way to brighten rooms during the day.

Sometimes small windows are installed by builders to prevent hot air or noise from entering, or because there are not sufficient available window materials, such as wood or glass, to make larger windows. It is useful to know how to light rooms even with small windows.

Below are a few factors that determine the quality of the lighting in a room:

**1**    The size of the window.

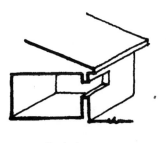
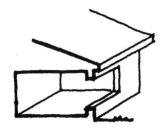

*small window*                                    *large window*

**2**    The shape of the room: A narrow room admits more light.

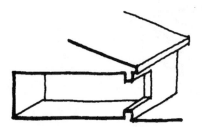

**3**   The orientation of the house: In regions south of the equator a room facing north admits more light than one facing south.

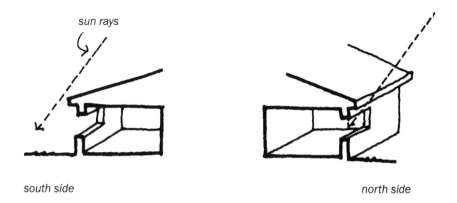

sun rays

south side                                                    north side

**4**   The sun's reflection on outside surfaces: A light-colored surface reflects more light into house, as well as heat. Vegetation absorbs sun rays.

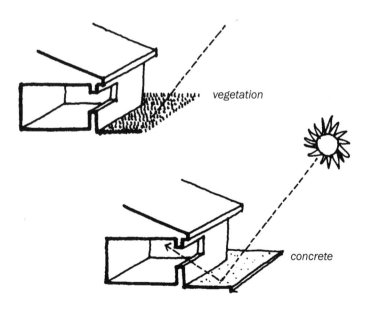

vegetation

concrete

**5**    The effects of the sun on other plants and buildings can improve or worsen the lighting of a house.

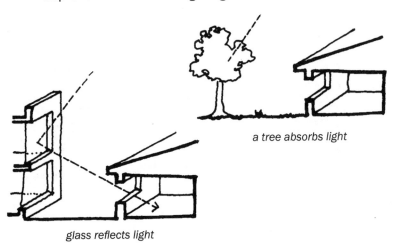

*a tree absorbs light*

*glass reflects light*

**6**    The type of materials and the colors of a room: A light color reflects light much more than a dark color.

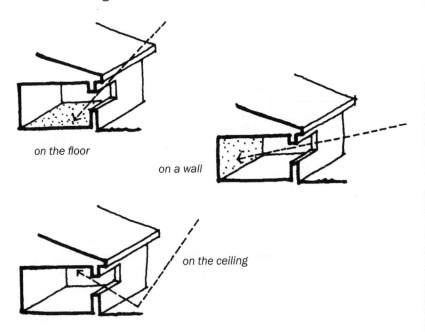

*on the floor*

*on a wall*

*on the ceiling*

**7**    The surrounding site topography affects the light intensity
during certain times of the day.

*In this example, there is little direct sunlight in the morning, but later on
the sunlight hits the house.*

**8**    The shade of other buildings or vegetation: The height of a
building, or the height and density of tree foliage, has an
impact on lighting.

*in the forest*                         *in the desert*

**9**    The climatic conditions: Overcast skies, typical of the humid
tropics, have a different effect than the clear skies of dry
tropics.

*humid tropics*                         dry tropics

Deciding on the size and location of the windows is therefore dependent on the site conditions.

However, if after considering all the site conditions, it is still difficult to resolve lighting issues, other measures can be used:

 When there is too much sunlight entering, use blinds, slats, curtains or plants.

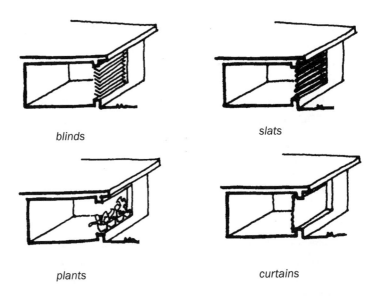

blinds                                          slats

plants                                          curtains

 When there is not enough sunlight entering, find other ways to create openings.

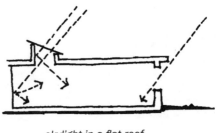

skylight in a flat roof

*another interesting solution:*

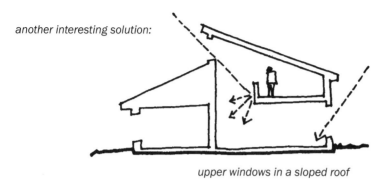

*upper windows in a sloped roof*

## WINDOW HEIGHT

The windows are located and sized to suit the type of activities that take place in each space of the house. Therefore each space may have different window heights.

For example:

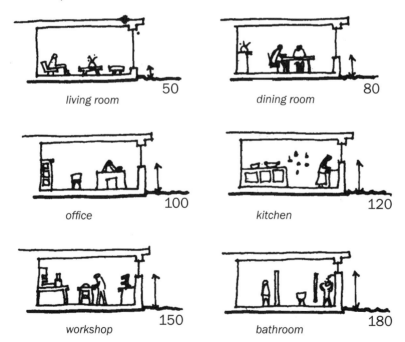

| living room | 50 | dining room | 80 |
| office | 100 | kitchen | 120 |
| workshop | 150 | bathroom | 180 |

All the dimensions above are in centimeters.

## SUNLIGHT IS HEALTHY

Mites, fungi, viruses and bacteria can grow in rooms which do not have enough sunlight, such as rooms with overly small or closed windows.

This can cause the occupants to become ill more frequently.

Therefore try to position the windows in such a way that sunlight can enter and purify the interior of the house.

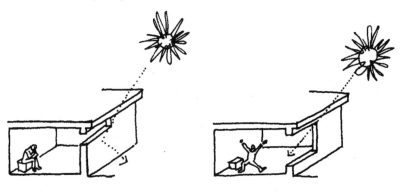

*here the air is impure*                    *here the air is cleaner*

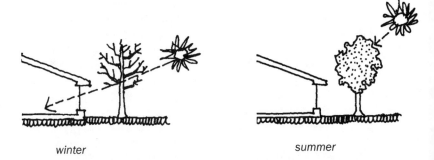

*winter*                    *summer*

To allow sunlight to enter through a large window only during cold seasons, plant deciduous trees (trees that lose their leaves in the winter).

## FRAMING VIEWS

Often large windows or glass walls are used to frame scenic views. However, sooner or later the pleasure of looking out these windows is exhausted and the view is ignored.

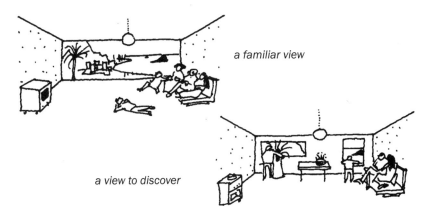

a familiar view

a view to discover

As it is difficult to imagine beforehand all the details for each room, some decisions can be made before or as the work begins, and others left for later on.

For example, when the sizes of the windows are known, they can be purchased, fabricated, or recycled windows can be found.

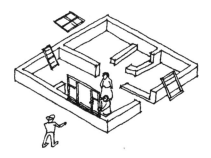

One way to be sure about the placement of the windows is to build the walls half a meter high, walk around the inside of the house, and then decide on their most suitable location and size.

# SITING A HOUSE

There are many types of site problems including odors, noise, smog, polluted water, unattractive zones, destroyed landscapes, and difficult infrastructure.

Industrial activities often are the cause of pollution in cities.

These industrial activities can be less harmful if they are located in areas that do not affect the population. All factories should install equipment to treat their waste before it is disposed of.

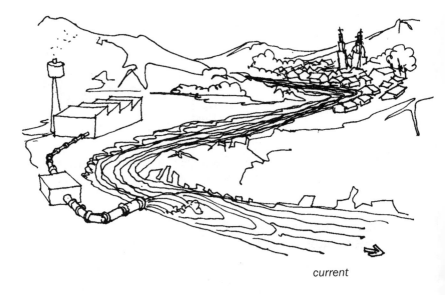

*current*

In the drawing above, the factory waste does not affect as many people since the river current is running away from the village.

Locate houses far away from the source of contamination.

## SUBDIVIDING LAND

A site's best areas should be used for public meeting places such as parks, squares, schools, theaters or markets. These areas are characterized by beautiful landscapes including small woods, views, or pleasant breezes. A town should be planned in such a way as to allow the public to have easy access to these types of areas.

The less interesting areas should be zoned for heavy construction, or activities that require substantial changes to the natural environment, such as bus stations, parking lots, factories, and highway access roads.

The town's streets and squares must be laid out and planned in a way that requires the least amount of earth displacement, and allows rainwater to be evacuated by following the natural drainage pattern of the site.

The small residential areas must include lots for the community's commercial activities. It is important to prevent a concentration of stores in a strictly commercial zone.

Lots should not be all the same size, since all sites do not have the same worth. The value of areas with trees, water, and great views should be considered. Since the financial situation of every buyer is different, a variety of lot sizes gives a buyer more choice.

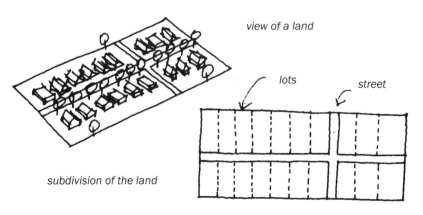

view of a land

lots          street

subdivision of the land

Therefore, instead of planning identical lots, it is preferable to subdivide in the following way:

 Plan streets so they follow the shape of the landscape.

 Then start delimiting a few lots by carefully marking off their property limits. If the street is curved, the edges of the lots which touch the street are curved. The property lines between lots can be irregular and vary in size depending on the amount of square meters each family purchases.

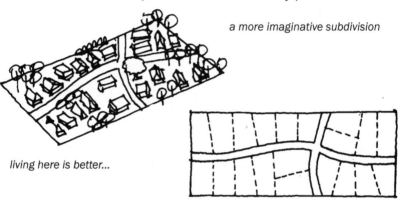

*a more imaginative subdivision*

*living here is better...*

Over time this land subdivision has a less rigid and a more pleasant appearance.

The value of a lot does not only depend on the amount of square meters, but also on the beauty of the site and its potential to accomodate a comfortable house.

## LOTS IN DIFFERENT CLIMATES

To improve ventilation and cool houses in humid zones, provide large front areas between the house and the street. In dry areas the lots should be narrower and longer, and the houses should have common walls. For more details see chapters 2 and 3.

Always conserve trees on a site for the future inhabitants. A tree's foliage provides shade and its roots protect the subsoil. Respect the trees.

In the humid tropics, the proportions of the residential lots are different than in the dry tropics.

street

Lots in the humid tropics: A garden surrounds the house and air from this outside space ventilates the house.

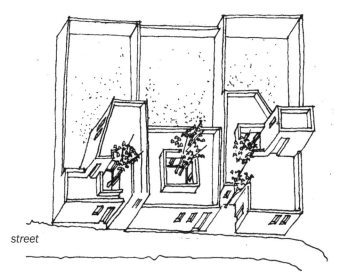

street

Lots in the dry tropics: A garden in the interior courtyard is used to ventilate the rooms, and the back space of the lot is reserved for future house expansion.

## SIZE OF THE LOTS

Dividing lots into equal sizes makes it easier to calculate their worth. However varied lot sizes are more inspiring for buyers to work with, and therefore create more attractive neighborhoods.

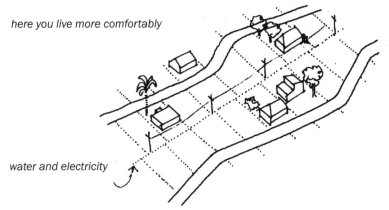

*here you live more comfortably*

*water and electricity*

The division between the two streets should be straight to facilitate the installation of services such as electrical lines and water piping.

With irregularly sized lots, the owners also have greater variety to choose from.

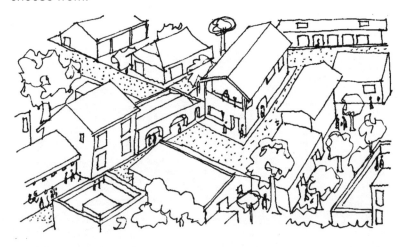

By using new types of sanitation systems there is no need for a sewage system, and therefore the streets can have less rigid shapes.

## INTEGRATING A HOUSE INTO A SITE

### Hills

 A house or group of houses should not be built at the top or bottom of a hill:

*middle zone for construction*

### River or sea

 Houses should be located where the water creates a bay and curves towards the land, rather than in areas where the land goes out towards the water.

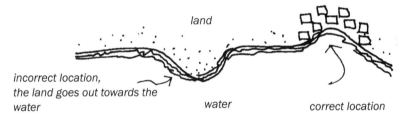

*land*

*incorrect location, the land goes out towards the water*

*water*

*correct location*

When a house is located on a slope, the path to the house should be curved.

*avoid direct access*

*use a curved path instead*

On a large property it is often difficult to decide where to place the house. There may be many possible locations and various reasons for locating it in one spot rather than another. In this situation, use intuition to guide the decision. Walk around the site. Look for clearings which are often good places to build.

The house should integrate with the existing elements.

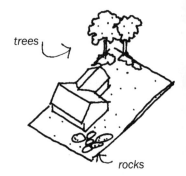

*trees*

*rocks*

Each site has different opportunities for locating the house:

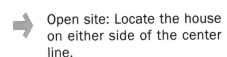

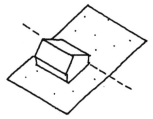

Open site: Locate the house on either side of the center line.

Site with one element: Locate house on the opposite side.

Unbalanced siting: The natural and the built elements are too close to each other.

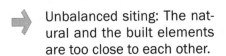

## THE SHAPE OF THE HOUSE

There are often some areas in a house where we feel more comfortable. Our enjoyment of spaces is a consequence of their orientation, the amount of sunlight entering, the ventilation, the type of materials, or the colors.

 The areas on either side of the entrance are used as living rooms or guest rooms.

 In "L" shaped houses it is better to locate beds or worktables on wall (a).

a

 (b) is a good area for the living room or main room of the house.

b

 Fill the empty space of the "L" with a tree, large rock or fountain.

The house is not just a building to protect the occupants from the rain, sun, or hot and cold temperatures. It should be a place where the family feels welcome and where guests and friends can be invited. A house should have smaller areas, inside as well as outside, where you can spend time alone, work or rest.

## HOUSES IN FLOOD ZONES

In flood zones and marshlands it is recommended to build houses on pillars or platforms. This is especially the case in non-urban areas with unpaved streets or improper drainage.

When streets are finally built, and there is less risk of floods or marsh-type conditions, the walls of the lower level of the house can be built to provide additional enclosed spaces.

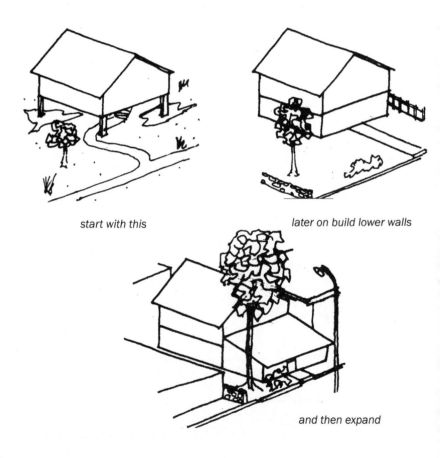

*start with this*                    *later on build lower walls*

*and then expand*

When the site is well settled, and more space is needed for a growing family, there are ways to build on more rooms.

Urbanization always develops in the following way: The first settlements are simple buildings, often for poor inhabitants, which in time are improved, expanded and renovated into beautiful houses along attractive streets.

*a settlement which is a few years old*

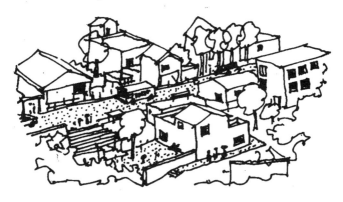

*the same settlement many years later*

"When you no longer improve your house, you are close to death."
*Arab proverb*

## ORIENTATION

 Well-ventilated houses always are planned with service spaces, such as the bathroom and kitchen, with one wall facing a garden, a courtyard or a street.

These service spaces should be located in such a way as to prevent prevailing winds from sending heat or odors towards the other spaces of the house.

 In hot, humid climates below the equator, the kitchen should be oriented to the south to avoid sun from the north and west heating up the walls.

 Bedrooms or sleeping spaces should be on the east side of the house. In cold climates the sun heats up the rooms in the morning when the occupants are waking up. In hot climates the afternoon sun, coming from the west, cannot heat up the bedrooms. The bedrooms remain cool and more comfortable to sleep in.

 Living rooms should be on the west side. In cold regions these are the warmest spaces of the house in the afternoon and evening when they are most used by the occupants.

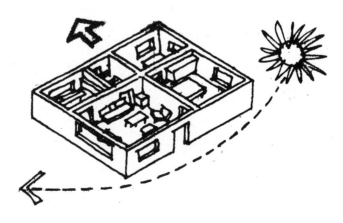

People living in a community often build their own public buildings. Problems arise when the community grows and these buildings need to be expanded. Additional space on the site for future construction should be foreseen.

To plan for this expansion, the following pages recommend several options, and provide examples for different types of public buildings.

Consider the consequences of designing a large building. One important factor is the increase in car circulation and the need for parking. The public spaces must be well differentiated away from these service spaces.

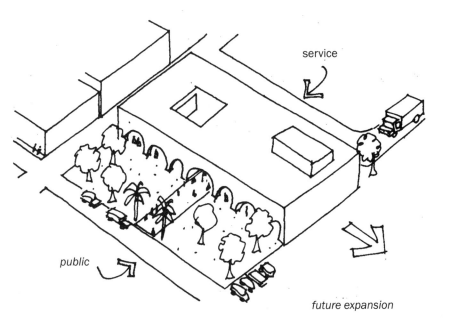

service

public

future expansion

## SCHOOLS

|   | FUNCTIONS | DIMENSIONS |
|---|---|---|
| A | classrooms (40 students) | 50 to 60 m² |
| B | teachers' room | 20 m² |
| C | boys' washroom | 10 m² |
| D | girls' washroom | 10 m² |

Space distribution:

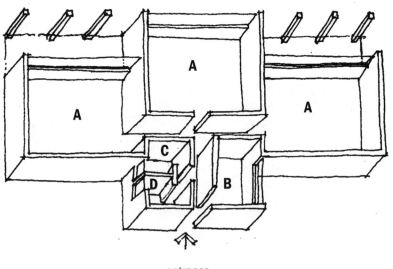

*entrance*

This basic plan can be repeated horizontally or vertically.

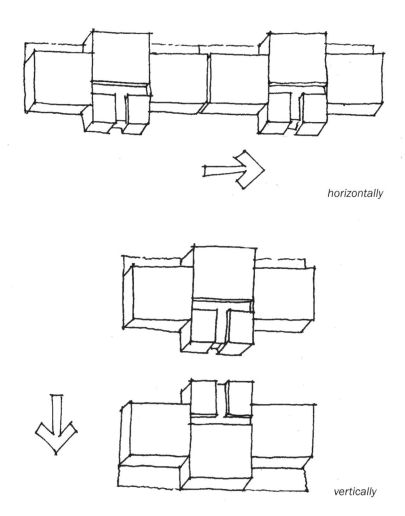

*horizontally*

*vertically*

The direction of the expansion depends on the site dimensions, the access location, the type of existing vegetation and the soil conditions.

This basic plan can be adapted to sloped sites as well:

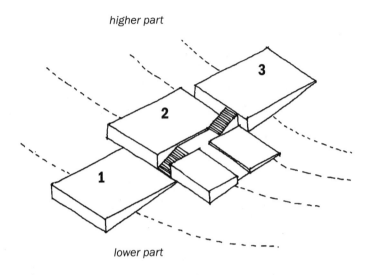

*higher part*

*lower part*

The spaces on the plan above are divided into three levels. Ascend from the left to the right to go from the lowest level (1) to the highest level (3).

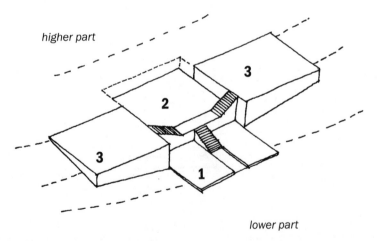

*higher part*

*lower part*

In the plan above, the spaces are also on three levels, but you ascend in the middle to level 2 and then turns to the right or left to level 3.

When a school expands, often there are additional functions which need special spaces, such as:

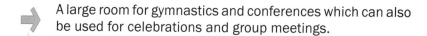 A large room for gymnastics and conferences which can also be used for celebrations and group meetings.

A workshop used for student and parent meetings, and for fabricating things, such as tools for the community.

## OBSERVATIONS:

Primary schools should not be too big. If a community grows, additional schools, in other areas, should be built. This prevents the young students from walking long distances.

Schools should be located in quiet areas, away from traffic and main streets.

Schools should also be far away from industrial zones or areas with loud and polluted activities, to not endanger the students' health.

A school's construction materials should be the same as the ones used for local housing. The school then integrates into the community and does have a strange visual appearance.

The recreational areas around the school should have trees which provide shade and fruit for the students.

## CLINICS

|   | FUNCTIONS | DIMENSIONS |
|---|---|---|
| A | reception/waiting room | 40m² |
| B | examination rooms | 10m² |
| C | laboratory | 20m² |
| D | dispensary, stores | 20m² |
| E | small surgery room | 20m² |
| F | infirmary | 40m² |
| G | kitchen | 20m² |
| H | washrooms | 20m² |
| I | employees' room | 20m² |

Space distribution:

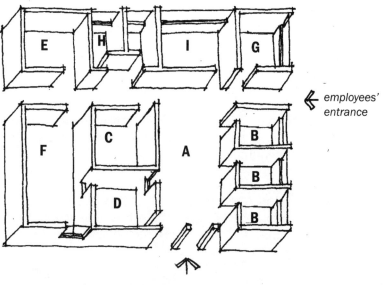

← employees' entrance

↑
public entrance

## DESCRIPTION OF THE SPACES:

**A**    The reception and waiting room is where the first contact is made with the patients. A nurse-receptionist decides if the case can be treated immediately or needs the attention of a doctor.

**B**    The examination rooms are used for examining patients and are furnished with an instrument table and a bed.

**C**    The laboratory is used for simple tests and to store instruments and medical equipment.

**D**    The storage is for medication and infirmary materials (towels, etc.). It is also used to distribute prescriptions to interned patients.

**E**    The small surgery room is for minor emergency operations.

**F**    The infirmary is used for patients recuperating from surgery, for example, after deliveries or local treatments.

**G**    The kitchen is used to prepare food for the patients and the employees.

**H**    The washrooms.

**I**    The employees' room is used to rest, to change clothes and to store personal belongings.

Starting with the basic clinic plan from the previous page, expand
the medical services in the following way:

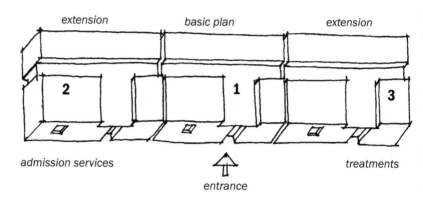

The central area (1) is expanded on one side for more beds (2) and
on the other side for additional consultation clinics (3).

For further expansion it is necessary to consult an architect since
a badly designed hospital plan can cause delays and traffic flow
problems. The local climate also needs to be well considered so
that the patients' rooms are not humid and hot.

A hospital uses equipment that consumes a lot of electricity and
water, so from the start, the design must take into account the
location of the plumbing pipes, wiring and ducting.

For example, a radiology room requires a special surface finish to
prevent the x-rays from harming the occupants of other rooms.

## OBSERVATIONS:

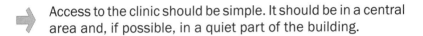

Access to the clinic should be simple. It should be in a central area and, if possible, in a quiet part of the building.

Many of the recommendations for schools also apply to clinics, such as using local materials, planting trees around the building, and avoiding contaminated and polluted areas.

There should be separate entrances for the different uses: one for the patients, one for emergency, and another for services (food and material delivery).

The front facade where the patients enter should be protected from the sun and rain with a large canopy or other type of device. In the event of emergency or disaster when the reception space must be used for exams and treatment, the patients can wait in this protected area.

*a view of the entrance*

## CITY HALL

|   | FUNCTIONS | DIMENSIONS |
|---|---|---|
| A<br>B<br>C<br>D<br>E<br>F | reception and security<br>administration<br>administrators' rooms<br>archives<br>conference rooms<br>service areas and washrooms | the size of the spaces is proportional to the size of the population |

Space distribution:

*one-storey building*

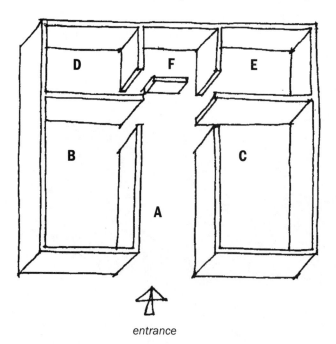

*entrance*

The distribution shows the relationship of the spaces. The reception area has only one entrance to control public access from the street. The public has access to the administration and the offices of the civil servants.

The municipal administration is on the same side as the archives, and the conference room is close by. The service areas, storage spaces, washrooms, and the kitchen with a dining area are in the back with a separate delivery area.

The city hall is often the largest building in a small municipality, so it should be carefully designed and executed. A city hall is frequently more than one storey high, and is generally located in a main square or a central location. The A, B, D and F spaces can be located on the ground floor, and the C and E spaces on the second floor.

*two-storey building*

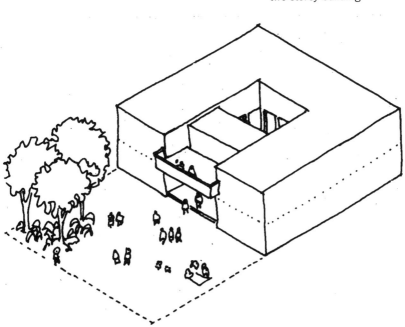

## HOTEL

|   | FUNCTIONS | DIMENSIONS m² |
|---|---|---|
| A | rooms | min 20.0 |
| B | restaurant | 2.0 |
| C | kitchen | 1.0 |
| D | laundry room | 0.5 |
| E | employees' room | 1.0 |
| F | office administration + reception | 0.5 |
| G | storage | 1.0 |
| H | parking | 16.0 |

Note: The areas are calculated in proportion to the number of rooms. For example, a hotel with 20 rooms has a kitchen of 20 x 1 = 20 square meters.

Space distribution:

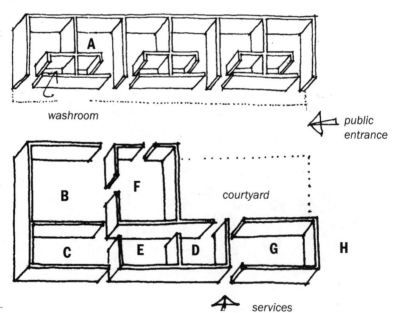

washroom

public entrance

courtyard

services

In this drawing above, not all the rooms are shown!

## OBSERVATIONS:

 A room for two people, with a bathroom, should be approximately 20 square meters.

 It is very difficult to have a model plan for a hotel project since each site has unique and prominent surrounding features that should be highlighted for the guests' enjoyment. The guest rooms, and public spaces such as the restaurant and waiting areas, should be designed to draw attention to the beauty of the natural landscape or historical buildings.

 The design of the guest rooms depends on several factors such as the surrounding landscape (a hotel with great views may have balconies, terraces or gardens), the time of day the rooms are used (a hotel close to a bus station has a night clientele), or the average length of stay of guests (guests may stay longer at hotels near beaches or tourist sites).

 Spaces can have multi-purpose functions; for example, a restaurant near a waiting area or a courtyard can be converted into large area for celebrations. Also service spaces, such as the laundry room, kitchen, and the personnel rooms, should be grouped together and their water pipelines located in one area.

 It is necessary to minimise exposure of tourists to noise pollution. There should not be any construction near tourist sites with features such as waterfalls, woods and monuments. Services like parking and stores, which produce traffic and noise, quickly diminish the appeal of these sites to visiting tourists.

## MARKET

| | FUNCTIONS | DIMENSIONS $m^2$ |
|---|---|---|
| A | storage of market stalls | variable |
| B | washing area | variable |
| C | public washrooms | $20 m^2$ min |
| D | garbage storage | $10 m^2$ min |
| E | covered area | $250 m^2$ min |
| F | overflow area | — |

Space distribution:

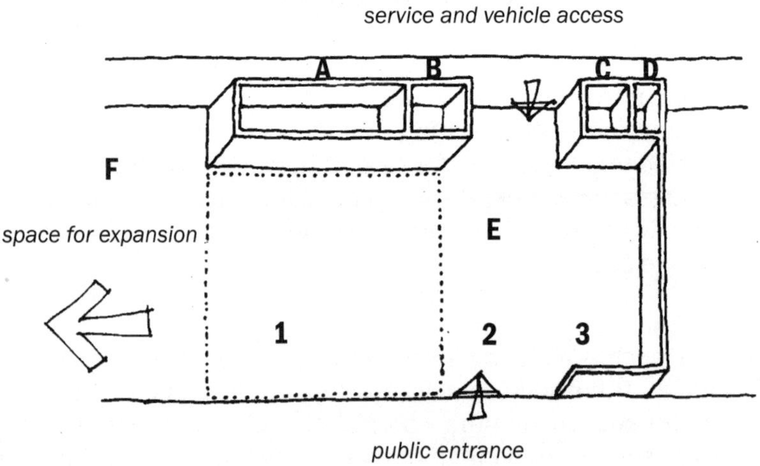
service and vehicle access
A
B
C
D
F
space for expansion
E
1
2
3
public entrance

## DESCRIPTION OF THE SPACES

**A**   A covered and enclosed area to store the market stall structures that are set up in the open areas of the market. A small room for the market's administration can also be located here.

**B**   A covered room to wash the market equipment and clean materials and produce.

**C**   Public washrooms.

**D**   A place to store the garbage that will be removed from the area by the city garbage trucks.

**E**   This area can be divided into three different spaces:

   **1**   The largest space is the market area where the vendors install their dismountable stalls. The stalls should be made with appropriate materials, or be rented from the city.

   **2**   A covered space, such as a large portal, where the vendors place their merchandise on tables.

   **3**   An area with permanent and enclosed stalls.

## OBSERVATIONS:

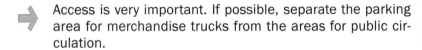 Access is very important. If possible, separate the parking area for merchandise trucks from the areas for public circulation.

Near the truck access areas where deliveries are made, locate services such as storage, washrooms, garbage and washing area. It is more economical to group these services together.

Foresee an area for expansion, which could be used in the meantime for parking.

The covered market area can be used also for expositions and celebrations. Therefore make the area attractive with terraces and trees.

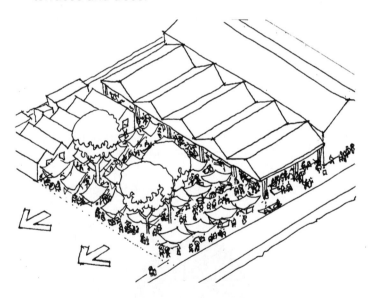

The drawing above shows one way to use the market spaces. There are many other possibilities depending on the site conditions, the road access, and the surrounding buildings.

As shown in the previous pages, housing design is different in each climate, whether in the humid tropics, dry tropics or temperate climate. Just as each of these regions has its unique conditions, so does every smaller region, settlement, village, or city. The type of housing in these areas depends on their specific local conditions, surroundings and environment.

## HUMID TROPICS:

1    Squares with trees.
2    Commercial areas with porticos for protection from rain.
3    Houses surrounding an open space for ventilation.
4    Large streets lined with shading trees.
5    Large covered areas for public activities.
6    Streets that follow the natural landscape level with drainage towards rivers or lakes.

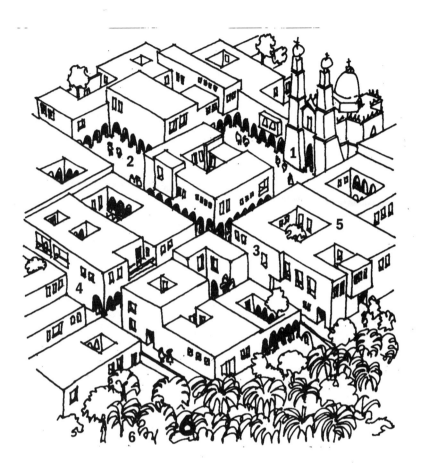

## DRY TROPICS:

| | |
|---|---|
| 1 | Small squares with high buildings shading the streets. |
| 2 | Commercial areas shaded by porticos. |
| 3 | Main streets running north-south so that one side is always in the shade. |
| 4 | Narrow streets, since they have more shade. |
| 5 | House are joined and have interior courtyards. |
| 6 | Parks located on lower ground level to receive drainage as irrigation. |

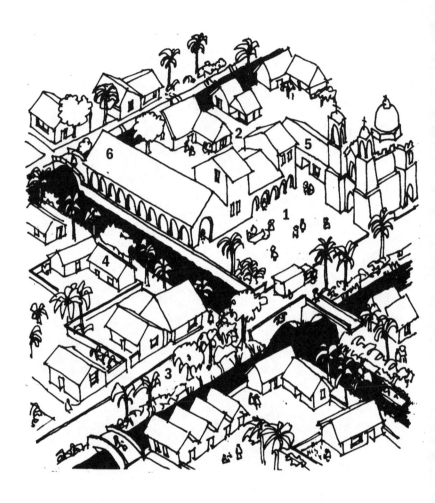

## MARSHLAND AREAS:

1   Small squares facing the canals.
2   Straight streets crossing over the canals.
3   Trees on the sides on the canals' edges.
4   Houses joined together, with ventilation from the canals.
5   Houses of various storeys with living space on the second floor and storage on the ground level.
6   Commercial areas located at intersection of the canals and streets near the bridges.

**FOREST AREAS:**

1       Islands of clearings with paths connecting them through the forest.
2       Settlements near the rivers to facilitate communication.
3       Every clearing has a square, or gathering area.
4       Buildings are separated for better ventilation.
5       Buildings located on the cleared and drained higher forest ground with drainage into the lower forest.
6       Elevated pathways to avoid flooding.

## BUILDING IN MARSHLANDS

Below are directions for starting a settlement in flood or marsh zones:

*section of the marshland*

**1**     Build dikes and plant trees to protect the banks.

**2**     Dig out earth from the smaller canals to make larger ones, and fill in the area between the two dikes to create an island.

**3**     When the earth is not stable, build lightweight houses. The rest of the buildings can be built when the ground settles.

## FOREST SETTLEMENTS

To prepare forest land for a settlement consider the following.

In a natural setting different types and sizes of vegetation grow together, as one species depends upon the other. In clearings there are smaller trees and plants around the border of the clearing or along the edge of rivers, and larger vegetation further into the forest.

Deforesting to make larger clearings can destroy the local ecology and turn a green healthy land into a desert without it ever growing back.

Houses built in this deforested type of environment are uncomfortable.

*a natural clearing has a "v" shape*

Below is an example of a badly built clearing settlement.

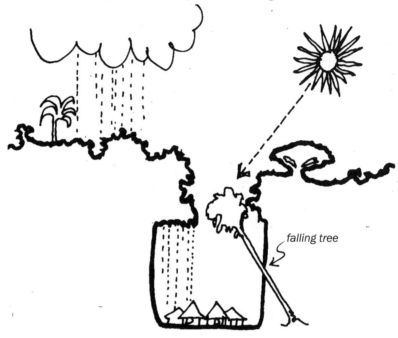

falling tree

Why is this settlement badly built?

➡ The roots of tall trees are usually not very deep; therefore without the natural support from shorter trees, these tall trees fall into the center of the clearing with strong winds.

➡ After a rainstorm, water continues to fall from the trees onto the settlement.

➡ The settlement is shaded and sunlight cannot penetrate the clearing to dry out the ground and the roofs of the houses.

Note: The drawing above shows a section of the forest with house facades. The section part is shown with heavy lines.

Illustrated below is the correct way to make a clearing settlement.

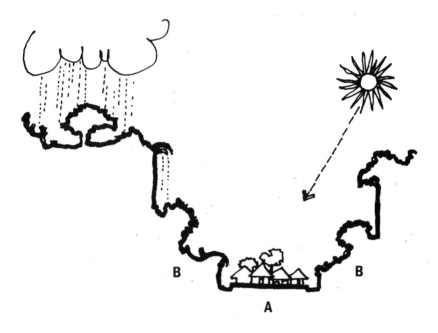

➡ The large trees are supported by the shorter ones. In part A of the clearing, all the trees are cut down and in part B, only the tall trees are removed.

➡ The rainwater runs in small canals between the clearing and the forest. It is important to prevent this water from becoming stagnant so that it does not breed mosquitos.

➡ The sun penetrates into the clearing and dries out the houses.

Between the houses, plant trees to provide the settlement with fruit and shade.

# CLIMATE                                    DESIGN

When designing a house, three aspects of the climate must be considered: sun, rain and wind.

SUN

Houses should be built so that they do not heat each other up from the sun's reflections.

Below is an example of a badly designed street and group of buildings. Their orientation, relationship to the sun and the positioning of their elements cause the following problems:

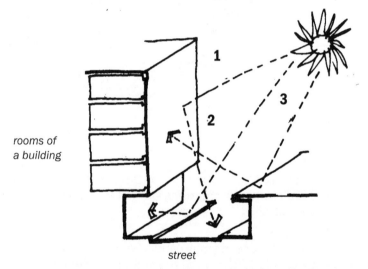

rooms of
a building

street

**1**   The sunlight falls onto the building with a glass facade and reflects out to the street and onto other buildings, therefore radiating heat all over the area.

**2**   The asphalt street absorbs a lot of heat and radiates it out into the air, therefore overheating the inhabitants.

**3**   The flat roof reflects the sunlight onto the facade of the building across the street, again overheating the rooms.

The drawings on these pages are perspective sections.

It is not much more difficult to build a comfortable design. Consider ahead of time how to avoid excessive heat gain from sunlight. Think of ways the heat may be deflected from entering. Of course all buildings heat up, but some designs are more efficient than others and do not need expensive cooling systems that consume a lot of energy.

When it is impossible to deflect sunlight, think of ways the heat can be evacuated from the spaces. Remember that hot air always rises.

Here is a better-designed area, for the following reasons:

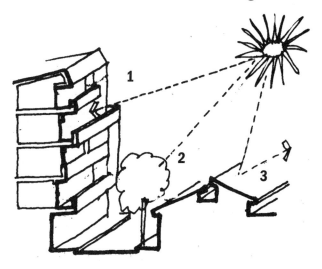

**1** The sunlight falls onto an irregular facade that creates its own shade from balconies and projections.

**2** The trees shade the asphalt.

**3** The different shapes and slopes of the roofs allow the sunlight to reflect in an irregular way.

**RAIN**

In heavy rain regions, groups of buildings and houses should be located on the highest ground level so that water flows down to the trees on the lower ground. In dry areas, the opposite approach is recommended.

The houses located at the bottom of a hill in a rainy zone are flooded.

Here the houses on the upper ground are safe from the floods.

## WIND

In hot regions, the cool air should be directed to flow through the houses or buildings.

When a building has large flat walls without windows, the wind passes over the building without entering it.

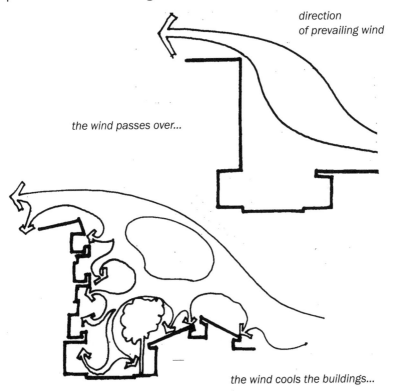

*direction of prevailing wind*

*the wind passes over...*

*the wind cools the buildings...*

The wind must have spaces to move through to cool facades and roofs, and enter into the building. Therefore buildings should have balconies, overhangs and sloped roofs to capture the wind.

A settlement must be located in the most favorable environmental conditions of the site and avoid the less desirable areas. For example, soil conditions must be verified when building on a hill, as well as sun and wind patterns.

Shown below are the effects of the sun and wind on a well-located settlement in a cold region.

*the sunlight warms up the settlement...*

The settlement must be situated in such a way that the sun heats up all the houses.

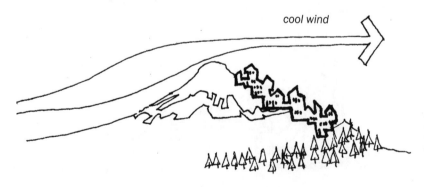

*cool wind*

*the cold wind flows over the settlement...*

A settlement in a cold region must be protected from the cold prevailing winds. A hill is a natural barrier against the cold winds.

A settlement in a hot region should be located on the opposite side of the hill, assuming that the wind and sun are in the same relationship to the hill as on the previous page. The drawing below illustrates how the hill protects the settlement from the sun by providing several hours of shade.

*the settlement is shaded*

In a hot climate, the settlement is better located on this side to benefit from breezes.

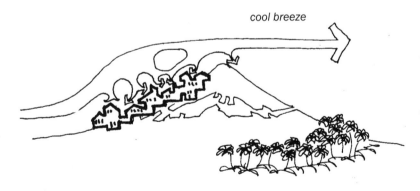

*the breeze enters the houses*

In the examples above, it is the climate and landscape that determine the location of the buildings.

Large buildings can be located in such a way as to help provide
other buildings with protection from prevailing winds.

## VENTILATION

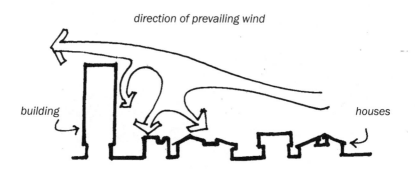

*direction of prevailing wind*

*building*                                                     *houses*

Above is an example of a neighborhood in a hot region. The cooling
wind blows through the area with low houses.

## PROTECTION

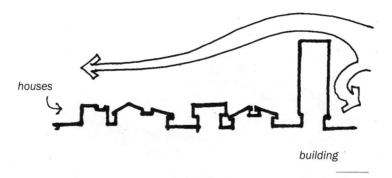

*houses*

*building*

In cold regions, the tall buildings act as a barrier against the cold
air, and therefore the wind passes over the houses.

## STREET ORIENTATION

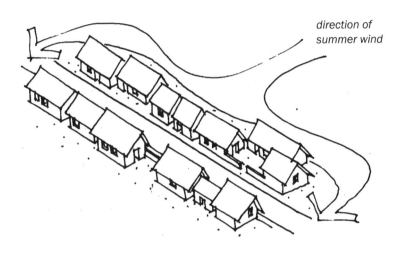

*direction of summer wind*

Incorrect street layout: The houses on one side of the street prevent the wind from reaching the other side.

Correct street layout: The prevailing wind reaches all the houses.

# URBAN SPACES DESIGN

Almost all cities begin as small villages, with some expanding quicker than others. It is important that the first settlement already contain the basic features for developing into an attractive and humane settlement.

Many large cities, and often small ones, have traffic problems:

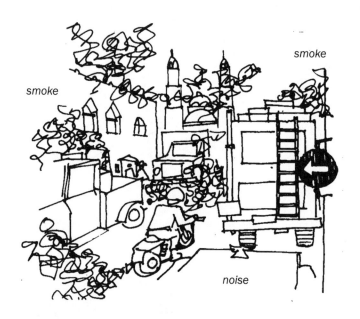

smoke

smoke

noise

To minimize traffic problems, make a selective choice of which buildings to place near each other. All buildings should have a clear access for moving, and reaching emergencies and fires.

In all pre-urban areas there are a certain number of activities that can at first be housed in one room, but which, with the growth of the community, eventually require a building (such as schools).

The type of space required for each function, and its vehicular access, should be well considered.

*the wind cools*

It is very important that cities have green spaces, not only on the outskirts, but in the centers as well. These green zones are called the "lungs" of the city.

The wind is cooled when it blows through the trees or bushes, thus cooling the inhabitants.

Below there are examples of activities and functions which can be located together in the city.

## PUBLIC SPACES

All cities have a main square. This section describes how to plan these public places.

The following three principal functions should have their own space:

Civic – the city hall
Religious – the church
Commercial – the public market

These functions are often placed around a central square or near each other.

The drawings on the following pages describe how to organize
public spaces for the community's activities. Of course each community and its site conditions require a unique solution.

> A – civic functions
> B – religious functions
> C – commercial functions

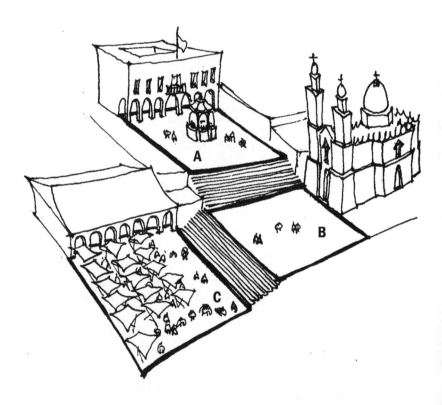

The layout above is often used in mountainous regions in order to
displace as little earth as possible during construction. This layout
also facilitates drainage, especially in humid regions.

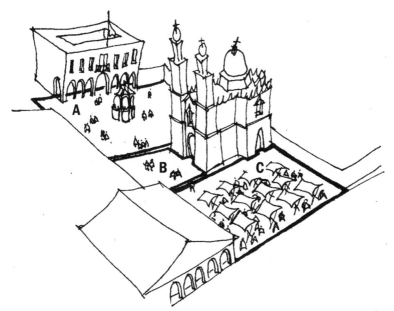

A building is placed in the center of a flat land, in this case the church, to create three distinct spaces, each with a different function.

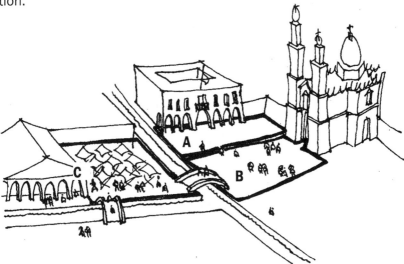

In marshlands, water can be directed into canals. These canals divide the spaces into different functions.

In small villages, there is often only one central square. In this case future squares should be planned for inhabitants in areas outside the center. A market, school, theater or store can be located in these distant squares.

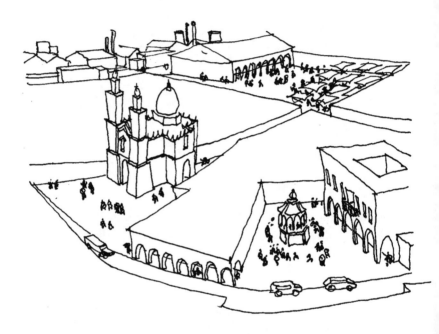

*each public space is surrounded by houses and stores*

## PUBLIC SQUARES

Public squares are located in the most attractive areas in a settlement since they are the spaces most used by the inhabitants. As seen on the next page, these areas are characterized by special features such as beautiful trees, views over landscapes or river banks.

Here are four examples of areas for public squares:

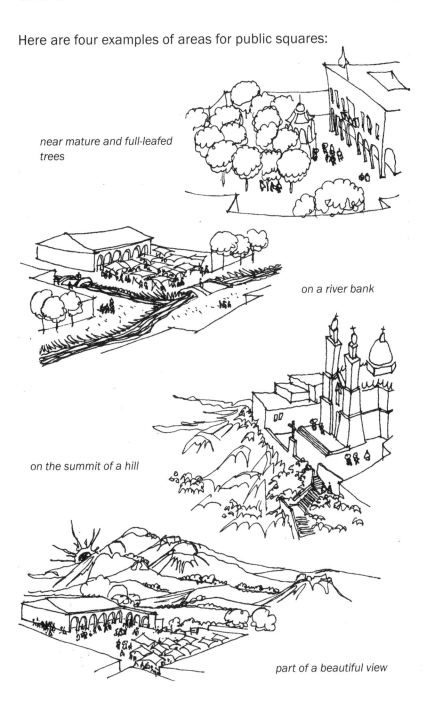

*near mature and full-leafed trees*

*on a river bank*

*on the summit of a hill*

*part of a beautiful view*

## SMALL SQUARES

Create small gathering spaces by enlarging streets at turns, corners, street crossings, or where there are special features such as beautiful views or trees.

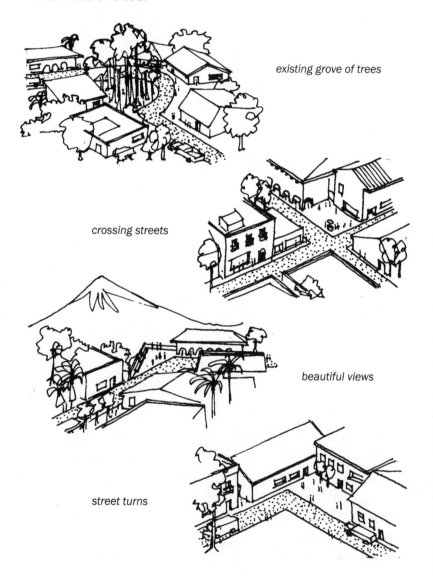

existing grove of trees

crossing streets

beautiful views

street turns

It is important to prevent a concentration of similar functions in one area. For example, an area with only commercial activities causes the inhabitants to walk less, and use their cars more, therefore increasing the traffic. Always combine functions; mix commercial and public areas within residential ones.

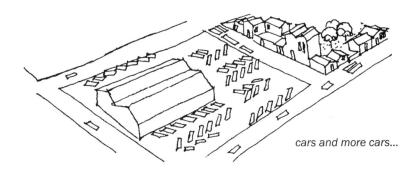

*cars and more cars...*

*this is a disaster: prevent this type of commercial center*

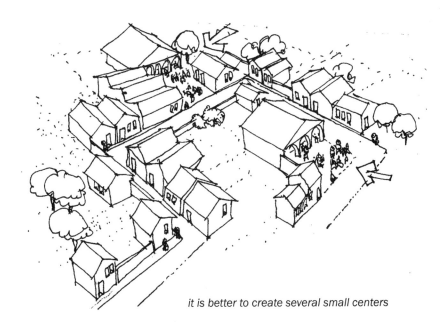

*it is better to create several small centers*

## PERCEPTIONS

We are not always aware of the effect our surroundings and built environments have on our daily lives and emotions. The source of this influence is difficult to identify. Our emotions are affected by several factors at once, including:

## SIZE

Buildings of different heights and volumes create visually lively and active surroundings...

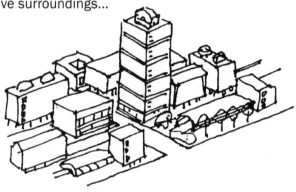

## CONTRAST

The contrast of different shapes and colors creates a dialogue between the built areas, pedestrian areas, squares and gardens which stimulates the visual senses.

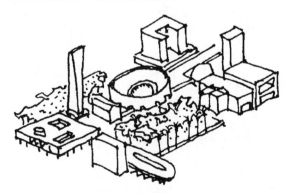

Of course always consider basic architectural composition...

## SYMBOLISM

Buildings represent a variety of spheres from religious to economic forces. Some constructions inspire and delight, others cause apprehension or even fear.

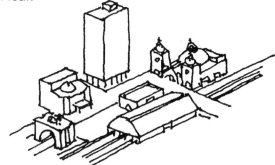

## COMPLEXITY

Dense and multi-functional areas with a variety of types of buildings can be interesting without feeling chaotic.

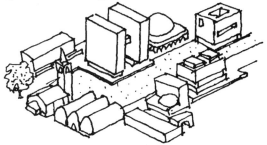

## SURPRISES

Urban routes can be built with a variety of environments, each with their associated sensations. There are spaces to work, contemplate, promenade and fall in love.

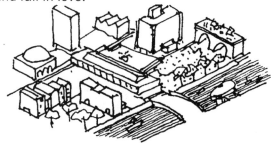

# CIRCULATION

Small towns usually do not have traffic problems. But as soon as the town grows into a small city, traffic issues develop. Often the additional traffic is not local but from people moving through the city to go elsewhere.

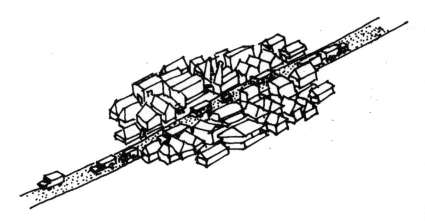

When the expansion of a settlement occurs near a transportation highway, many circulation problems arise if the city is divided in two.

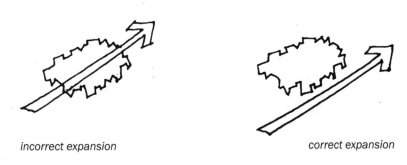

*incorrect expansion*                    *correct expansion*

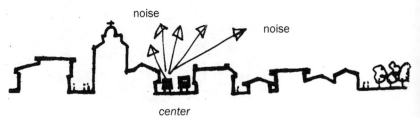

noise

noise

*center*

The access routes should be situated on the outside of the town; expansion then occurs on three sides instead of four:

*grove*             *center*

It is recommended that workshops and factories be situated on the other side of the highway:

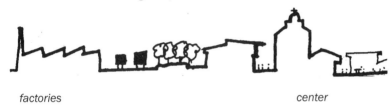

*factories*             *center*

As shown below, a new highway to an existing town should be built outside the town and with only one way to enter and exit.

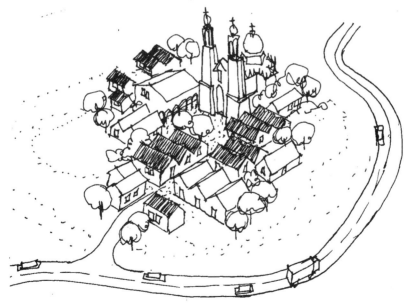

## SERVICES

It is recommended that houses be built with composting toilets which do not pollute potable water or contaminate rivers and soil. The water for bathing and kitchen use can be filtered and reused to irrigate gardens and parks. These green spaces can be located in the lower areas of a town. With this sanitation system it is not necessary to build sewers or water treatment stations. See chapters 8 and 9 for more details.

Many small communities use electricity for lighting, but rarely is this type of energy used for cooking since gas and wood are less expensive.

In rural regions where the inhabitants own animals, the animals' manure can be converted into gas. The waste from a group of houses – 10 or fewer families – can be collected together since it is easier to build and maintain one processor. See chapter 9.

Small oil generators should not be located near houses since they produce noise, odors and increase traffic on the roads. However, if they are too far away, energy is lost in the distribution.

Often, water and electricity distribution to all houses of a new community is difficult since they are far from each other. In this case there should be several electricity generating stations so that energy is not wasted during its distribution. The stations can use oil, gas or waste to produce energy.

Residential neighborhoods should be near the commercial and recreational facilities. Each one should have its own small center with stores and offices. This prevents excess traffic problems.

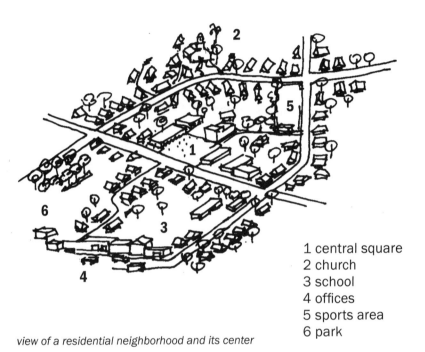

1 central square
2 church
3 school
4 offices
5 sports area
6 park

*view of a residential neighborhood and its center*

Below is a section of a small city showing residential zones between public zones, and work/service areas.

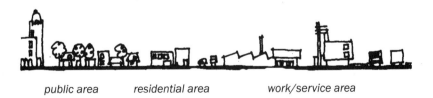

*public area*          *residential area*          *work/service area*

In the public areas, there are buildings for government functions, sports and other types of recreational facilities.

As seen in the previous pages, settlements must have, besides houses, services areas for schools, markets, clinics, administration, work and recreational buildings. While designing a settlement, the service and access infrastructure must also be planned. This means locating streets, potable water distribution and electricity lines.

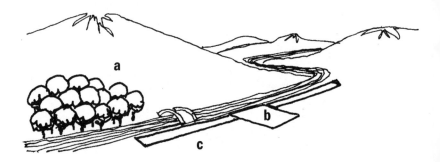

**1**    First locate the public areas, such as parks (a), ceremonial squares (b), and civic areas (c), near areas with beautiful natural features.

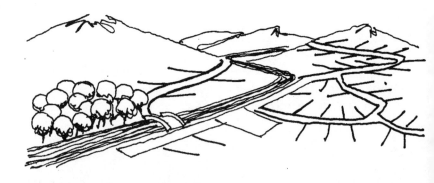

**2**    Then determine the circulation and lot network, such as the streets and roads, public areas and subdivision areas for lots. The land form, meaning ground level changes, should be maintained and preserved to facilitate rainwater drainage.

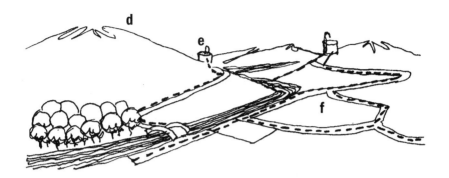

**3**    Determine the location of the watershed (d), the cistern (e) and the water distribution mains (f).

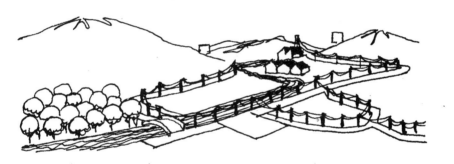

**4**    Then locate the electrical generator in an area that does not disturb the community, but is close to the principal users, such as workshops.

## MUNICIPAL GARBAGE

Compost is made from organic waste and can be used to fertilize the garden. Make a hole in an appropriate corner of the garden, fill it with the organic garbage and cover the hole with earth. In a few months remove the decomposed organic waste, which is called compost and looks like earth, from the ground and use it as fertilizer. Make other holes every few months for new loads of garbage.

Non-organic garbage is everything fabricated, such as objects made with plastic, tin, glass etc... This type of garbage can be used to fill the lower ground in the community. It is even better to recycle this garbage. There are some industries that re-use these types of waste.

Choose landfill areas for garbage that are not going to be used for construction, since this land becomes unstable. If compacted down, these areas can be used for paths but not roads.

Even better, cover the garbage with a layer of earth and make a park with lots of vegetation.

*today's landfills are tomorrow's parks*

The drawing below is not a site plan. It only shows the relationship between different zones of the city.

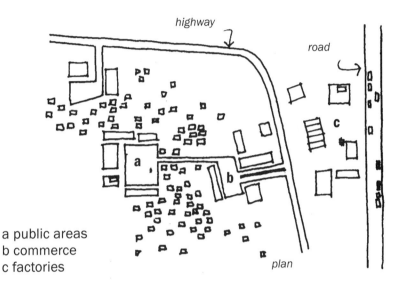

a public areas
b commerce
c factories

An accurate plan depends on the natural environment of the region, its hills, rivers and groves.

## STREETS

In planning road layouts, it is important to alter as little as possible the topography, meaning the shape and level changes of the land. In regions where there are earthquakes, roads can be destroyed by flooding or landslides if incorrectly located and built with inadequate drainage.

It is important that the street drainage be well planned so that even with torrential rains the rainwater is evacuated efficiently towards the lower ground, a river or valley. The streets should follow the natural shape and levels of the land. This method takes more time to plan, but the result is better for the inhabitants and more cost-effective in the long term.

*a layout that goes against the land's shape*            *a layout that follows the land's shape*

It is also important that wind circulates through the streets to cool and clean away dust. Therefore the orientation of the main streets should follow the direction of the prevailing winds.

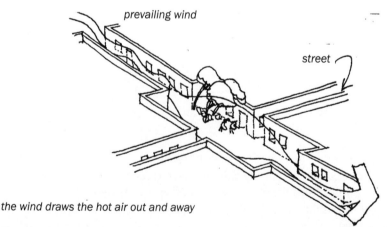

*prevailing wind*

*street*

*the wind draws the hot air out and away*

For the best result, enlarge areas at street corners to change the wind's velocity. This draws the air out from the less ventilated cross streets.

These open corners are ideal areas for small businesses.

It is important that the streets in the center of town offer shade and protection from the rain.

This can be done in the following ways:

 Use street orientation to shade

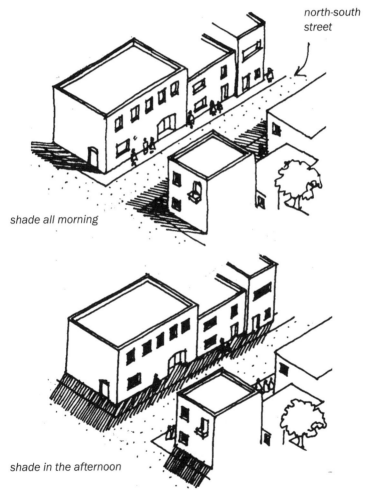

*north-south street*

*shade all morning*

*shade in the afternoon*

Two views of a street that runs north-south. The east side is shaded in the morning and the west side in the afternoon and evening.

Streets that run east-west:

→ Locate public buildings and businesses with porticos around squares, or in areas where there is a lot of pedestrian activity. (a)

→ Design houses and stores with large canopies. (b)

→ Plant trees on both sides of the street. (c)

→ Upper floors can project out over the ground floor. (d)

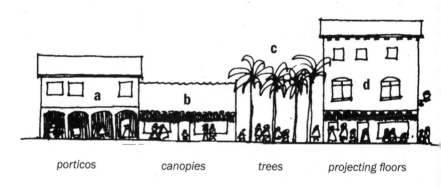

porticos          canopies          trees          projecting floors

*view of facades of houses and stores*

## SQUARES

Squares are areas to be enjoyed. Vehicles should be prohibited from parking or circulating in them. Therefore build enclosures or barriers such as stairs, trees, level changes, canals or porticos.

Vehicles should be able to come near the square, but not enter.

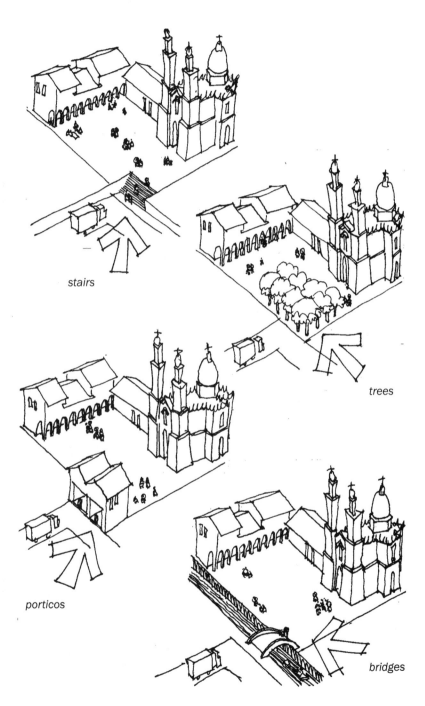

*stairs*

*trees*

*porticos*

*bridges*

There are two types of streets that lead to the main square and link smaller squares.The first type is lined with stores and is a highly pedestrian street with few vehicles; ample space is provided for pedestrians to circulate. The second has workshops for artisans with a larger road for vehicles and less space for pedestrians.

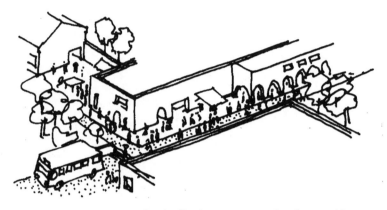

*street with stores: many pedestrians and few cars*

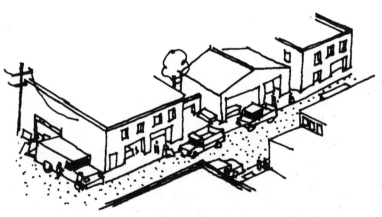

*street with workshops: few pedestrians and more cars*

After locating public areas, the squares and streets, preserve the existing trees that do not obstruct the circulation. Plant additional trees to shade and beautify these common spaces.

When all the streets in mountainous zones are paved, the rainwater that runs down the hill can cause flooding, while the upper trees die from lack of water.

*here the trees are dried out*

*here there is too much water*

Trees on sloped land should have several areas down the hill where soil absorbs and filters the water into the subsoil.

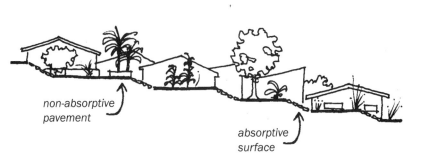

*non-absorptive pavement*

*absorptive surface*

When the street follows the shape of the land, the water is absorbed in:

1 paved area for circulation
2 drainage areas

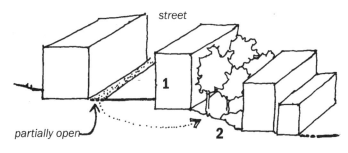

*street*

*partially open*

In very dry regions, the streets and squares can be used to collect rainwater in public cisterns.

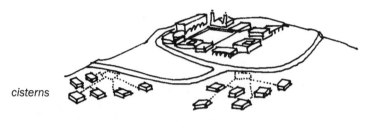

*cisterns*

➡ The street system should be designed so that the streets start at the highest point of the town and end at the lowest part, where the cisterns are located:

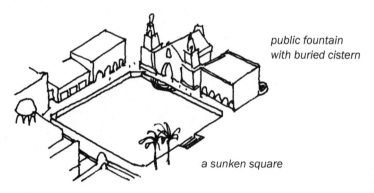

*public fountain with buried cistern*

*a sunken square*

➡ The squares should be on a lower sunken level. The public buildings around the square are built with underground cisterns.

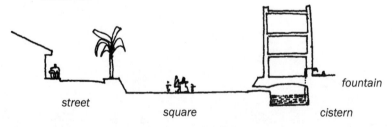

*street*

*square*

*fountain*

*cistern*

In a town with small population, the water may not be needed for domestic or other building use, and therefore can be used to irrigate plants and trees in the square.

Below are two planning examples.

The first is a badly designed plan. The inhabitants all need to walk a long distance or take a bus to get to the commercial area or the school:

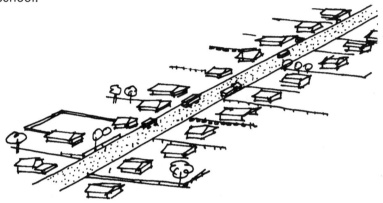

The second layout is well designed. The inhabitants live a short walk away from a small center surrounded by all the necessary services:

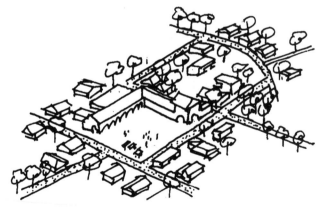

This layout is ideal for less fertile lands. In time the lot's earth can be improved by adding compost from dry toilets and water from the houses.

A community must serve its inhabitants and not the automobile.

## THE ENVIRONMENT AND OUR VISION

When your vision is not stimulated frequently, the eye muscles lose elasticity and stiffen.To improve your vision, move your eyes over objects as if they were touching every line.

Do the same when observing the shape and details of a house:

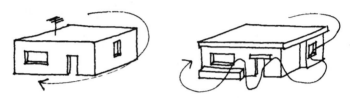

*here the eye movement is tense and stiff*      *here the movement is fluid*

The drawing below shows a badly designed city. The uniform and repetitious shapes stiffen the eyes since there are few details to exercise your vision.

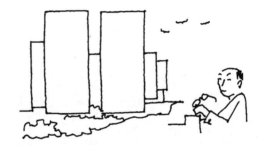

The outline of the buildings below stimulates eye movement...

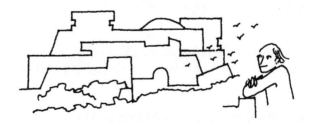

## GREEN AREAS

All expanding communities should have sufficient green areas. If a site planned for a settlement does not have beautiful existing natural features, some areas should be set aside to create future parks.

Planning green areas should be done at the same time as planning the layout of streets. New forest settlements should leave groups of trees untouched for the enjoyment of the future inhabitants.

In rural towns there is often a zone left for expansion between the houses and their small vegetable gardens, and the agricultural fields further away. These houses should not be aligned one after another along a main road because, with expansion, the town will become linear and the distance between the houses and the fields will increase. To maintain a comfortable walking distance between these two areas, the town should be concentrated in a circular layout, with the fields surrounding the town.

People who leave the countryside to find work and live close to large cities often use a lot of cement outside of their houses. There is a common belief that plants attract insects and bugs, and that a property should look "clean." But actually this reasoning is incorrect since the opposite is true. Paved areas are hotter and their flat surface creates pools of stagnant water. Also dust and dirt collect to further disturb the inhabitants.

Plants and trees, besides providing fruit and vegetables, help regulate the temperature. The drawings below show the temperature differences between a forested area and a field.

cold          hot                    hot          cold

during the day                    at night

In temperate climates, a dense forest is much colder than an open field.

dense forest                    open forest

cold day and night          comfortable day and night

In cold areas, the vegetation also is a barrier against the cold winds.

For example, in cold zones, when the wind temperature is 15°C, the temperature of the spaces between the houses is 10°C.

*settlement without wind protection*

With high vegetation as barrier, the temperature is higher since the heat from the walls is not blown away by the wind.

*settlement with trees as barrier*

This type of barrier, with additional trees and plants between the houses, further increases the temperature.

*settlement with trees on the outside and*
*more vegetation between houses*

Houses built in open areas or fields, such as farmhouses, should be protected with gardens.

In urban areas, the most economical and rapid way to improve the environmental conditions and local climate is using vegetation.

The following illustrations show the amount of pollution and dust that city dwellers breathe:

 Above the trees of a park, there are 1000 times less particles of dust.

 On tree-lined streets, there is 5 times less dust than streets without vegetation.

*a street without trees*          *a street with trees*

There are many advantages to urban parks:

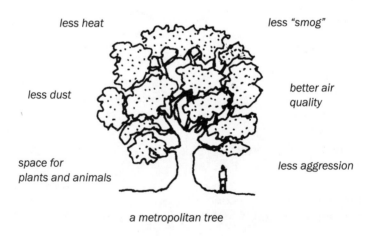

less heat                          less "smog"

less dust                          better air
                                   quality

space for                          less aggression
plants and animals

*a metropolitan tree*

## SUBSOILS

Carefully consider the subsoil conditions of a site. The type of subsoil must be known in order to decide on the materials and structure of a building's foundations. This information is also important for planning the areas between buildings.

The subsoil of the forest area is much richer in life than that of a field:

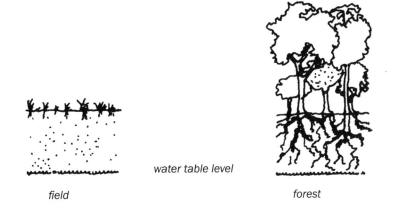

water table level

field                                          forest

"When you compare the total weight of the cows in a field with the total weight of the earthworms in the ground, you discover they are equal in healthy soil."

*–The New Scientist,* July, 1989

A 25-meter-high tree purifies air for 10 people!

We forget how long it takes for a tree to grow. Few consider the size of the trees. The drawings below describe the growing time of trees.

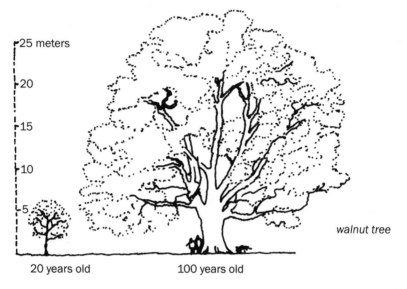

*walnut tree*

20 years old             100 years old

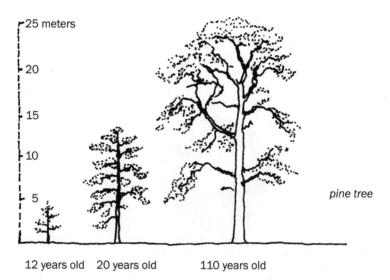

*pine tree*

12 years old    20 years old         110 years old

Trees, then, should be planted sooner rather than later...

## POLLUTION

There has been a lot of discussion about pollution. The air in today's large cities is far less clean than country air because of the
smoke and exhaust from factories, trucks, and cars, as well as
from other sources of contamination. To avoid direct contact with
this pollution, industries and high-traffic roads must be located far
from residential neighborhoods.

There is also the seldom-recognized problem of visual pollution,
such as piles of garbage, big bright signs and bad planning. To
prevent this visual pollution, create beautiful landscapes, public
areas and squares surrounded by carefully designed and well-
made buildings.

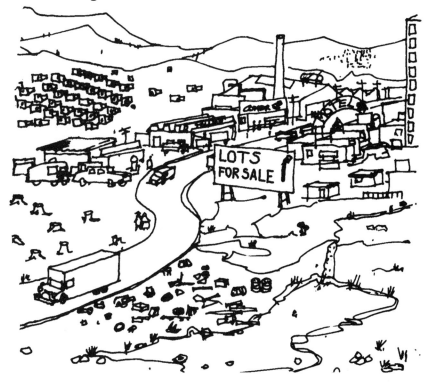

What types of pollution can be found in this drawing?

# HUMID TROPICS

2

## THE DWELLING IN A HUMID TROPICAL CLIMATE

There are many possible housing models to consider when building in the humid tropics. The shape of a building is determined by various factors, including:

the availability of materials, the type of workmanship, the local customs and traditions, the possibility of using materials from other regions, and the financial situation of the community.

 One example of this decision-making process is with the use of wood or clay for walls. If these materials are available, a house can be built with them in several ways:

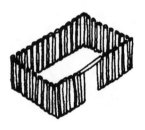

*all in wood*

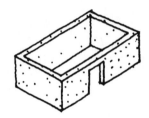

*all in clay*

 Or these materials can be combined:

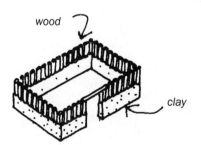

wood

clay

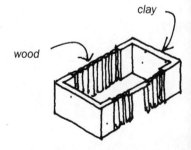

clay

wood

The shape of the house is dependent on several factors:

 the size of the family

 the availability of materials and the means to purchase them

 the traditional methods of building

 the imagination and creativity of the builders

 the regional climate

 the regional customs in the use of space

 the site conditions

This manual does not recommend one type of house which can be used as a model for many peoples and for all regions. Each valley, each hill, each grove has specific conditions. Differences are also found amongst the people within a community, since their activities vary greatly. The house of a carpenter is unlike the house of a merchant.

Therefore, the following pages explain several ways to build, and provide some ideas of what is possible. There are a variety of shapes and structures described, all of which are adequate for a humid tropical climate. The builder can choose the one that is most appropriate for his conditions.

*Before starting, study all the possibilities in order to create with your imagination a house that combines and integrates the methods and techniques for your project.*

# ROOFS

## DWELLING ROOFS

The roofs of houses in the humid tropics have steeper slopes than houses in other regions for the following reasons:

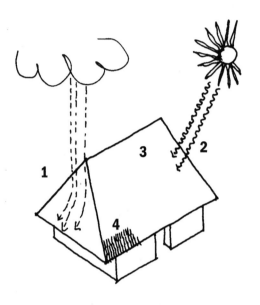

**1**   The rain drains off the roof more quickly.

**2**   The sun does not heat up the roofing materials as much; a sloped surface is less affected by the sun's rays than a flat surface.

**3**   The air space in the high area of the roof is a buffer from the penetration of heat.

**4**   Most of the time the available materials of these regions, such as thatching grasses, leaves and roofing tiles, can be installed on slopes.

The details below show a few ways to cool a house:

Start with the basic hip roof shape; 4 planes with 4 over-hanging eaves.

Make an opening in the upper smaller part of the roof to improve ventilation.

Extend the roof's ridge, on the longer sides, to prevent rain from entering the openings.

The ventilation opening can be partly closed with wood lathes or louvers, angled to prevent the rain from entering.

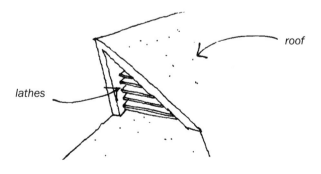

lathes

roof

## EAVES

The eaves protect the walls against deterioration from exposure to the sun and rain.

Since the eaves project out, a shallower pitch can be used in the lower part of the roof:

*roof with two different pitches*

Shown below is a section of a house with eaves with the same pitch as the roof:

*low windows*

This other section shows a house with eaves at a different pitch. In this example the windows are the right height:

*this is better...*

## PROPER VENTILATION

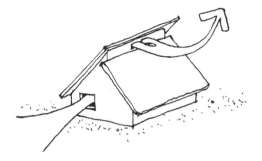

To properly ventilate a house, separate the two planes of the roof. The hot air exits the upper opening as the cool air enters the lower window.

Above is an example of a house in a humid tropical climate with one area of the floor higher than the others.

The roof has three planes. The fourth side is a separate roof in the opposition direction to the prevailing winds with an opening below the ridge for ventilation. The hot air in the top part of the roof flows out and the cool air at ground level enters.

To take advantage of the space between the roof and the ceiling, elevate part of the roof:

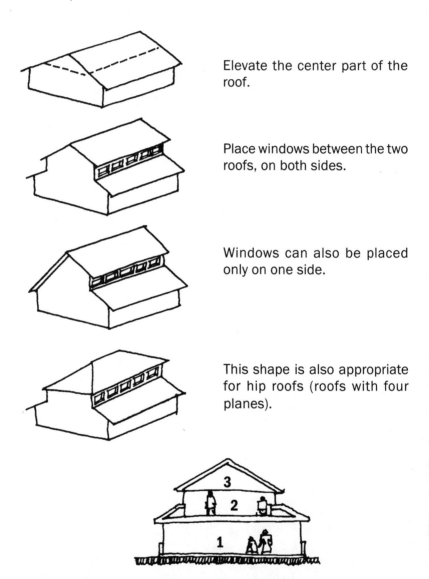

Elevate the center part of the roof.

Place windows between the two roofs, on both sides.

Windows can also be placed only on one side.

This shape is also appropriate for hip roofs (roofs with four planes).

This section of a house shows the rooms of the first (1) and the second (2) floors. The empty upper space is used as storage (3).

In regions where wood for building large roof structures is scarce, build separate roofs for each room, as shown below.

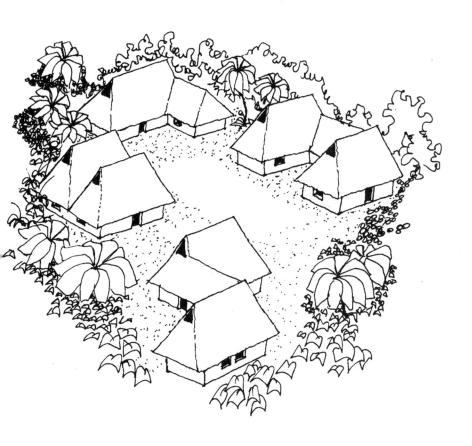

## LARGE ROOFS

In high rainfall zones, it is difficult for people to meet in exterior public places, such as squares, as is the custom in other regions.

Fortunately, there is adequate available material in these regions (large trees), to develop structures capable of sheltering large public meeting spaces.

Indigenous cultures have invented a great variety of architectural solutions, for construction, use of space and ventilation, which can be applied to building meeting spaces. Some of these solutions are included in the following three examples.

All of these examples of large spaces have openings for ventilation.

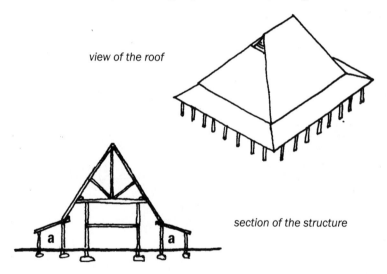

*view of the roof*

*section of the structure*

The first example, above, is a simple structure with center posts. Surrounding the space is a colonnade. Inside there are two floors with an area for storage. The side spaces (a) can be used for stores.

Note: The footings for the center posts are larger than the others.

This type of structure is suitable for sheltering markets or groups of small workshops.

*open a space for windows in the roofs where the two slopes meet*

Parts of the veranda can be enclosed for stores, while others remain open.

Another option is to elevate the center structure to create two levels (a) on either side.

*ventilation*

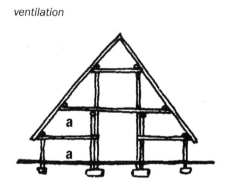

*section of the structure*

With a higher central area, the structure requires larger-sized logs. The interior side spaces become mezannines or elevated arcades. Since the roofs planes must be lower, a large central triangular window can be inserted to light the space.

To construct this type of building, first raise the structure of the second floor and use it as a work platform (1).

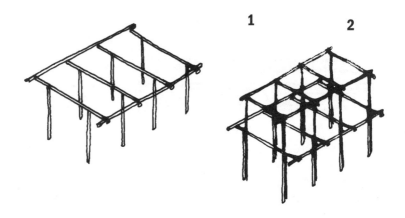

**1**

**2**

Then place the posts of the higher floor next to the others (2). Now install the columns for the exterior walls and the intermediary floor of the mezannine (3).

**3**

Finally, install the roof rafters.

This small building or shed contains a great variety of interior spaces for diverse uses.

The second example, a circular structure, is another interesting shape for a public building. This shape also allows for a variety of space uses. Below is a plan and a view of this type of building.

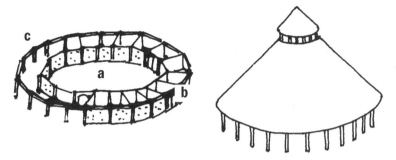

In this example, there is a sheltered interior (a) with upper ventilation; there are enclosed areas with entryways from outside and inside (b); there is a veranda to expand into (c). This type of space can be arranged to accomodate a market, a fair, a small school or a community center.

The structure shown in the drawing below is more elaborate than the first example. The posts (a) are driven into the ground and are well fastened to the roof beams, which are supported by other posts (b). The beams, located on the upper part of the posts, go around the whole circle. Above there is cupola made with a ring of logs connected together with diagonal reinforcement (c). The cupola has its own roof.

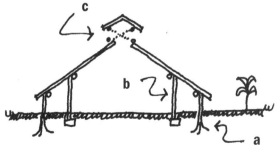

The stability of this type of structure is dependent on the strength of the connections. To understand the behavior of the forces acting on such a structure, it is recommended to first build a smaller building, such as a shed for fowl or cattle.

Naturally these techniques can be used for homes, as is shown in the third example below.

For the main structure, first install 15cm diameter columns, positioned at a 4-meter distance from each other:

*ridge beam*

Next install the smaller columns for the ridge beam. Install the ridge beam, and then mount the posts and beams of the exterior walls that support the lower part of roof rafters:

*roof rafters*

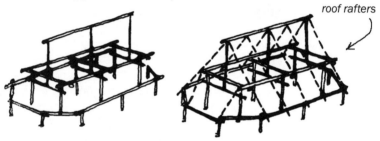

The roof planes on the shorter sides are square (a) with triangular corners (b):

*ventilation*

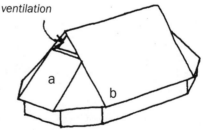

The result is a very comfortable, well-ventilated house. There is flexibility to plan the interior spaces to suit the occupants' needs.

In marsh or swamp regions, the houses are built on pillars, as described below. The roof structure is separate from the structure supporting floor and walls. This technique removes the roof weight from the walls, which can be damaged when the house moves slightly in the unstable ground.

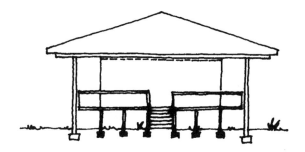

In the next chapter on the dry tropics, there are suggestions on how to prevent insects from entering a house. In those climates pests enter a house at ground level. However, in humid tropical conditions, the insects and unwanted animals enter through openings between the roof and the upper part of the wall. Besides insects, there are rats, possums, bats and lizards that often enter and make their homes in openings.

When closing off the space between the walls and the roof rafters, the board must be placed on the interior side of the sleeper so that the remaining space is on the outside of the building.

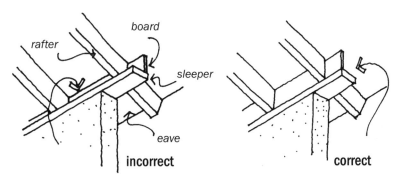

the interior space can house pests     the exterior space is a place for birds

## CONSTRUCTION PHASES

When your land is small and you wish to build a two-storey house, it is common practice to raise the structure, and build the floor of the second storey with a concrete slab. When you have limited funds to build the whole house at once, the first floor is built first, and later on the second storey.

In tropical climates, this type of house does not offer sufficient protection from the sun and rain; the house heats up, and during the rainy season it remains very humid, with water pools collecting on the concrete slab roof.

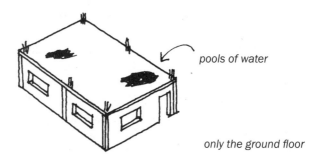

pools of water

only the ground floor

It is preferable to build the first and second storey at once with a good protective roof. With this approach, the walls can be made with lighter and less costly materials. At the same time, the lower space, under the slab, can be used as a rest area, a dining room or workshop.

only the second floor

Later on you can enclose the first floor and expand out to the sides.

*now the house is finished.....*

Instead of this way:

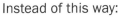

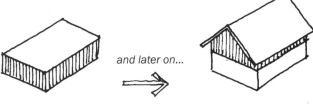

*and later on...*

try this method:

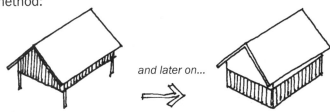

*and later on...*

Another solution is to build the ground floor with a green roof on top of a barrel-vaulted slab. This type of roof does not heat up or cool down the house as much. It can be reused later on as a green roof for the second storey.

## STRUCTURES

When the walls are made with strong and durable materials, such as bricks, stones, or concrete blocks, the roof structure can be supported by the walls.

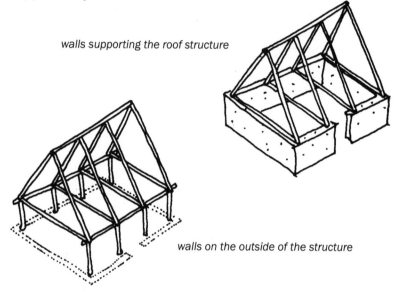

*walls supporting the roof structure*

*walls on the outside of the structure*

When the walls are not built as supports, or are built in phases, it is preferable to mount a structure which is independent from the walls to support the roof.

The roof should be sloped, with one or several planes, no matter which material is used for the walls. The edges of the roof should have wide eaves to protect the walls from the rain.

The structure shown below is for a basic roof of a small-sized house. Larger houses require additional main posts and beams.

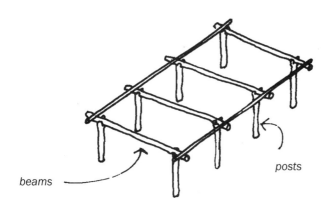

beams ——

posts

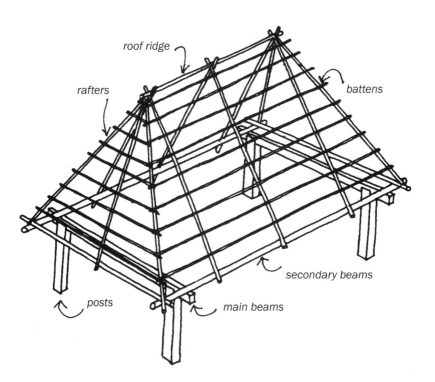

roof ridge

rafters

battens

secondary beams

posts

main beams

The posts supporting the roof structure can be positioned in various ways:

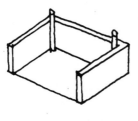

The posts are imbedded in the walls and therefore protected from humidity.

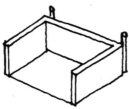

The posts are outside of the walls and do not take up any interior space of the house.

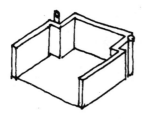

The recommended method is to position the posts a little outside. Walls with many corners are more resistant to earth movement.

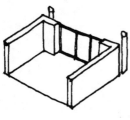

In this example the position of the posts facilitates the installation of a large window or an open wall. The wall is protected from the rain.

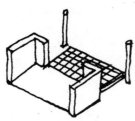

Pull the wall posts forward to create a covered outside veranda.

When large pieces of wood are not available to make posts or beams, join several smaller pieces together with wire or twine.

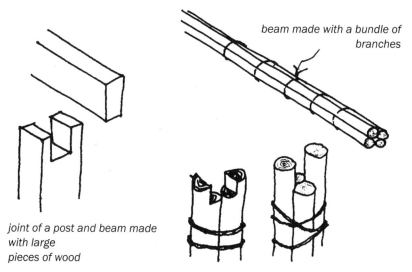

beam made with a bundle of branches

joint of a post and beam made with large pieces of wood

two ways to join the beam to the post

Attic floors can be part of the roof or wall structure.

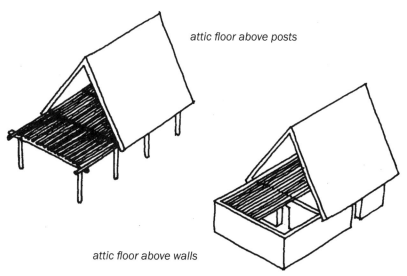

attic floor above posts

attic floor above walls

## ATTICS

Attics can be used to improve the ventilation of the rooms, to store objects, or to dry grain, seeds or fruit. They can be made with bamboo mats or reeds with a thin layer of plaster, or lathes with a thin layer of mud and straw.

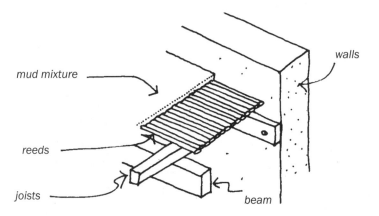

When possible, the ceilings of adjacent rooms should be at different heights to ventilate the spaces:

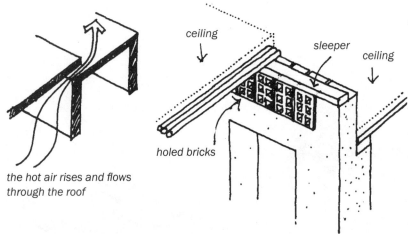

*the hot air rises and flows through the roof*

A construction tip: Use holed bricks to let the rising hot air escape. See chapter 6 for more information on building ceiling panels.

## JOISTS

The sleeper or joist to which the inclined roof rafters are attached is supported by a beam or wall.

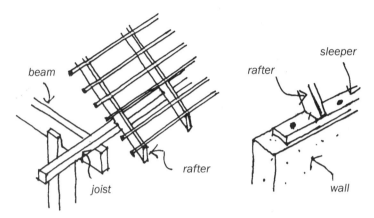

The sleeper or joist should be well attached. If it should slip, the roof rafters could loosen and the whole structure could fall.

To build a roof with two pitches, install three joists:

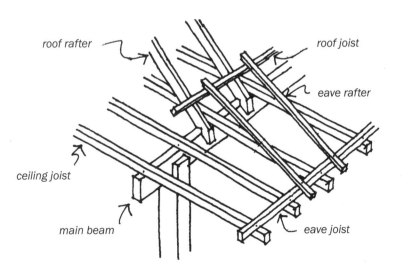

## EAVES

When the eaves are wide, the extension of rafter requires support posts. The roof beams can extend through the wall to support these posts.

In very wet regions, build roofs with wide overhanging eaves to protect the finishing of the wall, and to shelter pedestrians.

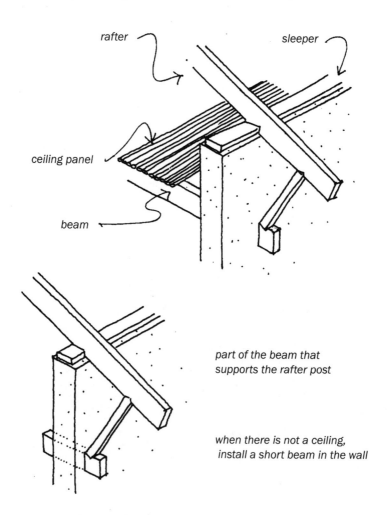

rafter

sleeper

ceiling panel

beam

part of the beam that
supports the rafter post

when there is not a ceiling,
install a short beam in the wall

## USING BAMBOO

In the fifth chapter there is a section on how to treat bamboo so that it lasts longer. Before using this material for house construction, it is recommended that you practice building with it by making small objects, such as the bench described below.

**1** Make two cuts in a piece of bamboo, then bend the thin and flexible "elbows." This piece is like a bridge, and is used as the leg and the beam of the bench.

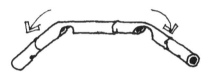

**2** Connect each of the legs with a piece of thin bamboo, held in place with two pegs, to prevent the legs from separating.

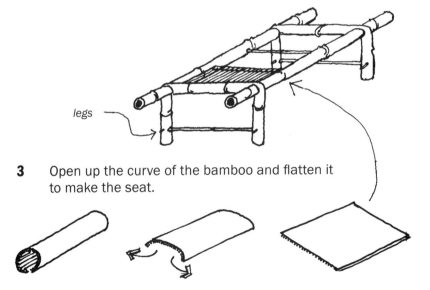

*legs*

**3** Open up the curve of the bamboo and flatten it to make the seat.

## BAMBOO STRUCTURES

Bamboo is an appropriate material for roof structures; however the joints must be carefully crafted. Not only must two joining trunks be tied together well, but each piece must be shaped to fit the other. The cuts for the joints must always made close to the knots. The middle part, between two knots, is more fragile than the area near the knots.

The most common connections used to join trunks are:

**a**  connection for simple joints
**b**  connection with a tongue
**c**  connection with a peg

Insert a peg of hard wood close to the joints and leave its ends extended to use as a support for ties made of vines, strings or wire.

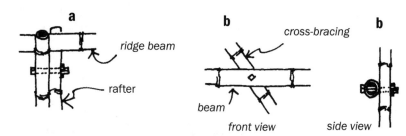

Structure of a small house without its interior partitions:

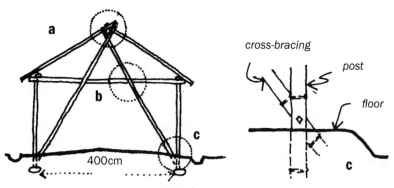

*Note: The circles identify details that are described in the larger drawings above.*

In a larger house, the interior walls should be located where there is cross-bracing to further strengthen the center of the beams.

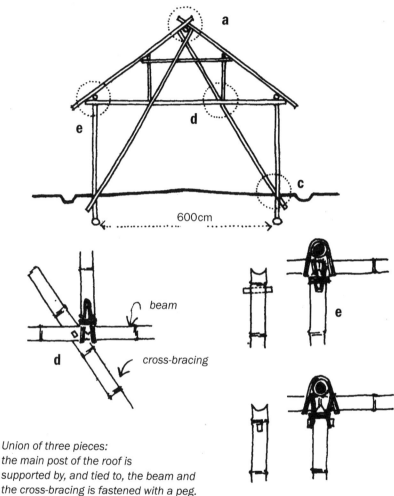

600cm

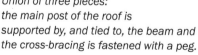

beam

cross-bracing

Union of three pieces:
the main post of the roof is
supported by, and tied to, the beam and
the cross-bracing is fastened with a peg.

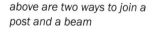

above are two ways to join a
post and a beam

another type of post and beam joint:
at the top of the posts there is a tongue

## OTHER BAMBOO JOINTS

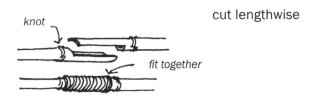

cut lengthwise

*knot*

*fit together*

Above is shown a type of bamboo joint that should not be used to support weight.

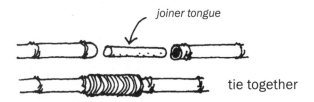

*joiner tongue*

tie together

Shown above is a type of joint which can be used when the bamboo is under compression. The tongue slides into both pieces between the knots. This is a very strong joint.

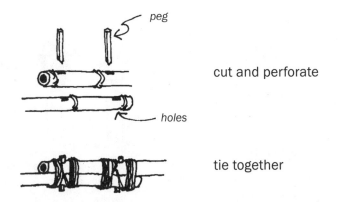

*peg*

cut and perforate

*holes*

tie together

When a structure requires a joint which can resist strong compression, it is better to use hardwood pegs. This ensures that the joint is sufficiently solid.

Bamboo joints are made with pegs and vines or strings. Normally the pegs are located close to the natural divisions in the bamboo (the knots). A depression is shaped above the knot to allow the two pieces to fit together well.

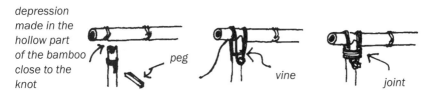

*depression made in the hollow part of the bamboo close to the knot*   *peg*   *vine*   *joint*

Join the post and beam so that they fit, and tie them together with vines which twist around the extended parts of the peg.

Another type of joint is made by cutting out a tongue in the post (above the knot), bending it over, and then tying the tongue to the rest of the post.

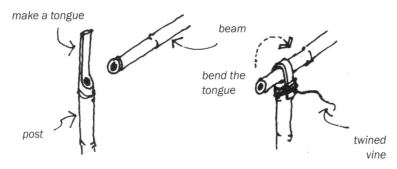

*make a tongue*   *beam*   *bend the tongue*   *post*   *twined vine*

The ridge beam is tied in the same way, by making a fitted joint and using pegs.

*simple ridge beam*          *reinforced ridge beam*

Never use nails in bamboo structures, for they weaken and split the wood.

The drawings below show details for a house built with central posts. This house has two, 4-meter spaces for rooms on either side of the center post. The interior partitions of the rooms are built around the posts.

Here are joint details for the roof rafters.

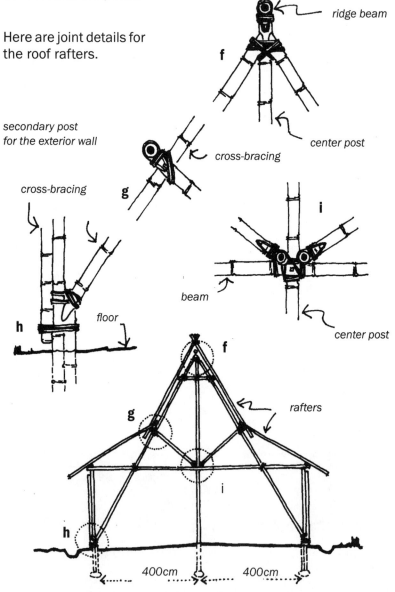

secondary post
for the exterior wall

cross-bracing

cross-bracing

ridge beam

center post

beam

center post

floor

rafters

400cm          400cm

Details of the rafters and ridge beam of the roof structure:

*basic detail*                      *tied together*

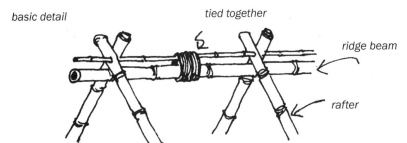

ridge beam

rafter

In regions with strong winds, use two ridge beams with a smaller bamboo pole in the center.

*reinforced detail*

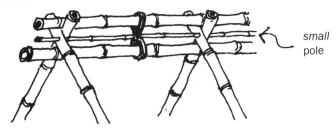

small pole

For steep sloped roofs, install the two ridge beams one on top of the other. For shallow slopes, install them side by side.

*steep slope*                    *shallow slope*

The two ridge beams must be tied together well to make a strong support for the rafters.

There are risks associated with the materials used to connect bamboo elements, or any other, together. Vegetal ties can be attacked by insects; and metal, such as wire, can rust. Therefore the connections should be visible to facilitate periodic inspection, and replacements when needed.

## WOVEN BAMBOO PANELS

To make woven bamboo mats for walls, dividers or floating floors, first start by slicing the bamboo trunk and removing the interior knots. Then open the bamboo, place a weight on top and leave it to dry out flat.

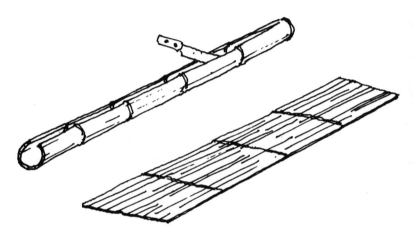

For modest houses, join full boards together to cover floors or walls.

To make stronger panels, cut the board into 3 cm wide strips.

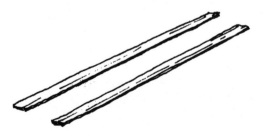

Generally, the panels have a height of half the height of a room, so approximately 1.50 meters and 50 cm large.

There are two ways to weave bamboo:

**A** This open weave is for a light panel that provides some privacy and allows breezes through (not for cold windy regions).

**B** This tighter weave can be used to make more finished walls. Cover the outer side with tar and apply sand. Then paint the two sides with a mixture of clay, lime and cactus juice.

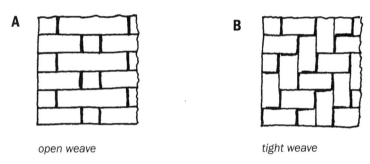

**A** open weave      **B** tight weave

After weaving a panel, torch the ends of the strips and lay it flat to apply the tar and sand. Before applying a second coat, allow the panel to dry in the sun. Wait until it is completely dry before installing it. Make sure the final coat covers the black tar. Reinforce the edges with other strips – one on each side – and tie the strips to the panel with string or wire to create a frame. One can also use a small trunk of bamboo with a slit which fits onto the edge, as seen below.

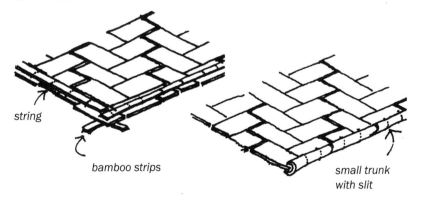

string

bamboo strips

small trunk with slit

## ROUND TIMBER FRAME STRUCTURES

Narrow the end of the timber to make a strong and fitted joints. For small structures, tie the joints with string, vine or metal wire. The wood logs must be straight and bark must be removed. For large structures, it is better to join the structure with nuts and bolts.

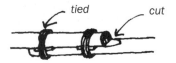

The strength of the joint above is improved with small wood fillers. Be careful with how the cuts are shaped.

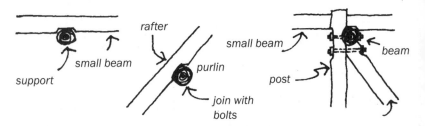

For a better-fitted joint, cut out a small notch from the rafters and the posts.

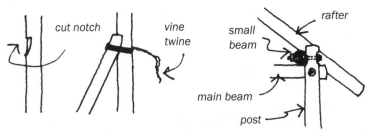

Shown below are details of log footings.

Be careful in the areas where the logs are notched.

The drawings below show another way to build roof structures. The columns can be made with bamboo or other materials. Whichever materials are chosen, the part that is below ground must be protected by using tar or by being torched with oil.

A small house with equal sides and a center support post is illustrated below.

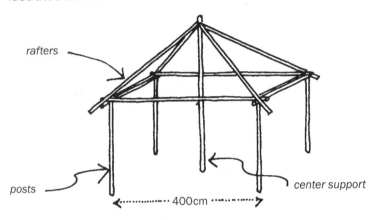

A house that is double the size of the previous one requires a more elaborate roof structure with additional posts and a doubled center post.

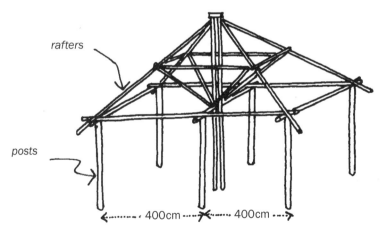

For a workshop or a shed, use smaller pieces, especially if there are no walls and the roof is lightweight.

*a large structure for a large space*

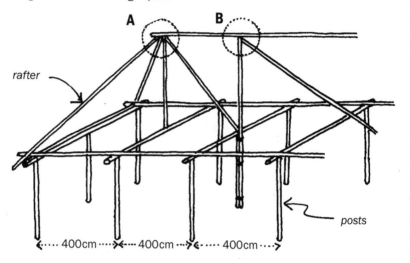

Below are some details of the ridge beam:

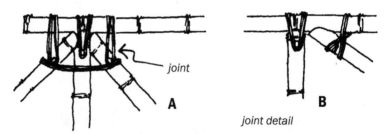

*joint detail*

The secret to making a good roof is to make well-crafted joints, meaning joints where the parts are well-fitted and tied together. Always cut bamboo trunks close to the knots and use projecting pegs to tie the strings. This takes more time, but the joint lasts much longer.

The basic roof structure is then reinforced with a lighter structure of purlins that supports the roofing layer.

For building even larger spans, reinforce the structure with bracing between the ridge beam and the rafter. The bracing starts at the center post at the height of the beams.

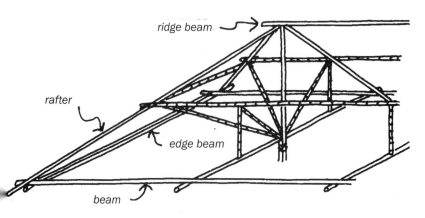

*...the posts are not shown here...*

In regions with damp ground, raise the floor above the ground:

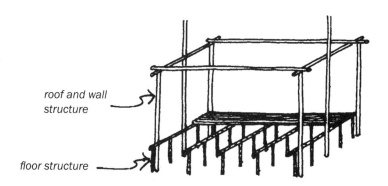

A raised floor has a separate support structure from the one for the walls and roof.

## SAWN TIMBER FRAME STRUCTURES

For public buildings, such as schools or clinics, it is preferable to use milled lumber. The lumber is joined with bolts and nuts, and toothed brackets.

The details below show a structure with a six-meter span. The floor can be made with polished cement or ceramic tiles.

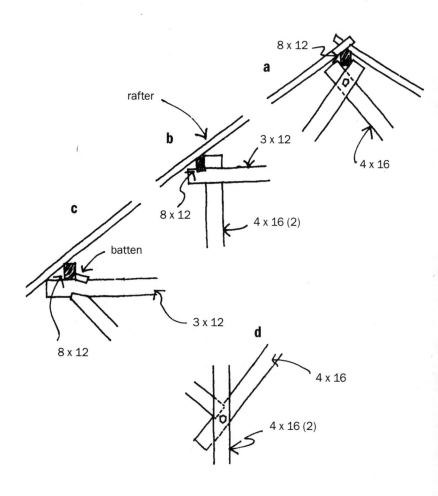

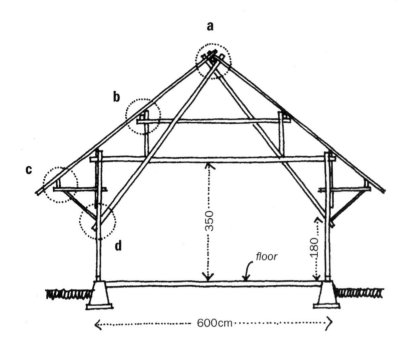

The ridge beam is 5½ meters above the floor. The columns and the cross-bracing are 4 x 16; the beams are 3 x 12, and the purlins are 8 x 12. The rafter can be 4 x 7, depending on the size of wood available. If their dimensions are smaller, they should be placed closer together.

The dimensions on the columns and cross-bracing are given in centimeters. For example, on the right is a 4 x 8 piece of lumber. The numbers in parentheses indicate the number of pieces that are joined together.

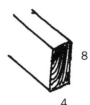

The ridge beam and purlins should not move with the weight of the rafters.

In this detail to the right, a batten is used to fasten the purlin and secure it to the beam, keeping it from dislocating.

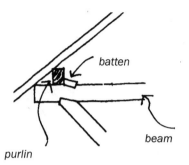

purlin

The drawing below shows a light structure, with a 12-meter span, that can be used as a factory or market. The joint details are the same as for smaller 6-meter-span buildings. This construction is actually two smaller buildings under one roof. The detail (e) shows the joints of the center columns.

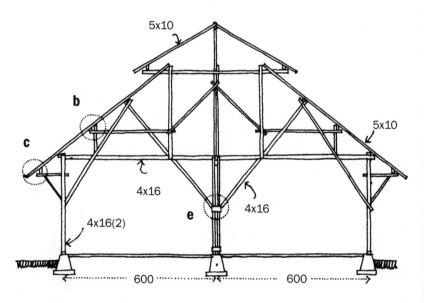

Note that the ridge beam extends to allow hot air to flow out. The drawings do not show the battens on the rafters nor the roofing materials.

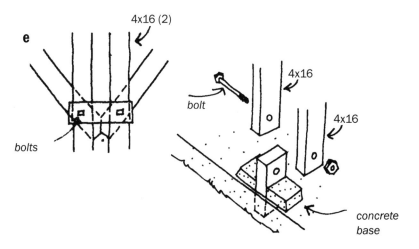

A continuous slab foundation must have a base to connect the two columns. Use concrete so that the wood does not rot. The base is also 4 x 16 and should be painted with oil or another type of protective seal. See chapter 6 for more details.

Below is another example of joint assembly:

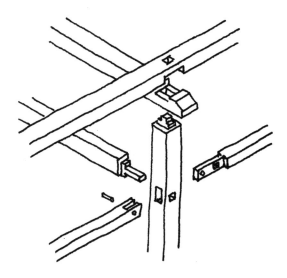

## WOVEN PALM LEAVES

First cut off the ends of the leaf, then divide the leaf in half, and round out the edges of the "spine" or stem, to prevent cutting your hands during the weaving.

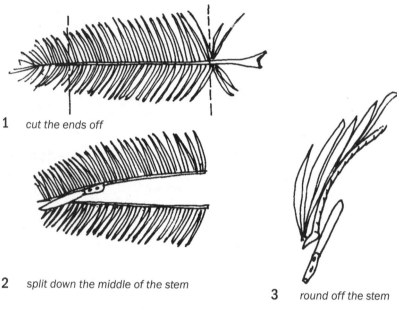

1  *cut the ends off*

2  *split down the middle of the stem*

3  *round off the stem*

Now weave one side at a time to make a large woven band of mat:

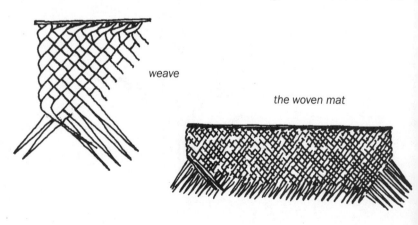

*weave*

*the woven mat*

Shown below is another way to prepare the palm leaves for roofing material. This method is a little more labor-intensive but gives a better result.

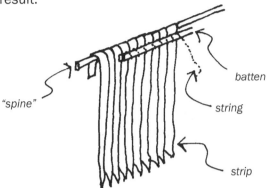

"spine"

batten

string

strip

Remove the strips of leaves (sometimes called fronds) from the large leaf. Then fold the strips around the "spine" or stem of the leaf. Place two battens on either side of the "spine" and tie the strips with a string to the battens.

A roof covered with this type of thatching can last for many years.

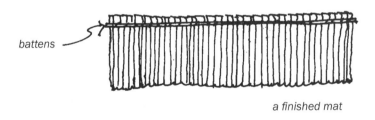

battens

*a finished mat*

To tie the leaves together, use a bamboo pole sliced into small string-like strips.

bamboo

*string-like strips*

To use this thatching as roofing, overlap the thatch pieces by placing the top one over one-third of the one underneath.

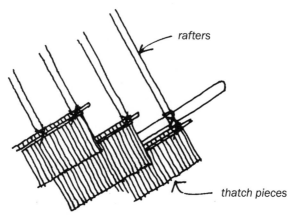

To reinforce the ridge beam roofing, install tightly joined and tied small bamboo rods on top of the thatching. Then tie this ridge cap assembly to the roof structure.

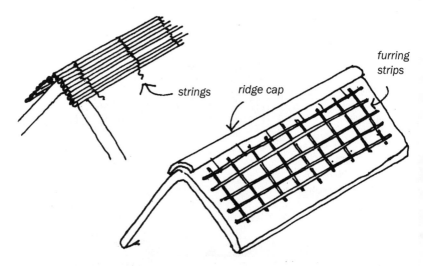

In zones with strong winds, make a grid of furring strips and place it on top of the thatching, starting at the ridge. This prevents wind from destroying the thatching.

## THATCHING THE RIDGE BEAM

Another way to protect the ridge beam is to build a thatch ridge "cap."

First make a roofing assembly of 4 thatches on top of which 4 strong bamboo battens are tied.

1  Layer 4 thatches:

2  Tie four bamboo battens, two on each side, leaving the center empty:

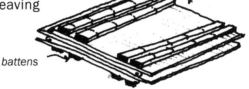

*center*

*battens*

3  Fold and tie the battens over the roof structure:

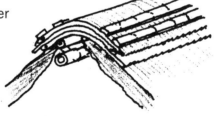

Below is a section showing how to thread wire through the battens and ridge beam:

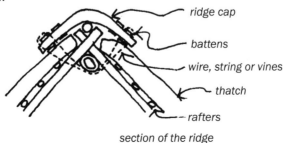

*ridge cap*

*battens*

*wire, string or vines*

*thatch*

*rafters*

section of the ridge

## A PALM TREE HOUSE

The fan palm tree grows in many regions. A comfortable house can be made with materials originating only from this one type of palm. Of course, more than one palm will be necessary.

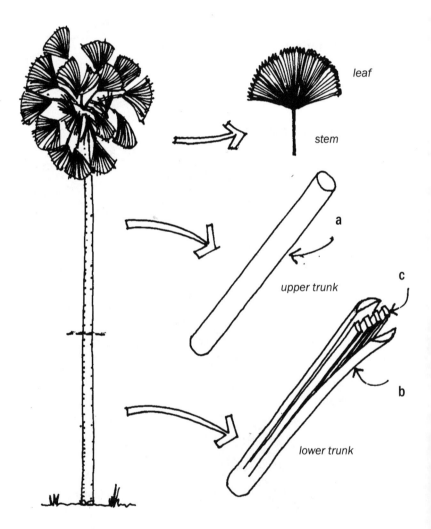

This palm tree is also known as the buriti or Mauritian palm.

When a baby is born, the parents can plant a number of palm trees so as an adult he or she can build a house from the materials made from these mature trees.

The leaves are used as roofing and the stems to cover the walls and:

> the trunk (a) for the posts
>
> the trunk (b) for the beams
>
> the trunk (c) for the purlins and the walls

The (b) and (c) parts of the trunk have the requisite sizes for the structure.

Shown below are (a) from the larger part of the trunk, and (b) and (c) from the smaller parts.

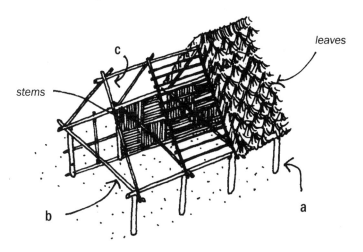

Note: In dry areas the trunk of the palm tree is used for posts. In humid areas it rots quickly, therefore a more resistant type of regional tree is required.

## PARTITIONS

These walls are used to separate rooms and are attached to the support posts.

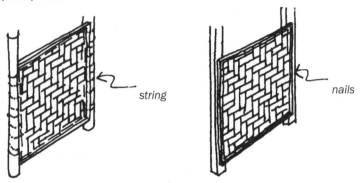

The partitions can be nailed when installed on solid wood posts.

The drawing below shows a small bamboo house where one-half of the floor space is used as a platform to sit or lie down, and to store things on:

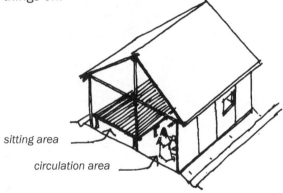

On a sloped site, on a hill for example, make several platforms as floor levels.

When the ground surface is very irregular, install rocks or concrete footings on the flattest or firmest area of the slope. This stabilizes the first floor posts.

## TIMBER AND MUD

Below is an example of a house made with various materials such as a tiled roof, and bamboo and mud walls. The construction phases for the exterior wall are the following:

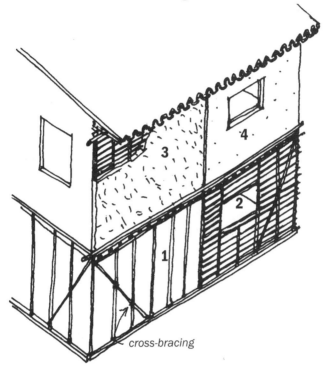

cross-bracing

1    The wall structure is made with long bamboo pieces.

2    On the exterior side, tie bamboo furrings, spaced 10 cm apart, to the vertical pieces.

3    Cover the furrings with mud and chopped straw.

4    Whitewash the final layer with lime.

Note that the wall has cross-bracing to strengthen it against earthquakes and strong winds.

Houses, streets and gardens can be built on sloped sites:

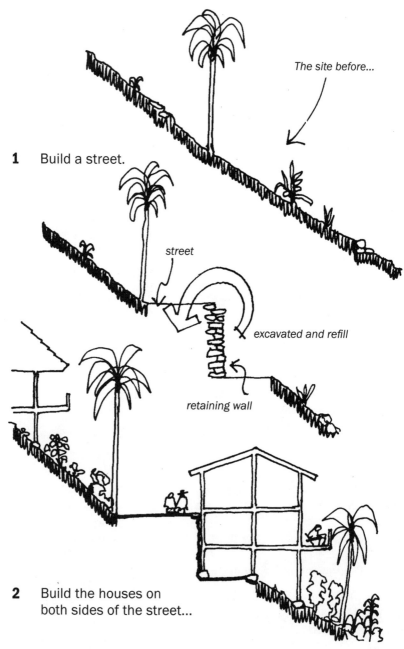

*The site before...*

**1** Build a street.

*street*

*excavated and refill*

*retaining wall*

**2** Build the houses on both sides of the street...

## TRIANGULATION

When the walls are made with wood posts, all the wall frames should be "triangulated."

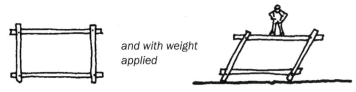

*and with weight applied*

If a carpenter does not use triangulation, the structure will not resist the weight of earthquakes, and might collapse.

With a diagonal wood member, the frame resists the forces exerted on the structure.

Shown below is an example of a triangulated floor structure:

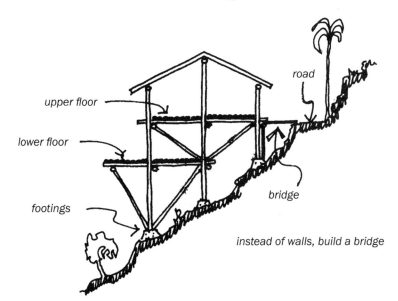

*road*

*upper floor*

*lower floor*

*footings*

*bridge*

*instead of walls, build a bridge*

In the humid tropics, floors made with stone, brick, ceramic or cement are preferable for the following reasons:

 They are simple to clean with water without getting damaged.

 They stay cooler.

 They are not inhabited or damaged by insects

## TILED FLOORS

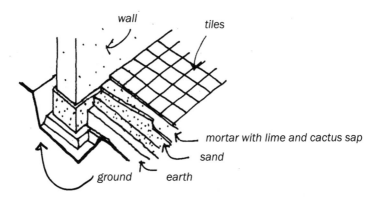

## WOOD FLOORS

In regions with colder winters, use wood parquet on top of a concrete floor:

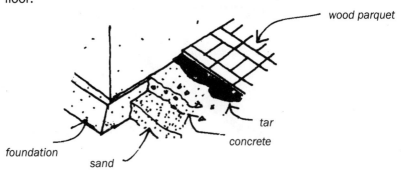

The parquet floors are made with hardwood, 2 cm-thick, 6 x 25 cm pieces. They are installed with fresh tar and sanded, and then protected with oil.

Use differently colored woods to create patterns:

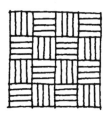  

## BAMBOO FLOORS

Raised floors for humid ground conditions can be made with mats over bamboo joists. The mats are pressed down with battens and fastened to the joists.

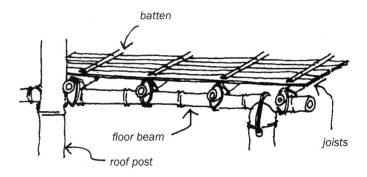

batten

floor beam

roof post

joists

# PESTS

Described here are ways to prevent pests, such as bats, rats and insects, from inhabiting structures:

Consider these two tips:

 Check that all joints do not have gaps or holes, to prevent animals from trying to build nests.

 Revise construction details in order to expose the corners of the structure from the inside. Also paint the ridge beam, inside the building, with lime to discourage the location of nests.

## EXAMPLES

A good example is the position of the ridge beam. If this piece is installed, as it usually is, in a square position, rats or other pests can build nests on the flat surface. If the rafters are bamboo, fill the open ends.

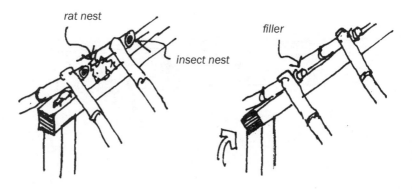

incorrect ridge beam installation          correct installation

Woven mats or bamboo should cover only one side of a wall to prevent animals from inhabiting the intervening space.

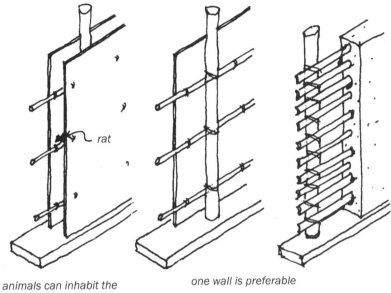

*animals can inhabit the space between two walls*

*one wall is preferable*

Another solution is to make walls with bamboo poles and then fill in the spaces with mud and thatch or straw. When the assembly dries, finish it with a lime whitewash.

Also slope the extensions of the main beam to prevent nesting on the flat projecting surface.

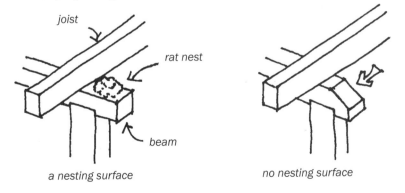

*joist*

*rat nest*

*beam*

*a nesting surface*

*no nesting surface*

When there are one or several levels of roofs below the main roof,
all support members of lower roofs should be cut on an angle.

*House with 2 roof levels*

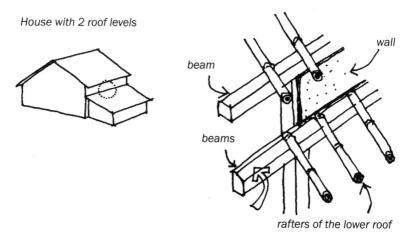

wall

beam

beams

rafters of the lower roof

The bamboo floor of the upper level should be visible. The mats
should be filled or tightly joined.

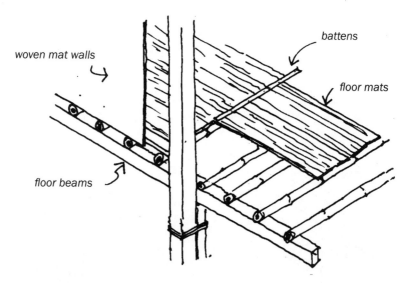

battens

woven mat walls

floor mats

floor beams

Also see chapter 5 for ways to prepare construction materials so
that they resist pests.

A row of bottles in concrete prevents scorpions from climbing the walls and entering through the windows.

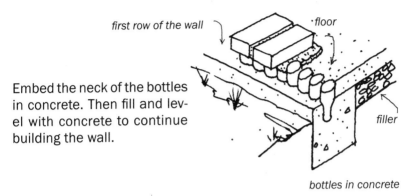

*first row of the wall*

Embed the neck of the bottles in concrete. Then fill and level with concrete to continue building the wall.

*·floor*

*filler*

*bottles in concrete*

The three steps of wall construction are:

**1**      Embed bottles in fresh concrete and prepare a floor base with gravel and sand.

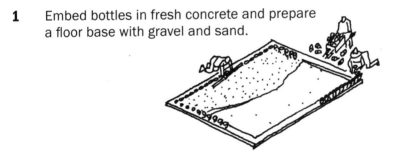

**2**      Fill in the space between the bottles and the floor area with cement.

**3**      Raise the walls.

This system is not recommended for houses over two storeys.

## SMOKE CIRCULATION

One of the problems with bamboo, reeds or other plants used for roofs is the destruction caused by insects such as termites and borers.

One way to deter these pests is to circulate smoke from the kitchen into the ceiling, the attic spaces, or wherever the insects are located.

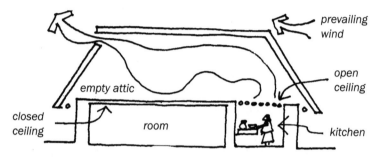

*section of a house with smoke circulation*

The kitchen and the roof openings are positioned in a way to allow prevailing winds to draw the smoke through the higher spaces. The kitchen ceiling is open, and the ceilings of the other rooms are closed.

## OTHER CONTROL METHODS

 Make a mixture of hot peppers, rolling tobacco and cumin. Burn a small amount of the mixture and close the house for a few hours. Eucalyptus incense also works.

 Around the house, near the walls, grow a garden of plants with fragrances that repel insects such as citronella, basil, common rue and germander.

 Paint areas with the most flies, such as the stable or the kitchen, in blue.

# DOORS AND WINDOWS

On the door frame, which is part of the wall structure, install another frame which is the structure for the door itself.

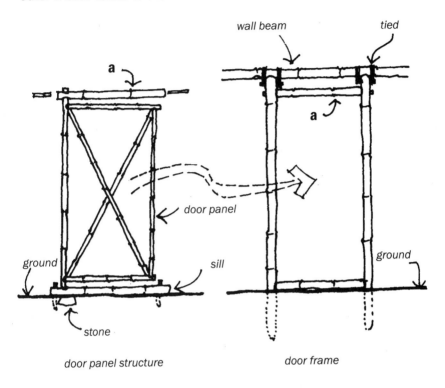

*door panel structure*  *door frame*

The piece (a) is the same in both drawings above. This piece has two tongues attached to the frame. The door sill is fastened to the ground with dowels, or secured to the vertical frame which has poles into the ground. The door structure is covered with woven bamboo mats, and turns on a stone placed at the bottom of the sill.

Note: With all these details, watch out for open ends in the bamboo which can house insects. The bamboo ends should be cut near the knots or filled in.

The same technique is used for windows. There are three types of hinges: The first example below is for a casement window, which is similar to the door system. The second is a sliding window, and the third is an awning window. Part (a), the window itself, is attached to part (b), the window frame.

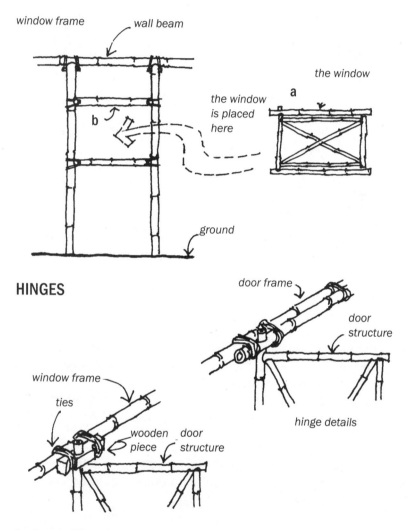

**HINGES**

hinge details

Instead of bamboo, use a piece of wood to attach the door to the frame.

The structure of a sliding window moves between two parts of the wall on a track made with hardwood battens. One section is covered with a mat and the other is left open for the window.

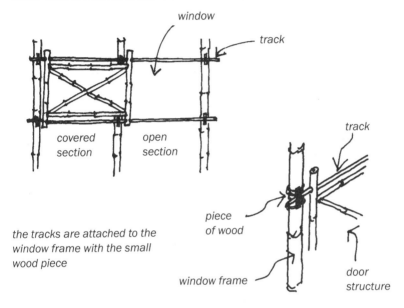

window frame with a sliding window

The window structure for an awning window is kept open with a pole or hook attached to the eaves of the roof. The hinges are loosely tied.

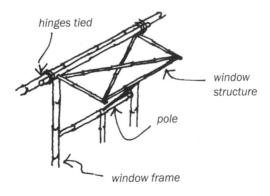

# VENTILATION

In a humid tropical climate, the ceiling can be closed off from the roof, but the space between the ceiling and the roof should remain open and well ventilated. The ceiling can be made with lath and plaster, or woven reeds.

Hot air rises, therefore openings should be made in the upper areas of the house to allow hot air to exit. It is also important to make openings in the lower walls for cool air to enter. See chapter 1 for more details.

There are many ways to ventilate depending on the available materials, the direction of the wind and the shape of the roof. The following drawings illustrate three examples:

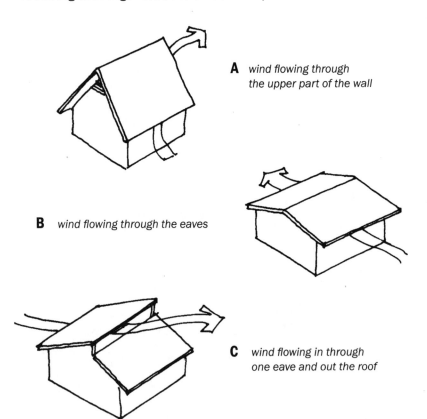

**A** *wind flowing through the upper part of the wall*

**B** *wind flowing through the eaves*

**C** *wind flowing in through one eave and out the roof*

## ROOF VENTILATION OPENINGS

In the upper section of the roof, make a triangular opening just below the ridge.

*gabled roof – 2 planes*

*hip roof – 4 planes*

Another method is to build an awning opening in the middle upper part of the roof, near the ridge. This opening can be permanently left open with the support of a pole.

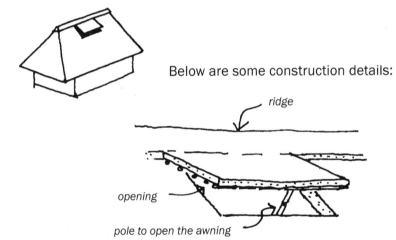

Below are some construction details:

*ridge*

*opening*

*pole to open the awning*

To leave the awning open when it is not raining, place the pole horizontally.

*pole*

# HUMIDITY

A wood house construction must be protected from humidity to be durable, therefore the wood should be maintained as dry as possible. Here are several ways to do this:

**A**    Build eaves. They protect the walls from rain and the sun's heat. They should be at least 60cm wide, and ideally 1.20m.

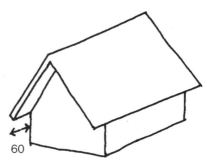

60

**B**    Protect the exposed ends of the wood boards with tar or stain. Humidity penetrates the ends more than the sides.

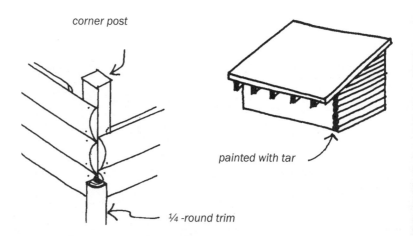

*corner post*

*painted with tar*

*¼ -round trim*

Another method is to cover the exposed corners with a log cut lengthwise in 4 pieces to make ¼-round trim.

**C**   Protect lower walls from ground humidity. Wall finishings made with reeds, fine boards and plaster are affected by ground humidity. Therefore the first 20 to 40 cm above ground should be made with durable materials such as stones, concrete, bricks or large lumber.

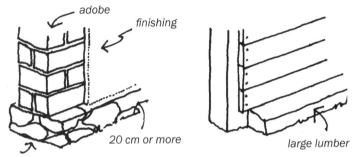

adobe

finishing

20 cm or more

stone foundation

large lumber

**D**   Prevent posts from being in direct contact with the ground. Protect the posts with tar or concrete, or sear the buried part.

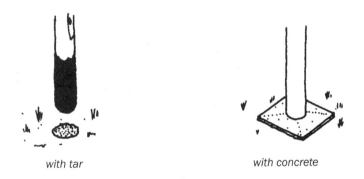

with tar

with concrete

## MASONRY IN THE HUMID TROPICS

It is not always possible to build large enough eaves to protect exterior walls from tropical rains. With two-storey houses, try cantilevering the second floor by extending it out beyond the ground floor wall.

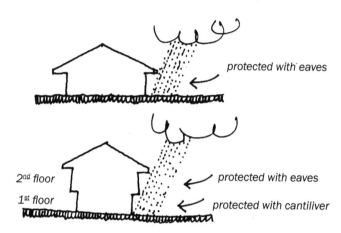

protected with eaves

2ⁿᵈ floor

1ˢᵗ floor

protected with eaves

protected with cantiliver

Other solutions for rain protection must be found for flat roofs, other roof shapes, or for higher buildings in urban areas. Humidity not only destroys wall materials but makes the interior of the house uncomfortable.

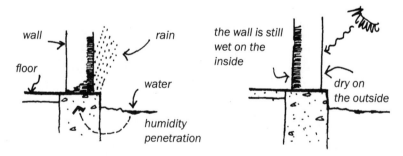

wall

floor

rain

water

humidity penetration

the wall is still wet on the inside

dry on the outside

wall in the rain: humidity enters

wall in the sun after the rain: humidity penetrates

The wall does not dry completely in the sun after a rainstorm since the humidity penetrates the walls.

Here are two ways to prevent humidity from penetrating the wall:

**A**   Build double exterior walls with an air space between the two layers.

Build the two separate walls with a 5 cm cavity space between them. Join the two walls with steel anchors. Place the anchors in the mortar joints at every meter, horizontally and vertically.

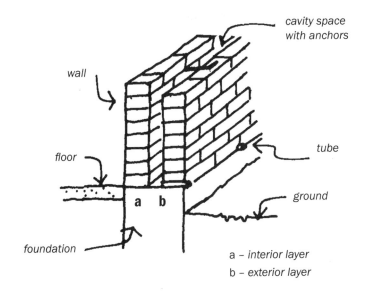

cavity space
with anchors

wall

floor

tube

**a   b**

ground

foundation

a – interior layer
b – exterior layer

With this method, humidity does not penetrate the interior wall layer and water is expelled in the cavity. In the lower wall place a piece of tube every 4 meters to allow water to drain out. This system improves substantially the interior climate.

**B**   Make an impermeable external wall finish with lime and cactus sap to prevent water from penetrating.

**C**    To prevent ground humidity from affecting lower walls, apply
tar to the top and outer sides of the foundation:

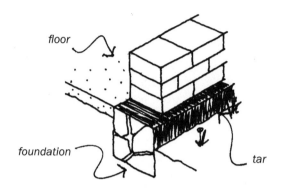

To deter water from penetrating, treat earth walls in the following
way:

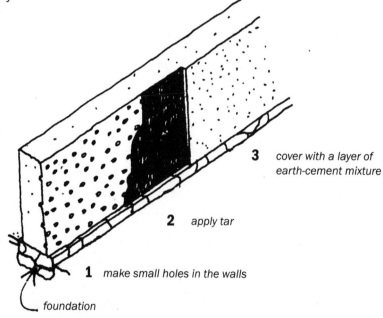

**3**  *cover with a layer of
earth-cement mixture*

**2**  *apply tar*

**1**  *make small holes in the walls*

*foundation*

In areas where there are no cactuses to make an outer protective
seal, use tar instead.

In urban areas, the lower parts of the walls are exposed to wear. Protect these surfaces with more durable materials, such as bricks.

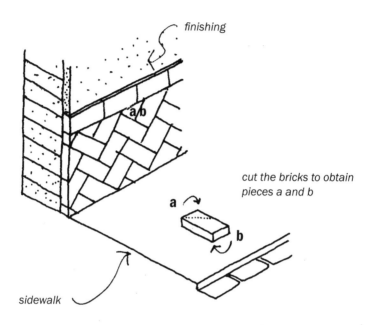

*finishing*

*cut the bricks to obtain pieces a and b*

*sidewalk*

In rural regions, as seen below, the lower part of an exterior wall is humid from rainfall and ground moisture. Animals such as pigs can destroy mud walls by digging into the base.

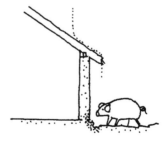

Reinforce this lower part with logs or with stones, or relocate animals in a pen.

# ROADS AND BRIDGES

In humid tropical areas, small rivers or streams often cross paths. The following pages describe construction techniques to build simple wood or bamboo bridges.

## ROADS

In tropical zones, paths are built during the dry season. Often part of the path is destroyed and its edges collapse during the rainy season. To prevent this erosion, water should be directed in ditches with banks retained by logs. The logs can be those cut down to clear the path.

**1** cut the branches from the trunks

**2** ram the logs into the ground

**3** fill in the path with earth from the ditches

**4** compact the earth down

Note: Leave some branches in the retaining logs to use as stakes to prevent them from slipping away.

When a water channel crosses a path, drain the earth bed with pipes made from large perforated bamboo trunks.

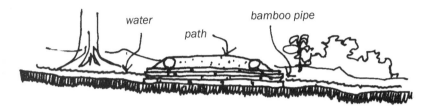

section of drainage pipe

A deeper water channel requires a bridge construction.

a pleasant stroll...

Cut as few trees as possible to keep the pathway shaded!

# BRIDGES

To make a solid durable bridge, first build strong supports on the river banks. These supports are made with four logs, two on either side of the bank. They are secured to the ground with stakes:

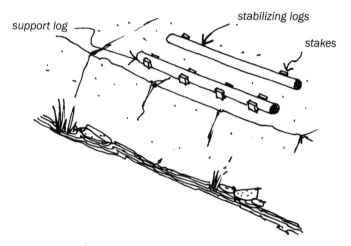

**1**     The support logs carry the weight of the beams that cross over the river. The stabilizing logs keep the beams in place when someone moves over them.

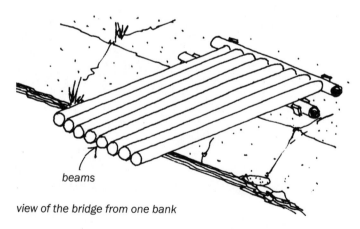

view of the bridge from one bank

**2**     After installing the logs on the banks, add the beams.

**3** Both sides of the bridge have retaining logs on top of the beams, to prevent the covering from slipping. Place leaves or bamboo on the logs before covering them with mud.

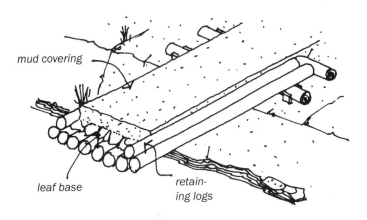

mud covering

leaf base

retain-
ing logs

A lighter bridge, for pedestrians only, can be made using fewer beams spaced farther apart. The bridge covering is made with reeds, branches or bamboo cut lengthwise into battens:

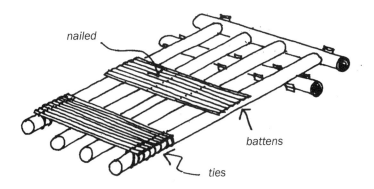

nailed

battens

ties

There are two ways to attach the covering: tie the strips, or battens, to the beams at both ends, or nail them only to the inner beams.

For bridge construction with joined beams, use the following table to determine spans:

| span in mts | PEDESTRIANS | | | VEHICLES | | |
|---|---|---|---|---|---|---|
| | 2 | 4 | 6 | 4 | 4 | 6 |
| size of beams in cms | 10 10 8 x 10 | 16 15 10 x 16 | 22 20 18 x 20 | 15 14 10 x 14 | 18 20 18 x 20 | 21 20 18 x 20 |

## LONG SPANNING BRIDGES

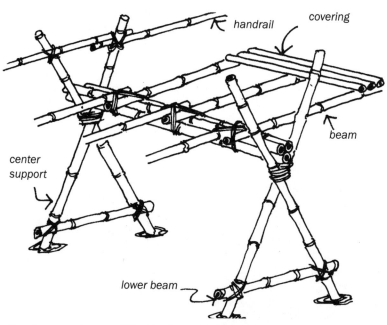

Bamboo can be used for the beams and all other parts that are not in contact with water. Use wood logs for the supports that are in the water. The lower beam prevents the posts from sinking into the river mud.

In areas where the riverbed is lined with stones, raise the lower beam so that the log posts sink a bit into the sand of the riverbed.

Bridges over larger rivers must have center supports spaced three meters from each other. For example, a bridge over a 12-meter-wide river has three supports.

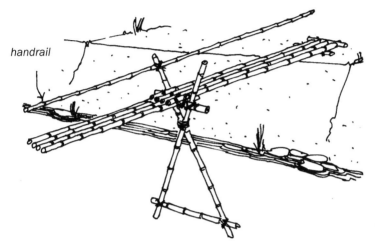

handrail

Above is a partial view of a light bridge over a wide river. A heavy bridge weighs more:

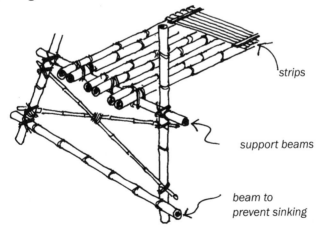

strips

support beams

beam to
prevent sinking

Note: To clarify the drawing above not all the required beams are shown, and the covering does not appear as it should over the strips.

## IMPROVING RIVERBANK CONDITIONS

To retain the banks of the river or make dikes, start by building basket-like containers with large bamboo trunks. These are filled with stones.

**1**     First cut the large trunk bamboo in 2-3cm strips leaving the solid ends as handles.

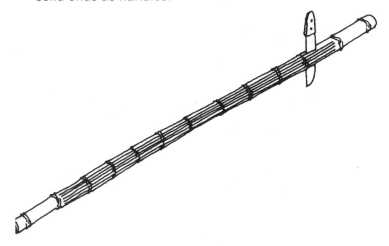

**2**     Open the bamboo strips by pushing them out and weaving in other bamboo strips to make a type of basket. Leave a small opening on one side.

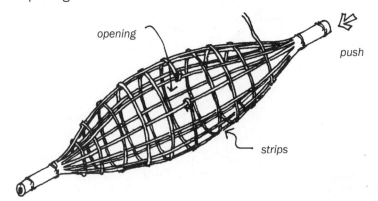

*opening*

*push*

*strips*

**3**     Through the opening, fill the basket with stones and place it
on the riverbank.

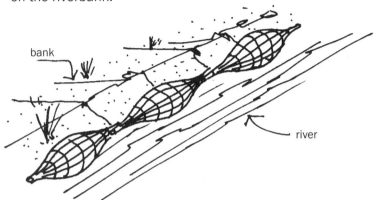

**4**     Make rows of baskets and cover the whole with stones and
earth.

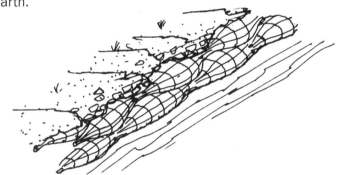

**5**     The bank is now retained. Dikes or dams can be made with
the same technique.

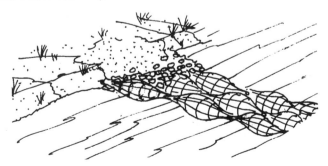

To cross over rivers that are deeper than one and one-half meters, build a bridge with rafts. There are three ways to build a lightweight and floating bridge:

**A**     With trunks from banana trees tied together with bamboo dowels. This type of bridge is quickly built but is not durable.

**B**     With logs or poles bound together with smaller logs placed perpendicularly.

**C**     With several layers of bamboo covered with a woven mat and tied together with strings.

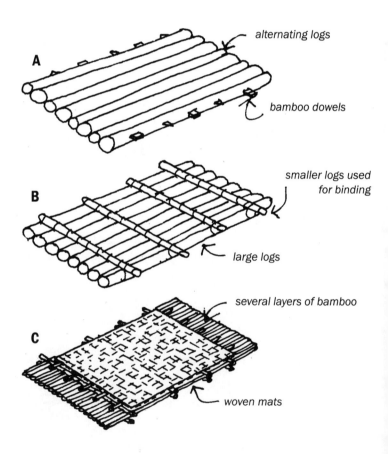

## SELF-PROPELLING TRANSPORT

Since regions with tropical climates have many rivers over which it is not always possible to build bridges, consider crossing over them with a self-propelling raft.

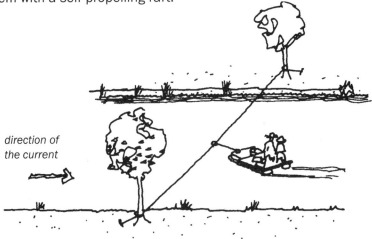

*direction of the current*

On one side of the raft, attach a strong rope or a cable with a metal bar. String a cable from one side of the river to the other to which the raft is connected. The force of the river current moves the raft.

To change direction, move the cable to the other side of the metal bar.

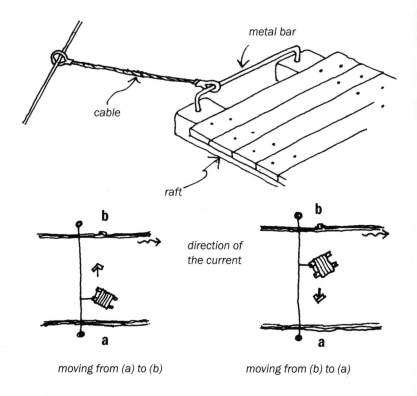

moving from (a) to (b)        moving from (b) to (a)

The above drawing shows how to change directions.

## FLOATING PENS

Water hyacinths grow in the rivers and lakes of many humid tropical regions. Despite their use in cleaning contaminated water, their rapid and dense growth impedes the passage of light, and the lack of oxygen kills fish. There is a way to control their growth by feeding livestock. This is made possible by building a floating pen that moves slowly over the plants.

The hyacinths continue to purify the contaminated water, while animals, such as pigs, are fed. Make sure there are no snails amongst the plants. Their ingestion by the animals causes illness.

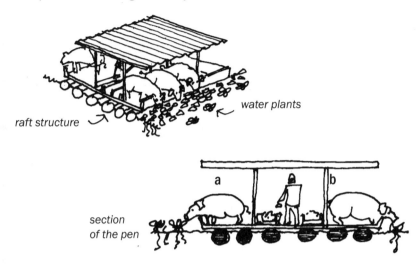

water plants

raft structure

section
of the pen

As shown above, there are two parallel spaces (a) and (b). More food can be placed in the central space. The floor boards have spaces in between them to evacuate the dung.

Shown below is an example of a different type of pen with a tilting grille. This grille collects the hyacinths when the raft is in motion, and is lifted when it is full of plants.

1    The motion of the raft and the lowered grille cuts the plants.

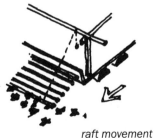

2    The grille full of plants is lifted to feed the pigs.

raft movement

Water plants also are used to feed biodigesters. For more information, see chapter 9.

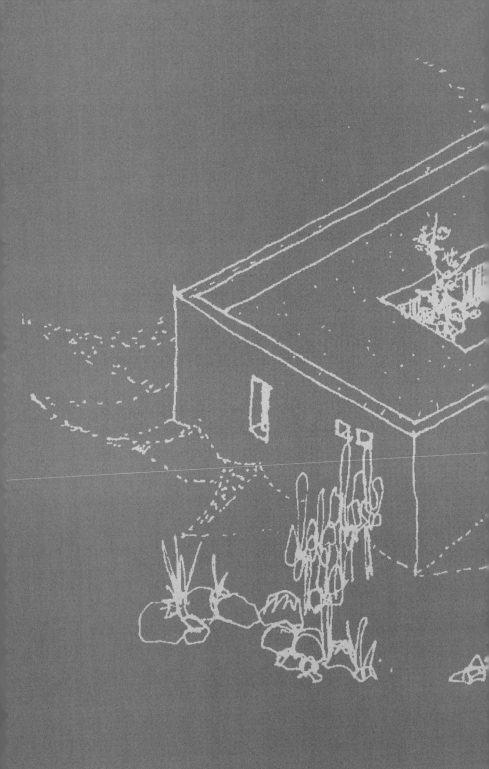

# DRY TROPICS

3

# HOUSE SHAPES

In a dry tropical climate, a good builder should use the following methods to design a house shape that keeps the interior of the house at a comfortable temperature:

The principal rule to remember is that hot air is lighter than cold air, and when hot air rises cold air is drawn into a space. This is how ventilation works.

 In regions with scarce vegetation, the house should have a shaded courtyard to cool the air.

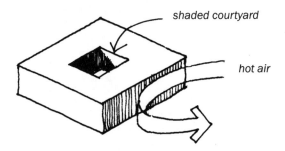

shaded courtyard

hot air

Shaded areas outside the house are quickly warmed when in contact with the circulating hot air.

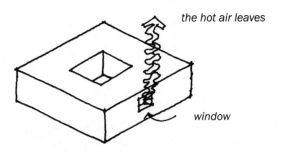

the hot air leaves

window

 When an opening or a window is made in a wall, the hot air in the room flows out of the house.

Therefore, the cooled air from the shaded courtyard enters the rooms as the hot air exits from the exterior windows. With this shape cold air currents circulate in all corners of the house. This method is further improved with plants and a fountain in the courtyard.

*plants further cool the air*

## COURTYARDS AND STREETS

Houses should be close together so that the sun heats up as little as possible of the wall surface. Narrow streets with as much shade as possible help cool the air.

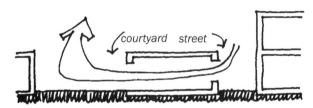

To improve air circulation, build two courtyards of different sizes. The air in the smaller courtyard is cooler than the air in the larger one where there is less shade. The warmer air of the larger courtyard rises, drawing the cooler air from the smaller courtyard through the rooms of the house.

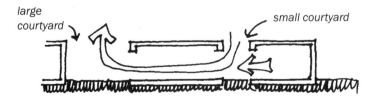

## USING THE EARTH AS AN INSULATION

In regions with dry tropical climates, there is another method to reduce the heat during the day and the cold at night, especially when the building has thin brick or cement block walls.

Since hot air moves quickly through thin walls, one way to insulate the house from the heat is to cover the lower parts of the exterior walls with earth. Build sloped mounds over the solid-walled areas and leave openings for the entrance to the house.

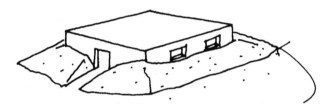

*solid parts of the walls with sloped earth mounds*

*partially earthed-in house in a mountainous region*

A roof covered with earth protects the house even further from temperature changes. There should not be any problems with humidity buildup, since there is little rain in these regions.

With very limited funds, save on construction materials by partially burying the house. Only the top half of the walls needs to be built, including the windows and doors and their lintels.

As shown below, the entrance door is on the side with steps down into the house. The excavated earth can be made into a sloped base for the water to run off. Unexcavated areas can be made into beds and benches. A low roof protects the house from winds.

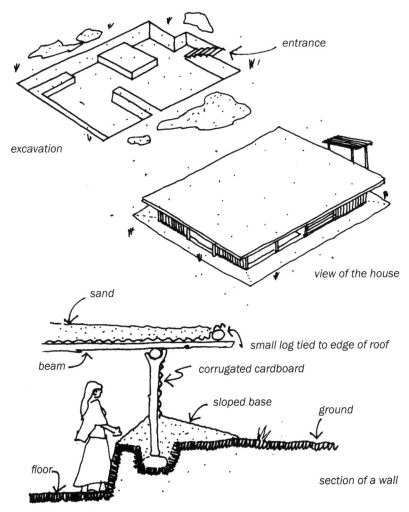

entrance

excavation

view of the house

sand

small log tied to edge of roof

beam

corrugated cardboard

sloped base

ground

floor

section of a wall

Asphalt paper is the cheapest roofing material, but cold or hot air passes through it easily. Painting it white can help reflect sun rays; however it is better to cover the paper with palm leaves, other types of leaves, gravel, or in very dry areas, with sand.

# VENTILATION

In dry tropical climates, the wind is stronger higher above the ground. In these regions there is generally not sufficient protection from dust and heat if the windows are as large as in humid tropical climates. Buildings with large roof eaves also accumulate dust.

One must understand local climate conditions. In humid and rainy zones, large sloped roofs are preferable; however in dry areas, flat roofs function better. Since there is little ventilation or vegetation in these dry regions, the air close to the ground is hot.

Therefore, the ways to ventilate a house with cool air are different in dry and desert-like regions.

In these regions, you try to catch the cool higher and cleaner air.

If there is wood available, build flat-roofed houses with a gentle slope to drain the rainwater and prevent pools of water.

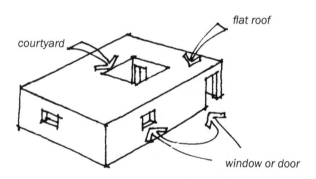

courtyard

flat roof

window or door

The doors and windows should be small, and the house should have an unroofed area, such as a courtyard, to ventilate the interior spaces.

## WINDCATCHERS

Illustrated here are ways to modify a roof in order to cool the rooms. The first method described is a simple ventilation system for a typical wood house in dry areas where palm trees are available.

**1**  To allow as much air as possible to flow through the house, extend the corner posts of the courtyard two meters above the roof.

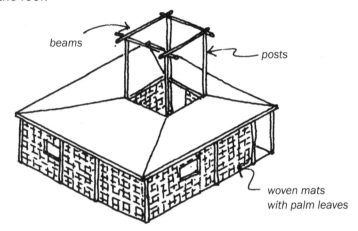

beams

posts

woven mats
with palm leaves

**2**  Join the posts with 4 beams, and add 2 other beams which cross over the center.

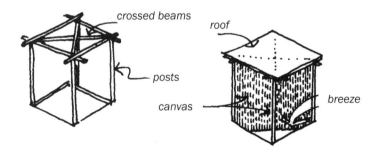

crossed beams

roof

posts

canvas

breeze

**3**  Make a small roof to cover the beams. On the 4 crossed beams place 4 woven mats or pieces of canvas which are joined at the center. The air is captured in these crossed elements and descends into the rooms.

With this method, the wind is captured whichever direction it is coming from. By opening some windows and closing others, the breeze is directed through the house while still protecting it from dust.

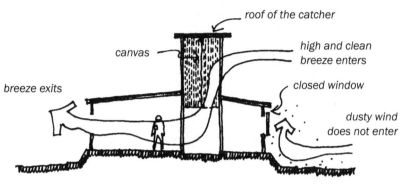

## POSITIONING THE WINDCATCHER

A catcher which is open on four sides, with a crossed center and horizontal roof, captures winds coming from all directions.

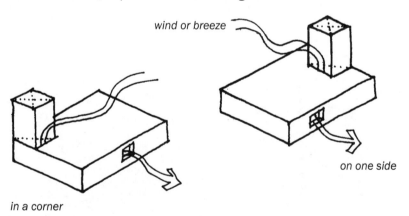

This type of catcher can be located on any part of the roof. Always place it so that the air flows through the most occupied or warmest rooms.

In regions where the wind always comes from the same direction, the windcatcher is open on the side of the cool summer wind.

*direction of prevailing wind*

The wind collectors can be built in different sizes and heights depending on the function of the areas in the house below the roof. The shape of the catcher is determined by local construction techniques and available materials.

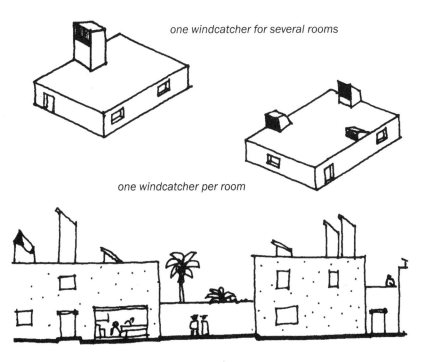

*one windcatcher for several rooms*

*one windcatcher per room*

*view of a street with houses and their windcatchers*

Shown below are two catchers made from wood or woven mats. On the left is an example of a catcher open on one side and made from wood boards. When the air is dusty, cover the opening with a thin cloth so that the dust adheres to the cloth and does not enter through the opening.

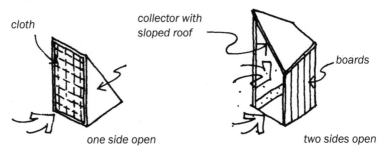

cloth          collector with sloped roof                               boards

one side open                                     two sides open

In regions with minimal breeze, the catcher should have two open sides and a sloped roof to direct the air downwards, as shown in the right drawing.

## OCCUPYING DIFFERENT SPACES DURING A DAY

Take advantage of the sun's motion to improve the comfort level in hot areas. In the morning when the sun is rising and its rays hit the east walls, inhabit the west areas of the house where the sun sets. In the afternoon when the west walls begin to be heated up, move to the east areas. In the summer, occupy the south* side as little as possible, and in the winter, avoid the north side.

The layout of a house is therefore also determined by the position of the sun. Different spaces, such as an office or a bedroom, are inhabited at different times of the day. They must be situated in the areas that are coolest when they are used.

The position of the walls is important when locating spaces in order to distinguish which ones should receive more sunlight than the others. The spaces most affected by sun need higher windcatchers, or larger openings in the wall.

*This applies to the Southern Hemisphere; do the opposite in the Northern Hemisphere.

## TWO-WALLED WINDCATCHER

This type of catcher has two tall walls at a right angle. There are two lower walls on the side the wind is coming from to prevent anyone from falling through the roof opening.

The sloped roof can be made with light materials such as a panel on a wood structure. A column supports the central beam.

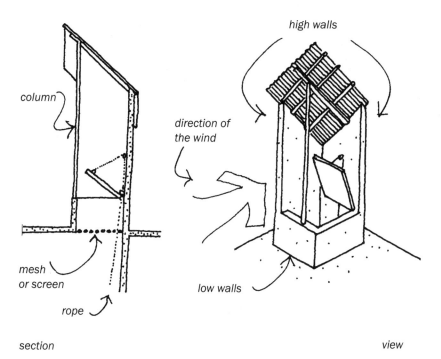

column

direction of
the wind

high walls

mesh
or screen

rope

low walls

section

view

At the height of the low wall, place a wood cover to regulate the air's circulation into the rooms. The angle of the cover is adjusted with a rope. Below the cover, install a mesh or screen to prevent birds and bats from entering the house.

## WIND TOWERS

The phrase "wind towers" is used to describe tall windcatchers built with durable materials.

Wind towers are appropriate for brick or concrete block houses. The form and function are the same as the windcatcher made with woven mats and canvas.

The tower works even when there is no significant breeze, since the temperature inside the tower is different from that outside and the hot air in the house is continuously moving upward. The section of the house below shows the air circulation pattern.

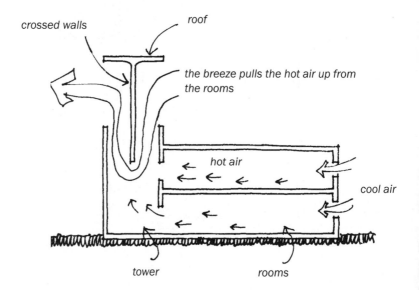

Since the wind enters one side of the tower and exits the other, the hot air from the rooms is drawn into the tower and cool air comes through the windows.

In the winter the openings between the tower and the rooms are closed.

The section drawing of the house below illustrates how to build a tower.

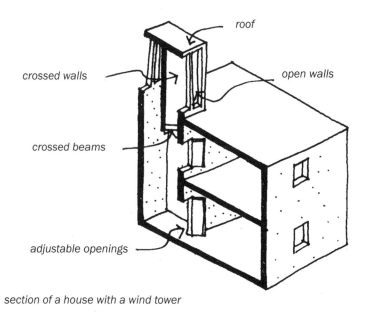

section of a house with a wind tower

The circulation of cool air is controlled by doors between the tower and the rooms, as well as by the windows in the exterior walls.

The crossed walls begin above the doors or the opening of the top floor. They are supported by a large concrete or wood beam. There are open walls in the upper part of the tower. Begin by building large-sized openings and test their efficiency over time. The size can be then adjusted and reduced, depending on the type of breeze, the neighboring houses and the quantity of dust in the air.

## POSITION OF THE TOWER

The tower can be located in any part of the roof of new or existing houses. When the tower is detached from the house, there is a subterranean connection.

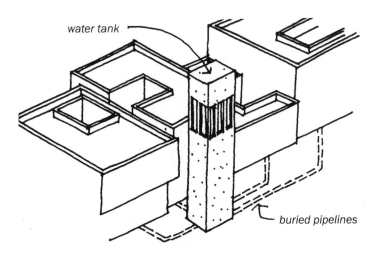

As shown above, one tower can cool many houses at once. The tower can also be used as a structure to contain a water tank.

## AIR CIRCULATION

One way to circulate air is through a central corridor. The cool air enters through the doors, and exits through the windows of the rooms.

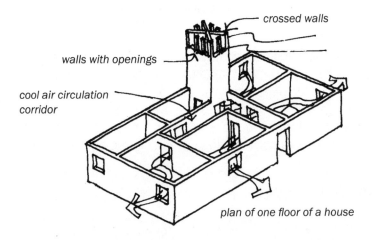

In the drawing above, the roof of the tower is not shown.

## TOWER CONSTRUCTION

The tower is built in the same way as the walls of the house:

**1**   Start by building the lower outside walls. For taller towers
the walls need to be thicker to support their weight.

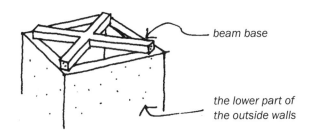

beam base

the lower part of
the outside walls

The base of the crossed walls is crossed wood or concrete beams
supported by the outside walls.

**2**   Build the crossed walls.

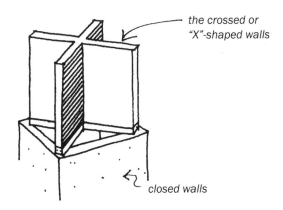

the crossed or
"X"-shaped walls

closed walls

**3**   Then build the exterior walls with the openings. The final element to build is the roof of the tower made with a horizontal concrete slab or vault.

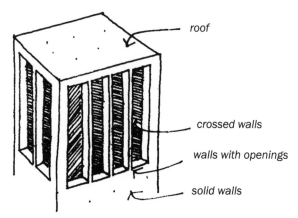

When the tower walls are built with holed concrete blocks, fill in the holes to reduce the entrance of the heat.

## WALLS WITH OPENINGS

There are many ways to make walls with openings:

**A**   With inclined bricks.

**B**   With bricks with premade openings.

**C**   With curved tiles.

## CISTERNS

In desert regions, it is worth considering building a house over cisterns. To accomodate several separate, but linked, cisterns, the foundation of the house must be deeper.

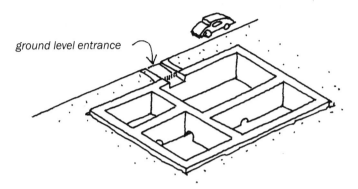

*ground level entrance*

To collect the rainwater that runs in the street, make a channel. The water at the start of the rainstorm should not enter the cisterns since it contains the most dust and dirt.

The openings from the street should be well protected with a mesh to prevent rats and other animals from entering.

Air flows over the water in the cistern.

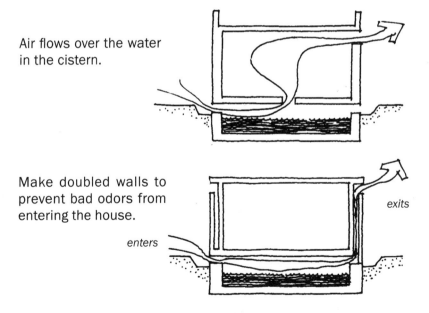

Make doubled walls to prevent bad odors from entering the house.

*exits*

*enters*

The entrances and exits are at opposite heights to create a cross-ventilation through the cistern.

## UNDERGROUND VENTILATION

Another way to induce cool air through the house is to take advantage of the difference between the air and the underground temperatures. On a hot day the ground is much cooler than the air, especially under the house.

This temperature difference can be used to make the rooms more comfortable on hot days.

How does this work?

 A house is like a box. The walls and roof absorb the sun and as the heat from the walls enters the house, the interior temperature increases.

 The outside air might be cooler, but it does not enter the house, even if the windows are open.

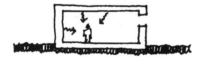

the heat from the walls and
the roof irritates the occupants

 Since hot air always rises, place openings in the roof or on the upper walls for it to exit.

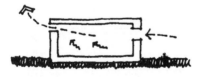

with two openings, the circulation
draws up the hot air

Now there is ventilation through the house, since the exterior air enters. It is worthwhile to examine how the temperature of the air could be lowered even further.

One way to do this is to circulate the air through the ground to cool it before it enters the house. The air must circulate at least two meters below the ground surface to be cooled.

To circulate the air, use 10cm clay or cement drainpipes.

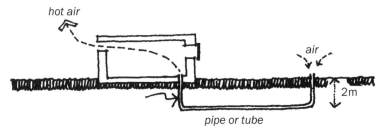

pipe or tube

The pipe opening is protected above ground with a metal cap to prevent rainwater from entering, while still allowing air to enter.

The exit into the room has a screen to keep insects from entering. This screen is attached to a frame, which is screwed to the wall in order to allow periodic cleanings. On top of the framed screen you fix a grille to control the amount of air entering.

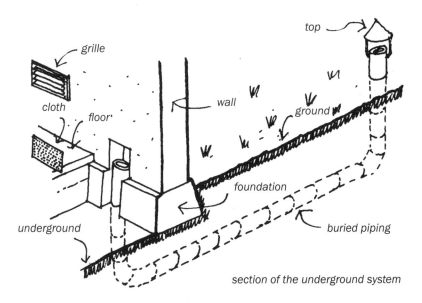

section of the underground system

The entryway for the air is located in a cool place, such as below trees or bushes. If you place it near a fragrant plant, a jasmine for example, the air in the rooms will have a perfumed scent.

Below is a drawing illustrating how the entryway of the air can be hidden under a bench or at the base of a closet.

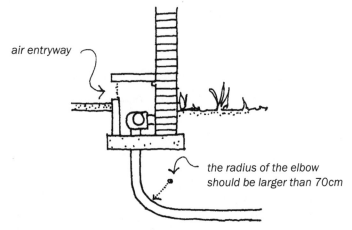

air entryway

the radius of the elbow
should be larger than 70cm

This type of ventilation system does not work when the level of the water table (the underground water) is higher than the buried piping. Therefore verify the depth of the underground water level before deciding what type of ventilation system to use.

There are no rules regarding the length of the piping. This decision depends on many factors, such as ground humidity, the size of the rooms, the vegetation, and the size of the property.

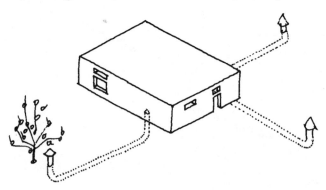

When the property is very large, the piping for each room is separate and shorter.

# DRY TROPICS

# ROOFS

The roofs in regions with dry tropical climates can be flat or slightly sloped. The structure of a flat roof does not require as much wood (a material which is scarce in dry regions) as a sloped roof.

For constructions built with earth and wood, the roofs are made with beams, branches and earth.

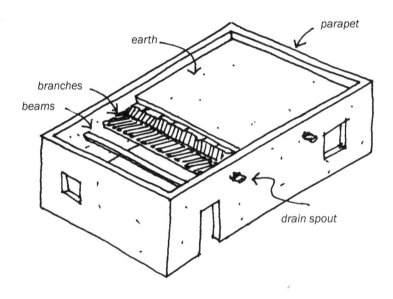

The beams have a 4 cm-per-meter slope, so that the rainwater runs toward the drain pipes.

On hot nights you can sleep on the roof. The parapet prevents falls and adds more privacy to the roof space.

## EARTH-CEMENT ROOFS

On the roof beams, install tied reeds or branches. On top of this pour a 10cm layer of an earth and cement mixture.

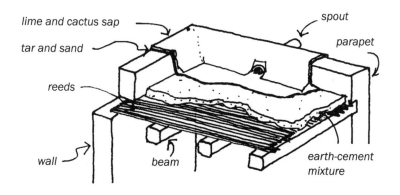

Apply tar and sand on top of the layer of earth-cement, as a base for the finishing layer. Then add a layer of whitewash with lime so that the final surface is light-colored to reflect the sunlight.

In regions where there are large temperature differences between day and night, first install a layer of earth on a sheet of plastic or asphalt paper to obtain a higher insulation value.

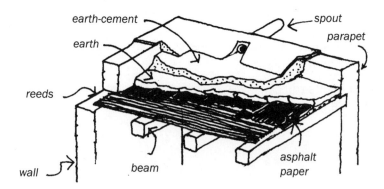

## ROOFED PORCH

In this example, the roof extends
over the entrance door to create
a porch area.

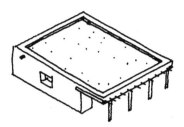

Below is a drawing showing the details of a house with an earth roof.

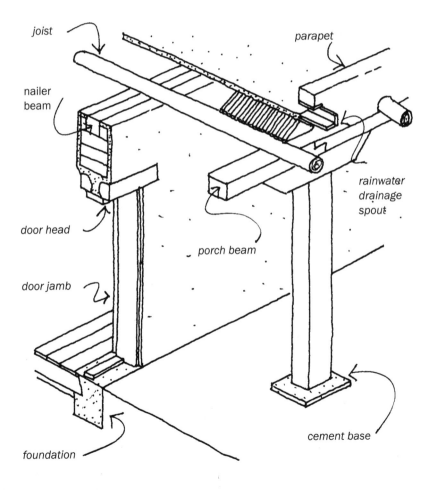

Since desert areas have few trees, it might be difficult to find large wood beams to span the full length of a roof. In this situation, the beams and joists can be made the following way:

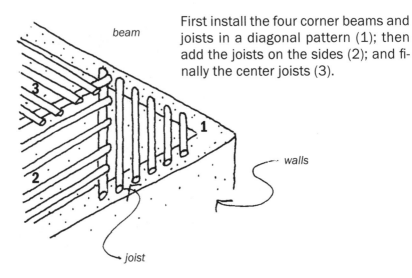

First install the four corner beams and joists in a diagonal pattern (1); then add the joists on the sides (2); and finally the center joists (3).

beam

walls

joist

A space of 4 x 4 meters can be covered by beams spanning no more than 2.80m. Finish the roof with reeds and earth. The roof from inside the house, as the drawing below shows, has an attractive appearance.

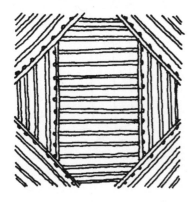

*the roof seen from inside below*

## TILE ROOFS

There are two ways to install the tiles on a roof. The drawing below shows the method for a larger type of tile. If they are smaller than the span between beams, use the second method.

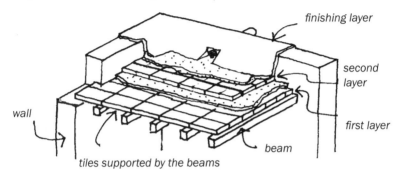

*finishing layer*

*second layer*

*wall*

*first layer*

*beam*

*tiles supported by the beams*

In the second method, the smaller tiles are installed in the following way:

**1**    The first layer of tiles is installed with a gypsum cement that is made with little water so it hardens quickly. The gypsum is applied on both sides of the dry tile and then it is joined rapidly to the tiles already set in place.

**2**    To install the second layer, use a mortar of cement and sand in a 1:3 proportion. The tiles are placed in the opposite direction to the first layer.

**3**    Finish with a final coat of cement plaster.

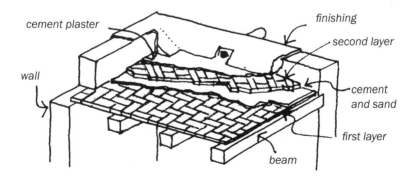

*cement plaster*

*finishing*

*second layer*

*wall*

*cement and sand*

*first layer*

*beam*

## BARREL-VAULTED ROOFS

The advantage of vaulted roofs is that they do not need wood structures and are cooler than flat roofs, since the curve of the vault increases the outside air flow. Barrel vaults should be placed in the opposite direction to the prevailing winds.

For large spaces, the roof can be domed. The dome cools no matter which direction the winds are coming from.

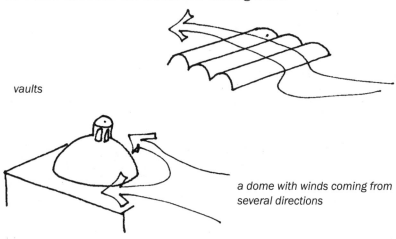

vaults

a dome with winds coming from several directions

Make a top cupola so that the hot air can exit.

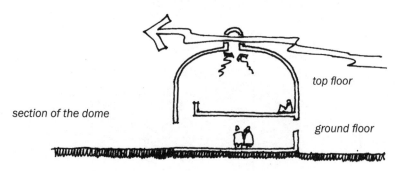

top floor

section of the dome

ground floor

Curved roof panels are easy to fabricate. When the walls are built, you can immediately install these panels.

The joints between panels are filled with an impermeable layer of tar or a thin layer of cement.

The inside curve at each end of the panel should be well supported by bricks. For more details, go to chapter 5 on materials.

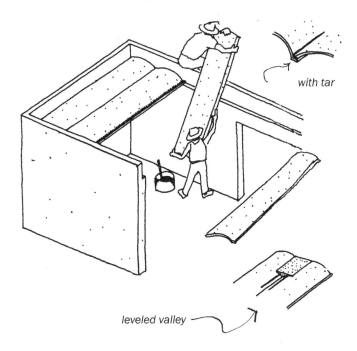

with tar

leveled valley

To use this roof as a floor slab, level it out by filling in the depressions between the curves with mortar. Strengthen the mortar with reinforcing rods or bamboo poles.

Whether the curved panels are left exposed as tiles, or made into a slab, install a temporary beam to support the middle of the panels until the cement has cured.

See chapter 6 for more details.

Below are a few precautions to take during construction:

**a**   Make sure the vaulted panels are joined together well; if there is a separation between panels, the roof may fall in.

**b**   When using the panels as roof tiles, insulate the roof from the heat by filling the valleys with an insulating material such as a mixture of sawdust and cement.

**c**   Apply a thin layer of cement to create an impermeable roof.

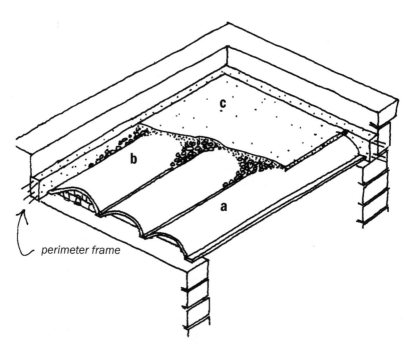

perimeter frame

When the ends of barrel-vaulted roof panels are exposed or extend past the walls, leave some of the ends open for the hot air to exit.

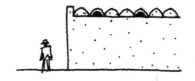

As described in chapter 6, the panels are usually 3 meters long. They can have any dimension up to 4 meters. The house must be planned with these dimensions in mind. In the example below, the living room is 4m wide, the bedrooms are 3m and the bathroom is 2m.

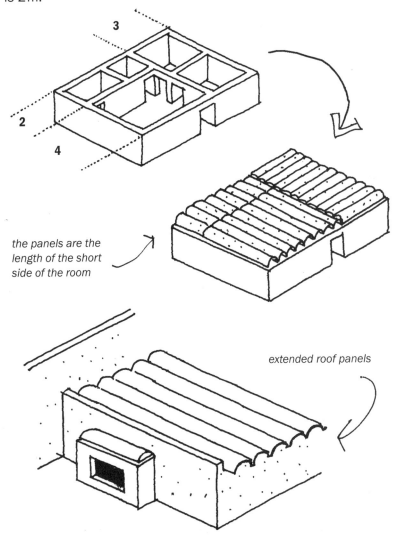

*the panels are the length of the short side of the room*

*extended roof panels*

The barrel-vaulted panels can also be used to make bay windows or roofs which extend past the main exterior walls.

## LOW-ARCH BARREL-VAULT CONSTRUCTION

To make a low-arch vault, use wood formwork during construction. Described further on is a technique to build vaults without formwork for regions where wood is scarce.

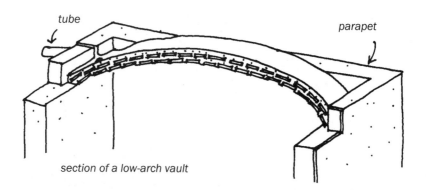

section of a low-arch vault

This vault is made with two layers of 3cm-thick bricks. There is a mortar mixture of cement and sand between the layers. The second layer is covered in a thick mixture of cement to create an impermeable surface. The bricks of the second layer are installed in the opposite direction to the first.

## HIGH-ARCH BARREL-VAULT CONSTRUCTION

To build a barrel vault without using formwork, build supporting walls on each end of the room. On this wall, draw a semicircle.

Against this wall, start building the arch of the vault using a mixture of gypsum cement and a minimum of water so that the joints dry rapidly. The first arch is leaning against the wall by using half bricks higher up. The second arch comes out a little more and third arch is a complete row of full bricks.

With the angled bricks, build one arch after another to the other end. One should add an impermeable finishing layer of a cement and sand mixture.

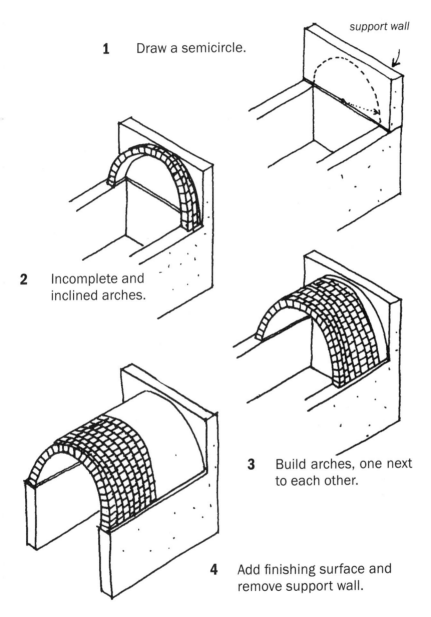

**1**   Draw a semicircle.

*support wall*

**2**   Incomplete and inclined arches.

**3**   Build arches, one next to each other.

**4**   Add finishing surface and remove support wall.

Remove the support wall when the vault is set, and fill in the opening with bricks, or install a window.

It is difficult to build a perfect arch. To make sure the arch of the vault is equal all the way along, do the following:

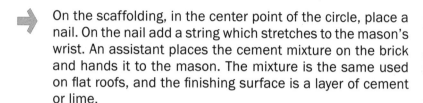 On the scaffolding, in the center point of the circle, place a nail. On the nail add a string which stretches to the mason's wrist. An assistant places the cement mixture on the brick and hands it to the mason. The mixture is the same used on flat roofs, and the finishing surface is a layer of cement or lime.

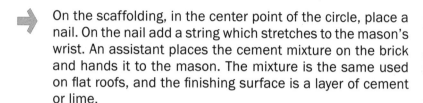 One can use smaller bricks made especially for this type of construction.

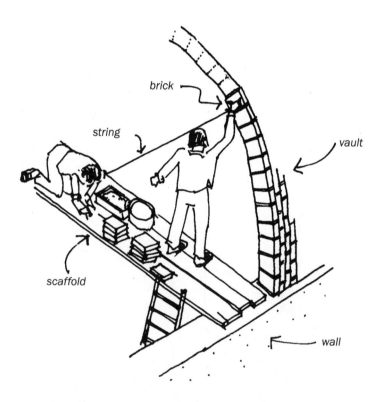

With the use of the string, the bricks are always at the same distance from the center, therefore making a perfect arch.

## DOMES

Domes are supported on the semicircular walls at ends of barrel vaults.

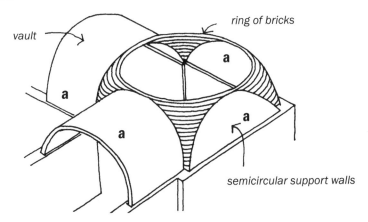

*a large space with barrel vaulting and a dome*

First build the support arches (a), then fill in the spaces between the arches to create a circular-shaped ring, build up the dome in rings of decreasing radiuses, and add a cupola or windows and the finishing surface.

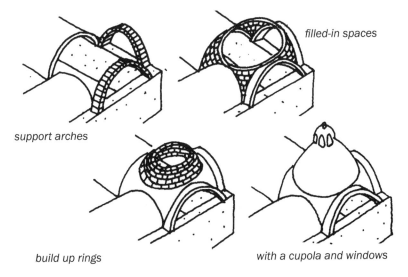

## CROSS-VAULT CONSTRUCTION

The bricks for this type of construction are similar to those used for walls, but are of a thinner variety (3cm thick).

The brick layer receives a brick which already has gypsum mortar on two sides, having been put there by the mason's assistant who is constantly making a new batch as this mortar dries very quickly. The mason then presses the brick against the others (1).

The brick must be well positioned against the sides of the bricks already installed. Hold the brick in place until the gypsum starts to dry.

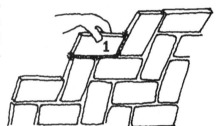

The next brick is installed as shown in the drawing to the right.

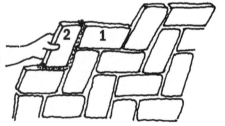

The bricks are dampened so they do not absorb water from the gypsum plaster. When the gypsum hardens, add another brick and remove the excess gypsum. Since the bricks will not have a finishing surface of plaster on the interior side, make sure the joints are cleaned.

The mason has a string tied to his wrist to maintain the curve of the arch. To position the bricks, the assistant holds the other end of the string at the same point along the opposite end wall.

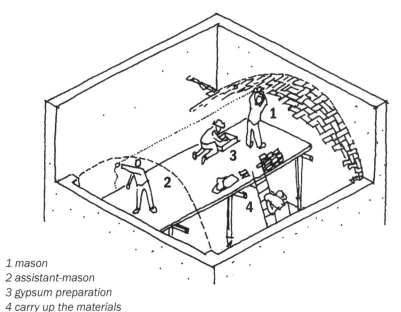

1 mason
2 assistant-mason
3 gypsum preparation
4 carry up the materials

Barrel vaults are simple to build; however for larger spaces, cross-vaults are recommended.

Always start to position the bricks at the lowest point along the arch. Then work upwards at the same time on an adjacent vault in order to make a junction. See drawings on the next page.

The drawings below show the steps for building a cross-vault:

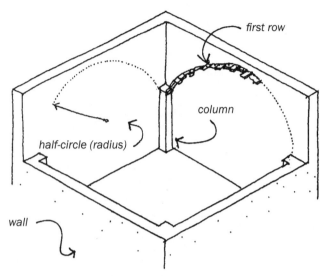

**1**     Start building the vaults in the corners where the walls and columns meet.

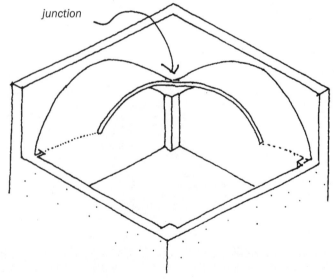

**2**     The meeting of the two arches begins at the lowest point of the arch. Build the junction with broken pieces of bricks.

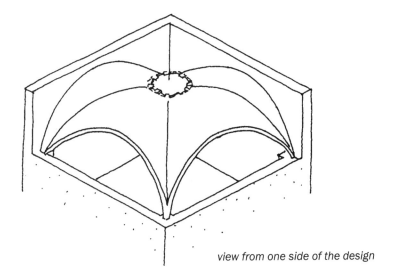

*view from one side of the design*

**3**  Close the central opening by building it up a little higher so it does not sink when it settles.

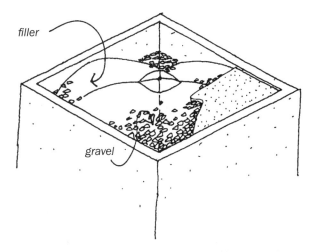

*filler*

*gravel*

**4**  The bricks are exposed on the interior surface of the vault. On the outside, fill the valleys with rubble and mortar. Before filling them, though, add a layer of diluted cement to prevent contact between the lime and the gypsum.

As seen in previous chapters, small windows prevent the entry of heat and dust. Therefore, in dry tropical regions where it is very bright, fewer openings in the walls are needed to illuminate the interior.

The larger openings to the rooms should be on the interior courtyard side where they are protected from dust and from sunlight by trees and plants.

If large openings are used, for example in a corridor that looks out onto a courtyard, build louvers, slats or venetian-type panels in the lower part of the opening in order not to block the view. Often sunlight from the reflection off the lime roofs or the facades is stronger than direct sunlight.

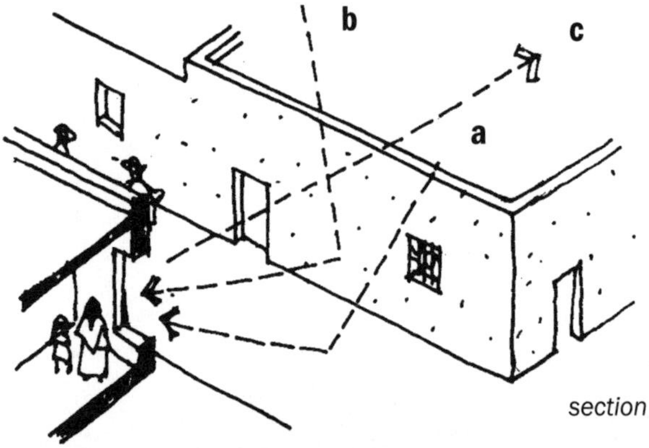


*For the people inside the room, the bright light from the flat lime-covered roof (a) and the facade (b) is much stronger than direct sunlight (c).*

For the slats, use round wood rods instead of square ones. The round shape allows more light to filter in and promotes better visibility towards the outside.

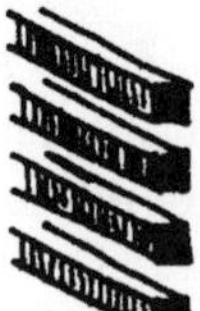

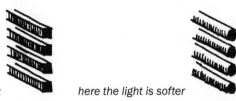

*strong contrast of light*

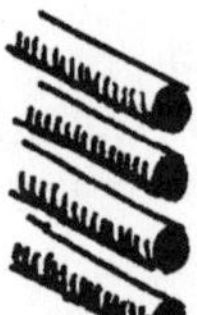

*here the light is softer*

## VENTILATION

Besides providing a softer and more diffused light, this type of window ventilates the spaces. This window can be made the following way:

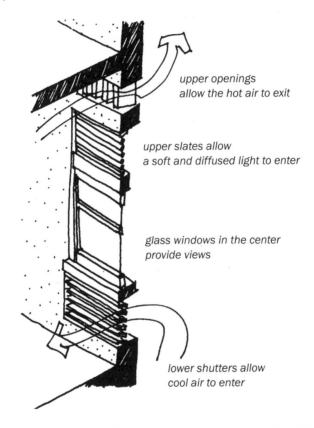

upper openings
allow the hot air to exit

upper slates allow
a soft and diffused light to enter

glass windows in the center
provide views

lower shutters allow
cool air to enter

section of a window in an urban setting where there is less dust as the roads are paved

To even further improve protection from the sun, place the venetian slats as a separate element from the window, so that the hot air exits from the top.

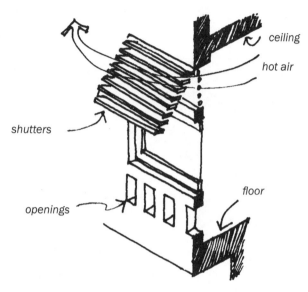

ceiling

hot air

shutters

floor

openings

*section of a well-ventilated room*

Wood shutters are better than concrete, as they do not absorb the sun's heat. Concrete absorbs heat and increases the temperature of the exterior walls, thereby heating up the rooms.

## WINDOWS WITH WATER CONTAINERS

The incoming air temperature of a room can be controlled with clay jugs or containers which do not have an enamel or a varnish finish. Fill the container with water, and place it in the lower part of the window, or any other opening in the wall.

The air is cooled as it moves over the water and enters the house, thus cooling the rooms.

Two examples of containers:

*inside the room*

The drawing above shows the position of two jars which are part of the opening in the space of the wall. Place a plate under the containers to collect the water that filters out from their porous sides.

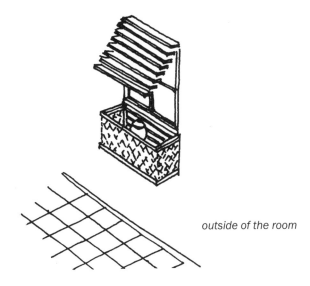

*outside of the room*

Jars can also be placed outside on balconies or in boxes under the window. The container is shaded by a roof or an awning over the window. Louvers below the window can be closed or opened to control the air circulation.

## WINDCATCHERS WITH WATER

Another method to cool rooms is to combine the water jars and
the windcatcher systems:

**a**    This type of air conditioning requires very little maintenance.
The water evaporates slowly and the jars are refilled as
needed.

**b**    One can build a small water reservoir at the base of the
catcher shaft near ground level.

**c**    In regions where the winds are minimal, you can create a
stronger air current by making the entrance opening larger
than the shaft and narrowing the shaft halfway down.

**d**    A more elaborate system consists of placing the water jars
at the top of the shaft near the opening. Drops of water fall
slowly down a charcoal grating and then into a container.
The charcoal filters dust from the air.

**e**    In dusty regions, build several rows of bricks projecting out
from the shaft. When the air descends in the shaft, the dust
settles on the surface of the bricks.

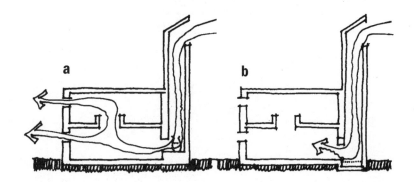

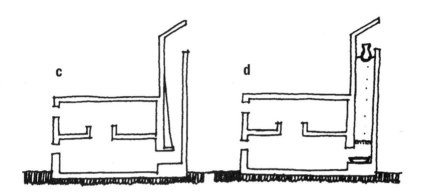

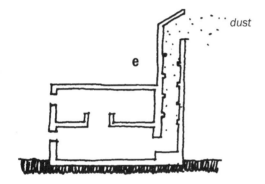

dust

When you has understood how to control the cool air circulation in a house, you can further improve the system by placing water jars at other air entryways and openings.

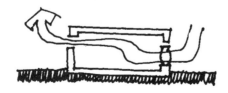

## HOW TO COOL AIR

→ Build small shaded courtyards or narrow streets.

→ Build hallways around courtyards for more shaded areas.

→ Use light colors which do not absorb heat.

→ Install small windows.

→ Plant vegetation and trees.

→ Use underground pipes.

→ Use water reservoirs or jars.

→ Build wind towers.

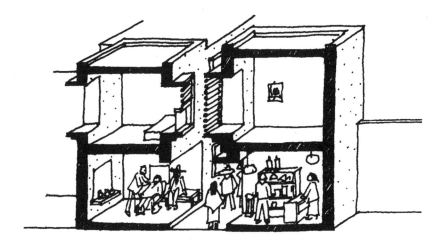

The drawings above illustrate many ideas and methods for cooling
a house in dry tropical regions. Try to find them!

# TEMPERATE ZONE

4

# CLIMATE

In cold climates houses need to be heated, therefore the house designs seen in this chapter are different in many ways from the houses described in the previous chapters.

To heat a house, it is important:

 to prevent cold outside air from entering the house

 to prevent the hot inside air from escaping from the house

To achieve this, the walls and roofs must be made with durable materials that are resistant to the passage of the heat or the cold. See the table in chapter 10 on the thermal value of materials.

*hot summer:*
*the heat should not enter*

*cold winter:*
*the heat should not escape*

In temperate zones, it is not always cold. At certain times of the year for several months the temperature is hot. In the hot summer, the heat should not enter, and in the cold winter, the heat should not escape the house.

The way a design uses the wind is also different from that in other climates. In windy hot regions, the walls are designed to allow air currents to pass through and cool the house. In cold regions, the design is the contrary; the walls must be resistant to cold winds.

Cold strong winds not only cool the rooms of a house, but draw heat out through gaps in the walls or roofs. To keep heat from escaping, it is important that all the doors and windows close well.

## SPACE ORIENTATION

In the following examples, the house orientations are based on Southern Hemisphere conditions.

A house's orientation is very important. For example, a large glass window on the south side cools a room, whereas the same window on the north side warms up a room. As the sun moves throughout the day, the north walls of a house receive the most sunlight and are the hottest, while the south walls remain in shade and never heat up.

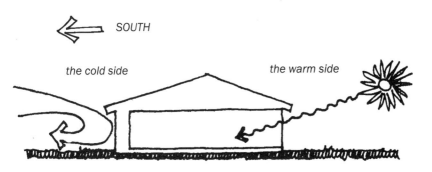

SOUTH

the cold side          the warm side

Taking into consideration the effects of orientation, the design must prevent the northern heat from escaping from the south side. Also the inside heat, which always rises, should not escape through the roof. The roof and ceiling should be insulated, and few openings should be made in the south walls.

The sun heats up the rooms with north-facing windows. Prevent this heat from quickly escaping by insulating the walls and ceilings.

Besides cold air, ground humidity also cools the floor. The floor should be built with insulation and a vapor barrier.

 In wood houses with raised floors, the cold air from the ground flows under the house.

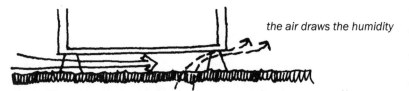

*the air draws the humidity*

 In houses with masonry walls and stone floors, cover the foundation with tar or impermeable material to prevent the infiltration of humidity.

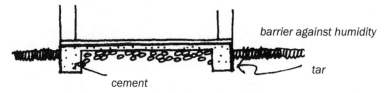

*barrier against humidity*

*tar*

*cement*

The rooms that are less used by the occupants should be located on the south side of the house. These rooms could be be pantries or bathrooms, or areas that generate heat such as kitchens. The living areas should be situated on the north side.

Below are more suggestions for keeping a house warm.

 As in hot climates, the bedrooms should be located on the side of the rising sun, so that the occupants rise with the heat of the sunlight. Since the heat from the lower rooms rises during the day, locate the bedrooms on the second floor and they will be warmer in the evening.

 Since hot air always rises, the rooms with lower, rather than higher, ceilings are more comfortable for the occupants. Therefore ceilings in cold regions should be lower than those in hot regions, as the example below illustrates.

hot air

cold air

high ceilings

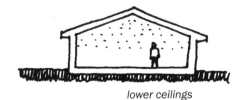

lower ceilings

Roof ventilation is different in cold climates. It should not be directed through the roof as in hot climates.

*hot air is lost through the roof*

*cold air enters at ground level*

 In cold regions, close and seal all openings to prevent hot air from escaping.

*do not ventilate in cold climates*

 It is important to protect the house from the cold south-prevailing winds.

If possible, build houses near elements that are barriers from prevailing winds:

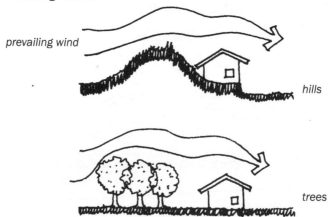

*prevailing wind*

*hills*

*trees*

Or use the following techniques:

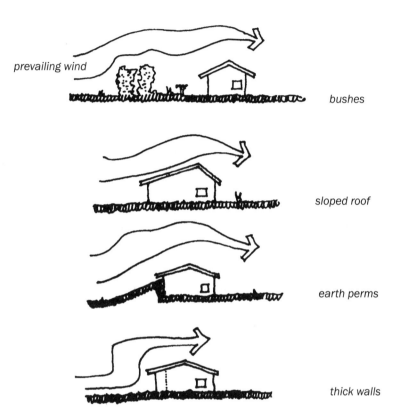

*prevailing wind*

*bushes*

*sloped roof*

*earth perms*

*thick walls*

On the south side, the walls should be thicker and the windows smaller.

*on the south side of this house there are no windows*

There are other ways to conserve heat.

## STORING SOLAR HEAT IN THE FLOOR

A house can take advantage of the sun's north heat by storing it overnight. Part of the floor can be built to absorb and store the heat.

To do this:

 Use dark colors for the floor, such as black or a dark green, which absorb more heat than light colors.

 Use floor material that absorbs heat, such as stones or ceramic tiles.

 Prevent heat from escaping through the ground.

The floor is acting as a heat transfer, since it receives, absorbs, stores, and then radiates the heat.

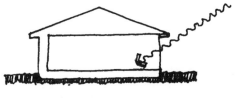

The heat enters the cold house during the day and heats up the floor.

By late afternoon, the floor has absorbed the heat and starts to release it.

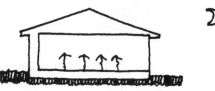

At night, as the oustside temperature drops, the floor continues to radiate heat, keeping the house warm.

## USING THE EARTH'S HEAT

The same type of underground piping used to cool houses in hot climates can be used to heat houses in cold climates.

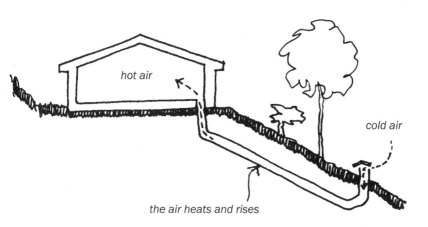

hot air

cold air

the air heats and rises

On flat terrain, install a small fan to draw the hot air through the rooms.

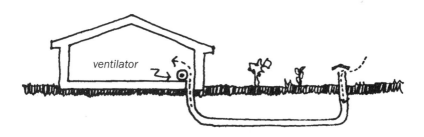

ventilator

Use asphalt or plastic to cover and protect the piping from humidity which reduces the air temperature in the pipes.

## HEATING WITH GARBAGE

Garbage that is not thrown into a composter or dry toilet can be used to generate heat. This heat is released when it decomposes.

 Install two plastic pipelines which start inside the house and end in the hole where the garbage is disposed of.

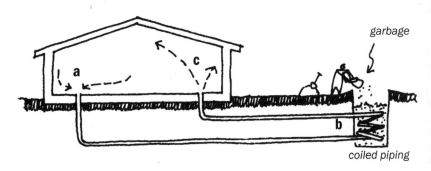

*garbage*

*coiled piping*

 In the hole connect a coiled pipe to the two pipelines. This coil is made with plastic tubing. The coil increases the amount of air in contact with the heat.

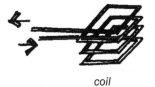

*coil*

Cold air, which is heavier than hot air, falls to the floor and into the entrance of the piping (a). The heat from the garbage is transferred to the air inside the coil and then rises (b). This rising warmed air exits the upper pipe and is drawn into the house (c). When the hot air enters the house, the cold air is drawn into the lower pipeline.

Raise the edge of the garbage hole and cover all with a wood or metal top to prevent rain from entering.

## HEATING WITH A FIREPLACE

A fireplace should be installed in such a way that it heats as many rooms as possible.

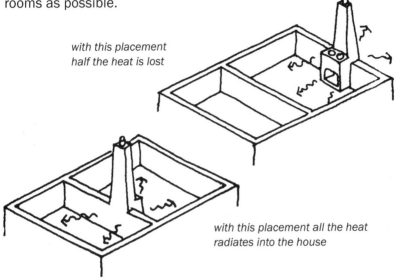

*with this placement half the heat is lost*

*with this placement all the heat radiates into the house*

In the first example, the fireplace is incorrectly located since it loses part of the heat it generates. In the second example, the heat radiates to adjacent rooms, so there is no loss.

## CAPTURING SOLAR HEAT WITH THE ROOF

The shape of the house, the location of the windows, and the slope of the roof can all be designed to collect the sun's heat. In the example below, the roof and ceiling are light-colored and have the correct inclination to reflect the sun's rays from an upper window.

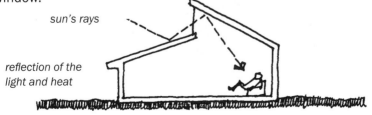

*sun's rays*

*reflection of the light and heat*

# SOLAR COLLECTOR ROOMS

A very efficient way to heat up a house is with a solar collector room.

During the day the sun heats up the air in this glass enclosure. At night the hot air flows into the other rooms of the house. The opening should be staggered (one on top of the wall and the other at the bottom) to circulate air.

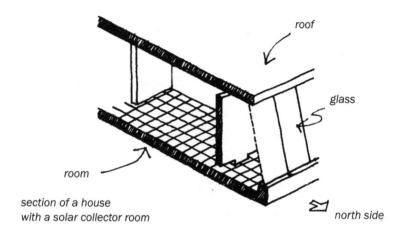

roof

glass

room

section of a house
with a solar collector room

north side

Plastic can be used instead of glass. It is less expensive, but also less durable. At night, cover the windows to prevent the heat from escaping. If it is not possible to cover them, close the openings between the solar room and the rest of the house to keep the heat inside.

The drawing below shows a house with a solar room. This house can be built in two phases. The first phase is part A and the extension is part B.

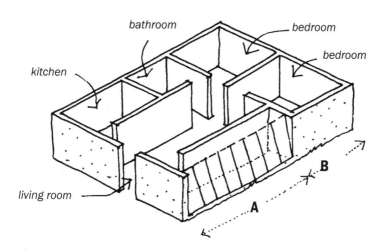

Existing houses can add the solar room onto the north side of the house.

 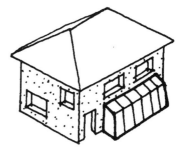

## SOLAR WALLS

These walls work the same way as a floor that stores heat. The house has a space on the north side with a large window. The interior wall, made of mobile panels, absorbs the sun's heat during the day. At night, the wall panels are turned around and the heat radiates into the interior of the house.

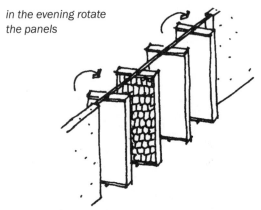

*in the evening rotate the panels*

The solar panels are made with a frame which has a solid board on one side. On the lower shelf-like part of the frame, install several rows of cans painted black, filled with water. Tie them together with wire. The back board can be painted any color.

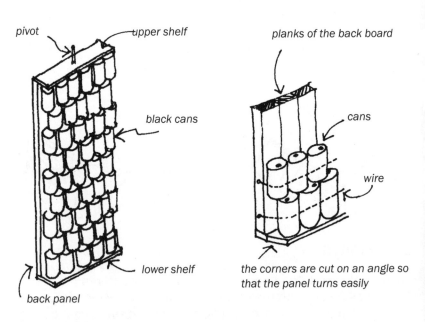

*pivot*  *upper shelf*  *planks of the back board*

*black cans*  *cans*

*wire*

*lower shelf*  *the corners are cut on an angle so that the panel turns easily*

*back panel*

The whole panel works like a door that turns in the center instead of to one side.

In the example below, the wall of solar panels is located near a large window:

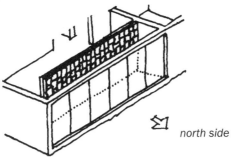

north side

Another method to make a solar wall is to cover the opening of a large window with the same type of cans. At night, cover the window from outside with an insulated wood shutter to keep the heat inside. In the summer, remove the cans from the window.

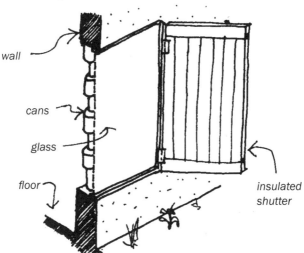

wall

cans

glass

floor

insulated shutter

Although there are always small leaks, heat loss from inside the house should be prevented as much as possible. The windows and the doors often lose a lot of heat; therefore, ensure they close tightly. There should not be gaps between the frames of the openings and the doors and windows themselves, nor between the roof and walls. If air leaks through the roof, through tiles for example, build a ceiling to keep the heat in the rooms.

## SOLAR WINDOW

This "blind" window is made with a pane of glass and dark-colored stones. If the stones are naturally light-colored, paint them a mat black. The air circulation is controlled by upper and lower boards.

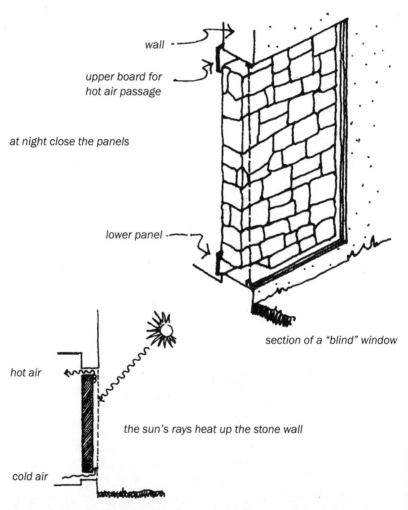

wall

upper board for
hot air passage

at night close the panels

lower panel

section of a "blind" window

hot air

the sun's rays heat up the stone wall

cold air

The air between the wall and the glass pane heats up, rises and flows through the open upper board into the room. This same air soon cools and falls to the floor, and the cycle starts over.

There are other ways to capture the sun's heat and circulate it through the house. One method consists of building a box below the windows on the north side of the house. This box works in the same way as the heated floors. There is a pane of glass covering the box and a wood board that can be closed or opened to control heat circulation.

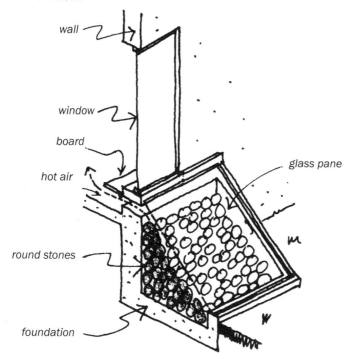

Fill the box with fist-sized round stones. They should be piled loosely to leave spaces for air to circulate between them. The cold air enters into this box through channels under the floor.

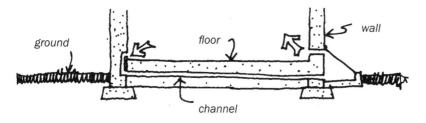

# HEATERS

## FLOOR HEATER

Between the foundation walls pour a 5cm layer of cement. On top and on the sides of this layer apply a layer of tar mixed with reeds. Fill this space full with round stones to store the heat.

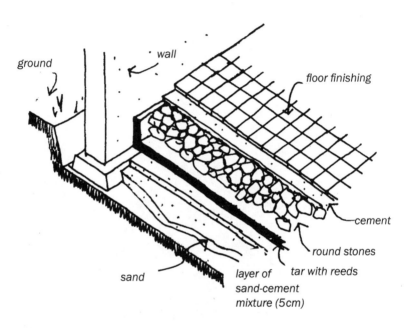

ground

wall

floor finishing

cement

round stones

sand

layer of sand-cement mixture (5cm)

tar with reeds

On the stones apply a layer of mortar and install a floor finishing such as dark ceramic tiles or dark-colored cement.

In very cold climates, a fireplace can also be used; see next page.

## HORIZONTAL CHIMNEY

To take full advantage of the heat generated by a fireplace, the hot air can be circulated under a floor before it exits the house. Build a stone floor over a canal or "horizontal chimney," through which the hot air flows before it finally enters the vertical chimney.

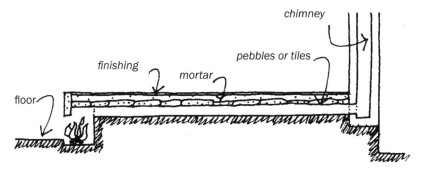

This construction creates an area with a heated, raised floor that is very comfortable to sit on.

An enclosed room can be made in the raised area with a mattress placed on the floor.

## FIREPLACES

Fireplaces should be built in interior walls to ensure no heat loss. The chimney can be made with bricks with an opening between 20 cm x 20 cm and 40 cm x 40 cm. Plaster the chimney to improve its efficiency.

If the fireplace is to be used frequently, embed a coil in the chimney to heat water.

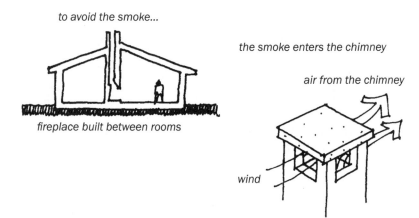

*to avoid the smoke...*

*fireplace built between rooms*

*the smoke enters the chimney*

*air from the chimney*

*wind*

The chimney has a small roof or cap to protect it from rain and to improve the draft.

The mouth of the fireplace should be 10 times larger than the area of the chimney opening. For example, if a chimney opening is 20 cm x 20 cm ($400 cm^2$), the mouth of the fireplace will be $4000 cm^2$ and therefore could be 50 cm high by 80 cm wide. The depth of the mouth should be about half the dimension of the height, so in this case, 25 cm.

To improve the efficiency of the fireplace, the sides and back of the mouth should be slightly sloped so that the fire's heat does not immediately rise into the chimney, but is reflected into the room.

To avoid smoke gettting drawn into the room through the throat by the wind, make a shelf inside the chimney at its base.

The smoke enters the chimney and passes through the throat. This throat has a rectangular opening which is a little larger than the chimney. This throat below is 10cm x 50cm.

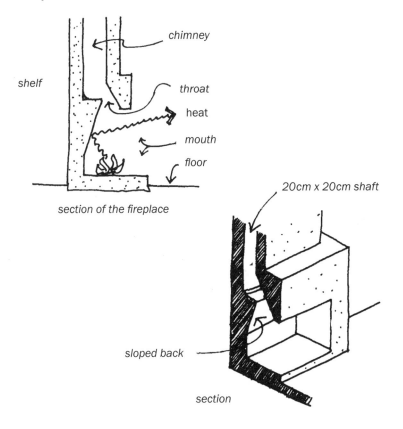

section of the fireplace

section

## CLAY FIREPLACE

A clay fireplace generates a lot of heat with small quantities of wood. This type of fireplace is made with clay and a mixture of ground pieces of ceramic (chamote) molded into a large bottle shape. In the lower part, there is an oval opening to place the wood.

The throat is slightly conical and ends in a 10cm-diameter opening which attaches to a metal duct. A little metal box, which is used as a small stove, can also be added.

Use two stacked bricks as a base. They should be removable to be able to lower the fireplace and clean the box and duct.

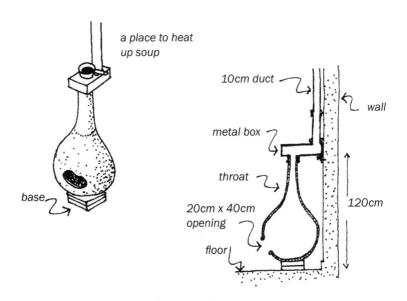

a place to heat up soup

10cm duct

wall

metal box

throat

base

20cm x 40cm opening

120cm

floor

## BARREL FIREPLACE

A fireplace can be made with a 120-liter metal barrel (see the next page for details). First make a opening for placing wood and removing ashes. On the other side, make an opening for the smoke and weld a metal duct.

Install a bottomless and topless smaller barrel into the larger one and fill the space between them with clay. This will hold the heat longer. In the bottom section, weld metal rods to support the wood and to allow for air circulation. Use bricks as a base for the barrel.

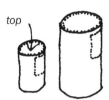

**1** Cut out the tops and make openings for the duct and door.

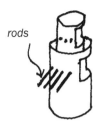

**2** Install the smaller barrel and the metal rods.

**3** Fill the space between the barrels with clay.

**4** Weld on the top.

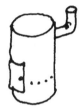

**5** Install the duct and the door.

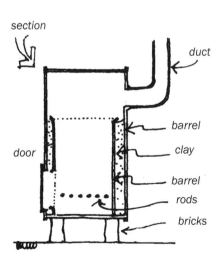

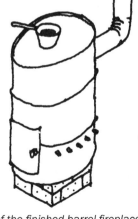

*view of the finished barrel fireplace*

## HEAT CONSERVATION

The previous pages described ways to heat a house in a temperate climate. It is also important to consider how to prevent the produced heat from escaping.

To keep a house comfortable, remember to:

 Prevent the passage of ground humidity.

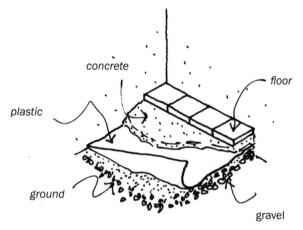

 Prevent the entrance of cold air.

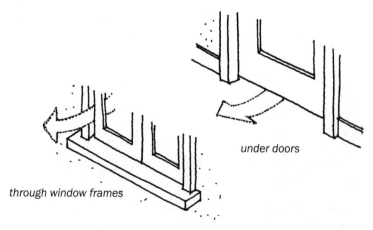

Prevent hot air from leaking out through roof tiles by installing a layer plastic and bamboo.

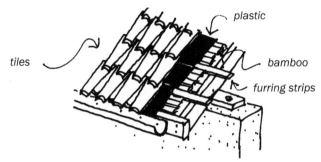

plastic

tiles

bamboo

furring strips

*to not see the plastic from the inside, install reeds or bamboo*

 Avoid building high ceilings in rooms.

studio

Human beings are fountains of heat, so when it is very cold invite more friends over...

*it's cold!* *now it's hot!*

If the windows and doors don't close properly, hang curtains in front of them, and in the evening, when it gets colder, add blankets.

Don't forget that emotions change your body temperature. In cold regions, give rooms a warm glow by painting them orange, yellow or ocre.

# MATERIALS

5

# SELECTING MATERIALS

Before selecting construction materials for houses or buildings, consider the following:

→ The maintenance of the building materials: Consider the long-term effort and cost to maintain the materials in good shape.

→ The effect of temperature on materials: Consider how the materials react to the heat and the cold and if they contribute to making a comfortable house or building.

→ The availability of the materials: Consider using regional materials that are abundant to avoid depending on others, fabrication conditions or transport. This applies to basic construction materials, since ordinarily some new materials and products are from outside the region.

→ The fabrication of the materials: Consider whether the region has the facilities or the equipment to convert raw materials into construction materials, such as mud into bricks.

→ The availability of the proper tradespeople to work the chosen material: Consider if there is the manual labor required to work with the selected materials in the community. For example, don't install steel windows without an ironworker; instead, hire a carpenter to make wood windows.

→ The use of materials from other regions: When there are not sufficient local materials, and materials from outside the region are used instead, consider how to transport them so they don't get damaged and how to store them so they don't deteriorate.

→ The durability of the materials: Consider how the materials will last over time and if they are adequate for the regional climate. Some materials get damaged quickly and others are more durable in some climates than in others.

The combination of materials: Consider how materials work together. For example, a heavy roofing material covering lightweight walls requires a larger and more expensive structure. However a lightweight roof covering massive walls does not work very well, since heat and cold are impeded from entering through the walls but come and go through the roof.

 The phases of building: If you do not have the means to build a house all at once, consider building in steps and living in a partially finished house. This requires planning the type of materials that can be used to build a house to live in immediately, while slowly finishing the rest.

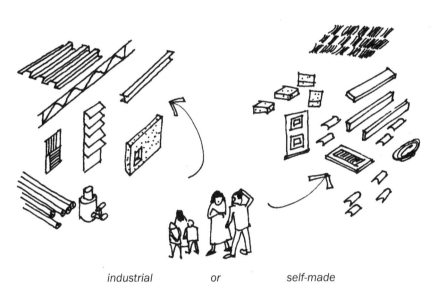

industrial          or          self-made

## MATERIAL TESTS

Almost all types of earth can be used to build walls, such as adobe brick, and wattle and daub walls. The quality of the earth is determined by the proportion of clay to sand. There are many types of earth in the composition of an earth sample. It is often necessary to combine earth from one area with some from another part of the site, even when the lot is small. A rich earth which has a lot of clay needs to be balanced out with sand, and a poor earth needs to be enriched with clay.

To know if a soil is adequate for adobe bricks try the tests below:

Several points on a site need to excavated to perform these tests. First remove the upper layer of earth that contains organic material and vegetation. Then remove samples of earth from different depths.

## TESTS

| | | |
|---|---|---|
| COLOR | dark (oily)<br>white (sandy) | not good for<br>adobe bricks |
| | red<br>brown | can be used for<br>adobe bricks |
| | light yellow | best for adobe<br>bricks |
| ODOR | do not use earth that smells moldy<br>since it has vegetal matter | |
| TEXTURE | if it does not grind, it has a lot of clay<br>if it grinds a bit, it has a lot of mud<br>if it grinds a lot, it has a lot of sand | |

## SEDIMENTATION

**1**   Fill ⅔ of a cylinder glass cup
with earth. Add water to the
top and 2 teaspoons of salt.
The salt helps to separate
the parts of clay and sand.

**2**   Stir the contents vigorously
for a few minutes.

**3**   Watch the parts separate.

water
clay
sand

**4**   If the separation is not very
clear, stir it again and let it sit
for a few hours.

**5**   If the separation is clear, measure the proportion of clay to
sand (for example, here the
proportion is 2 to 1).

4cm
8cm

## SHRINKAGE

The next step is to make a malleable mixture to pour into a test
mold of 4cm x 4cm x 40cm.

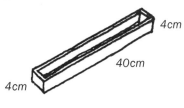

4cm

40cm

4cm

Leave the filled box to dry in the shade.

If the mixture curves in the center like a rising cake, it is not
to be used and another type of
earth should be found.

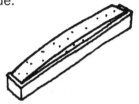

Normally the earth should shrink and crack. Push the whole block
to one side and measure the size of the shrinkage.

The mixture should shrink more
than $\frac{1}{10}$ of the whole length, so
in this case, 4cm.

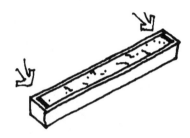

## TEST STRIP

Knead the earth with water and make a 20cm-long, 5cm-wide and
2.50cm-thick strip. Push down on the end of the strip, pushing it
forward out of your hand with the thumb to see when it breaks.

If it breaks before reaching
5cm of length, it is too sandy.

If it breaks after 15cm, it has
a lot of clay.

If the strip breaks between 5
and 15cm, it is good for making
adobe bricks.

Now make some adobe bricks to test their strength:

To make an adobe brick which is resistant to humidity, you can cover it with tar or apply burnt oil instead, using only half the quantity of tar. The best solution is to use small quantities of manure. Straw, grass or pine needles can also be added to the adobe mixture.

If the quantity of sand is equal to or up to two times greater than the amount of clay, the earth is good for adobe construction without adding sand or clay.

When the earth is not adequate, follow the table below to adjust proportions:

| MATERIAL | PROPORTION |
|----------|------------|
| sand | 4-8 parts |
| clay | 4 parts |
| water | 4 parts |

The recipe of this mixture must be adjusted for each type of earth, but the basic recipe remains the same.

The proportions for a wall that is 20cm thick, 3m high and 12m long using a 20-liter bucket, for example, are the following:

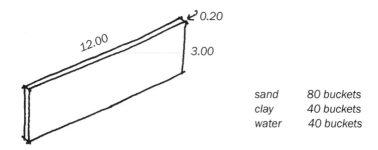

0.20

12.00

3.00

| | |
|-------|-------------|
| sand | 80 buckets |
| clay | 40 buckets |
| water | 40 buckets |

After the mixture has been stirred, it should have a uniform texture and color without marble-like streaks of different colors.

## TESTING THE ADOBE BRICKS

To test the adobe bricks to know if they are strong enough to use for construction, do the following test:

**1**  Place an adobe brick on top of two others spaced apart and step on it heavily. It should bear the weight without breaking.

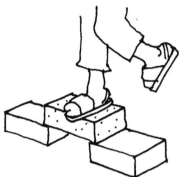

**2**  Soak a whole adobe brick in water for 4 hours. Then break it in half and measure the thickness of the dampened surface. It should not be greater than 1cm.

**3**  Soak another whole adobe brick in water for 4 hours and place it on top of two other ones spaced apart. Pile up 6 other adobe bricks on top of it. The adobe brick being tested should withstand the weight for at least 1 minute before breaking.

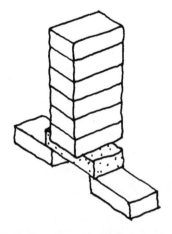

When adobe bricks do not pass the test, the recipe mixture should be adjusted or be used for interior, non-structural brick walls.

## PREPARING THE EARTH

Horse or mule manure, when available, should be mixed with cut straw and added to the adobe mixture. The manure increases the durability of the adobe, since it is resistant to humidity and erosion over time. Also the manure deters termites and assassin bugs from penetrating earth walls.

Find the place where the best earth is found, then:

**1**    Excavate the earth.

**2**    Cover the approximately 30cms-high earth mound with straw.

**3**    Put on a 10cm layer of sand and 5cm of dry manure.

**4**    Remove one or two wheelbarrows, add water and mix.

**5**    Mix all the materials together by treading with the bare feet.

## MOLDS

Adobe bricks can have many dimensions. The most common sizes are: 5cm x 10cm x 20cm, 8cm x 10cm x 40cm, and 10cm x 15cm x 30cm. The molds can be made with wood or metal. At the ends, add handles to facilitate carrying.

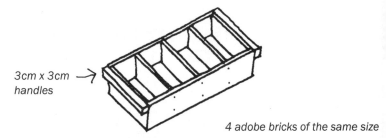

3cm x 3cm
handles

*4 adobe bricks of the same size*

The wood used for the molds should be clean and smooth. Make the mold impermeable by applying a layer of burnt oil or a mixture of tar and oil or kerosene.

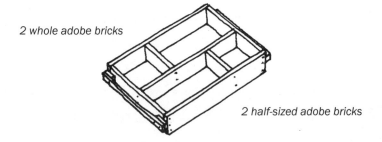

*2 whole adobe bricks*

*2 half-sized adobe bricks*

When the adobe bricks are thinner, a mold can be made for 2 whole bricks and 2 half-sized bricks.

## THE MIXTURE

Let the mixture settle with a little bit of water for 3 days to cure. Then add more water until it is malleable enough to place into the molds.

The adobe bricks should maintain the shape of the mold. If they bulge, there is too much water in the mixture.

 If one part of the brick sticks to the side of the mold, there is not enough water in the mixture.

## MOLDING THE ADOBE BRICKS

1   Wet the molds with water.

2   Shovel the mixture, throwing it well into the corners.

3   Add more of the mixture, and level out the top.

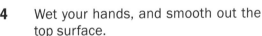

4   Wet your hands, and smooth out the top surface.

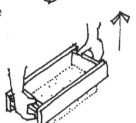

5   Remove the mold carefully.

6   Let the brick dry for 1 or 2 days, depending on the weather.

7   Let the bricks harden for 20 days before using them.

## DRYING THE ADOBE BRICKS

The adobe bricks should not be left out in the sun to dry. If there is not a shaded place to dry them, cover them with leaves and wet them every once in a while.

When they have dried, line them up in rows that are spaced to aerate. Leave them in this position for some days, depending on the local humidity.

It is always better to dry out the bricks slowly to prevent splitting or deformations.

*with splitting*
*the brick breaks*

*with deformations*
*the brick curves*

In dry climates, the bricks must be watered in the afternoon so that they dry overnight. Also sprinkle them with water every once in a while or cover them with straw. Two days after they are removed from their molds, they should be turned to the side as illustrated below.

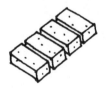  

*drying position*          *covered with straw*          *turned to the side*

Round adobe bricks can be made for the corners of walls, including those around the doors and windows. These curves create a beautifully shaped house.

## MOLDS FOR ROUNDED ADOBE BRICKS

Corners of walls made with adobe bricks are especially susceptible to breaking from impacts or the effects of the climate. Consider making the corners round to diminish the fragility of exposed corners. To make rounded bricks that fit together well, the proportion between the length and the width of the other bricks should be 2:1.

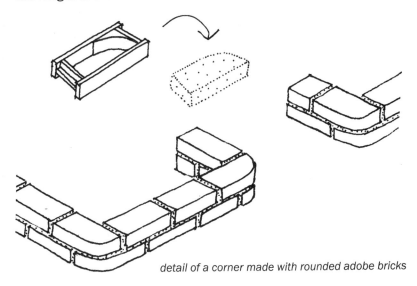

*detail of a corner made with rounded adobe bricks*

## ADDING DISCARDED MATERIALS

Lighter-weight adobe bricks can be made by adding discarded materials inside the bricks, such as cans, bottles, milk cartons, and corncobs.

cans                 bottles               cartons              corncobs

## REINFORCED MOLDS

To make molds that are more resistant to the weight of the mixture, reinforce them with steel or wood rods. As shown below, the holes in the bricks are for the placement of the reinforcing.

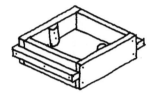 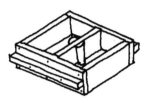

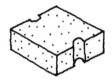 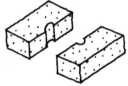

The brick above is square since the four sides are the same dimension. Half-sized bricks can also be made.

## LARGE MOLDS

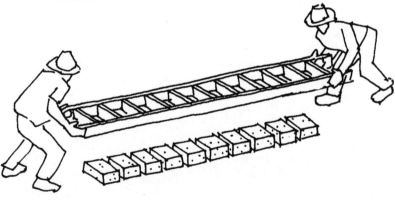

Large molds can make many bricks at once.

## OTHER TYPES OF MOLDS

There are many other shapes of molds that can be made:

You can build a mold for trapezoid-shaped bricks where one side is longer than the other. The mold should have 3 or 4 brick spaces.

Adobe bricks shaped like this can be used to build walls with round corners.

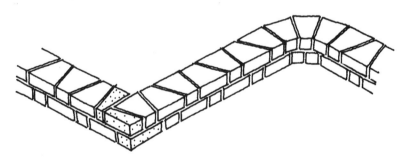

Square corners require half-sized bricks.

*walls with rounded corners*

## EARTH-CEMENT BRICKS

Stronger as well as hollow bricks can be made with an earth-cement mixture and metal molds.

The mold is made with sheet metal with rods welded to the sides as handles:

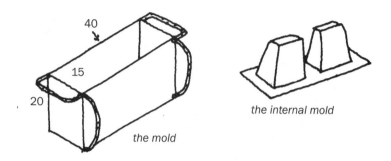

40

15

20

*the mold*

*the internal mold*

Use a heavy hardwood stick to press the mixture into the mold.

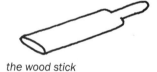

*the wood stick*

## FABRICATION

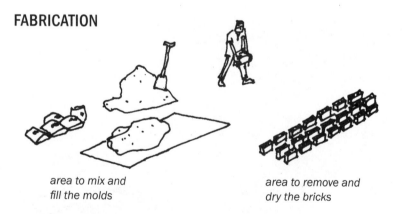

*area to mix and
fill the molds*

*area to remove and
dry the bricks*

See chapter 10 for the proportions of the mixture.

# MATERIALS

**1**  Bring the molds to the area where the mixture is prepared. Place the internal mold inside the other one.

**2**  Fill the mold with the mixture using the stick and a shovel.

**3**  Hit firmly with the wood stick to make sure all the corners and spaces of the mold are filled.

**4**  Move the filled mold to the drying area.

**5**  Place the mold down. Turn the bricks that are already dry on their sides.

**6**  Turn over and remove the mold carefully.

**7**  Pull out the internal mold carefully.

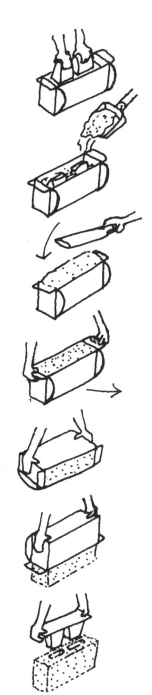

To improve the quality of an earth, add cement by increasing proportions to 1 part cement for 12 parts earth. Lime can also be added to make a mixture of 1 part cement, 2 parts lime and 24 parts earth.

| cement | lime | earth |
|--------|------|-------|
| 1      |      | 12    |
| 1      | 2    | 24    |

When the earth is very sandy, the mixture can be improved using 1 part cement for 10 parts earth. Since cement irritates the skin, it should not be mixed with bare feet but with mechanical mixers.

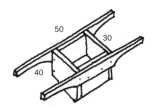

To the left is a measuring box with dimensions that facilitate making a proportional mixture. Ten of these boxes produce one cubic meter.

*inside dimensions of the measuring box*

## LIME AND CEMENT MIXTURE

| | |
|---|---|
| 6 | boxes of sifted earth (8mm sieve) |
| 1 | bag of cement |
| 2 | bags of lime |

**1**   Prepare the dry earth and cement mixture.

**2**   Mix the lime with water.

**3**   With a watering can, add the water and lime to the earth-cement mixture.

## BRICK PRESS

Build a brick press machine to make sandy earth into bricks strong enough for building.

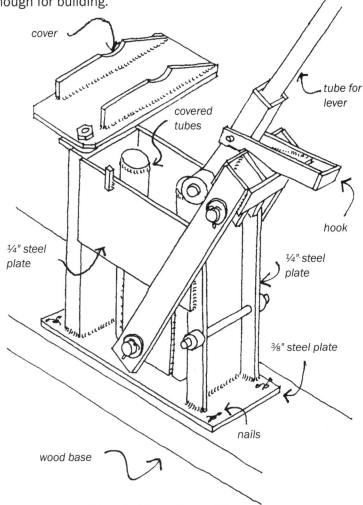

The interior of the mold size is 10cm x 14cm x 29cm.
The galvanized tubes have a 5cm diameter and are spaced 15cm center to center.

There are several types of machines available. The original and most well-known model is Inva-ram.

## ASPHALT MIXTURE

An earth-cement mixture produces strong bricks. However asphalt can also be used to reinforce the earth. For every 2 cubic meters of earth, use 15 liters of asphalt.

**1**     Mix the asphalt with river sand and add water to obtain a liquid mixture.

**2**     Add ⅓ of earth and mix again with more water.

**3**     Add the rest of the earth without water. The mixture should have the consistency of mortar.

Never soak the mixture. Always use the watering can to add more water.

The mixture must be used within one hour. Each time a block is made, the metal plate must be placed in the mold.

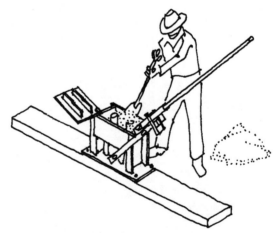

**4**     Fill the mold with the wet mixture, close the cover and place the lever in a vertical position.

Now the brick is ready to be pressed.

**5**   Remove the hook to free the lever and lower the lever to press the mixture.

**6**   Place the lever back in its original position and open the cover.

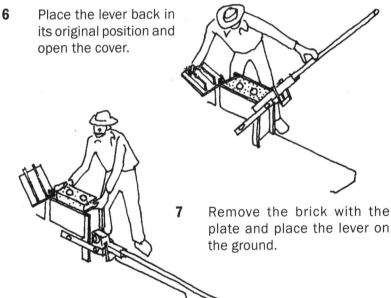

**7**   Remove the brick with the plate and place the lever on the ground.

**8**   Place the brick on its side on flat ground and remove the plate.

# FERROCEMENT

Ferrocement is a structural concrete material which uses chicken wire instead of steel reinforcing rod armature. With this type of cement, it is possible to build roofs, panels and reservoirs.

Chicken wire with small openings is stronger than the type with larger openings:

There is an economical substitute for chicken wire which can be used in most situations. Use common mesh plastic bags that are used to transport fruits and vegetables and are often found at markets.

The mixture of ferrocement should have a 2:1 proportion: two parts sand and one part cement. It is important not to over-water the mixture. Add water slowly to control the consistency.

## CONCRETE SHELL PANELS

Concrete shell panels are vaulted panels that can be used for roofs and slabs. The most common size is 50cm wide, which can span up to 4m.

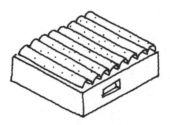

These panels are prefabricated using the plastic cement system, which has the advantage of saving on basic materials. The panels are 1cm thick at the center and increase to 3cm at the extremities.

## CONSTRUCTION OF THE CONCRETE SHELL PANELS

**1**  The 50 cm-wide concrete shell panels are usually molded to 2, 3 and 4 meter lengths.

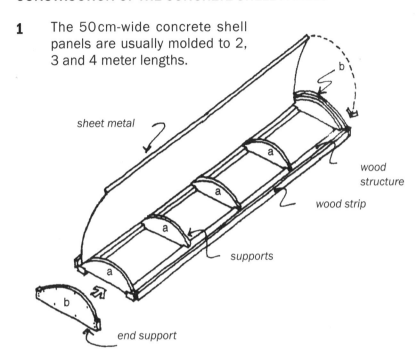

The concrete shell panel mold is made with two pieces of lumber for the frame, wood strips, intermediary support plates and a sheet of zinc or aluminum that covers the whole surface.

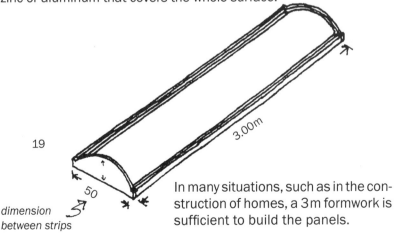

In many situations, such as in the construction of homes, a 3 m formwork is sufficient to build the panels.

**1**    The vault is made with a 60 cm-wide sheet of metal. On each side the metal is folded 3 cm and is supported by the wood frame. This creates a space between the curve and the wood strip where the cement will be poured.

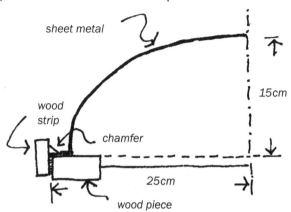

**2**    Chamfer the joint between the wood piece and the strip. This makes it easier to remove the panel from the mold.

The mixture is made with 1 part cement and 2 parts sand.

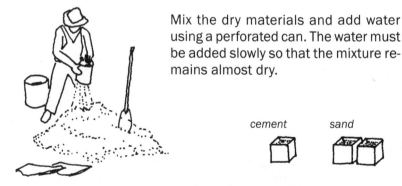

Mix the dry materials and add water using a perforated can. The water must be added slowly so that the mixture remains almost dry.

**3**    Cover the outer curve with a sheet of thick plastic that is stretched out smoothly over the formwork. Apply a first layer of ½-cm-thick cement.

Over this first layer, place a stretched-out piece of plastic mesh from recycled bags.

Cut out strips of mesh the same size as the formwork and soak them in a bucket containing pure cement mixture.

*Along the edges on each side of the conshell, place a ³⁄₁₆" reinforcing rod.*

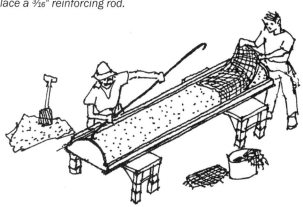

**4** On top of the plastic, add a second 1cm-thick layer of cement. On the edges, at the base of the vault, there must be enough mortar to cover the reinforcing rods.

Thicken the whole lower edge area of the vault.

**5** Let the panel dry in the shade for 3 days before removing it from the formwork.

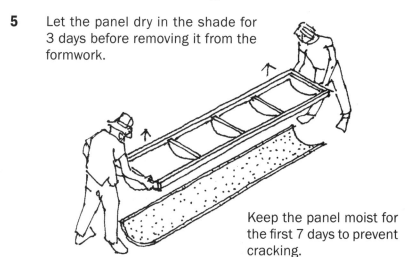

Keep the panel moist for the first 7 days to prevent cracking.

## TUCON LINTELS

Pre-molded elements can be fabricated for door and window lintels. This saves on formwork and reinforcing rods, therefore making construction time shorter and less expensive.

One mold can be used to fabricate all the lintels of a house. This type of lintel is called a "tucon."

The mold box contains a steel tube which is 40 cm longer than the box. Decorative designs and patterns can be made on the inside panels of the box to imprint on the lintel.

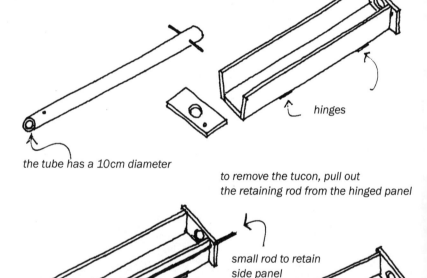

hinges

the tube has a 10 cm diameter

to remove the tucon, pull out
the retaining rod from the hinged panel

small rod to retain
side panel

closed mold

open mold showing the side panel with a decorative design

## MAKING TUCONS

**1**    Cut a piece of plastic mesh the length of the mold and 100 cm wide, and fold it over to make a double layer.

**2**    Apply burnt oil to the inside of the formwork and to the tube, or line it with a sheet of plastic or banana leaves.

 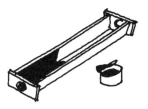

**3**    Before installing the plastic mesh, place 2 cm of cement in the bottom of the mold.

 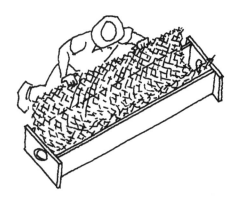

**4**   Install the plastic mesh and the tube.

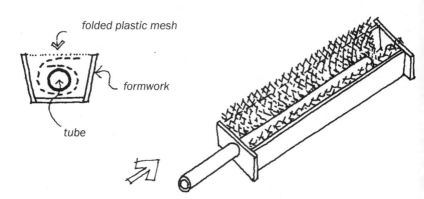

folded plastic mesh

formwork

tube

**5**   Fill the mold with the cement mix and level the surface. The plastic mesh is rolled around itself.

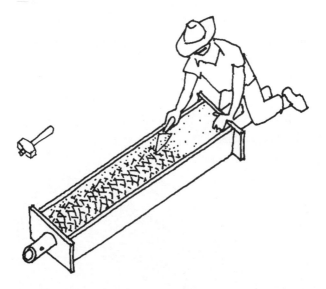

**6**   Let the mixture set for one day before removing the mold. Then dry it out in the shade, or cover it for two weeks, always keeping it damp.

## PRECAUTIONS

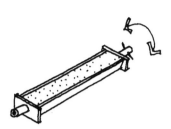

➡ During the first hour of curing, rotate the tube every once in a while. At one end of the tube there are two holes through which a small rod is placed as a handle.

➡ After one hour, remove the tube core carefully. Do not leave the tube in the mold since it will not be able to be removed once the cement dries.

➡ When fabricating many lintels, remember to reapply the burnt oil to the mold and the tube every time a lintel is made.

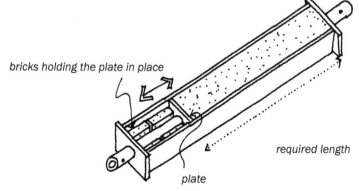

bricks holding the plate in place

required length

plate

To make tucon lintels of different lengths, only one mold with a movable plate is needed.

Below are a few comments on the correct use of ferrocement:

➡ The mixture composition is 2:1 sand and cement, respectively. Add water very carefully to not overwet the mixture.

➡ The chicken wire should be the type with the smallest openings: 14.3mm x 19mm.

➡ Before pouring the cement mix, the wire mesh must be lifted and stretched so it does not stick to the mold.

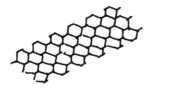 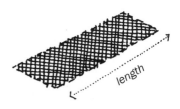

➡ The wire mesh is 3 times stronger in tension if it is used as illustrated above.

➡ There should be one layer of mesh for every centimeter of cement.

➡ Tap the sides of the mold for 4 minutes to settle the mix and fill up the mold completely.

➡ Remove the mold after 24 hours.

➡ Keep the cement damp by covering the panel with a sheet of straw or paper.

➡ Once the panel is removed from the mold, let it cure for 7 days, always keeping it damp. The best conditions for curing are 22° C with 100% humidity.

When using a mixing machine, add 10% of the required water to the sand and cement, then add the rest of the water.

# SAND

Sand is used to make mixtures for masonry. For walls or partitions, use unsifted coarse sand; for finishing, use fine or sifted sand.

| coarse sand | 1 to 3 millimeter grain |
|---|---|
| fine sand | ½ millimeter or less grain |

Clean river sand is good for construction. Sand from the sea is not.

 To select the right sand, test different sands by placing a little of each in glass cups with water. Stir the mixtures and let them settle to see which has the least amount of dirt.

 To clean sand, sift it through a metal wire mesh.

If the size of the site is adequate, place the sifter as illustrated below:

In this set up, the sifted sand falls directly into the wheelbarrow.

# LIME

Lime comes from a soft white stone which becomes a brittle block when heated.

The simplest way to make lime is by placing pieces of limestone in a fire. Make sure the fire is even. Keep the stones in the fire until they crack but still remain in one piece.

Sprinkle water over the stones slowly to cool them while spreading them constantly with a rake to break up the burnt pieces.

Then let the liquid settle until a putty forms.

Cover the lime with sand so it does not harden, and let it sit for 6 days before using it for the cement mix.

## THE OVEN

To make large quantities of lime, build a stone and brick stove 4 meters high with a 2.5 meter base. Make openings in the base to let hot air exit.

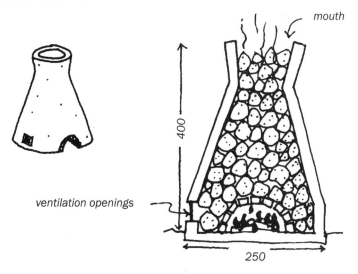

mouth

400

ventilation openings

250

Feed the stove through the upper mouth, ignite the fire and heat the limestones. When smoke stops exiting the mouth, the lime is ready.

## FIRED CLAY TILES

These tiles are made with malleable clay. The thickness of the formwork should be between 1cm and 2cm, depending on the quality of the clay.

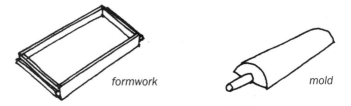

*formwork*                              *mold*

Place the formwork on top of a wet stone and fill it with clay. Then place it on top of the mold (1). Remove the mold (2). Let it dry (3).

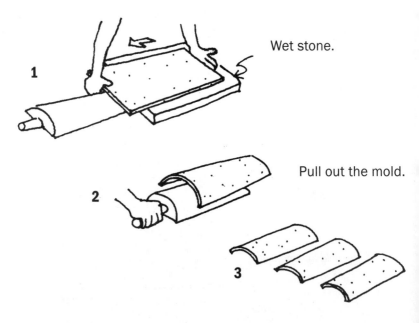

Wet stone.

Pull out the mold.

When the tiles are dry, place them in the oven. It is recommended to make them impermeable to rain by varnishing the upper side.

In humid tropical regions, there are many types of wood which are long-lasting and resistant to insects.

Unfortunately the best types of wood are now scarce, and less resistant wood must be used.

To ensure that wood used in house construction lasts as long as possible, do the following:

**1**      Cut trees on the days between the full moon and the new moon for wood that is more resistant.

**2**      Dry out the wood in a position where the whole piece is exposed to air.

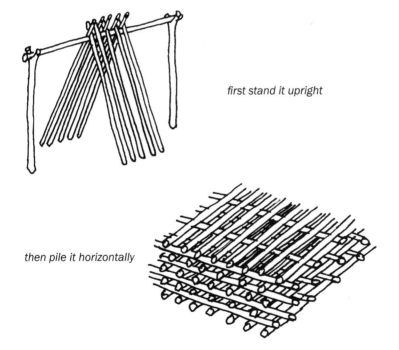

*first stand it upright*

*then pile it horizontally*

## WOOD SHINGLES

In the humid tropics, shingles or wood tiles can be used for finishing roofs or walls.

The wood used for shingles must have a straight grain and be easy to split.

## FABRICATION

**1**    First cut the tree trunk in a 40cm-long stump, and then divide each stump into eight pieces the following way:

*First divide in half (1), then in quarters (2) in the center (3), and then divide the quarter in two equal parts.*

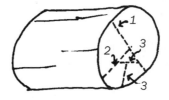

**2**    Remove the bark from the pieces, dry them out for several weeks in a place where they are protected from sun and wind.

**3**    Now they are ready for splitting:

Divide each piece in two until each slice is 2cm thick and 16cm wide.

**4** The final shingles are:

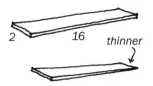

**5** A better finishing is made with a shingle that has one end thinner than the other.

A special cutter is needed to make the shingles.

Hammer the metal bar into the log and move the handle to split the log.

## CUTTER

The way to make the cutter is described below:

Use a thin ½-inch-thick steel plate sharpened on one side.

On one side weld a handle made with a one-inch reinforcing rod.

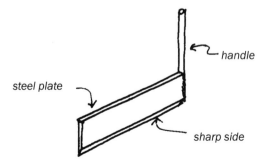

# CACTUS

Mixing cactus juice with other construction materials can improve the quality of walls, floors and roofs by making them more resistant to deterioration from rain and humidity. The prickly pear cactus with large, flat, oval pads produces the best results.

## PREPARATION

**1** Fill a bucket with cut cactus and water up to the rim.

**2** After one week, filter the liquid. It is ready to use.

**3** Make a shallow pit and place the cactus liquid and fresh lime in the pit. Use 1 part liquid to 2 parts lime.

Every one ton of quicklime produces 2½ tons of hydrated lime.

## MIXTURES

| | MATERIAL | PARTS |
|---|---|---|
| cement mix for mortar | earth<br>coarse sand<br>lime | 3<br>1<br>1 |

| | | |
|---|---|---|
| smooth walls, floors and roofs | coarse sand<br>hydrated lime | 4<br>1 |

| | | |
|---|---|---|
| whitewashed walls | granular salt<br>hydrated lime | 1<br>20 |

## USING CACTUS WATERPROOFING

When using only cactus juice as wash, add more salt to the mixture to make its application easier. The indigenous people of Mexico used this techniques to make their temples impermeable. Centuries later the walls are still in perfect condition.

To make smoother wash, the mixture must have more water than juice at the time of application. Also it is preferable to allow the mixture to settle for a few days so that the sand absorbs the juice.

Without doubt there are other types of vegetation with the same impermeable or waterproofing properties. Often when inquiring in the region where you are building, you discover other similar, traditions.

# BAMBOO

Generally the word "bamboo" is used to describe the larger varieties of bamboo and "taquara" to describe the smaller types.

Bamboo trunks reach their maximium height in 3 or 4 months, after which their walls grow thicker and stronger. Within the next 3 to 6 years, depending on the type of bamboo, the trunks reach their maximum strength. At this point they can be used for construction.

## CUTTING BAMBOO

→ Cut the plant when it has reached its maximum hardness; otherwise it will be weak.

→ It is best to cut the bamboo during the colder time of the year when there are fewer insects. It is also recommended that it be cut during the waning moon.

→ Cut the tree 20cm from the ground before the knot, to prevent the retention of water in the trunk where insects, especially mosquitoes, breed.

*do not leave a place for mosquitoes*

*before cutting*          *after cutting*

## PREPARING THE TRUNKS

There are two ways to prepare bamboo trunks, one with air and the other with water.

 Once cut, stand the trunks upright inside an enclosure and leave them there to dry with all their leaves. They must be protected from the sun so that they do not dry too quickly. The trunks should dry in this position for 4 to 8 weeks, depending on the climate.

With this curing in air, the bamboo maintains its natural color and will not grow fungus.

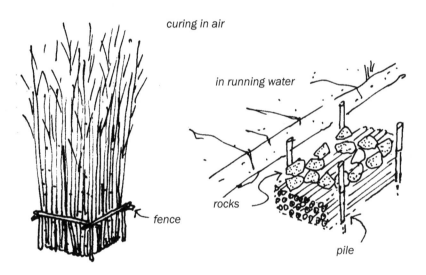

curing in air

in running water

rocks

fence

pile

 The second way to prepare cut trunks is to soak them without leaves in any stream for at least 4 weeks.

To keep them together in one area, make a few piles and use rocks as weights to keep the trunks submerged.

## DRYING

After the first preparations described previously, the bamboo trunks must be dried with the following procedure:

 Air-dried: Pile up the trunks in layers separated by larger trunks in a ventilated area where they are protected from the sun and rain for 2 months.

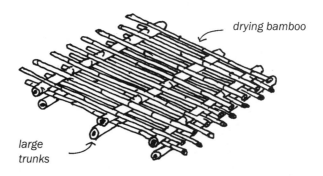

*drying bamboo*

*large trunks*

 Heat-dried: Use fire when the days are overcast and it is necessary to dry the bamboo quickly.

Make a shallow hole and cover the ground and the sides of the hole with bricks so that the fire does not spread. The bamboo should be placed at 50cm above the fire. To dry the trunks uniformly, rotate the pile every once in a while. This method produces trunks more resistant to insects. But be careful! If the fire is too hot, it can deform or crack the bamboo.

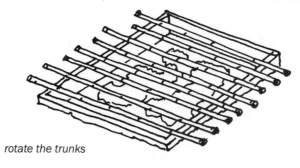

*rotate the trunks*

Hot air: This is the quickest method to dry bamboo. Build a storage space with a solar air heater. The heater is built with blocks, black painted cans and glass or plastic.

 The storage space must have insulated walls so that the heat does not escape at night. The air circulation is controlled during the day with panels that close at night. See chapter 7 on solar heaters.

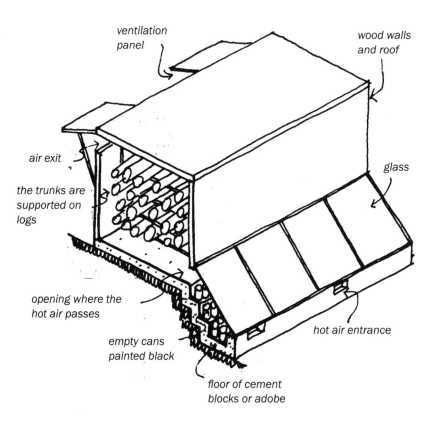

ventilation panel

wood walls and roof

air exit

glass

the trunks are supported on logs

opening where the hot air passes

empty cans painted black

hot air entrance

floor of cement blocks or adobe

Note: This storage space can also be used to dry wood.

## LIQUID PROTECTOR

To protect soft wood, bamboo, tall grasses and leaves against insects and rot:

It is recommended to use non-toxic materials such as manure, creosote or borax which can be dissolved in water to facilitate the treatment of wood. Undiluted whitewash, beeswax or linseed oil can also be used.

When using toxic chemical products in extreme cases, be very careful since they are poisonous and should never be used on interior wood construction or finishings.

It is better to avoid using toxic chemicals altogether by making intelligent construction decisions such as those that prevent humidity and ground contact, provide good ventilation and allow for simple maintenance.

For the immersion treatment, use barrels cut in half and welded together end to end into a trough:

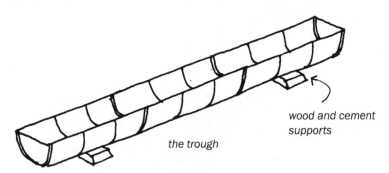

wood and cement supports

the trough

Before treating materials, they should be air-dried and cut to their final size.

Grass must be soaked in the liquid for 30 hours, and leaves and bamboo for 40 hours.

To test small quantities, use only one-half barrel.

For longer-sized wood, soak one half in the liquid first and then the other half.

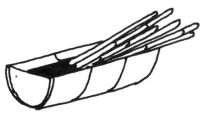

A mixture of earth with asphalt can also be used to treat wood posts.

Dig a small hole in the ground and line the inside with plastic. Fill the hole with a liquid asphalt. Place the posts in the liquid and leave them to soak for several days.

Another method is to fill the hole with a mixture of tar and sand, and apply the treatment to the posts.

## SCORCHING

A quick way to protect the base of undergound wood posts is to scorch their outer surface in a mild fire until they are blackened.

*scorching*        *installing*

# SISAL

The fiber of the agave plant (also named American aloe or century plant) is called sisal. This fiber can be used to tie wood roof structures together. Sisal connections must be carefully crafted and well protected from rainwater.

To know if a century plant leaf has fibers adequate for building, fold the tip of the leaf back without breaking it off. If the end moves back to its original position, the leaf's fibers are good.

this leaf should
not be used

this leaf is
good to use

There are many ways to extract the fibers from the plant; one example is described below:

**1**    Cut the leaf at its base and remove the fibers from the skin or bark starting from the base.

**2** Let the fibers dry for a day or until they harden.

**3** When using the fibers for construction, wet them in a bucket of water so that they regain their elasticity.

A roof structure:

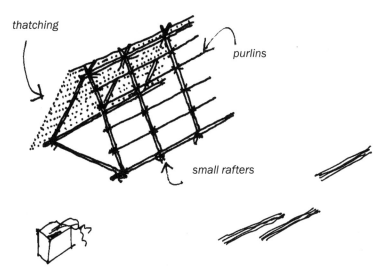

Sisal should only be used in areas that are protected from the rain. For example, when using sisal fibers to fasten rafters to purlins make sure that all the connections are covered by tiles, tall grasses or leaves. Exposed joints must be treated with tar or covered with thatching.

Caution: Do not use fresh sisal, since its fibers contain a sap that damages the skin. The fibers must be well dried before they are used.

# SEACRETE

For construction close to the sea, seacrete can be used to make things like water reservoirs, other types of containers, etc.

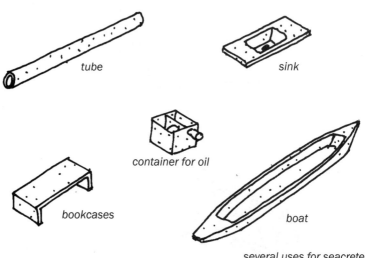

tube

sink

container for oil

bookcases

boat

*several uses for seacrete*

**1** To build a water reservoir, first make a frame with wire or reinforcing rods and cover the structure with metal mesh to shape the container. For the best results use a sheet mesh with 12mm x 12mm openings.

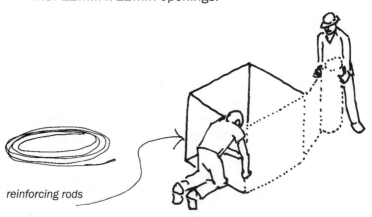

reinforcing rods

**2**     Submerge the box in a calm part of the sea where there are few waves. Connect a wire to one side of the container and connect the other end to the negative pole of a car battery.

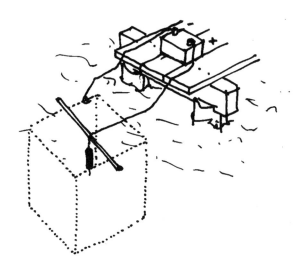

On the positive pole, connect another wire. Tie a piece of charcoal to the end of this wire and suspend it in the center of the container.

**3**     After several weeks, depending on the composition of the water, the metal mesh will be covered with a layer of sea minerals that looks similar to coral.

**4**     Remove the container from the sea when the desired thickness is formed. The salt layer needs sun to harden, so be careful when pulling the object out from the water. Now let it dry.

The salts must be left to harden and settle for several weeks before the container or object can be used.

The surface can be smoothed out before it completely dries.

To recharge the battery, use the energy provided by a windmill since coastal zones are commonly windy.

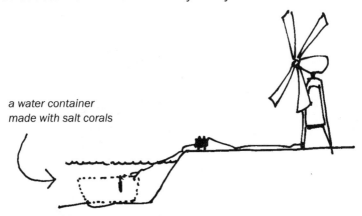

a water container
made with salt corals

Since the electrical current does not need to be constant, the wires can be directly connected to the windmill without using a battery.

Since the charge needs to be between 2 and 12 volts, old car parts can be used to build the windmill.

The charge is not constant, and its mild current does not endanger marine life.

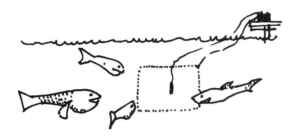

With this method you can make tubes, sinks, tanks, benches, canoes, and so many other things!

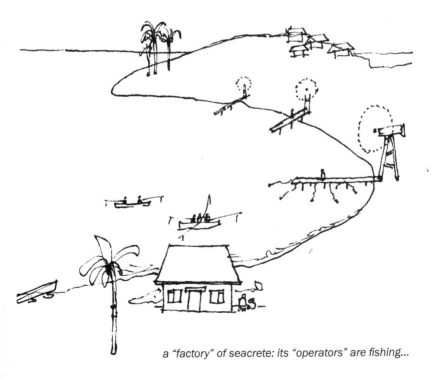

*a "factory" of seacrete: its "operators" are fishing...*

# CONSTRUCTION

6

## GETTING STARTED

Building is similar to travelling; your destination and route may be planned, but it is impossible to foresee what will happen along the way. A construction project can run into problems; it can cost more than calculated, take more time than predicted, materials or techniques may change, or the weather may slow down the work.

Therefore many variables must be taken into account when planning a construction project: the available funds, materials, labor, as well many other considerations. When in doubt, build in phases, which means planning the project in several steps. Start with building immediately only the basic and necessary spaces.

There are three basic building elements that must be well designed and built from the start:

➡   A good foundation, so that the building does not sink.

➡   A good structure, so that the building resists earthquakes and strong winds.

➡   A good roof that protects from sun and rain.

The rest, such as lightweight walls, can be built slowly and with less expensive and less durable materials.

A well-made roof, with strong large rafters, allows for more flexibility with the wall materials. The wall can be made with lighter and less durable materials, since they are well protected from rains and wind.

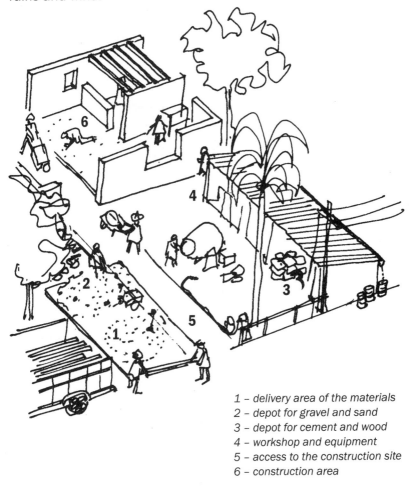

1 – delivery area of the materials
2 – depot for gravel and sand
3 – depot for cement and wood
4 – workshop and equipment
5 – access to the construction site
6 – construction area

Illustrated above is a construction site showing where each activity takes place.

## CONSTRUCTION MANAGEMENT

All construction materials must be stored to protect them from rain and vandalism. They should be kept in a place close to the area where they are delivered and used.

When access to materials is not planned, the workers waste time carrying them from one area to another.

The same thing applies to preparing materials, such as mixing cement and sand. All these types of activities must be planned so that the storage, preparation and application of the materials are done at a short distance from each other.

It is important to organize the arrival of materials. If they arrive earlier than planned, they can be damaged from exposure to sun and rain. If they arrive late, the workers will have nothing to do and hours or days can be lost.

Often it is necessary to build a workshop on the construction site to fabricate construction elements, especially those made with wood such as door and window frames, parts of the roof structure, posts, or cupboards. The workshop can be very simple and must always be located in an area with shade and flat ground. It should be kept clean, and all equipment and tools must be near at hand.

Tools are always getting lost on a construction site. After being used, they should always be placed back immediately in a pre-determined area. A lot of time can be wasted looking for tools or working with inadequate or broken tools.

When building many houses at once, or when engaged in any large construction, it is recommended to prefabricate some of the construction elements. Time is saved when repeated elements are all made at once.

An example of a useful and simple "tool" that saves time on the site is an apron. Worn mostly by carpenters and masons, an apron is used to hold tools, including tape measures, T-squares, plumb lines, strings, hammers, wrenches and screwdrivers.

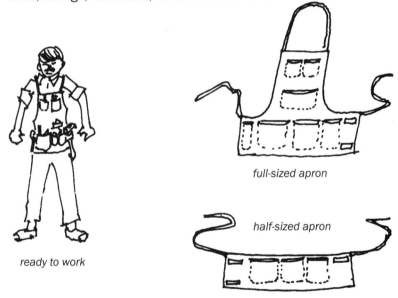

*full-sized apron*

*half-sized apron*

*ready to work*

It is easy to make an apron out of canvas, leather or any other durable fabric or material.

## PLANNING CONSTRUCTION

Before deciding on the shape and size of a building, consider:

➡️  The function of the different spaces, the quantity and size of rooms, and the type of workshop.

➡️  The amount of funds available. Often it is necessary to build in several phases.

Then gather the following information:

➡️  The access to electricity, potable water and sewer system.

➡️  The costs and the availability of materials and labor.

➡️  The municipal and state building and planning laws and soil conditions.

With this information, determine:

➡️  The location of the building, the type of foundation and the connections to the service network.

➡️  The location of accesses, especially for vehicles, during construction and for the finished project.

➡️  The preservation, or in some cases the improvement, of the site with trees or land levelling.

➡️  The way to direct rainwater away from the site so it does not flood the construction site.

➡️  The best area for storing materials during construction.

➡️  The best location for the workshop, so there is the least amount of movement between the storage, the workshop and the work area.

Often the city allows construction to proceed without plans or permits when the site is in an area that does not have service infrastructure such as water, electricity or sewers. The permits, when solicited, are done with drawings of the building (plans, elevations etc.) which indicate the area of construction, the building's location on the site, and the site's relationship to streets.

## LABOR

It is not that difficult for a family to build their own house. There are a few difficult tasks, such as lifting the roof structure, that are more challenging, but this work can be accomplished with the help of neighbors and friends.

When building for other people, the labor needs to be organized. A timetable or schedule should made to determine when the specialized trades need to arrive on the site, such as carpenters, masons, or plumbers. Construction must be prepared and ready for them to start working as soon as they arrive on site.

For the work to advance smoothly, it is important to know when equipment and machines are needed and who will operate them. Some private companies and government agencies rent equipment that they do not use on the weekend.

It is important to be organized so that the construction process is efficient. Small communities can set up communal volunteer projects to build parks or sheds that serve the whole town.

## ORGANIZING THE WORK

   SITE PREPARATION:

Construction location, protection of the existing vegetation, planting trees (for fruit and shade), and excavation.

   FOUNDATIONS:

Including the construction of service systems and piping for water, drainage, and ventilation of underground spaces.

   STRUCTURE:

Construction of columns or supporting walls. Supporting walls must have angles:

It is always convenient to place the kitchen and bathroom together. In this way their filters for used water (grey water) can be combined. See chapter 9 for more details.

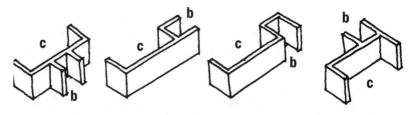

*several ways to combine kitchens (c) and bathrooms (b)*

ROOF:

The roof has its own structure and finishing material.

 WALLS:

Storage or closets can be integrated into walls.

between rooms                    between the kitchen

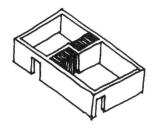 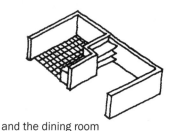

and the dining room

 SERVICES:

All plumbing for water distribution and wiring for electricity can be installed during construction of the walls and must be easy to access in case of repair. These service elements are located in partition walls and not support walls.

 DOORS AND WINDOWS:

The frames are installed during the construction of the walls.

 FINISHINGS:

Floors, walls and kitchen and bathroom surfaces.

# USING MATERIALS

## THE USE OF MATERIALS

There are two important points to consider when deciding on the the type of materials to use for construction:

 If the materials protect from the climatic conditions: e.g., rain, heat and cold, insect attacks and earthquakes. Also if they are durable and easy to maintain.

 If the materials come from the region. Regional materials are more available and less expensive, since the price does not include transportation. Also their availability makes them easier to obtain for repairs.

It is important to use recycled materials from agriculture or industry in combination with more commonly used materials. For example, cactus juice can be used as an impermeable finishing or bottles to replace bricks.

A material should not be chosen only because it looks good or the neighbors used it. A material must be appropriate for its function.

Often you build without knowing how long you will stay in the same place. In this case, light materials can be used and "closet-walls" that have demountable structure and roof can be built. When moving, parts of the house are taken apart and rebuilt in another place. The other walls can be made of adobe or earth.

A movable box which converts into a shelving unit when installed:

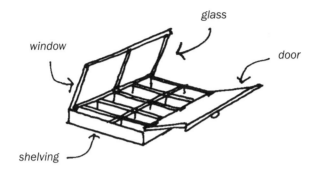

When this movable box is installed between two walls, it creates a window (1), a shelving unit (2) and a door (3).

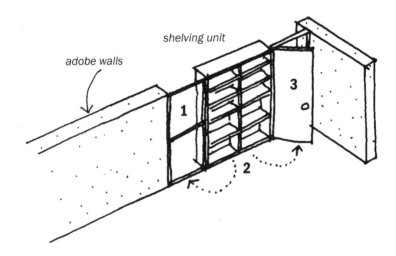

A wooden roof structure can be covered in corrugated metal that is easy to move and reuse.

This system is practical for people working temporarily on large construction sites. When the work ends, the house can be moved to another place, leaving only a few earth walls behind.

## QUANTITY OF MATERIALS

To calculate the quantity of bricks that will be used for a project, the size of the building, the size of its partitions and openings, and the size of the chosen brick must be known.

For example, when using 10cm x 20cm x 40cm bricks for a 20cm-thick wall, the following quantity of bricks is needed for every square meter of wall:

>For each horizontal row there are 2½ bricks. Vertically the wall is 8 bricks high, and with the mortar joints the total height is one meter. Therefore the number of bricks is 8 times 2½ which equals 20.

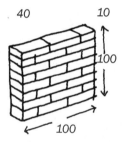

*1 square meter of brick wall has 20 bricks*

If a plan looks like this:

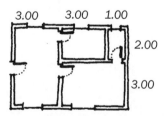

this house plan is 5m x 7m

Let us consider that the interior walls should have a height of two and a half meters.

There are 3 + 3 + 1 + 2 + 3 + 4 + 3 + 5 meters = 24 meters of exterior walls. Inside there are 2 + 2 + 4 + 3 meters = 11 meters of interior walls.

This makes a total of 35 meters 2.5m high or 2.5m x 35m = 87.5m² or 88 square meters of bricks.

Now the the size of the openings needs to be deducted from this total.

There are 4 doors (of 2m² – two square meters each one) which equals 8m² – eight square meters – and minus the 5 windows (with a size of 1.5m² – one and a half square meters each one) which equals 7.5m². This makes a total of 15.5m² or approximately 16m².

The walls, 88m², minus the openings, 16m² gives a total of 72m².

72 square meters, with 20 bricks each, makes 1440 bricks. On top of this calculate an additional 10% for waste during transport and construction.The total is therefore 1600 bricks.

The broken bricks can be crushed into powder and used in plaster mixtures.

## SURVEY LINES

The first step to building is placing the lines of the walls with stakes. These lines will be used as a base for the construction of the foundations.

To correctly locate the trenches for the wall foundations, a few simple instruments are required:

1       a metric tape measure

2       a string with twelve knots spaced a meter apart

3       a plumb line

4       a transparent rubber tube

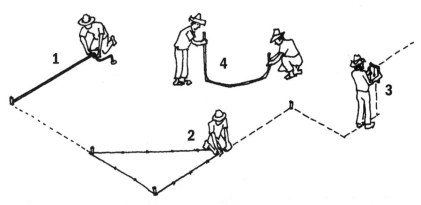

These tools are used to mark the lines of the construction and indicate the center of the trenches where the foundation walls will be built.

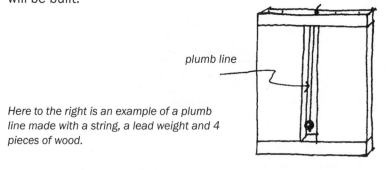

plumb line

*Here to the right is an example of a plumb line made with a string, a lead weight and 4 pieces of wood.*

Mark the width of the trenches using stakes and lines.

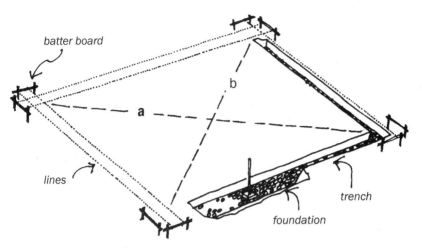

To verify if the lines are 90 degrees for a plan with square corners, place two strings between opposite corners. The dimension of half of one line (a) must be equal to half of the other line (b).

Excavate the earth and press it down with a compacting machine.

Then add a base of sand, gravel or crushed rock.

A compacting device can be made with a pole and a bucket filled with fresh concrete. Place nails at one end of the pole, insert it into the bucket, and let the concrete set.

# FOUNDATIONS

Often wood or clay walls are built directly on the ground with buried trunks; however, it is best to support the wall and roof structure with a foundation. With foundations there are fewer problems of damaged materials caused by settling and ground humidity.

Clay and hard soils are unstable since when they swell they absorb a certain amount of water. This swelling moves the foundation, causing cracks in the walls.

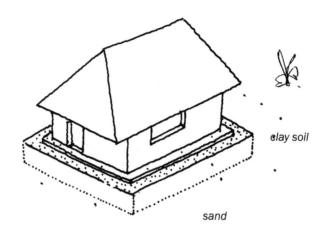

clay soil

sand

To build in clay soils, remove all the earth in the area of the future house and replace it with sand.

In regions where the soil is very humid and there is wood available, such as in marshlands, it is preferable to build the floor above the ground on stilts or pillars.

A wooden house with well-crafted joints can be built loosely connected to ground. During earthquakes this type of house "dances" over the ground but does not collapse. All the joints must be braced. See chapter 2.

The type of stilt house below can also be built in mountainous areas where the ground surface is irregular, hard or very sloped.

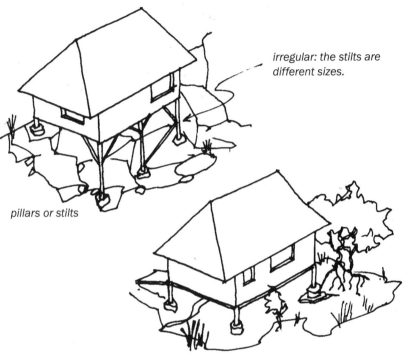

*irregular: the stilts are different sizes.*

*pillars or stilts*

*marshland: the pillars are on footings*

In situations where the ground is flat and firm, make a continuous foundation:

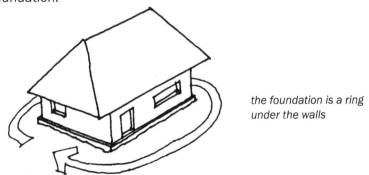

*the foundation is a ring under the walls*

## HEIGHT AND WIDTH OF FOUNDATIONS

The lower floor must be built above the ground level to prevent rain-water from entering. The base of the wall should be 20cm above the ground level. Water then runs over the ground and does not damage walls that are usually made with less durable materials than the foundation.

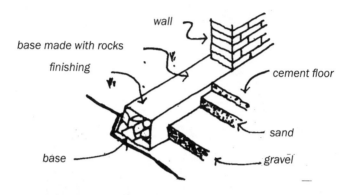

The width of the foundation depends on the stability of the soil, and the weight of the walls and roof. A house made with bamboo walls and a thatched roof requires a narrower foundation than a brick house. The foundation wall can be inclined, with the top part narrower than the base.

## RETAINING WALLS

Walls for retaining land at a higher level must also be larger at the base than at the top. This slanted wall provides additional strength to resist the earth's pressure.

## DIMENSIONS

| SOIL TYPE | FOUNDATIONS | FOOTINGS |
|---|---|---|
| soft | 60 | 90   90 |
| medium | 50 | 60   60 |
| hard | 40 | 40   40 |

The table above shows concrete wall bases. For a wooden house the dimensions can be smaller, and for a heavy brick house they should be a little larger.

 Foundations can also be made with other materials:

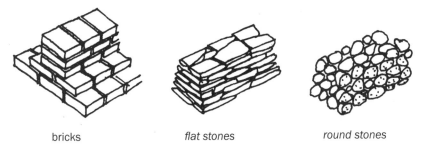

bricks     flat stones     round stones

*use only good-quality bricks*     *more mortar is necessary than with other types*

A more elaborate foundation is required for houses in earthquake zones.

**1**     First build half the foundation with stones on a base. Make a 20cm trench and install a reinforcing rod armature along the whole length.

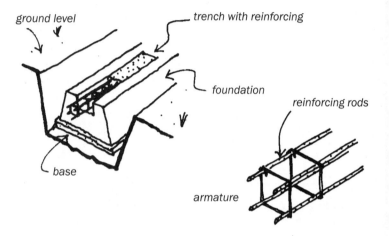

ground level

trench with reinforcing

foundation

reinforcing rods

base

armature

**2**     Fill the trench with concrete. When it is dry, build the other half of the foundation with stones and mortar to the required height. When planning to build concrete columns, connect their armature to the armature of the foundation.

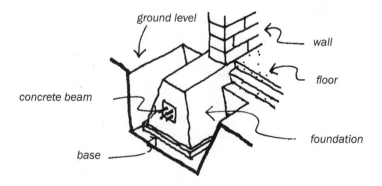

ground level

wall

floor

concrete beam

foundation

base

In very soft soils that do not support the weight of a building, improve the base of the foundation with a 40cm-thick layer of sand at the bottom of the trench. This prevents building large foundations and wasting materials.

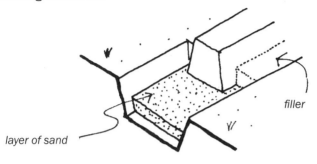

*filler*

*layer of sand*

Then fill the spaces around the foundation and between the trench edge and foundation wall with earth.

## EXCAVATION

The earth that is removed from the trench is used to fill the spaces between the foundations to make a flat surface.

It is therefore preferable to place the excavated earth in the center of the trenches.

When building continuous foundations on a sloped site, the base should step down the slope.

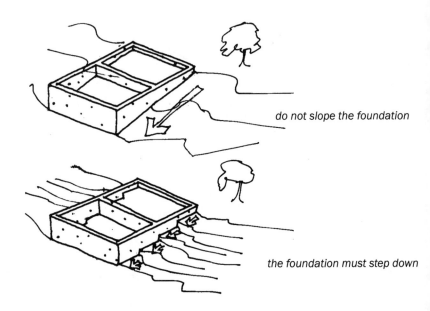

*do not slope the foundation*

*the foundation must step down*

Another way to work on a slope is to make different levels of floors, each with a different foundation height.

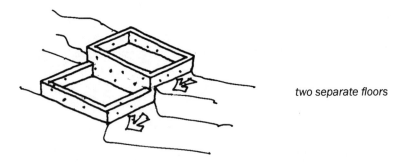

*two separate floors*

It is worthwhile to reinforce foundations. Often house owners waste a lot of time and money repairing floors and walls that break or shift because of badly built foundations.

## PREPARING THE BASE

 Make a foundation by filling the trench with stones and a mixture of cement and sand.

 The foundation should rise 20cm to 40cm above ground level. Use a square tool made with wood pieces to verify the corner angles.

## MORTARS

See chapter 10 on mixtures for finishes.

If the stones for foundations are small and irregularly shaped, it is worth making blocks out of them.

To build these blocks, make a 30cm x 20cm x 15cm mold or form-work. Place the stones in the mold with sand and a small amount of cement or lime.

## CLAY AND BAMBOO FOUNDATION

**1**    Excavate the trenches.

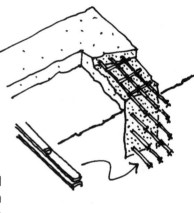

**2**    Wet the excavated earth.

**3**    In the trench place several pieces of bamboo with 10cm spaces between them. Then fill the trench with the wet earth.

Foundations can be raised 40cm above ground to create benches.

## EARTH-CEMENT

One- or two-storey houses can be built with earth-cement foundations.

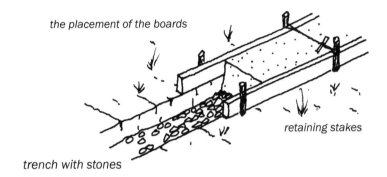

the placement of the boards

retaining stakes

trench with stones

In dry or semi-dry regions, make the foundations with a 10:1 mixture of earth and cement. Compact the mixture with a 5kg compactor.

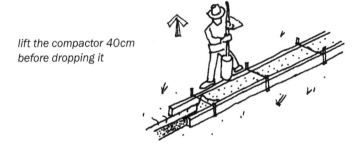

lift the compactor 40cm before dropping it

The mixture must be used immediately, since the cement hardens very quickly with this type of mixture. After pouring it in place, keep it damp for one day and slightly humid for a week.

Earth rich in clay should not be mixed with cement. Instead use a lime mixture of half a part lime for every 20 parts of earth.

## BUILDING ON SLOPED SITES

Badly built retaining walls will collapse with the first landslide or rainstorm. Since making concrete columns is costly, described below are other ways to build safely on sloped sites.

When the land is very sloped, the house must be built to project out like a very large step support. This reduces the cost of structure and cement.

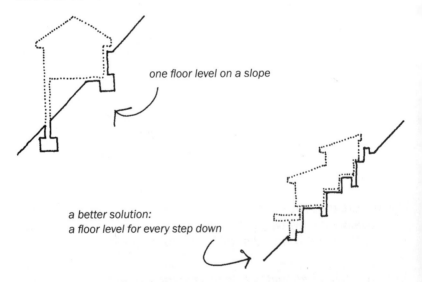

*one floor level on a slope*

*a better solution:*
*a floor level for every step down*

This second method is more work to design, but the construction can be less expensive, especially if the area or wall where the level changes is used for storage, closets, benches, etc.

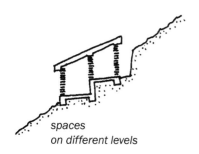

*spaces
on different levels*

*spaces and furniture
on different levels*

for example:

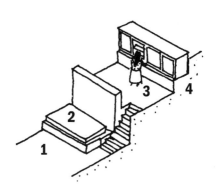

level 1 floor of the bedroom

level 2 base for a bed

level 3 floor of the livingroom

level 4 base for closet

Build footings in the corners to prevent the foundation from sliding in soft soil.

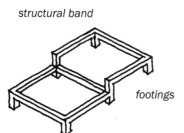

*structural band*

*footings*

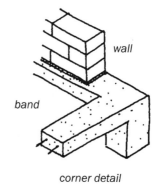

*wall*

*band*

*corner detail*

## LOG OR POST COLUMNS

Posts can be installed in solid and firm soil.

When the soil is sandy and less firm, the posts do not have a pointed end but are supported by a rock or block.

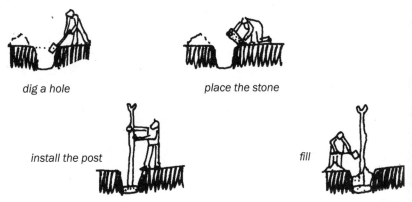

*dig a hole*                              *place the stone*

*install the post*                              *fill*

In regions without rocks or blocks, use logs of durable or treated wood, as explained in chapter 5 on materials.

*dig a hole*        *place a log*        *install the post*        *fill*

*detail of bottom log*

Make a notch in the bottom log to insert post.

Logs can also be used for the inclined posts.

*inclined post*

## CONCRETE COLUMNS

Columns can be built with bricks and concrete or with broken bricks with concrete in the center. When the columns are supporting more than one floor, install several reinforcing rods in the concrete.

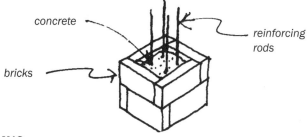

*concrete*

*reinforcing rods*

*bricks*

## BRICK COLUMNS

Brick columns can be various sizes, depending on their spacing and the weight of the structure that they support.

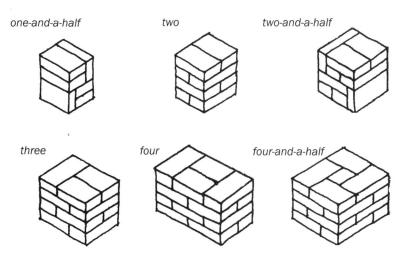

*one-and-a-half*   *two*   *two-and-a-half*

*three*   *four*   *four-and-a-half*

Illustrated above are a few ways to build brick columns.

To build walls, many materials can be used. Choose the ones which are available in the region of the project.

## STONE WALLS

The joints in stone walls must be offset from one row to the next so that the wall does not crack during earthquakes.

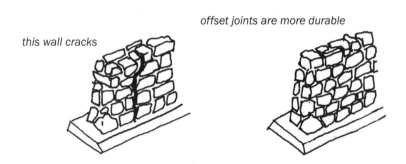

*offset joints are more durable*

*this wall cracks*

On one side place a crosspiece with two strings attached to the corner to make sure the wall is level during its construction.

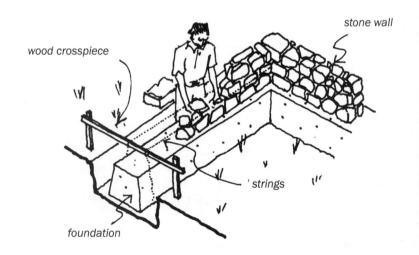

*stone wall*

*wood crosspiece*

*strings*

*foundation*

## ADOBE WALLS

In adobe wall construction, a thick layer of tar must be applied to the top of the foundation to prevent humidity from penetrating and weakening the wall.

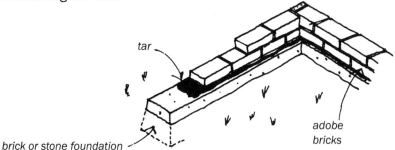

tar

brick or stone foundation

adobe bricks

In regions where wood is available, the adobe bricks can be combined with wood elements to fill spaces within the wood structure.

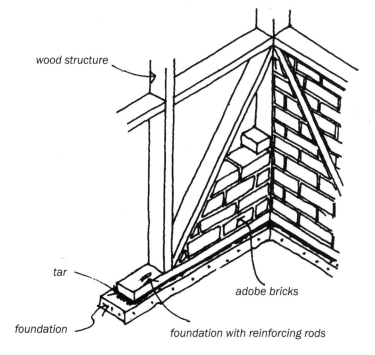

wood structure

tar

foundation

adobe bricks

foundation with reinforcing rods

## ADOBE BLOCK SIZES

The traditional size of an adobe block is 10cm x 40cm x 40cm. The most common size used today is 10cm x 20cm x 40cm.

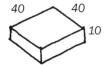

The drawings below show traditional wall construction patterns. In the block wall, the upper course is raised above the wall to show the position of the lower courses.

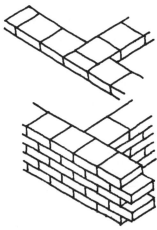

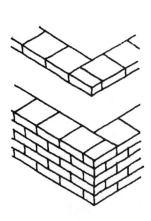

*the course layout at the corner*

*the course layout at the junction with another wall*

The adobe bricks are placed in offset courses to prevent vertical cracks in the walls.

In earthquake zones, reinforce the walls by crossing corners and projecting walls across walls.

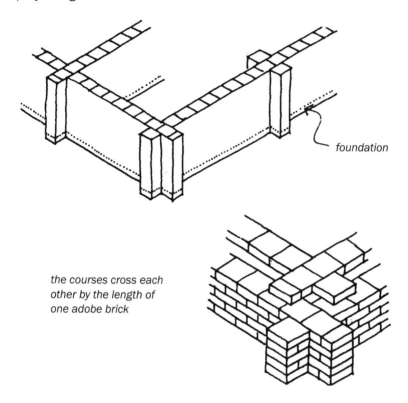

foundation

the courses cross each
other by the length of
one adobe brick

The installation method for adobe bricks depends on their size. Below is a wall made with large adobe bricks.

a narrow wall with adobe
bricks placed on their
sides requires larger-
sized bricks

It is recommended to reinforce the corners of the adobe walls with fired clay bricks to prevent them from breaking.

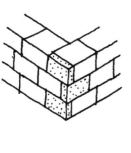

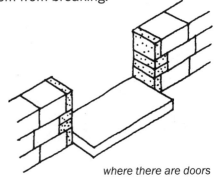

*on corners*

*where there are doors and windows*

The fired clay bricks must be wetted before they are installed so that they do not absorb water from the mortar. It is very important not to wet the adobe bricks before using them.

There are many advantages to using adobe bricks and blocks:

They are impermeable if the clay and sand mixture is well proportioned and blended.

They are good insulators from the cold, heat and noise.

They are resistant to insects.

They are resistant to fire.

They are simple to mold.

They are simple to work with, drill and repair.

The earth of your land can be the building material for your house!

## WATTLE AND DAUB WALLS

To build wattle and daub walls, it is recommended that:

➡ The foundations be made with bricks or stones that rise at least 30cm from the ground (1).

➡ The joints between the walls and the foundations, windows and doors should be made impermeable with asphalt and adjusted to prevent water leaks (2).

➡ The corners and tops of walls be strengthened with reinforcing rods, wood or bamboo (3).

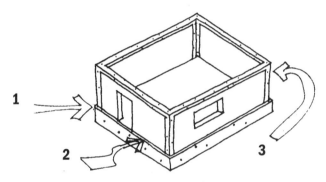

The simplest wattle and daub is made by weaving a wall with reeds and split or whole bamboo, and then applying earth.

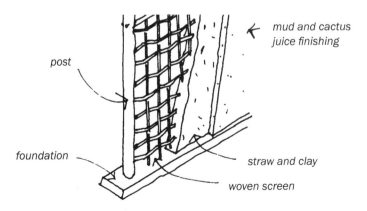

post

foundation

mud and cactus juice finishing

straw and clay

woven screen

Another way to build with mud is to make a rammed earth wall with a formwork of wood boards and braces. Fill the space between the boards with a drier type of mixture and ram it down.

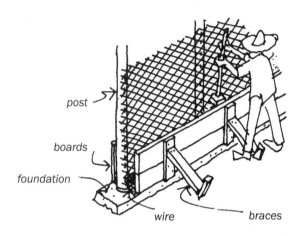

post

boards

foundation

wire                              braces

Place the boards on both sides to make a 30cm-high box that is adjustable to the thickness of wall. The boards are held in place by angled bracing.

The wall structure is made with chicken wire nailed to the posts. The boards must be wetted with water every once in a while so that they can be removed easily.

A good mixture is: 1 part cement, 1 part lime and 8 parts earth. The earth must be sifted beforehand through a wire mesh with 0.5cm openings.

Many elements can be added to the mixture, including sawdust, eucalyptus seeds, nut shells, straw, pieces of corn, coffee or sugar cane. Also the outside can be made different from the inside by adding elements or by using clay of another color.

The outside can be a mixture of earth with asphalt, tar or cactus juice.

In regions with few earth tremors, it is not necessary to use chicken wire. The drawings below show a type of sliding formwork with wood vertical pole supports tied together with wire.

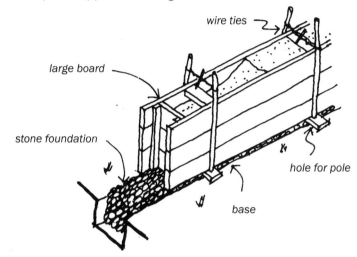

Start with the lower part of the wall. When the earth is dry, remove the boards and build the upper part.

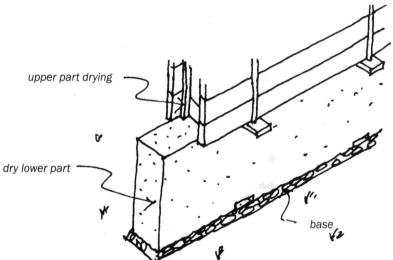

The wall is made in sections built one on top of the other until the wall reaches the desired height.

## MUD AND THATCH WALLS

Mix thatch, which has been drying in the shade for several days, with a handful with mud and then hang it on a rod tied to the posts. The thatching mixture should not be too dry because that will cause it to crack.

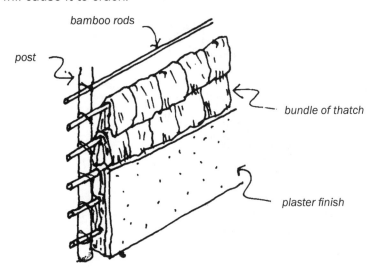

## PREPARING THE MIXTURE

When preparing a second batch of mixture with a different type of clay that will combine with the first, leave the mud in the shade for a few days to cure. Before mixing this mud with the thatch, add enough water to produce a liquid consistency. Then make the bundle of thatch with the mixture and hang it over the rods.

When the wall is half dry, add a thin layer of mud to make a smooth finish.

## MUD AND BAMBOO WALLS

There are two ways to make a weave with strips of bamboo, either horizontally or vertically. With this technique the wood structure, the foundation, the wall mixtures, and the finishing are the same as in the previous example.

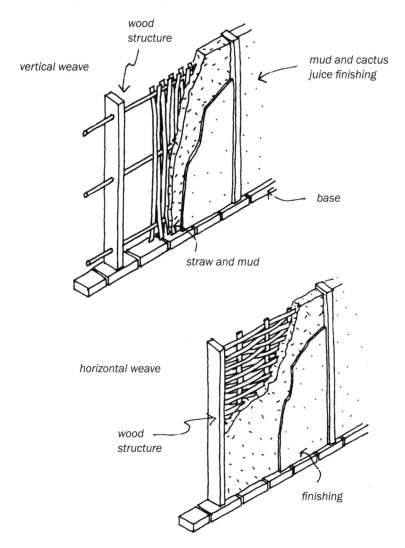

vertical weave

wood structure

mud and cactus juice finishing

base

straw and mud

horizontal weave

wood structure

finishing

## PLANT FIBER WALLS

In humid tropical climates where the walls must be lightweight, use bamboo rods, branches and thatch bundles.

The walls must be lightweight:

 to absorb less heat

to dry quickly after a rainstorm

to well ventilate the rooms

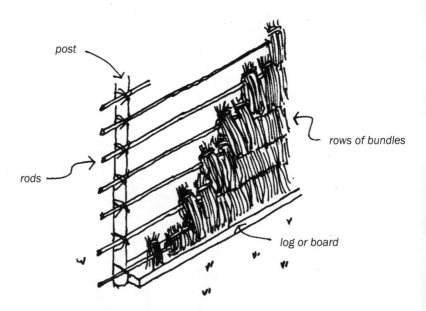

The thatch is tied at the top to make a bundle and then hung in rows on the bamboo rods that are connected to the posts.

A wall made with branches or sticks:

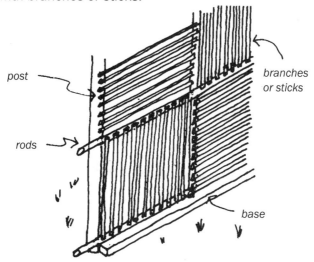

The stems of palm leaves are nailed or tied with twine to a branch or wood structure.

A wall made with thin split bamboo:

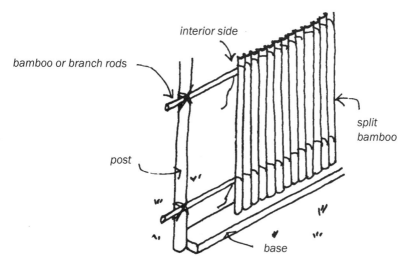

Since whole bamboo sticks may harbor insects, bamboo should be split in half.

A wall made with agave (century plant) leaves:

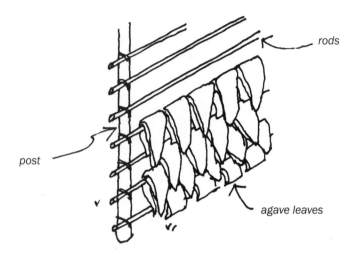

*post*

*rods*

*agave leaves*

The leaves are folded over the rods in offset rows.

A wall made with bamboo panels:

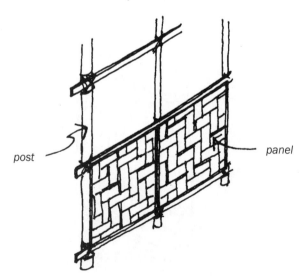

*post*

*panel*

See chapter 2 on how to weave bamboo.

## WOOD WALLS

In temperate climates where there are abundant sources of wood, walls can be made with large boards tightly joined to prevent cold air from entering.

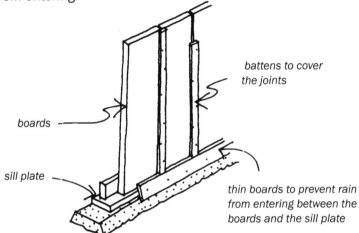

boards

battens to cover
the joints

sill plate

thin boards to prevent rain
from entering between the
boards and the sill plate

A good-quality wood can be left exposed to the sun and rain.

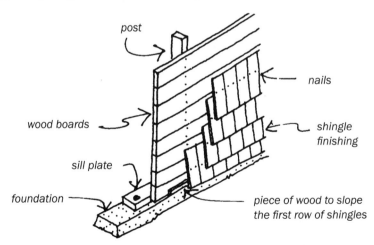

post

nails

wood boards

shingle
finishing

sill plate

foundation

piece of wood to slope
the first row of shingles

A low-quality wood needs a covering such as wood shingles. They are installed in such a way that the upper row covers the nails of the lower row.

## BRICK WALLS

Fired clay bricks are generally better than adobe bricks. There are many ways to lay bricks.

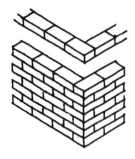

*next course (row)*

**A**  A simple way to build straight walls is by setting the bricks lengthwise.

**B**  For thicker walls, the bricks are set crosswise. The corners are finished with two ¾-sized bricks.

**C**  When the bricks are exposed without another finishing, alternate the direction of the bricks to create a pattern.

**D**    A more elaborate way to lay bricks. Note: The pattern of the courses changes at the corners.

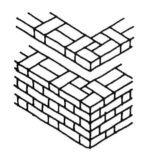

**E**    Another pattern uses bricks that are ¾, ½ and ¼ of the original size.

Bricks can also be combined with concrete blocks of the same length but with a different thickness. Make a pattern alternating one course of blocks with two courses of bricks.

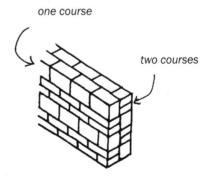

*the corner joints are simple*

*section of a wall showing the alternating courses*

## SPECIAL WALLS

With concrete blocks:

The blocks are on the interior side and are covered with finishing bricks on the exterior side.

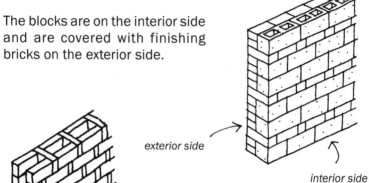

exterior side

interior side

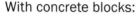

For humid zones:

Build cavity walls in hot and humid zones. The humidity will take longer to penetrate and drying is quicker after rain.

In a cavity wall, the humidity stays in the exterior wall. Reinforcing ties must be used to join both layers of the wall.

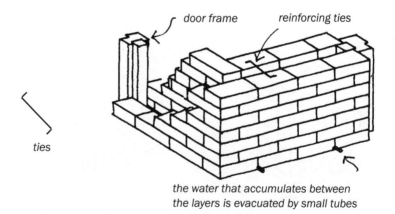

door frame          reinforcing ties

ties

the water that accumulates between the layers is evacuated by small tubes

The support ties should be placed every 8 courses and be one meter apart.

When using concrete blocks, the cavities can be used to make columns and beams by filling the corners and the tops of the wall. The reinforcing rods of the columns are tied into the foundation and the continuous beam.

A special type of block is required for the beam. These blocks are open at the top and are half the size of a regular block.

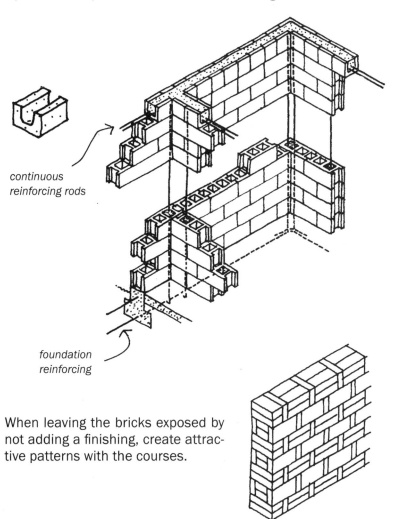

continuous
reinforcing rods

foundation
reinforcing

When leaving the bricks exposed by not adding a finishing, create attractive patterns with the courses.

When the bricks are irregular sizes, install them so that the exterior side is flat.

Then fill the holes and joints with an interior finishing and make an attractive pattern.

Slanted bricks can be made with a different mold. This does not require much more work and gives a nicer finishing to walls and parapets.

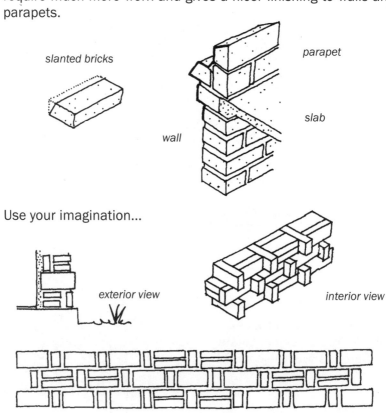

slanted bricks

parapet

slab

wall

Use your imagination...

exterior view

interior view

## JOINTS

Other materials can be added to the joints when the courses are being layed and the mortar is still fresh.

With this technique, less mortar is used and the walls are better protected from the rain. Also any finish applied to these walls will stay on better.

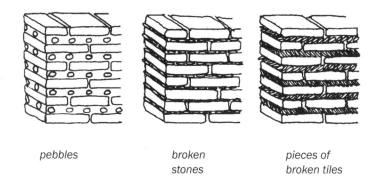

pebbles                   broken                    pieces of
                          stones                    broken tiles

## JOINTS AGAINST RAIN

To make good joints in exposed masonry walls, remove excess mortar from the joints and clean the bricks well with a stiff brush after building an area.

This work must be done when the joint mortar is still fresh. Later a finishing joint can be made that is more resistant to water. The mortar for this joint is a mixture of cement, lime and sand in a 1:2:6 proportion.

newly made joint          remove a little           apply the 1:2:6
                                                    mixture

## BUILDING ON UNSTABLE LAND

In areas with unstable soils, such as on hills, the corners and joints of the walls must be reinforced with concrete pillars and columns.

With this strengthening system, the thickness of the walls can be decreased, and only one layer of bricks is required.

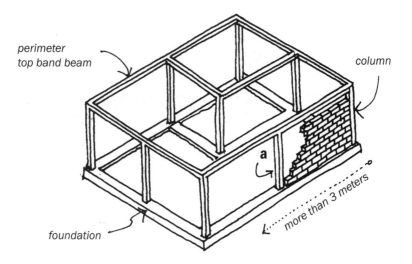

perimeter
top band beam

column

a

more than 3 meters

foundation

When a wall is more than three meters long, an intermediary column must be built (a).

In dry tropical or temperate climates, it is recommended to build thick walls that provide more protection from temperature changes.

Below are a few recommendations for building with bricks in earth-quake regions:

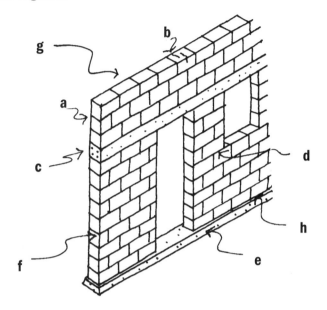

**a** Use good-quality mortar (see chapter 10).

**b** Do not use broken bricks.

**c** Build a continuous concrete beam at the height of the upper part of the doors and windows.

**d** Leave a minimum of 100cm between the doors and the windows.

**e** Build a stone or concrete block foundation.

**f** The minimum thickness of a wall should be $\frac{1}{12}$ its height.

**g** The length of a wall without internal supports should not be more than 20 times its thickness.

**h** Apply layers of tar or cement plaster to prevent ground humidity from penetrating the bricks.

## EARTHQUAKES AND LANDSLIDES

To build a house that is resistant to damage caused by settling, consider the following:

 A wall with no support will fall with the first earthquake or landslide.

 Walls with corners are more resistant.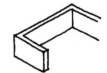

 A wall weakens when it is too long.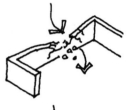

 Walls get damaged when there is a small space between the doors and windows.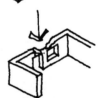

The walls must have "ins" and "outs" and use the roof or slabs to brace the walls.

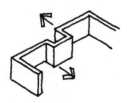  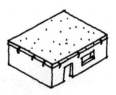

*a continuous strengthening band*

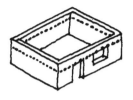

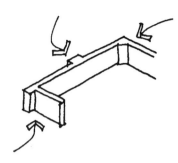

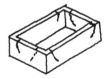

*or thickening of certain sections*

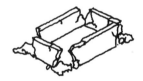

*between the roof and the continuous reinforcing band, leave openings in the wall for the hot air to exit*

During earthquakes the walls crack and the corners are the first part to fall.

## A BADLY DESIGNED HOUSE

The doors and windows should not be so close to each other, nor to the corners.

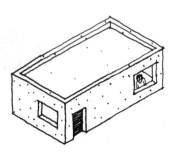

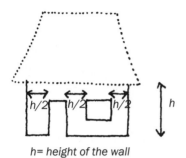

*h= height of the wall*

For stronger construction use these guidelines to determine the spacing between openings.

For those who like equations:

$$D + W = L/2$$

The sum of the width of the door and the width of the window should not be greater than half the length of the wall.

For example, with a 4m-long wall and an 80cm door, the window can not be larger than 120cm.

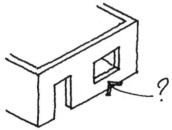

half the length of the wall = 200
door length = 80
what is left for the window = 120

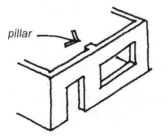

*pillar*

When a larger window is required, a pillar must be built.

It is worth building strong corners and walls to strengthen the house in case there is no time to exit in an emergency. A small secure area can be made to store valuables. In a disaster situation such as flooding, collapses or earthquakes, inhabitants are often trapped while attempting to save their valuables.

Usually houses do not collapse with the first tremor, but the door is often unopenable since its frame is bent. In unstable zones, the door frame must be made with a thicker wood frame.

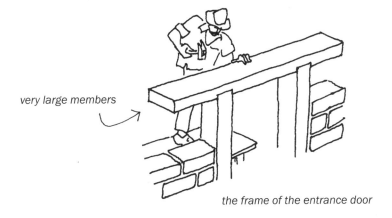

very large members

the frame of the entrance door

Many people do not wake up at night to leave the house in this type of emergency. Hang a bell in the bedroom that rings at the very first tremor of the earth.

## CORNERS

In areas with little stable ground, it is best to reinforce the corners of the walls with small structures:

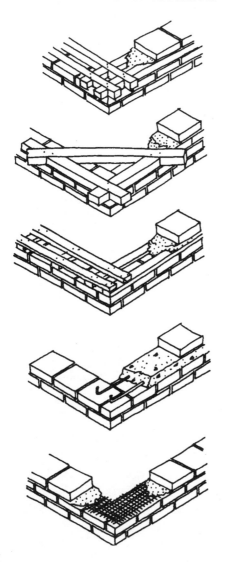

The lumber members are installed at the same width as the wall.

Place larger wood members on an angle above the door height.

The same technique with smaller members.

A layer of concrete and reinforcing rods that hook together at the corner.

For a simpler reinforcing technique, use a metal mesh that crosses over at the corners.

When the masonry walls are made with earth-cement blocks, it is necessary to reinforce the corners. If reinforcing rods are not available, use bamboo rods or palm leaf stems covered in tar and coarse sand to bind them together.

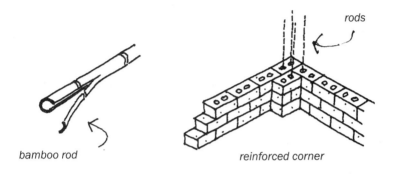

bamboo rod                    reinforced corner

The same technique can be used to build adobe walls with openings at the joints.

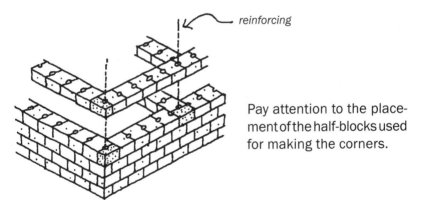

reinforcing

Pay attention to the placement of the half-blocks used for making the corners.

Place bamboo rods or reinforcing rods in the holes to reinforce the corners and the meeting points of walls.

When building a continous structural band for large adobe walls, also build corner feet to increase the strength.

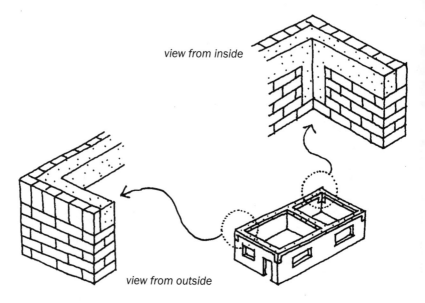

*view from inside*

*view from outside*

But really the best way to reinforce corners of adobe walls is with concrete columns.

To prevent damage at the corners, which always occurs, use rounded adobe walls.

*reinforcing*

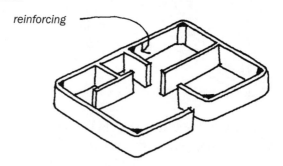

On the interior, build triangular-shaped reinforcing columns.

## REINFORCED ROUNDED CORNERS

**1**   The foundations must have a triangular angle at every corner. Reinforcing rods from the foundations should connect to the column's reinforcing.

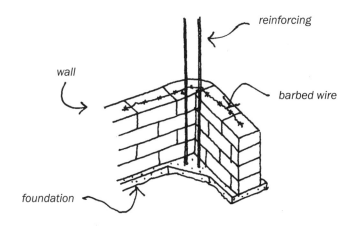

**2**   Every four courses add two meters of barbed wire in the joint. The wire must also be tied around the rods.

**3** Every 10 courses install a board in the corner and fill the space with concrete. Hit the board to prevent bubbles from forming in the concrete.

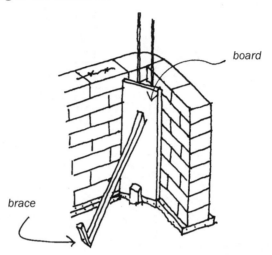

board

brace

**4** At the top end of the wall, connect the reinforcing rods to the perimeter band.

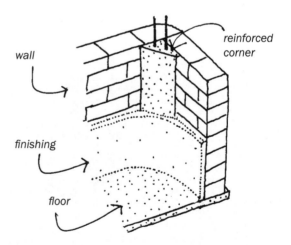

wall

reinforced corner

finishing

floor

**5** Later add the interior finishing with a smooth curve at the corners.

## WOOD AND BRICK WALL

In regions where wood and bricks are about the same price, try combining these two materials to make walls:

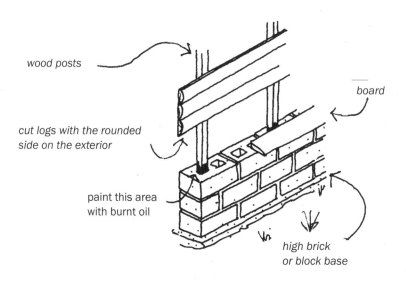

*wood posts*

*board*

*cut logs with the rounded side on the exterior*

paint this area
with burnt oil

*high brick
or block base*

In rain zones, the masonry is higher and the roof must have adequate eaves to protect the wood. In dry zones, the masonry can be only two or three courses high.

*rain zones*

*dry zones*

## INSULATING FROM HEAT AND COLD

A wall made with adobe provides better protection from the heat and cold than a brick wall. Improve the insulation of hollow concrete blocks by filling the holes with earth or sand while installing each course.

Before installing the second course, fill the first. This technique's insulation value (resistance to heat and cold) is 32 to 40. See chapter 10.

## FOOD WALL

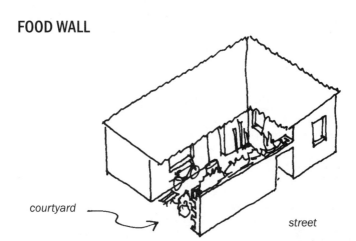

*courtyard*

*street*

In areas where the houses are close together and there are very small gardens, build a wall with bricks or blocks which can be used to grow food. This wall can be located between the street and the entrance courtyard.

The top part can be a small garden for growing vegetables and food for the chickens or rabbits that are in the lower compartments. The animals produce fertilizer for the garden.

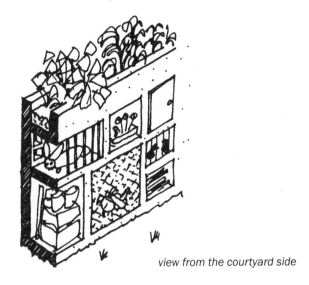

*view from the courtyard side*

This wall can also be used to store things such as tools and materials. The animal compartments can be built in bricks with openings towards the outside.

*a view of an ecological wall along a street*

## VERTICAL GARDEN

When good earth is not available and space is limited, build vertical gardens inside tubes.

**1**     In a metal tube 2.5 meters long, make alternating cuts 20cm from each other.

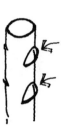

**2**     Pull the upper part of the cut in to make little shelves.

**3**     Fill the tube with earth and plant different types of plants, such as strawberries, vegetables or medicinal herbs.

It is also possible to use bamboo instead of metal. In chapter 8 on water, see how to remove the knots in bamboo trunks.

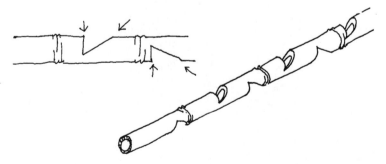

Another way to build a vertical garden is to install clay vases one on top of the other as illustrated below:

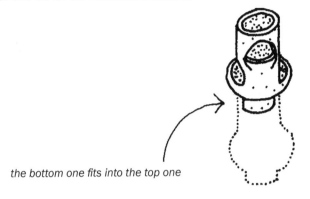

*the bottom one fits into the top one*

This type of "garden" requires very little earth and water. The garden tubes are watered by wet strings which hang from a gutter bringing water.

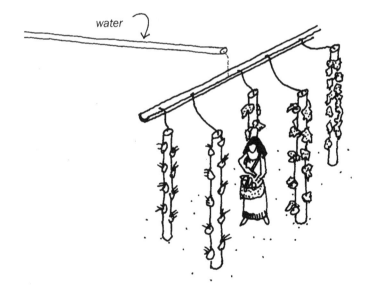

water

The lower parts of the tubes are buried in the ground.

## CLAY JAR WALLS

First build a wall with posts and strips tied horizontally on both sides of the posts. Place the clay jars top-down between the strips.

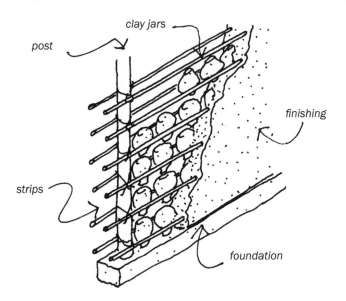

Apply a finishing made from a mixture of mud, sand and grass or cut straw.

## ADOBE BRICK JOINTS

The joints should not be larger than a half or a third the thickness of the adobe brick.

*proportions of the adobe*

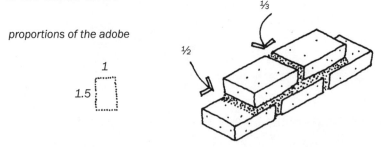

## WALL OPENINGS

Openings in the walls for windows or doors should have lintels. Lintels can be made with wood, bricks or concrete.

An opening of a meter wide or less can be made with bricks, but a larger window or door frame must be installed.

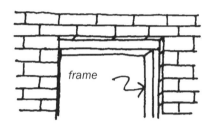

Larger openings must have lintels made with concrete and reinforcing rods.

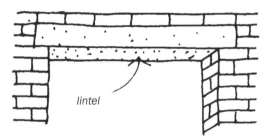

Bricks can be installed to make a kind of a compressed beam:

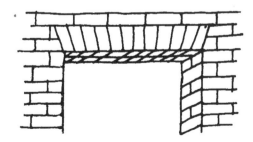

This brick lintel is a traditional way to span an opening.

Another way to span an opening is to corbel the bricks by projecting each course half-way over the opening towards the center.

Bricks can also be used as a mold for a concealed concrete lintel.

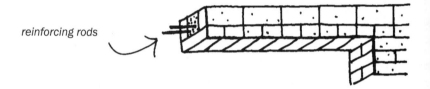

*reinforcing rods*

## THE TUCON

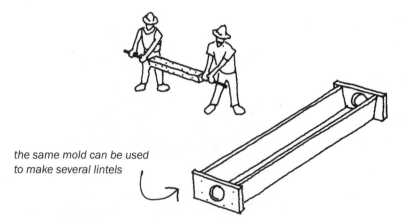

*the same mold can be used to make several lintels*

See chapter 5 on materials for directions on making tucons.

A tucon can be installed without formwork or bracing.

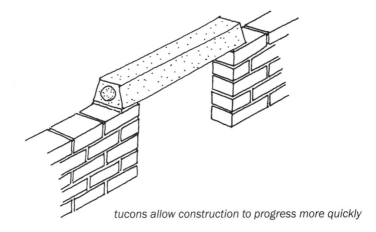

*tucons allow construction to progress more quickly*

When the weight above an opening is very heavy, reinforcing rods must be placed in the hole and the hole filled with concrete.

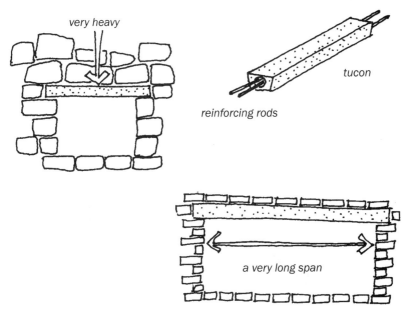

The same goes for large openings...

## ARCHED WINDOWS

Here are two ways to build arched windows.

**A**      Support made with bricks:

Place the bricks in an arch without mortar. They will be removed after the finished brick arch is dry.

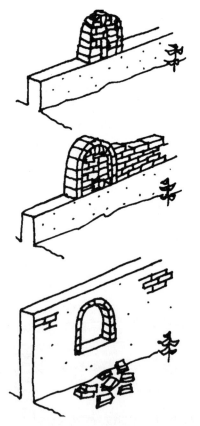

**1**  Install bricks in the shape of the opening without mortar.

**2**  Build the brick arch of the opening with mortar and install the other courses of the wall.

**3**  Remove the loose bricks in the opening, and then apply the finishing.

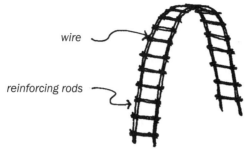

*wire*

*reinforcing rods*

**B** Support with a formwork:

Make a simple curved formwork with reinforcing rods connected with wire. The advantage of this type of support mold is that it can be easily modified for other window shapes.

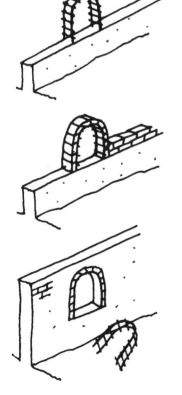

**1** Place the formwork in the desired curve.

**2** Build the brick arch and the courses of the wall.

**3** Remove the formwork.

## DECORATIVE WALLS

With good-quality bricks or concrete blocks that do not require a finishing, take the opportunity to build walls with patterns.

In very dusty regions it is recommended that walls be flat. In other regions the masonry can be installed on different angles to create zig-zag patterns. Besides being decorative, these walls are less hot since they create shade and air movement.

*a flat wall gathers less dust*

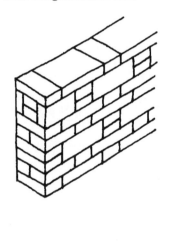

a zig-zag wall makes its own shade

The lower part of the wall must be flat to prevent the masonry from being damaged by vehicles, gardening equipment, animals or children wanting to climb up.

area with projecting wall pattern

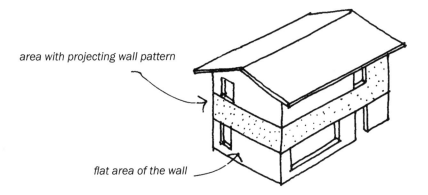

flat area of the wall

## EXAMPLES

Trapezoid-shaped adobe bricks can make interesting walls or partitions.

The bricks can be made with differently colored sands. The result is illustrated on the right:

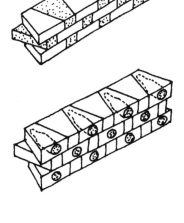

Another idea is to install glass bottles in the bricks, leaving their bottom ends exposed.

*install a glass bottle*                    *with an exposed bottom*

Even bricks without decoration can be installed to make patterns:

One brick faces in and the other out.

A wall with a flat and finished interior and a patterned exterior.

A wall with both sides patterned by bricks installed in the same direction.

A wall with alternating course directions.

An alternating pattern with offset courses.

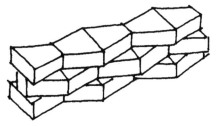

A wall with openings for partition or garden:

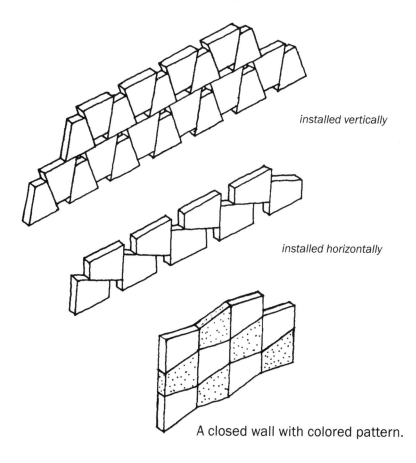

*installed vertically*

*installed horizontally*

A closed wall with colored pattern.

Rectangular bricks can also be used to create patterns:

*a slightly angled wall*

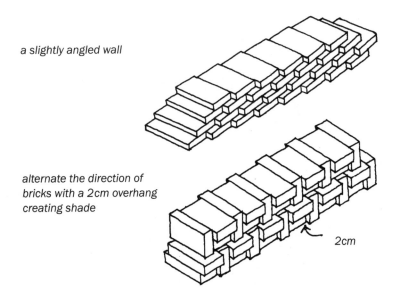

*alternate the direction of
bricks with a 2cm overhang
creating shade*

2cm

Concrete blocks can also be installed to create decorative patterns:

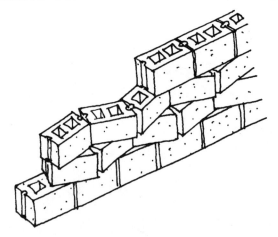

In a flat wall, one or two courses can have a different pattern.

Always use good-quality bricks which do not easily break.

## OUTDOOR WALL COPING

To prevent rain from entering into the joints of outdoor brick walls, cap the top of the wall with a special top course made with bricks.

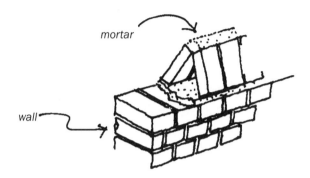

Garden walls can have open-pattern courses in the upper part of the wall:

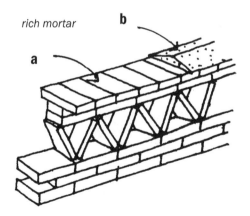

In rain zones use a richer type of mortar on the coping to prevent water from damaging the joints (a). Another solution is to add a sloped cement finishing coping (b).

Often curved tiles are used for coping veranda walls:

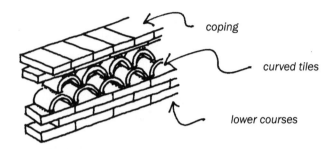

coping

curved tiles

lower courses

The spaces can remain open or be filled with mortar and painted with lime.

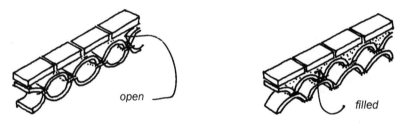

open

filled

To close off the top of the wall, add a course of bricks placed in the other direction.

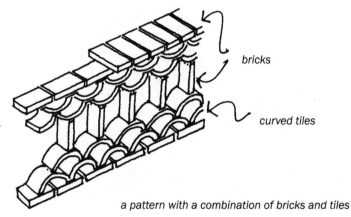

bricks

curved tiles

*a pattern with a combination of bricks and tiles*

With this technique, many different patterns can be created to decorate a balustrade:

These patterns can also be used for garden walls:

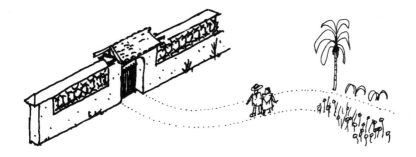

They also work well for interior partitions:

## WALLS MADE WITH SEVERAL MATERIALS

The walls of a house or building do not need to all be made with the same materials and techniques.

Neither is it necessary to build the final walls immediately. One can start by building with lightweight materials and then change them for other, more durable materials later on.

It is important that a construction begin with a well-made foundation and structure to support the roof. The walls can be part of the structure or not. The materials for the walls should alternate in clear patterns.

*not* like this

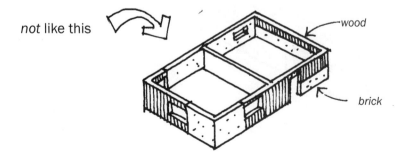

wood

brick

This is better.

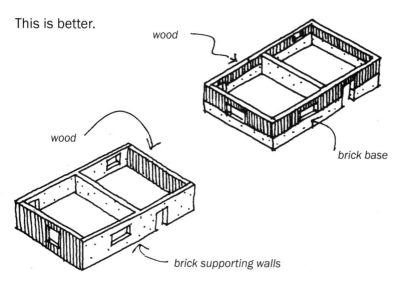

THICKNESS OF ADOBE WALLS

The first-storey walls of a two-storey house should be one-and-a-half times thicker than the walls of the second storey.

Another way to calculate the thickness of a wall is based on its height. For example, a 3 meter-high wall will be 30cm thick.

The thickness of a wall also depends on the quality of the materials and the regional climate.

## LIME PLASTER

Some special tools are required to apply plaster. The technique is explained below.

**1** Dampen the masonry wall and apply plaster mixture.

**2** Verify the level of the wall with a plumb line.

**3** Smooth out the surface with a wood board.

**4** Finish the surface with a wood or metal trowel.

## SLAB FORMWORK

Often material is wasted in the construction of concrete floors and roofs due to incorrect space planning.

By designing a house with modular units, the same formwork can be used for the whole slab. This saves wood which often cannot be reused after it is cut.

A concrete construction can be more expensive than planned due to the high cost of wood that is not reusable.

Shown below is a house based on a 50cm unit:

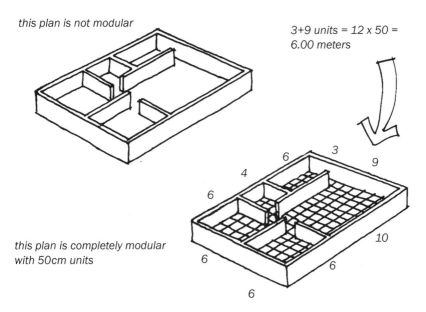

*this plan is not modular*

*3+9 units = 12 x 50 = 6.00 meters*

*this plan is completely modular with 50cm units*

## MODULAR CONSTRUCTION

To build with a modular construction technique, first decide on the most convenient unit to use. This module is based on the size of wood boards available, so that wood is not wasted by cutting. Design the plan of the house with the chosen module.

Below is an example of a module of one meter by one meter and a half. The plywood formwork panels must not be too large or heavy, so as to be easy to manipulate. Panels made with boards are usually smaller since they are heavier.

A typical plan of a small house could be:

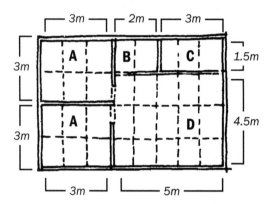

Note: The size of the rooms in meters is measured from one wall to the other. These are the inside dimensions of the spaces, and they do not include the thickness of the walls.

| ROOM | FUNCTION | MODULES | DIMENSION |
|------|----------|---------|-----------|
| A | bedroom | 12 | 3 x 3.0m |
| B | bathroom | 2 | 2 x 1.5m |
| C | kitchen | 3 | 3 x 1.5m |
| D | living room | 15 | 5 x 4.5m |
| | TOTAL | 32 | |

There are 32 modules of formwork required.

There are two ways to build formwork panels:

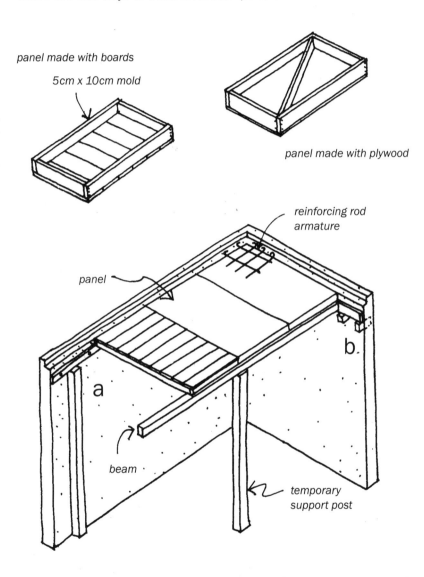

panel made with boards

5cm x 10cm mold

panel made with plywood

reinforcing rod armature

panel

a

b

beam

temporary support post

If wood is not available for posts (a), the panels must be supported by projecting bricks (b).

# PANELS

Prefabricated panels are often convenient for closing off the space between the roof and the upper part of the wall. These types of panels are called ceiling panels.

There are several ways to build ceiling panels using clay and grass, gypsum and sisal fibers, or bamboo and cement.

## CLAY AND THATCH GRASS PANELS

Clay and thatch are materials used to build durable ceilings and upper storage surface.

**1**    Make a row of holes in the joists before they are installed.

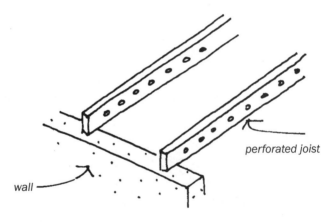

*perforated joist*

*wall*

**2**    Then wrap straw or thatch grass soaked in clay around branches which are longer than the distance between the joists.

*wrap around*

**3**     Install the branches wrapped in grass and clay between the joists. Place one end of the branch in one side and then in the other.

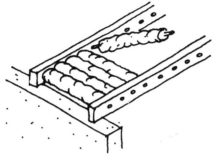

**4**     Add a smooth finishing layer of a sand and clay mixture above and below the panel.

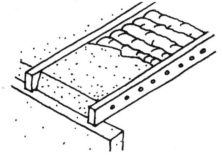

## BAMBOO, MUD AND THATCH PANELS

This type of panel is made with bamboo split lengthwise and a mixture of mud and cut thatch:

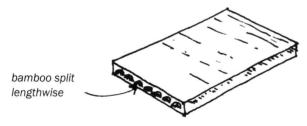

bamboo split
lengthwise

The round side of the bamboo is placed upward and the lower part is well embedded in mud.

## BAMBOO AND MORTAR PANELS

This type of panel or slab can also be used to make interior partitions.

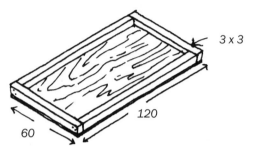

**1**    Build a mold with plywood with a 3cm x 3cm wood frame.

**2**    Apply burnt oil to the panel and the frame.

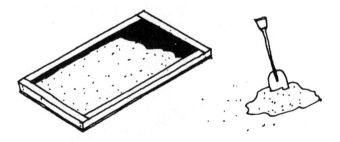

**3**    Add a fine layer of mortar in the mold. The mortar is made from one part cement and two parts sand.

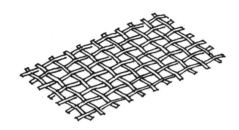

**4**   Install a woven bamboo mat made with 2mm thick and
one centimeter wide strips spaced 4cm to 5cm apart.
When the bamboo is dry, coat the mat with tar and spread
a fine layer of sand on top. Press the mat into the cement
mixture. Let the panel dry.

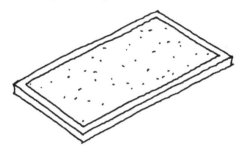

**5**   Cover the whole mat with the cement mixture up to the edge
of the frame and remove the excess with a piece of wood.
Then finish the surface.

**6**   Let the panel settle for 8 days and wait 3 weeks before
installation.

To save on wood, make a 3cm x 3cm wood frame and use flattened
cardboard or newspaper as a base.

Note: The slabs for kitchen counters are 5cm thick.

## GYPSUM AND SISAL PANELS

Lightweight and non-supporting gypsum and sisal fiber panels for ceilings can be built during construction.

On a table or work bench place a sheet of glass approximately 50cm x 100cm. Build a frame with 1cm-thick strips of wood held in place with clamps made from reinforcing rods.

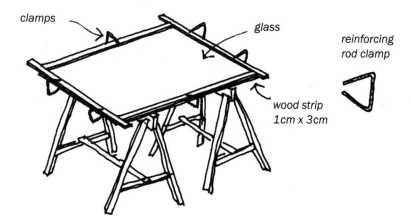

clamps

glass

reinforcing rod clamp

wood strip 1cm x 3cm

**1**    Mix a small quantity of gypsum, just enough to cover the sheet of glass.

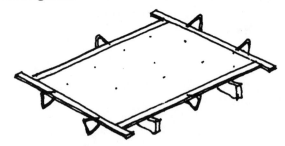

**2**    Fill the frame with the gypsum to the top edge of the wood strips.

**3** Cover the surface with a thin layer of sisal fibers.

sisal fibers

**4** Let the panel dry for a few minutes.

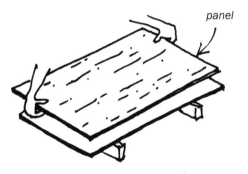

panel

**5** Remove the wood strips and then lift the finished panel.

Placing the panels:

These gypsum panels can be hung from the roof joists. Two people should be on hand to install them. One person holds up the panel while the other dips sisal fibers in the gypsum mixture, places it over the joist and glues each end to the panel (see illustration on the next page). The person below supports the panel for a moment until the attachment is dry.

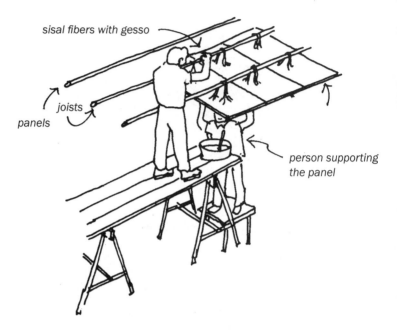

When all the panels are installed, apply gypsum to the joints for a smooth finishing.

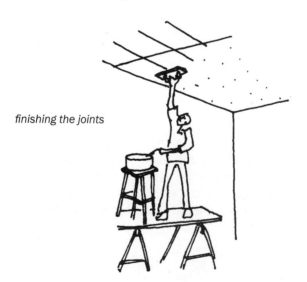

To prevent the panels from cracking at the joint with the wall, leave a 2cm space betwen the wall and panel. This space can be concealed with a strip of wood or a cove molding.

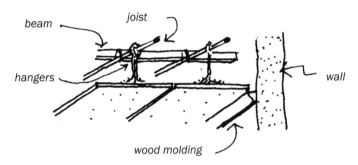

Another technique is used to install the panels below concrete floor slabs. The panels are hung from dowels or stakes inserted in holes in the slab.

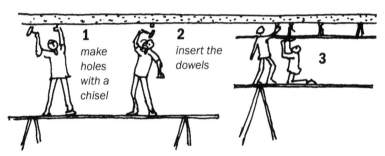

**1** Make holes with a chisel and a hammer.

**2** Solidly install the dowels with the hammer.

**3** Connect the panels to the dowels with sisal fibers soaked in gypsum.

These panels are easy to pierce and to cut when installing electrical wiring. Remember, though, it is always preferable to install wiring before closing off the space with the suspended ceiling.

# FLOORS

## EARTH FLOORS

The floor area between posts must be higher than the outer area. The wall will be protected from rainwater that runs along the flat outer wall of the house.

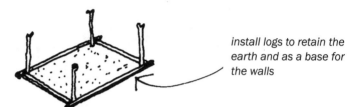

install logs to retain the earth and as a base for the walls

The mixture for the earth floor is earth, gravel and water/asphalt in a 10:2:1 proportion, respectively.

Another way to build a good floor is to use pumice stone sand which provides a thermal insulation base for very cold or very hot regions.

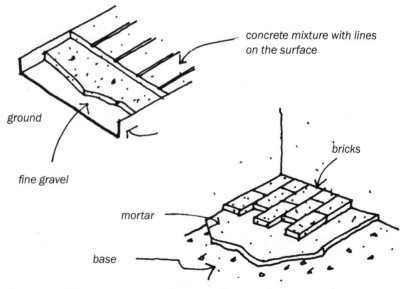

concrete mixture with lines on the surface

ground

fine gravel

bricks

mortar

base

To harden an earth or clay floor, build a fire with branches or straw on its surface.

## VENTILATED FLOORS

To insulate a floor from the cold or heat, make openings in the floors to let air circulate. In very hot zones, the openings or channels allow the cool breezes to circulate. In cold zones or during cold seasons, these openings can be closed off at the base of the walls.

The channels run from one side of the house to the other. At the place where they meet, build a collector channel in the opposite direction. This type of ventilated floor has a thin layer of concrete, and a ceramic or wood floor.

The channels can be built with various materials:

Connected hollow blocks or bricks:

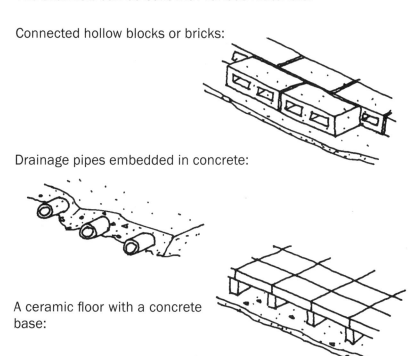

Drainage pipes embedded in concrete:

A ceramic floor with a concrete base:

Note: Plant certain types of vegetation, such as lemongrass, around the exterior walls to deter insects from entering the channels.

## ROOF SLAB

On the beams, install channel-shaped roof tiles so that the large end of one meets the large end of the other tile, and in the next row the inverse occurs.

Install chicken wire mesh on top of the tiles and cover the whole area with a 3cm layer of concrete. Lift the wire mesh slightly to make sure the concrete settles and adheres to the assembly.

*view from above*

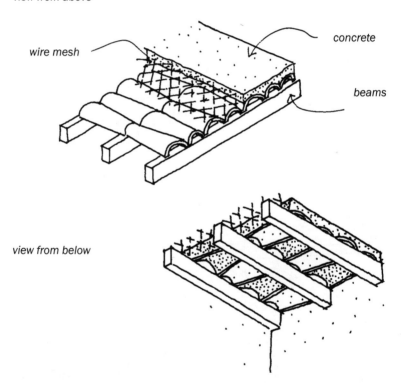

*view from below*

To decorate the ceiling which is seen from below, paint alternating tiles with lime.

The house decoration should not be limited to the walls or floors. The ceiling is also an area to be admired.

## BRICK AND BAMBOO SLAB

In the chapter on materials there are instructions on preparing bamboo for construction. The drawing below shows how to build a strong and low-cost floor.

1    Install bamboo parallel to one of the walls.

2    Install bricks as shown
     on the right.

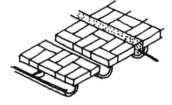

3    Place reinforcing rods in
     the bamboo channels.

4    Fill the channels with concrete.

5    Finish the surface with a layer of cement.

→    Before combining concrete and bamboo
     to build slabs, it is recommended to
     build 1m x 2m test plates. Not all types
     of bamboo are suited for construction,
     and some must be treated beforehand
     to be strengthened. See chapter 10 for
     more details.

## CONCRETE AND BAMBOO SLAB

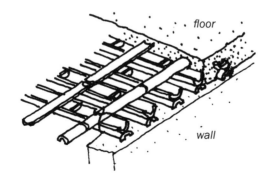

floor

wall

Leave a 5cm space between the pieces of bamboo.

## CASCAJE SLABS

*Cascajes* are lightweight concrete, prefabricated slabs used to make floors and roofs. The idea was invented at TIBÁ and proved to be substantially more economical than typical concrete floor slabs, which use more cement and steel reinforcement. It offers a pleasant visual aspect, has durability and space for ducts and wiring.

Install the con-shells and support them with an intermediary post and beam during the construction. Then fill the valleys using bamboo to save on reinforcing rods.

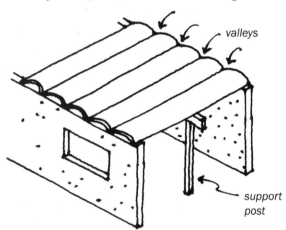

valleys

support post

1    Apply 3cm of cement mix and a ¼-gauge reinforcing rod to the bottom of the valley. The cement mix is 1:2 cement and sand.

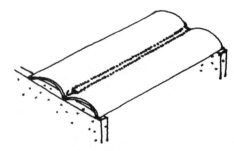

2    Install a few sticks of bamboo.

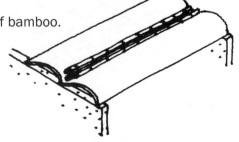

**3**    Now fill the valley with a cement mixture of 1:6 cement and sand/clay.

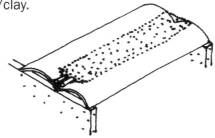

**4**    When all the valleys are filled, cover the whole with a 2cm cement mixture of 1:4 and then apply a cement finishing.

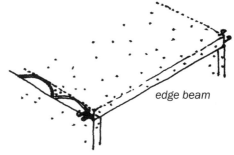

edge beam

Build a concrete beam with two reinforcing rods on the exterior edges to prevent the floor from breaking (conshells lose their strength with lateral forces). Then build a low wall above the beam (1). Now fill the open curved space at the end of the conshell (2).

## BAMCRETE BEAMS

Bamboo can be used instead of steel reinforcing rods to make concrete beams.

**1**     Build a formwork with boards.

**2**     Install nails near the knots in the bamboo pole and wrap it with barbed wire.

**3**     Fill the bottom of the formwork with a 2 cm layer of cement mixture (cement, sand and gravel), install bamboo and fill the form. If the beam is large, use more bamboo.

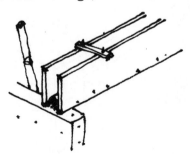

**4**    Compact the cement and make sure the bamboo remains in the center of the beam.

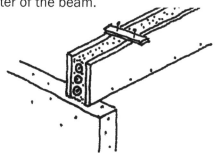

**5**    Remove the formwork side boards in 2 days. The bottom board should remain for 2 weeks.

The drawing below shows a house that is built with several ecotechniques, such as conshells and green roofs:

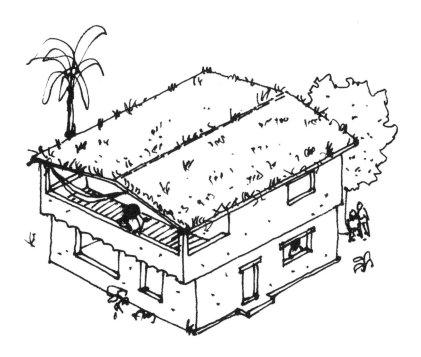

# ROOFS

Below is a description of how to build a basic roof with wood posts and beams. The wood dimensions depend on the type of lumber and the size of the house.

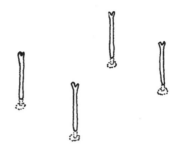

**1**     Install the posts on flat rocks embedded in the ground.

**2**     Connect the main beams solidly to the posts to make sure they resist earthquakes and strong winds.

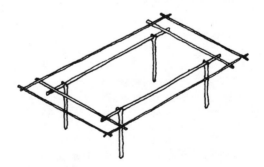

**3**     Install the secondary beams that will support the eaves.

**4**    Install the main roof structure.

**5**    For a stronger structure, install diagonal and center bracing to the sloped members.

**6**    Install the rafters which create the eaves. On the rafters install purlins to which the roof finishing will be fastened.

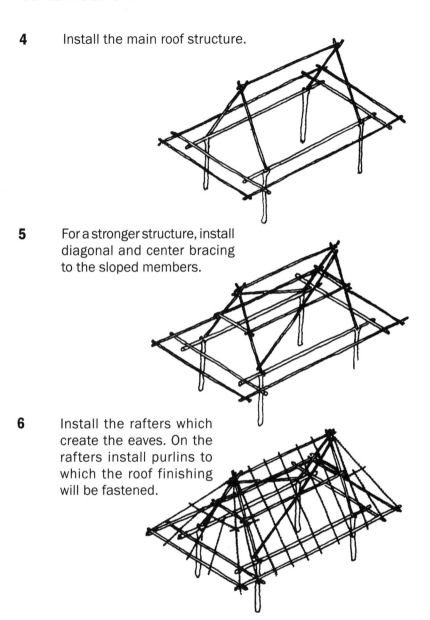

Woven mat walls can be made independently from the structure.

Shown below are other types of roofs. The structure is similar but the spaces below are different. The posts that structure the walls are the same as those that support the roof.

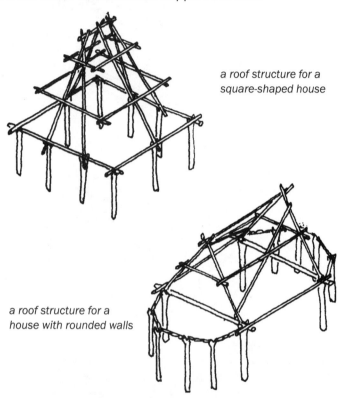

*a roof structure for a square-shaped house*

*a roof structure for a house with rounded walls*

## ASSEMBLING THE BEAMS

When working with wood logs and forked trees are not available, connect posts, beams and rafters by cutting notches into the joint areas and shaping them into interlocking pieces.

*post*

*rafters*

Assemble all members in the following way:

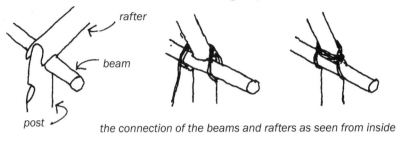

*the connection of the beams and rafters as seen from inside*

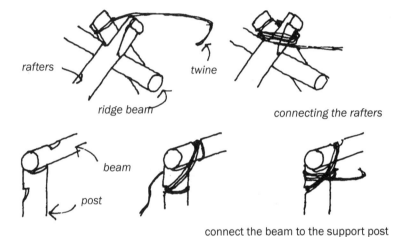

*connecting the rafters*

*connect the beam to the support post*

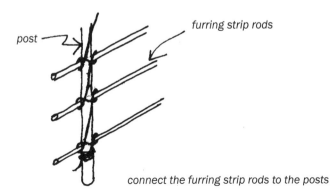

*connect the furring strip rods to the posts*

## THATCHED ROOFS WITH REEDS

To make a thatched roof with long bundles of reeds use wire, string, and reeds with stems 1 meter to 2 meters long.

Let the reeds dry, but not too much, to prevent them from breaking.

 Below are details of this type of roof construction:

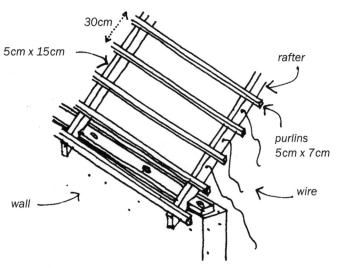

Start by sewing a bundle of reeds to the first rafter and make a row. Sew on the next layer of reeds with a fine string which also goes through the previous bundle. Each layer covers ⅔ of the previous one and is tied down at three points. The stiches should be on an angle so that there are not any spaces between the bundles. A wooden needle with the following dimensions is used:

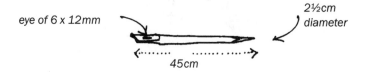

The diameter of a bundle of reeds is 15cm.

The first row and layer:

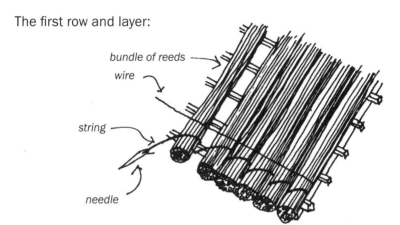

bundle of reeds
wire
string
needle

The lower part of the next layer covers the wire and the string of the previous layer.

The second layer:

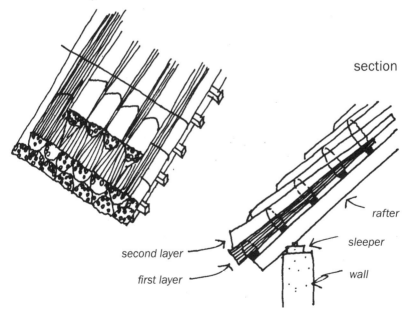

section

rafter
sleeper
wall
second layer
first layer

## REED AND MUD ROOF PANELS

**1**      First build a work table.

**2**      Place the reeds on the table with the thinner ends all to one side and allow them to extend beyond the mold. Complete the mold at the thin end with a stick installed as shown below.

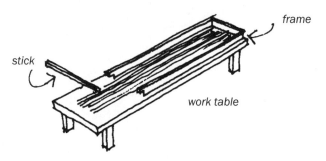

**3**      Then fill the mold with mud and bend the thin end of the reeds over the stick towards the inside, pressing it into the layer of mud.

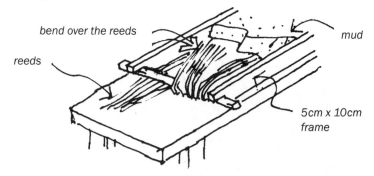

**4**      Remove the panel and place it on a flat surface to dry. Pull the stick out carefully to maintain the molded tunnel.

Bind the panels to the roof's purlins with wire. The wire passes through the molded tunnel.

This type of roof must be sloped more than 45 degrees for the rain to properly run off its surface.

## SHINGLE ROOFS

A shingle roof must have a slope greater than 15 degrees to prevent winds from lifting up the shingles. Each shingle should have two nails in the center and be installed starting from the eaves to the ridge. Each shingle is nailed in two areas and is supported by three purlins.

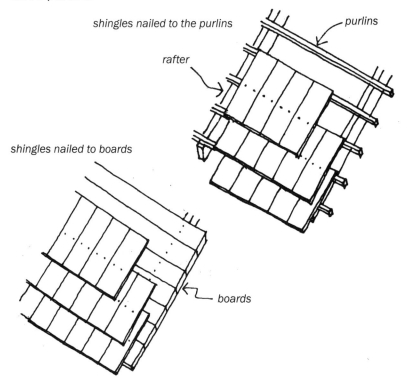

shingles nailed to the purlins

purlins

rafter

shingles nailed to boards

boards

Another way to support shingles is with a board sheathing made with a durable type of wood. With this method, the shingles must be absolutely dry.

Installing a board sheathing is a good way to make a base for shingles, but in regions where there is no equipment to cut boards, the shingles can be nailed directly to the roof structure.

The size of the shingles depends on the quality of the wood and the local climate.

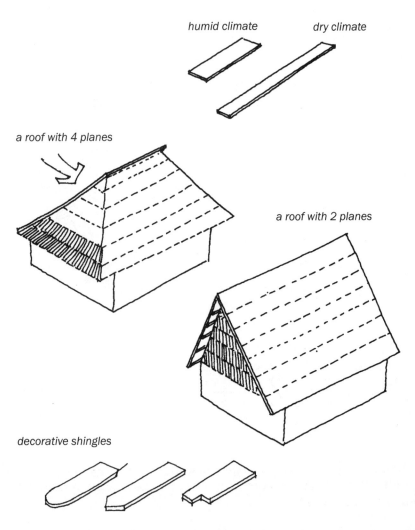

humid climate    dry climate

a roof with 4 planes

a roof with 2 planes

decorative shingles

Usually roof shingles are larger and thicker than the shingles used for walls.

The detail below shows a way to place shingles to prevent rain and wind from entering.

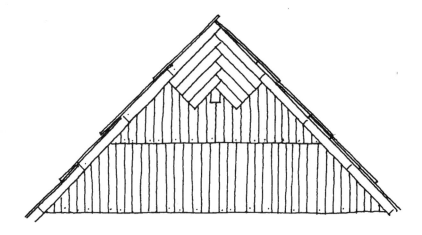

In regions with heavy rains and strong winds, it is important to orient the roof in relation to the prevailing winds.

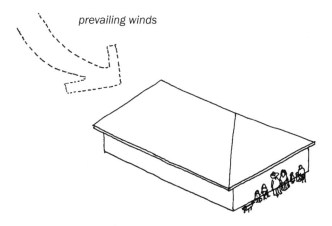

prevailing winds

The wind hits the smaller part of the roof...

## FLAT ROOFS WITH CORRUGATED SHEATHING

Shown here are details for flat roofs made with corrugated metal sheathing. The flat roof must have a slight slope so that rainwater does not accumulate.

Since corrugated sheathing does not insulate from the heat and the cold, other ways must be found to protect the house:

**A**   Build a a second roof or suspended ceiling below the roofing to allow air to circulate between the two layers. In hot regions the moving air cools the roofing. In cold regions use insulating materials to prevent the heat from escaping from the rooms.

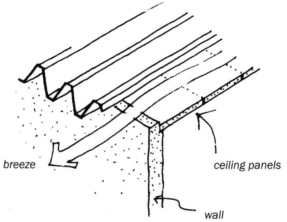

breeze                                                    ceiling panels

wall

**B**   Use insulating materials on top of the roofing. First orient the corrugated roofing so that the grooves are in the opposite direction to the prevailing winds. Fill the grooves with palm leaves, reeds or grass.

In regions with strong winds, the insulating materials must be tied to the roof with wire.

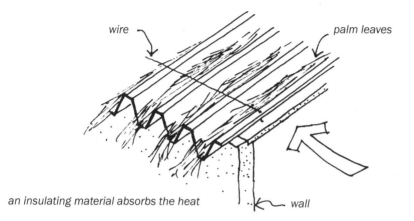

wire

palm leaves

an insulating material absorbs the heat

wall

In regions with heavy rains where buildings have large eaves to protect the walls, extend the beams to support the roofing. Without this additional support, the ends may break off.

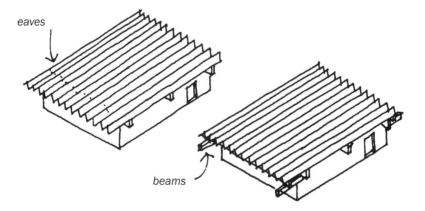

eaves

beams

Warning: The roof structure, joists and purlins must be straight and well levelled to prevent problems when installing tiles or any other roofing material.

## THATCH OR LEAF-COVERED ROOFS

To cover a roof with thatch, first make bundles of thatch that are tied at one end.

Then bind the bundles to the purlins of the roof structure.

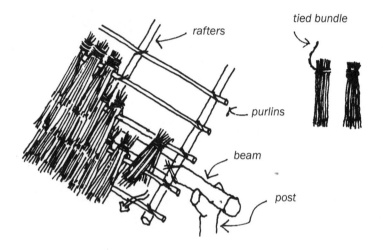

Another method is to fold one end of the bundle over the purlin and tie the bundle together.

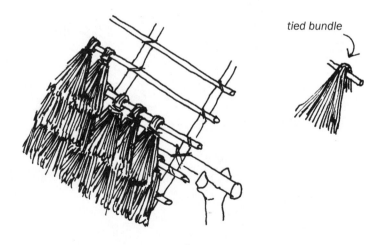

Palm leaves such as the fan palm can be used in many ways. The strips of leaves can either be woven or tied together.

*the stem is used to weave*

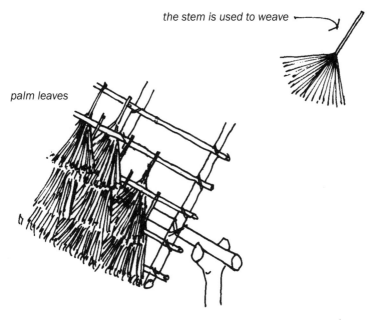

*palm leaves*

*the stem is cut and...*

*the palm is tied to the purlins with a strip of leaf*

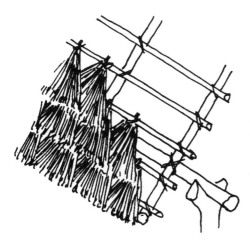

The palm leaves are folded or cut lengthwise. They are then tied directly to the rafters, which can be a smaller size but spaced closer together.

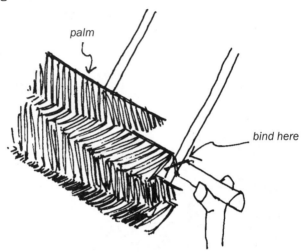

Tie bundles of straw or reeds to purlins with a wooden needle.

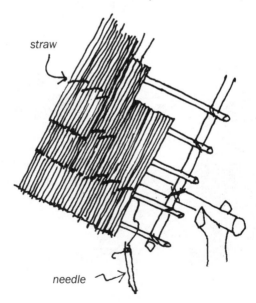

Agave leaves can also be used as roofing.

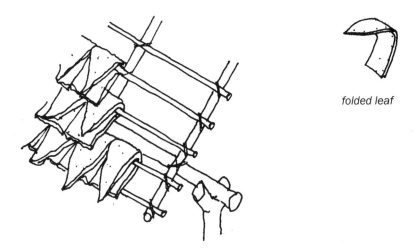

*folded leaf*

... or part of the stem of imperial palms can be used as tiles.

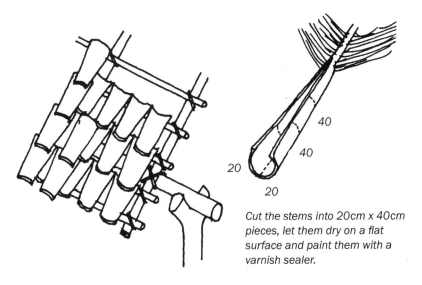

40

40

20

20

*Cut the stems into 20cm x 40cm
pieces, let them dry on a flat
surface and paint them with a
varnish sealer.*

See chapter 2 for other types of roofs for humid tropical regions.

## CLAY TILE ROOFS

Clay tile roofs must have a slope between 30 and 45 degrees.

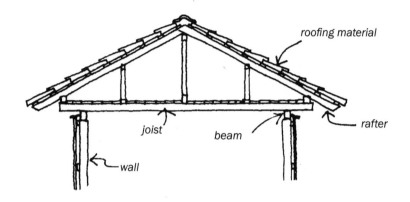

A roof without a ceiling:

Here the sloped rafters are nailed to the wall sleeper.

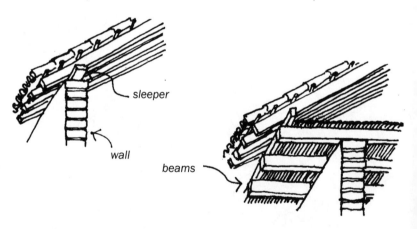

A roof with a ceiling or an attic space:

This solution is preferable if there is enough wood available for beams. It provides better protection from temperature changes, and the wider eaves protect the walls from rainwater and sun. The extended beams support the ends of the rafters.

There are three ways to install clay tiles on rafters.

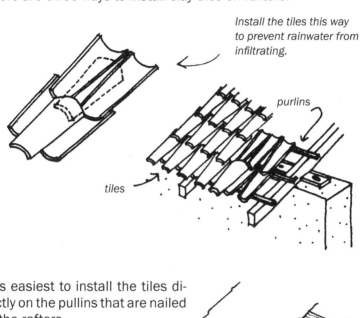

*Install the tiles this way to prevent rainwater from infiltrating.*

*purlins*

*tiles*

It is easiest to install the tiles directly on the pullins that are nailed to the rafters.

To reduce the circulation of hot or cold air through the tiles, install them on a sheathing of small bamboo installed on the rafters.

In regions where there is wood available, the sheathing can be made of boards on top of which the tiles are laid.

## ROOF GUTTERS

To collect rainwater, install roof gutters to the ends of the roof rafters.

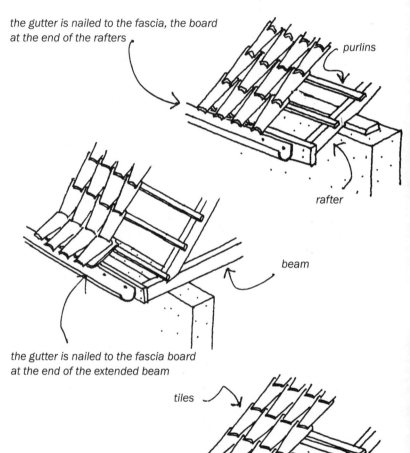

*the gutter is nailed to the fascia, the board at the end of the rafters*

*purlins*

*rafter*

*beam*

*the gutter is nailed to the fascia board at the end of the extended beam*

*tiles*

*a gutter made with three boards*

A gutter can also be installed at the junction of the roof and wall:

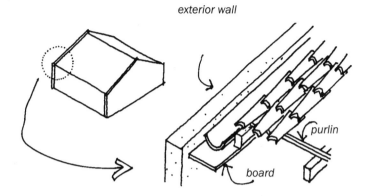

*exterior wall*

*purlin*

*board*

Half of a 10 cm drainage pipe can also be used as a gutter.

## CONCRETE TILE ROOFS

Many types of roofs can be built with long concrete tiles:

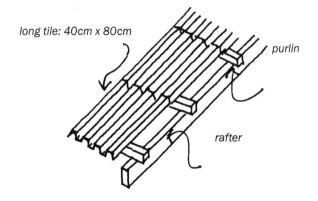

*long tile: 40cm x 80cm*

*purlin*

*rafter*

The same tiles can be used to make a concrete slab or a flat roof:

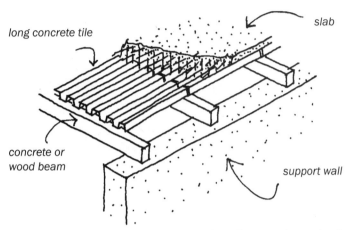

long concrete tile

slab

concrete or
wood beam

support wall

Place a chicken wire mesh over the tiles and apply 4 cm of concrete.

Lift the tile slightly to allow the concrete to settle. To build a stronger floor, install continuous reinforcing rods in the grooves of the tiles.

## GREEN ROOFS

A beautiful roof can be made with natural materials such as bamboo, earth and grasses. This type of roof has a high thermal value and therefore is a good insulation. It is inexpensive and can be built in a day.

cold

heat

**1** Build the wood and bamboo structure with a slope of a least 1:10.

For greater slopes, it is preferable to use bamboo rods of different diameters which make an undulated base and help prevent the earth from sliding.

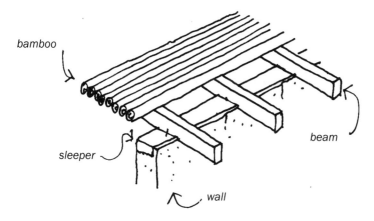

**2** Nail an upright fascia board at the end of the rafters, and install a sheet of plastic to prevent water from infiltrating.

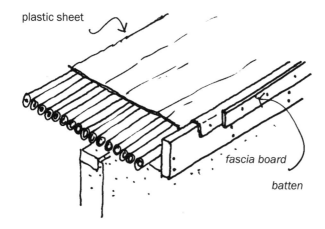

Fold the end of the plastic sheet over the fascia board and secure it with a batten nailed to the board.

**3**    Along the lowest end of the roof place a tube perforated every 20 cm that drains the rainwater. Cover the tube with gravel so the holes do not get clogged.

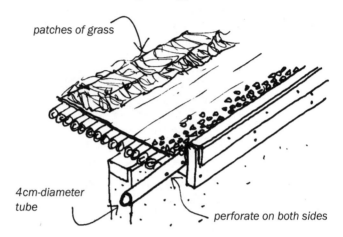

patches of grass

4 cm-diameter tube

perforate on both sides

**4**    Cover the plastic with pieces of grass.

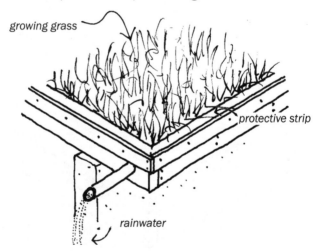

growing grass

protective strip

rainwater

To protect the piece of the plastic from exposure to sun, cover it with a strip of wood on the horizontal surface.

During dry months, irrigate the roof with a perforated hose installed on the highest part of the roof.

A green roof can have many shapes, and it is very flexible:

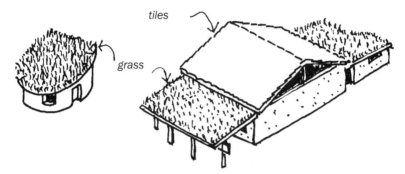

It can be combined with other types of roofs.

➡ Choose the most appropriate local grasses available in the region. Test some varieties. Since there is not much earth, be careful that the roots do not dry out.

➡ Tree and bush seeds can fall onto the grass roof. It is recommended that their seedlings be removed.

Plant flowers or differently colored grasses to enliven the roof even more:

...or fragrant and medicinal herbs to cook with and keep us healthy.

A green roof is the ideal solution for roofing a building in a tropical climate. In dry seasons, it is necessary to irrigate the roof.

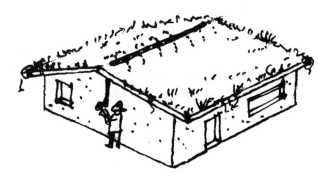

In dry regions, install a perforated tube on the ridge and a valve on the wall below.

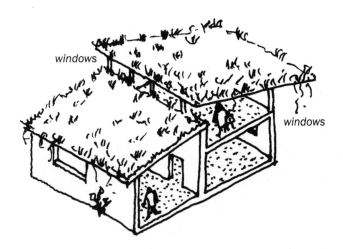

*a house with windows on the 2nd floor*

A good-quality plastic sheet must always be installed. The sheets that are commonly used in the construction of dams or pools are recommended.

Green roofs also provide a shelter for birds.

Usually green roofs are slightly sloped. If the slope is steep, such as up to 45 degrees, certain details need to be considered to prevent sliding.

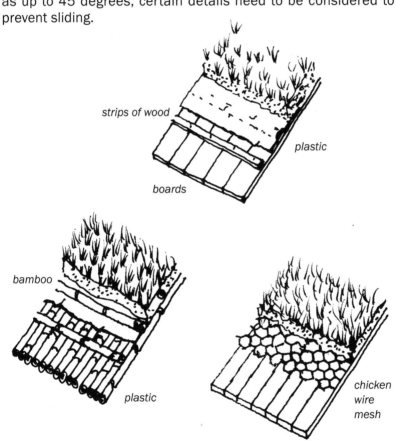

strips of wood

plastic

boards

bamboo

plastic

chicken
wire
mesh

## TRUSSES

Trusses must be built when only pieces of wood are available for roof structure. Recycled wood, such as railroad ties, can be used to build trusses.

Here are a few ways to cut railroad ties which are usually 20cm x 20cm into lumber:

*8 pieces 5cm x 10cm*

*4 pieces 5cm x 20cm*

*4 pieces 5cm x 15cm*
*2 pieces 5cm x 10cm*

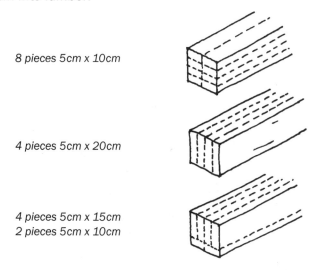

Use rectangular pieces placed upright. A square piece is equivalent to two rectagular pieces, so it is a waste to make square pieces. It is better to span the spaces with lighter pieces of the same height.

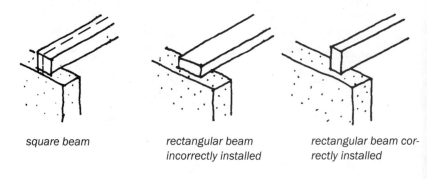

*square beam*        *rectangular beam incorrectly installed*        *rectangular beam correctly installed*

The truss lumber is joined with nuts and bolts.

*bolts*

*nuts*

Shown below are a few examples for assembling lumber into truss-es that can span 6 to 20 meters. Trusses are convenient when one has different-sized lumber and nothing long enough to span the whole space.

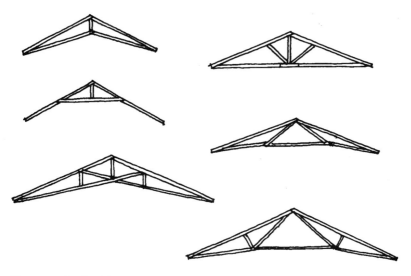

They are built this way:

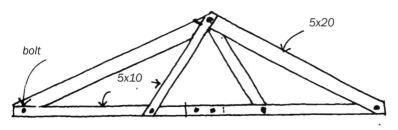

A truss that is 5cm x 20cm along the top diagonal and 5cm x 10cm below can span larger distances.

## WOOD AND WIRE BEAM

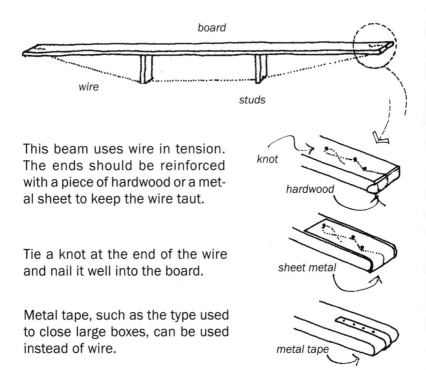

This beam uses wire in tension. The ends should be reinforced with a piece of hardwood or a metal sheet to keep the wire taut.

Tie a knot at the end of the wire and nail it well into the board.

Metal tape, such as the type used to close large boxes, can be used instead of wire.

Below the studs, hold down the wire with the same type of metal reinforcing.

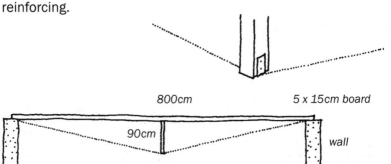

To build a roof over an 8-meter span with 5cm x 15cm wood, the wood stud must be at least 90cm long.

The longer the stud, the less tension in the wire.

Here are two examples for a 3-meter span. With a 15cm stud, the beam supports a 50-kilo load. The same beam with a 60cm stud supports a 200-kilo load.

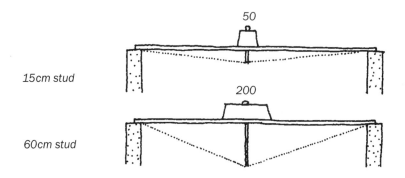

15cm stud

60cm stud

To assemble the beam, first nail the wire to both ends. Then calculate the length of the stud. Since the studs are in compression, it is preferable for them to be square, such as 5cm x 5cm.

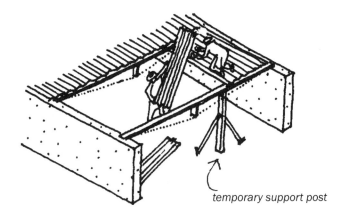

*temporary support post*

During the construction the weight of the workers on the structure makes the load heavier than it is designed to be. Therefore, work posts should be installed temporarily during construction.

478

When wood of an adequate size to span spaces between walls of a house is not available, and there are insufficient tools or connectors, such as bolts, build with columns or pillars.

Install the columns or pillars away from the center of the room to provide as much free space as possible.

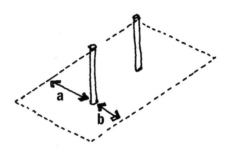

The dimension (a) is larger than (b).

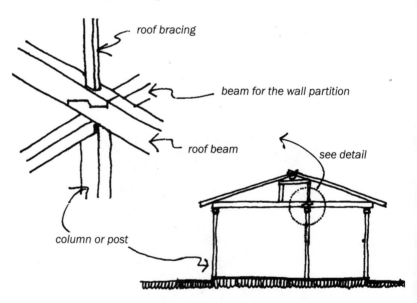

First install the beam for the shorter span, then the longer one. Next install the small posts supporting the roof.

Illustrated below are several types of wooden joint details:

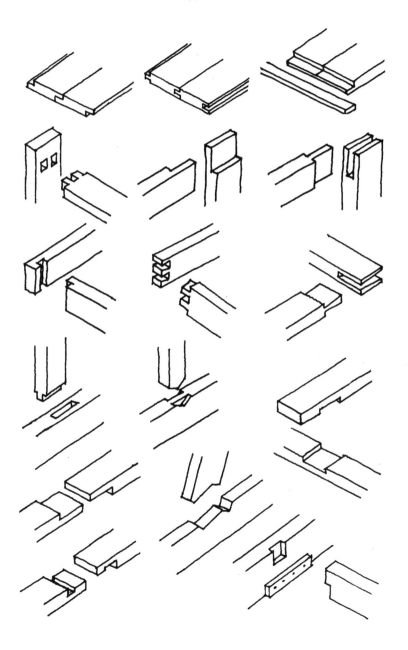

In previous chapters there are descriptions of how to design and build houses for different climatic conditions.

The climate must also be taken into account when deciding on the type of doors or windows for a project.

In this book, three climatic conditions are considered:

 humid tropical climate: hot and rainy regions

 dry tropical climate: hot and arid regions

 temperate climate: mountain regions

See chapter 1 for more details on the differences between these climates.

## A    HUMID TROPICAL CLIMATE

The inhabitants of the humid tropical regions are comfortable when there are breezes passing through their rooms and the rooms are well ventilated. Making openings in wood or bamboo walls is one way to circulate air.

However, in the colder season of this climate the occupants prefer to close their house to the exterior, and in very populated areas it is, of course, usually important to lock up the house completely before leaving.

There are regions where the cool breeze comes from a certain direction during the hot season and the humid and cold winds come from another direction during the cold season.

In these regions, two walls can be built: one half-open that allows the cool air to circulate, and another closed that prevents the cold air from entering.

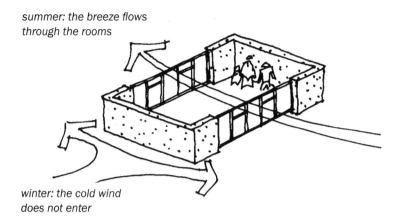

*summer: the breeze flows through the rooms*

*winter: the cold wind does not enter*

The same considerations must be made for the placement of the windows: they must be on the side of the summer breezes and not on the side of the winter winds. At the very least, the windows on the side of the cold winds should be smaller.

The height and positioning of the windows can make a significant difference for regions where there is a temperature change between the night and day.

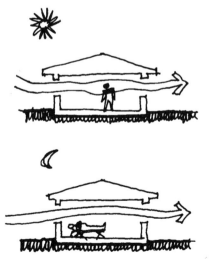

*during the day the breezes are felt by the occupants*

*at night the air flows over the sleeping occupants*

To allow air to flow through the house even when the windows and doors are closed, use slatted shutters or venetian windows.

Illustrated below are a few examples of venetian-type openings:

Doors:

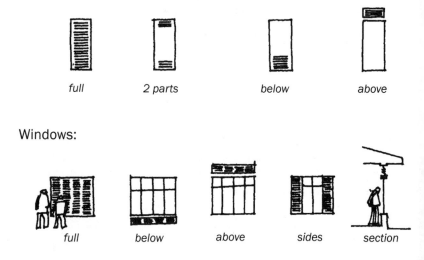

full          2 parts          below          above

Windows:

full          below          above          sides          section

Cross-ventilation is a term used to describe a breeze that enters from one side of a room and exits through the other side. This type of ventilation is possible with venetian-style openings.

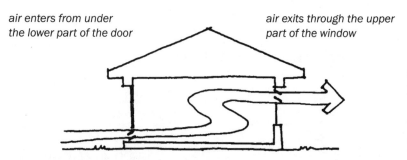

air enters from under                          air exits through the upper
the lower part of the door                     part of the window

Shown above is an example of cross-ventilation with venetians.

## B DRY TROPICAL CLIMATE

A dry tropical climate has other types of conditions. Since there is scarce vegetation and few cloudy days, the sun is constantly reflecting off flat surfaces and the ground, and into the buildings.

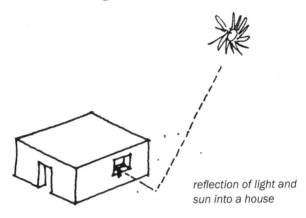

*reflection of light and sun into a house*

The dryness of these regions also produces dusty winds. It is therefore preferable to have smaller windows on the outside. Large windows should be placed in walls of courtyards where there is less dust.

As the walls in these regions are usually thicker, a fixed glass window can be receded so that the sun's rays do not heat up the glass.

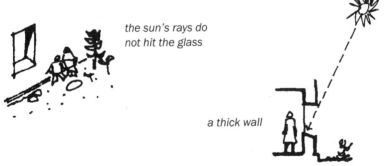

*the sun's rays do not hit the glass*

*a thick wall*

Go to chapter 3 to find out how to cool rooms by building openings below and above windows.

## C   TEMPERATE CLIMATE

In colder regions, most of the heat from inside the house escapes through the doors and windows. Windows on the south side, the cold side of the house, should not be large. However the windows on the north side can be larger to let the sun enter and warm the house. This applies to the Southern Hemisphere; do the opposite in the Northern Hemisphere.

Also it is important that the frames be well built and installed. There must not be gaps between the frame and the wall so that heat does not escape and cold does not enter through these areas. On the following pages, there are details on how to install frames properly.

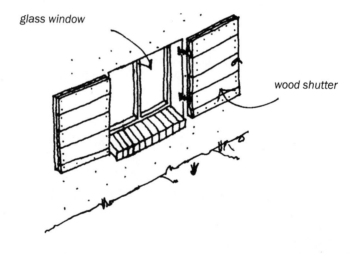

All windows must close well. To reduce the loss of heat during the night, install wood shutters outside the glass windows.

## POSITIONING DOORS

In traditional houses where there is one room with one or two doors and few windows, if any, the doors should be located in the center of the wall.

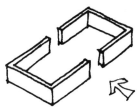

In houses with many separate spaces where there is more furniture, the doors should be located at one end of the wall.

This provides more space for furniture and circulation.

Here is an example of a room:

*a central door leaves little space to position furniture*

*with the door in the corner there is more space*

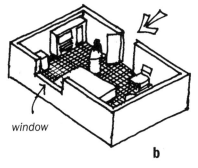

*window*

**b**

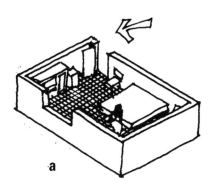

**a**

It is easier to place the wardrobe and bed in example (a) than in (b).

Don't forget that the doors always open towards the inside of a room or house and never towards the outside!

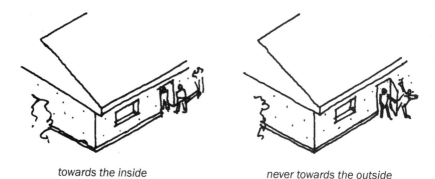

*towards the inside*                    *never towards the outside*

## AWNING WINDOWS

Awning windows have the advantage of being left open when it rains, or it is overcast and there is little light entering the rooms. They can simply be opened up further.

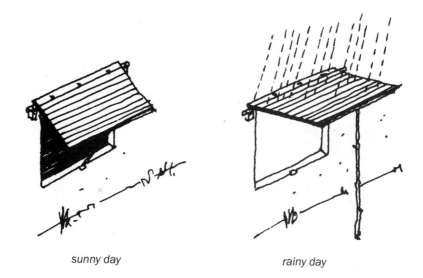

*sunny day*                              *rainy day*

## STORE WINDOWS

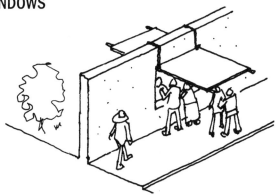

Small stores can be located in the wall of a courtyard or garden by making an opening for a large window and using two suspended poles and an awning or woven mat.

On the interior side, set up the store with a table.

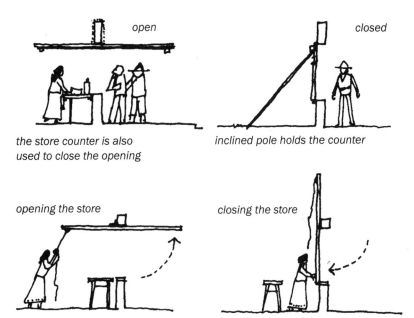

*open* *closed*

*the store counter is also used to close the opening*

*inclined pole holds the counter*

*opening the store* *closing the store*

Another way is to make a small wooden awning on hinges which also is used to close the opening.

In hot and rainy climates, the humid part of the kitchen can be located outside the house and the awning window is opened under the eaves.

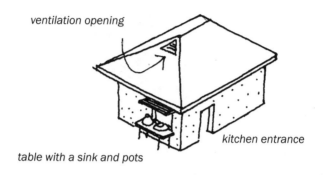

ventilation opening

kitchen entrance

table with a sink and pots

hook to hold up the awning

The outdoor floor is sloped so that water drains away from the house.

## WINDOW FRAMES

When the walls are built before the windows are placed in, leave a space around the openings to properly install the windows. If possible, install the framing while building the walls to avoid gaps between the wall and the frame through which air can flow.

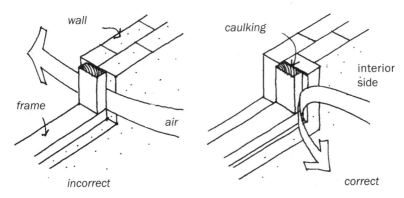

*incorrect*         *correct*

Apply caulking between the wall and frame to seal the joints.

In cold regions the wind blows through gaps cooling the interior of the house.

Adobe bricks, without a finishing layer, should have protected corners so they don't get damaged and break.

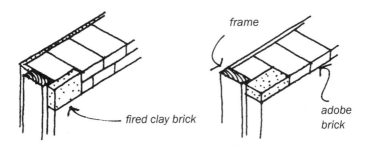

Shown above are ways to protect the corners with fired clay bricks.

It is simpler to protect the corners of openings with rounded adobe.

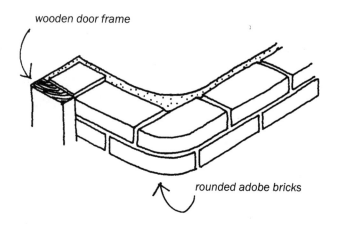

*wooden door frame*

*rounded adobe bricks*

The door can be receded to create a welcoming entrance where visitors are well protected from the rain.

The windows also have rounded corners.

*...a doorway for lovers*

## WINDOWSILLS

Sills should be located in the lower part of the window to protect the wall from rainwater.

Windowsills can be made with stone, concrete, bricks or wood. The upper surface of the sill should be slightly sloped towards the outside to drain rainwater.

A little channel or groove on the bottom surface of the sill collects rainwater and directs it away from the wall to protect it from water and dirt.

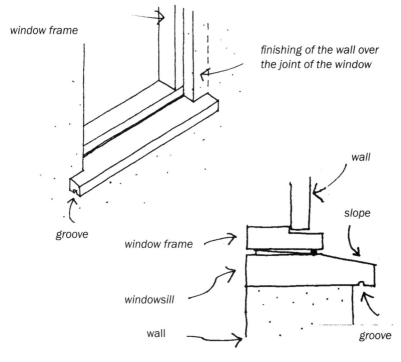

*window frame*

*finishing of the wall over the joint of the window*

*wall*

*slope*

*groove*

*window frame*

*windowsill*

*wall*

*groove*

*section of the lower part of a window*

The windowsill must be a little larger on the outside of the opening. It is embedded in the bricks of the wall so that it does not become loose or damaged.

## CONSTRUCTION DETAILS

Simple panels can be made with wooden boards. The frame can be installed in the wall during construction or fastened to the wall later with small wooden blocks.

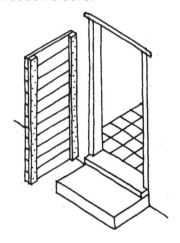

## HINGES

The windows can open the following ways:

➡ nails or bolts

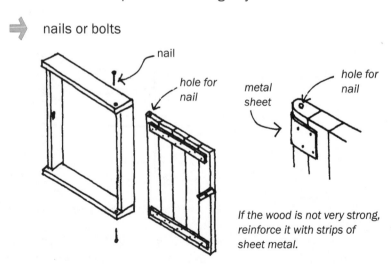

*If the wood is not very strong, reinforce it with strips of sheet metal.*

This window opens outwards.

leather

Hinges can be made out of leather:

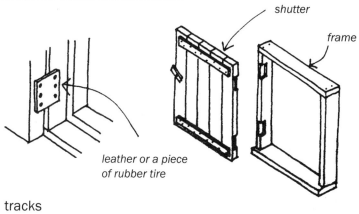

leather or a piece
of rubber tire

tracks

In dry regions where the windows are protected by roof eaves, the windows can be built to slide on tracks.

A groove is made in the upper and lower part of the window or the shutter so that it runs along a strip of wood.

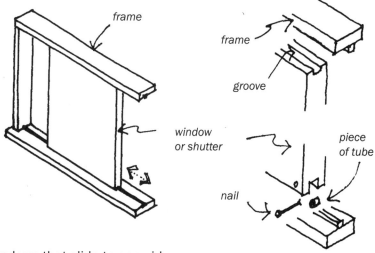

Windows that slide to one side.

Another way to build sliding windows is to nail strips of wood to the frame and round off edges of the window, as shown below.

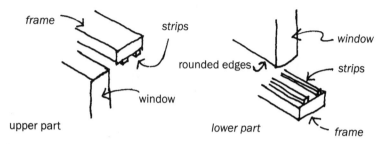

Note: upper part — frame, strips, window; lower part — window, strips, rounded edges, frame

## HEAVY DOORS

Heavy doors for walls or gates often become warped in time. To prevent them from changing shape, build these doors with bracing. The bracing is a board installed diagonally from one corner to the other. Instead of hinges, use a strip of wood nailed to the door. At the bottom of the door, this strip rotates on a stone, and at the top it turns in a loop of wire.

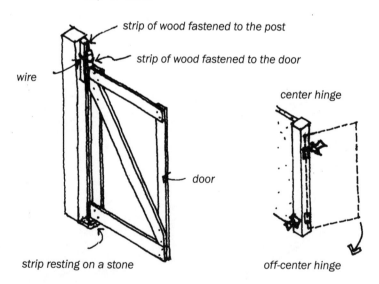

strip of wood fastened to the post

strip of wood fastened to the door

wire

door

strip resting on a stone

center hinge

off-center hinge

Note: Install the top hinge out of line with the bottom hinge, so that the door closes with its own weight.

## WINDOWS AND DOOR PANELS

Windows and doors can be solid or have trellised panels, venetian louvres or sheets of glass.

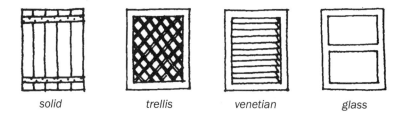

solid          trellis          venetian          glass

The tools for making frames must be adequate so that the windows and doors are well crafted.

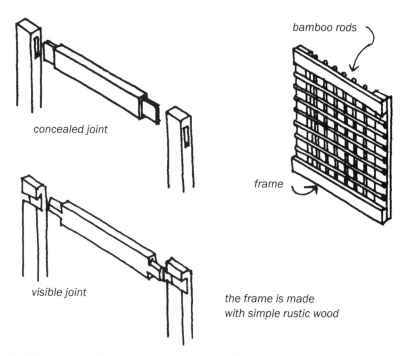

bamboo rods

concealed joint

visible joint

frame

the frame is made
with simple rustic wood

The hinges are placed so that they are impossible to remove from outside the house when the windows and doors are closed. The closed windows or doors must cover their hinges completely.

Another type of venetian is made with bamboo split lengthwise. The curved and shiny side should be on the outside to prevent reflections on the inside.

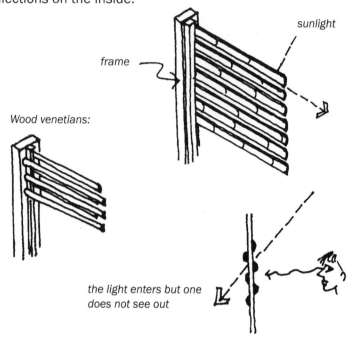

*sunlight*

*frame*

*Wood venetians:*

*the light enters but one does not see out*

The sunlight enters but there is little visibility through the opening.

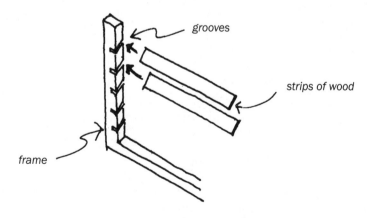

*grooves*

*strips of wood*

*frame*

A frame with venetian slats placed in angled grooves.

In chapter 1 there are more ideas for building door and window openings.

## TUCONS

The size of the concrete tucon lintels is based on the width of the window plus the length of two bricks (one on either side).

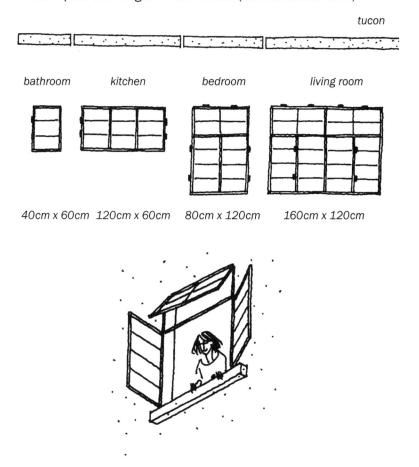

*tucon*

bathroom          kitchen          bedroom          living room

40cm x 60cm   120cm x 60cm   80cm x 120cm      160cm x 120cm

The window dimensions above are for a house built in a temperate climate. These sizes need to be reduced or increased depending on the local climate conditions.

## FRAMES IN BRICK WALLS

It is recommended to install the window and door frames during the construction of the walls, rather than after.

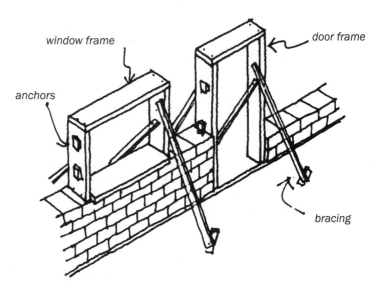

Install the frames in the wall with anchors or nails. If building with adobe bricks, make grooves on the side that is near the frame.

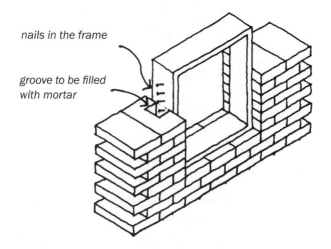

## DOORSILLS

Doorsills are used to prevent rainwater from entering the house through the lower part of the door.

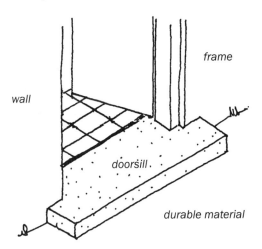

A durable material should be used on the ground area in front of the door. Doorsills can be made with the same materials as windowsills.

## SIMPLE DOOR CLOSURES

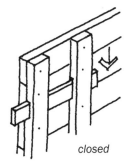

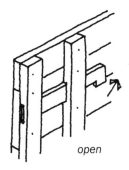

When the lever is pushed down and out, the bar locks the door. When it is lifted and pulled in, the door opens.

To prevent scorpions from entering the house, embed glass bottles in the doorsill. This technique prevents the scorpions from climbing up.

**1**     Excavate the doorsill area.

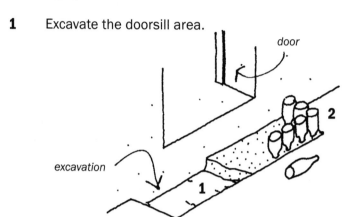

**2**     Fill the hole with concrete and place the bottles with necks down.

**3**     Fill the space between the wall and the bottles with concrete.

**4**     Add mortar and make a brick or tile doorsill.

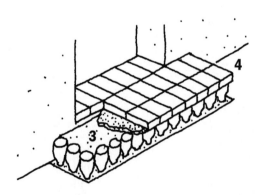

Not only is the house now protected, but the entrance is more attractive and colorful.

## EXTERIOR FLOORS

Courtyard and exterior floors around the house, such as a garden path, can be made with hollow blocks which allow the water to pass through.

Hollow blocks used for walls are equally well suited for floors.

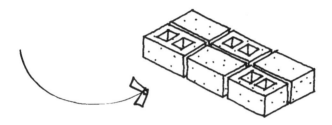

In garages or other areas in which cars circulate, a more durable and strong type of block should be used.

Interlocking blocks, as shown below, do not loosen as quickly with the weight of vehicles

Install the blocks in a layer of sand, leaving a small gap between them. Then add more sand or earth to fill the joints and cavities.

# SERVICES

## ELECTRICITY

For lighting and electricity, a few items are required:

➥ A service panel: The main panel is where all the circuits tie into the incoming electrical supply line and where the electricity for the house is controlled. Usually this panel is located at the entrance of the house near the meter.

➥ Fuses or breakers: They blow apart or break the circuit if an overload or short circuit occurs, preventing occupants from being harmed by shock.

➥ Light socket: The component where lights are screwed in.

➥ Switches: An interrupter switch for each light socket or group of sockets.

➥ Wall outlets: To plug in appliances or lights.

## INSTALLATION

All pieces require two wires, one direct and one with a switch.

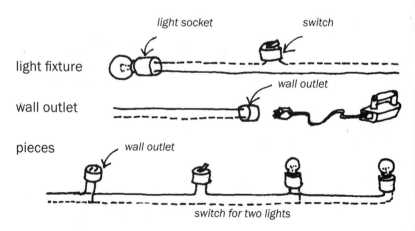

light socket          switch

light fixture

wall outlet

wall outlet

pieces          wall outlet

switch for two lights

Only use wiring that is covered with a protective plastic coating.

Use insulated staples or bent nails to install wires, being careful not to pierce the plastic coating which could damage the wiring. Hammer the nails down with a lightweight hammer.

*bent nails holding down the wiring*

*staple*

Bamboo split lengthwise can also be used to cover and protect wiring installed at the base of the wall.

*electrical wiring*     *bamboo*

The joints of wiring must be well covered with insulating electrical tape. Do not install light fixtures or wire connections near grass ceilings or roofs. Water leaks could wet incorrectly installed wiring and start a fire. In humid regions, it is recommended to install the wiring in tubing or hoses embedded in the walls.

In a building designed with exposed brick walls, you must decide beforehand where the plugs, the fixtures and the switches are located so that the wiring can be installed during the wall construction. When a house has an outer plaster, cement or other finish, the wiring can be embedded in this finishing layer.

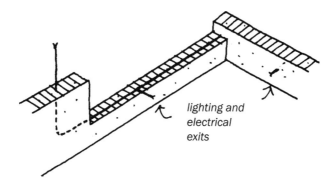

*lighting and electrical exits*

Here is an example of a simple electrical installation:

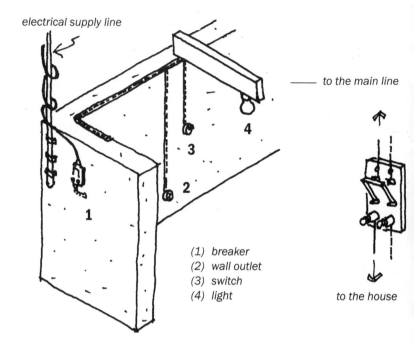

electrical supply line

to the main line

(1)  breaker
(2)  wall outlet
(3)  switch
(4)  light

to the house

The wiring is installed at the tops of the walls out of the reach of children and to prevent humidity from reaching the wires.

It is always preferable to first install the tubes or the hoses on the wall and later insert the wires through them.

Insulation must be installed in walls which have unprotected wiring. The insulation is fastened with wood blocks around the plugs and switches and in places where the wiring changes direction. In the drawing below, note how the plugs are installed higher above the floor in the kitchen and bathroom.

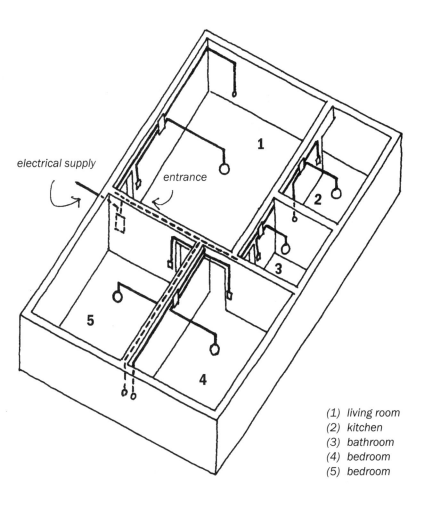

electrical supply

entrance

(1) living room
(2) kitchen
(3) bathroom
(4) bedroom
(5) bedroom

## POSITIONING PLUGS AND LIGHTING FIXTURES

*in a square room*

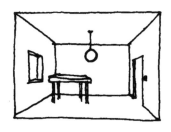

*in a rectangular room*

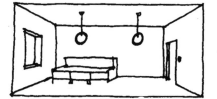

The switches are near the door to the room, so that it is easy to turn the light on or off when entering or leaving the room.

The wall outlets must be 20cm above the finished floor.

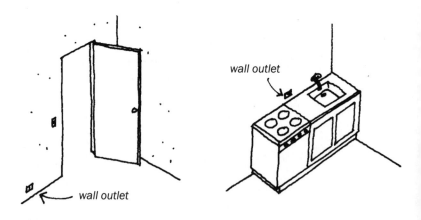

*wall outlet*

*wall outlet*

Wall outlets are placed above built-in elements such as sinks and stoves.

## INSTALLING PLUMBING FOR POTABLE WATER

In a house the plumbing for potable water must reach the bathroom sink and shower, the kitchen sink, and the washbasin in the service area.

Water can be heated in a solar heater. See chapter 7 for how to build one.

It is recommended to install dry toilets to conserve water and not contaminate local waterways and soils. See chapter 9 for more information.

Usually ¾-inch tubes are used for general water distribution and ½-inch tubes at specific points.

As with the electrical wiring, the plumbing is installed inside the walls.

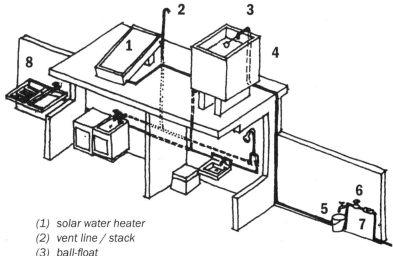

(1) solar water heater
(2) vent line / stack
(3) ball-float
(4) water tank
(5) tap
(6) valve
(7) water meter
(8) basin

In house plans, place the bathroom and kitchen back to back or above and below each other to save on piping. Also consider the future expansion of the house, so that piping will be easy to extend to other bathrooms. All piping should be easily accessible, which means walls and floors should not require excessive demolition to repair the piping.

Water leaving the sink and the basin in drainage pipes must pass through a p-trap to prevent sewer odors from entering the house.

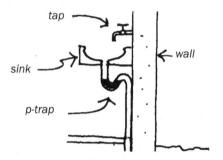

A p-trap is made with a curved tube installed in such a way that there is always a small amount of water in the bend that impedes the upward passage of odors.

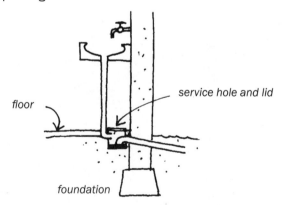

When premade p-traps are not available a trap can be made in the floor with two L-shaped end pipes and an open service hole with a lid. This hole must be accessed to be cleaned and to remove dropped items.

# SPECIAL ITEMS

## OVENS

An oven is great for making bread and cakes. One can be built with an arched bamboo structure. The outer layers can be made with plaster and a final finish with a mixture of mud and cut grass or straw.

After applying the plaster, warm up the oven for the first time. Ignite the wood to burn the bamboo which was part of the structure.

The fired mud becomes a solid structure.

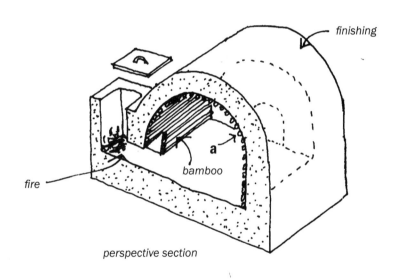

*finishing*

*fire*

*bamboo*

*a*

*perspective section*

On one side of the oven install a small door (a) for placing food.

## STAIRS

To make a comfortable stair, the width of the stair tread should be 25cm and the height of the riser 17cm.

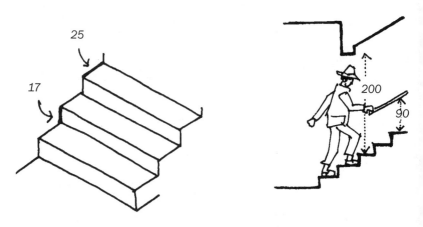

The distance between the stair and the ceiling or roof should not be less than 200cm.

To build simple wooden stairs, you can use two 5cm x 15 cm lumber supports.

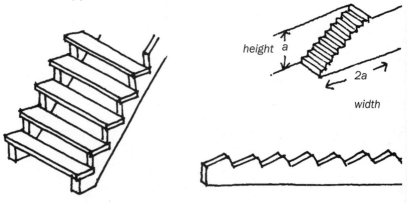

The treads are made out of 3- or 4cm-thick boards.

Stone, brick or concrete stairs can be built in many shapes, depending on their use. For example:

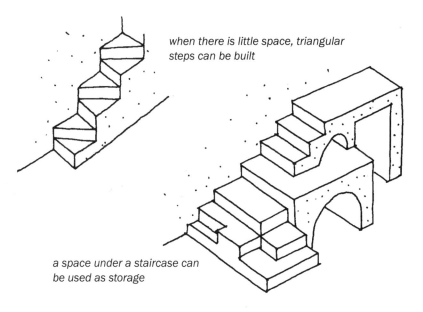

*when there is little space, triangular steps can be built*

*a space under a staircase can be used as storage*

In small spaces, a staircase can have a steep angle.

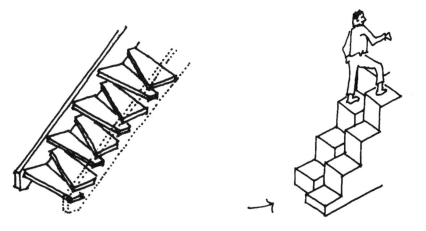

Or when using bricks, it can even have this shape.

When building many houses at once, the staircases can be pre-fabricated with ferroconcrete.

A staircase, that takes up little space, is built with two different formwork modules: one for straight stairs and another for corner stairs.

**1** Cut triangles out of a 90cm x 90cm piece of plywood.

**2** From the same sheet of plywood cut four 18cm-wide pieces for the turning risers.

**3** Cut more 18cm x 90cm pieces for the risers of the straight steps and 25cm x 90cm pieces for the treads.

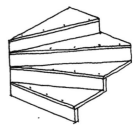

**4** Nail the pieces together as illustrated.

Nail a strip of wood along the joint of the riser and tread to strengthen the formwork.

When ready to apply the cement mixture, place the formwork on the ground as illustrated below.

**5** Prepare the cement mixture of 2:1 sand-cement and apply a first 1cm-thick layer onto the form. Place the plastic mesh (see page 316) and apply the second 1cm-thick layer of the mixture.

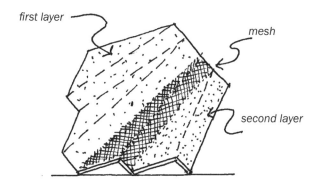

first layer

mesh

second layer

**6** Once the cement is applied, let the stair dry in the sun for three days and then remove the formwork. Let the stair dry two weeks before installing it.

## PROTECTION

Wood is often damaged by insects that breed in humid soil.

To prevent this type of damage, the wood roof and wall structure must not be in contact with the ground.

The parts of the wood that are near the ground must be protected by raising them on concrete bases, or waterproofing them with tar.

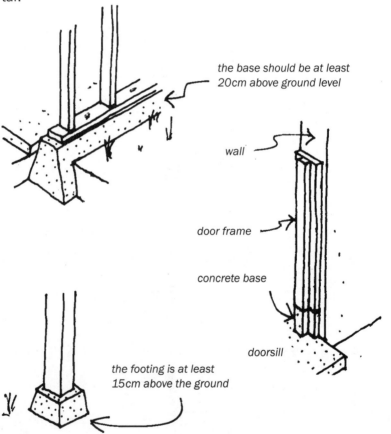

the base should be at least 20cm above ground level

wall

door frame

concrete base

doorsill

the footing is at least 15cm above the ground

The base of the door frames is 15cm above the floor level.

Houses built on pillars or in marsh areas need to be protected.

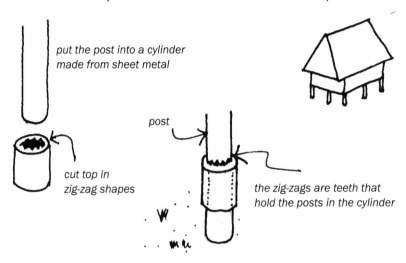

put the post into a cylinder
made from sheet metal

cut top in
zig-zag shapes

post

the zig-zags are teeth that
hold the posts in the cylinder

Termites cannot climb a thin border and will return to the ground.

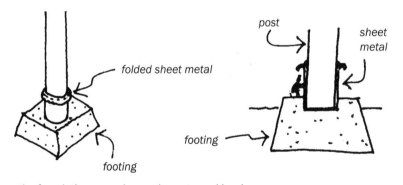

folded sheet metal

footing

footing

post

sheet
metal

footing

the foundations are always above ground level

Before installing the post in a concrete footing, slip on the metal cylinder whose edges are slanted out and downwards.

For more details, see the chapter on humid tropical climates. In these regions, wood is the most available material for construction.

## SILO CONSTRUCTION

Silos, containers for storing corn or wheat, can be built out of mud and grass or straw.

Round silos deter rats or other pests from climbing up them.

The round shape also prevents the silo from being overexposed to sun and rain.

The silo illustrated above has a stone base and a grass roof.

## PREPARATION

Make a mixture for the silo with equals parts sand and clay while adding water until the mixture is malleable. Leave it in the shade for a few days to cure.

Then mix grass or straw into the mixture in the following way:

**1** Place some grass on the ground.

**2** Add two handfuls of the mud mixture.

**3** Knead the mud into the grass.

**4** Roll the mixture.

**5** Make a roll that looks like a fish with two tails.

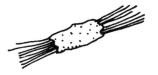

**6** Shape the roll into a curve.

Now leave the rolls to dry out for one day:

**7**    Build a 2-meter-diameter ring by placing the rolls one next to the other. They should be slightly inclined towards the center of the circle.

Join all the rolls with mud, leaving the tails out and alternating from inside to outside.

**8**    Place another ring of rolls on top of the first.

**9**    Place a third ring. All the rolls should be installed with a slight inclination towards the inside of the ring, so that the top diameter will be less than the base. The grass tails remain uncovered.

**10**   Now cross the tails and cover them with mud to unite all three rings. The covering is applied to the inside and outside of the rings until the surface of both sides is smooth.

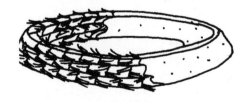

Then cover the upper surface with ashes so that the second series of rings does not stick to the first.

**11** On the next day, install a second large ring composed of the series of the three smaller ones. This large ring should be more inclined towards the inside to make a smaller ring than the one below.

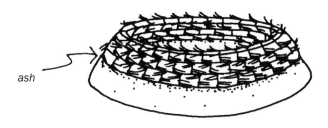

ash

*add ash and let the construction dry out overnight*

**12** Now make an even smaller ring. There should be a total of three large rings separated with layers of ash.

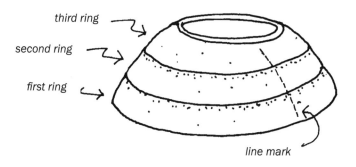

third ring

second ring

first ring

*line mark*

After building the rings, mark them with a line. The line helps reassemble the rings correctly later on.

**13**   Now build another three large rings with the same process.
         The rings are dried out for one week. During this wait, build
         a stone or a rammed earth base to support the silo.

**14**   The roof is built on the top ring. The roof structure is made
         with wooden poles tied together with sisal.

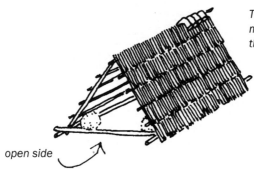

*The closed side of the roof
must be oriented towards
the prevailing winds.*

open side

Use the same bundles of grass to cover the structure. Two sides
remain uncovered, one of which is used to fill the silo.

**15**   Assemble the six rings of the silo, starting at the base with
         the smallest.

Before placing the next ring, apply a small amount of mud to the
first ring to bind the two together. Coat the inside with mud so that
it is very smooth.

**16**    After assembling the silo, coat the entire inside and outside with mud mixed with cactus juice.

**17**    The upper part of the silo is then covered with two rows of bundled grass. Add a layer of mud to the upper area, so the grass binds to the silo.

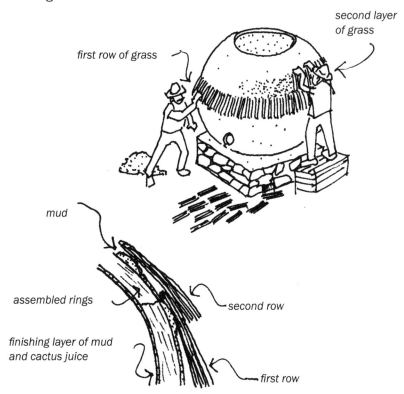

second layer of grass

first row of grass

mud

assembled rings

finishing layer of mud and cactus juice

second row

first row

**18**    On the lower part make a hole to remove the grains. The upper and lower openings have covers made with mosquito mesh so that animals and insects do not enter but the grains are aerated.

Finally, install the roof with a stone in each corner. A strong wind may beat on the roof but will not damage the silo.

## PLASTO SILOS

A silo can be built using a cement mixture and plastic mesh bags such as the kind used to transport vegetables. This technique is called plasto. With a bag of cement, it is possible to build a 3-cubic-meter silo.

This type of silo is in the shape of a soccer ball. This shape is composed of six-sided panels (hexagons) and five-sided panels (pentagons). The silo requires 20 hexagons and 12 pentagons.

**1** First build the molds with ½cm-thick and 8cm-wide strips of wood.

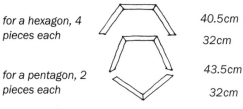

for a hexagon, 4 pieces each          40.5cm

                                       32cm

for a pentagon, 2 pieces each         43.5cm

                                       32cm

**2** Make a 2:1 mixture of sand and cement.

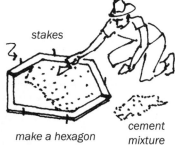

stakes

make a hexagon          cement mixture

**3** On flat ground, lay down newspaper and place the strips for the first mold on the paper and secure them with stakes. Fill the mold up to its edge with the cement mixture.

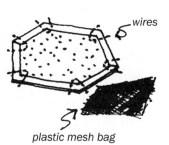

wires

**4** Place pieces of thin wire in the corners and cover the mold with a plastic mesh bag.

plastic mesh bag

**5** Place the second mold on top of the first and fill the mold with more than ½cm of the cement mixture. Then remove the strips of the molds, sliding them out from the sides.

*leave 3cm of the bag around the edges*

**6** Dry the cement panel for one week, keeping it well protected from the rain.

**7** With bricks or stones, make a support base with a opening for the grain. Install an inclined 10cm pvc tube and make a little mound with the cement mixture. Sliding the tube up or down will close or open the exit.

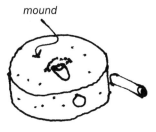

*mound*

**8** On the ground assemble the lower part of the silo upside down starting with the bottom hexagon.

**9** The panels are joined by first twisting the protruding little wires to keep the plates in place. Once done, the extruding plastic mesh edges are covered with cement mix.

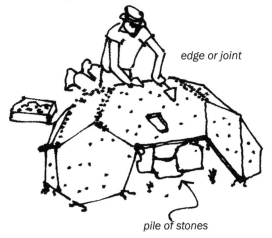

*edge or joint*

*pile of stones*

**10**     Wait one week, then install this part of the silo on the base.
           While in place, the inside joints can be covered with cement.
           Cut a hole in the bottom hexagon to connect to the PVC exit
           tube.

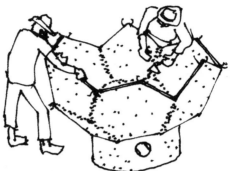

**11**     Now assemble the other panels, one ring at a time. Let each
           ring dry for three days before installing the next to allow the
           joints to harden.

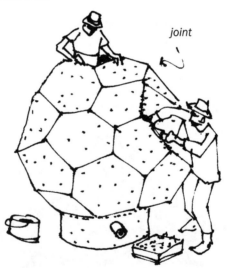

*joint*

**12**     The last hexagon is a lid for pouring in the grains and should
           not be sealed. To protect the silo from sun and rain, many
           types of roofs or covers can be built, such as thatch, tiles or
           sheathing, depending on available materials.

A PVC tube is used at the base as a channel to remove the grains. When the tube is pulled out, it opens the channel and the grains spill out. The tube is closed when it is pushed back in.

*closed*                                    *open*

## OTHER USES FOR A SILO

This silo can also be used as a water reservoir. Reinforce the base with brick supports. The silo can store around a thousand liters.

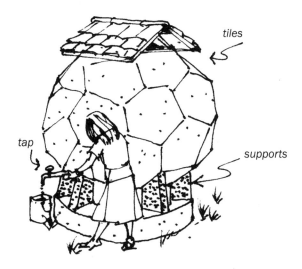

*tiles*

*tap*

*supports*

The water can be cleaned with sand and gravel filters beforehand, so that only clean water enters the reservoir.

## PREMOLDED SINKS

A similar technique as that used for making the silos can be used for premolded sinks and basins. Use a rounded-bottom clay bowl placed upside down as the mold.

1      On a flat surface, covered with newspaper, place the bowl upside down and cover it with plastic so that the cement does not stick to the mold. The mold of the sink counter is made with ½cm-thick strips of wood that are placed on the flat working surface.

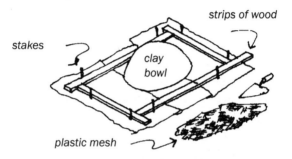

2      Fill the mold of the counter with a ½cm-thick layer of the 2:1 cement mixture. Apply the same thickness of mixture to the bowl.

3      Soak the plastic mesh in a bucket of the cement mixture and then place it on top of the cement already applied.

4      On top of the plastic mesh, apply a second ½cm-thick layer of cement mixture.

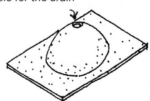

Let the sink dry in the shade for a week before installing it. Once installed, apply a white or colored cement finishing.

It is important to use the right tools for each type of work. Often construction is delayed because of inadequate tools. This chapter decribes how to make tools to facilitate construction.

## LEVELLING TOOLS

This instrument is used to verify the ground level in order to build foundations or streets.

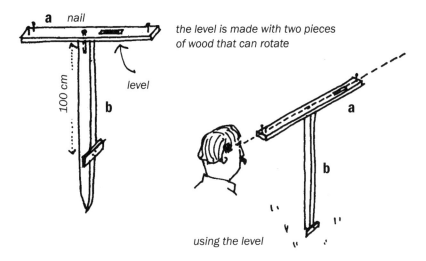

a   nail

the level is made with two pieces
of wood that can rotate

100 cm

level

b

a

b

using the level

On piece (a) fasten a slightly curved transparent plastic tube with an air bubble inside. Place two nails at one end of this piece and one nail at the other, making sure they are at the same height. Piece (b) has a small strip of wood crossing it at one meter below piece (a).

## OTHER TYPES OF LEVELLING TOOLS

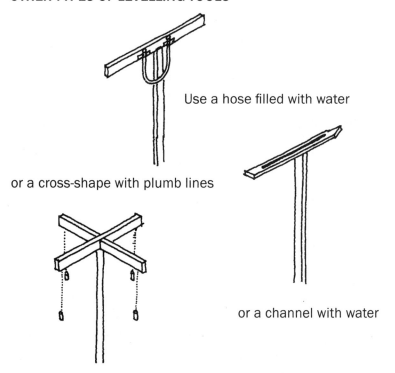

Use a hose filled with water

or a cross-shape with plumb lines

or a channel with water

All these tools are installed on support poles.

On the site, use a transparent hose filled with water to level heights.

*making the windows the same height*

The level can be used in combination with a two-meter levelling rod painted with 20cm-wide black and white stripes.

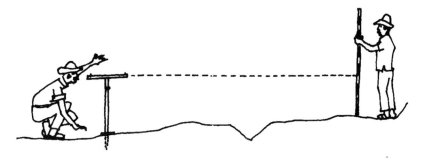

Place the level in the ground and turn part (a) so that the air bubble is always level.

In the drawing above, the man standing up with the levelling rod is 20cm higher than the area where the other man is kneeling.

Another type of level can be made with a plastic tube or hose in the following way:

Cut a 5cm piece of transparent plastic tube. Insert a cork or a stopper and at one end make a hook around the tube and stopper, slightly bending the tube.

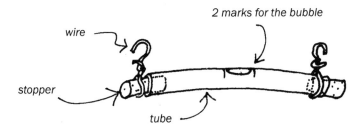

Fill the tube with alcohol and place a stopper at the other end, leaving an air bubble in the tube. Make another wire hook which is attached only to the stopper to be able to open up and adjust the bubble later. Apply a little wax to the stopper so the alcohol does not leak out.

Now the level needs to be calibrated with a carpenter's level. Install a level string between two posts, using the carpenter's level. Then hang the level on the string and adjust the hooks so that the air bubble is exactly between the two marks.

 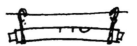 

*mark the center with two lines*          *the bubble is on the right side, so raise the left hook to center it*          *correct position for the air bubble*

Example: To verify the height at which to build a wall so that it is level with an existing one, stretch out a string and hang the level from it. When the air bubble is in the center between the marks, measure the height. Now the right height is known.

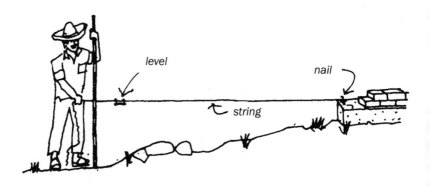

Rivets made with nails:

*a nail...*          *sliced...*          *opened...*          *add a washer..*          *bend the nail...*

## CUTTING TOOL

A cutter or can opener can be made with a piece of steel.

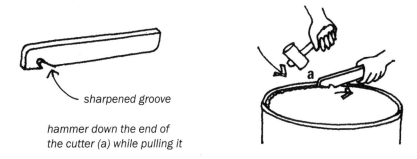

sharpened groove

*hammer down the end of the cutter (a) while pulling it*

## COMPACTOR

To compact down soil, a metal drum can be used.

Weld a 3mm-thick steel cross to both ends of the metal barrel to make a connection for the axle. The axle is made with steel rods flattened at one end; at the other end, make a hook.

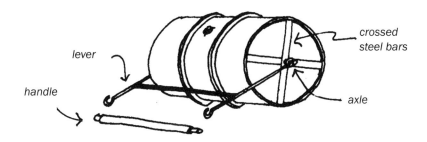

lever

handle

crossed steel bars

axle

Install a wood handle to facilitate moving the compactor by hand. An animal can also be used to move the compactor.

Before using the barrel, fill the compactor with water. After the work is done, empty it so it is lighter to transport.

## BUILDING A LATHE

The lathe described below is an example of a basic tool. If there is constant wind or a source of moving water in the region, the power of this lathe can be increased with a water or windmill. Find out more details in chapter 7.

The base of the lathe is made with large-sized lumber. On top of the table build a support with two boards for the cylinder. Place the cylinder between the boards with a metal axle. The smaller the diameter of the cylinder, the quicker the lathe will turn. On one side of the table fasten a flexible pole. Tie one end of a string to the top of the pole, turn the string around the cylinder and tie the other end to the pedal at ground level.

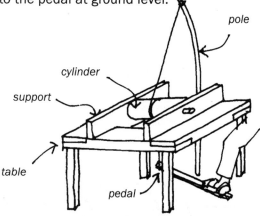

When the pedal is pressed down, the string is pulled down and turns the cylinder. The string's tension in the pole turns the cylinder the opposite way, creating a continuous rotation movement around the axle.

## MEASURING BUCKET

A bucket without a lid can be used to prepare cement mixtures and mortars. Nail a 2cm or 3cm strip of wood to the inside edge of the container for easier handling.

## WHEELBARROWS

A wheelbarrow can be made to transport construction materials.

*platform type*

*for transporting bricks, blocks, wood, stones, adobe*

*box type*

*for transporting earth, concrete, sand*

Reinforce the corners of the platform and box with metal.

The wheel can be a motorcycle tire, or one can be made from wood with a metal ring.

Half of a wooden or metal barrel can be used as a container. Cut the barrel down the middle with a torch on a slant so one end is higher than the other.

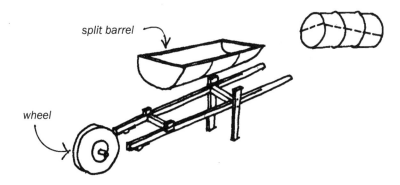

*split barrel*

*wheel*

# WELDER

Tie a wire from the switch box to the piece that is to be welded as a ground wire. Install another wire to a bucket filled with18 liters of water with 5kg of salt.

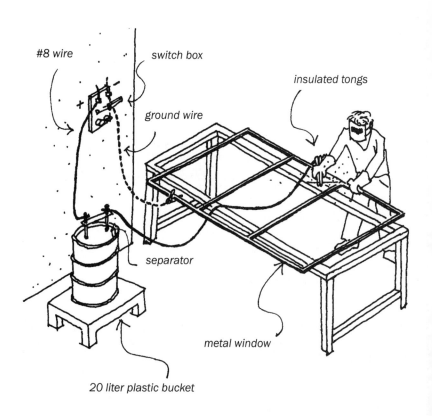

#8 wire
switch box
insulated tongs
ground wire
separator
metal window
20 liter plastic bucket

The energy capacity of the welder depends on the depth of the metal rods in the water. The lid of the bucket should be plastic, and an insulator must separate the metal rods from each other.

## LADDER

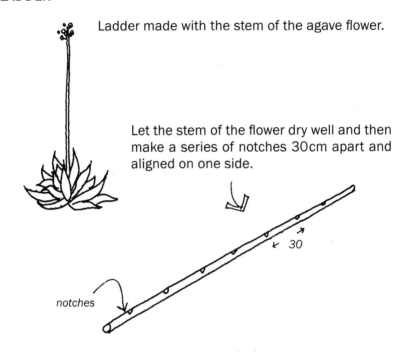

Ladder made with the stem of the agave flower.

Let the stem of the flower dry well and then make a series of notches 30cm apart and aligned on one side.

30

notches

Make the steps out of hardwood:

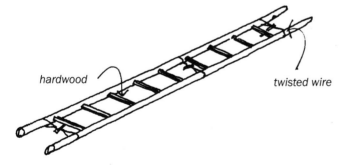

hardwood

twisted wire

Tie the two sides of the ladder together with three pieces of wire twisted close. Large bamboo poles could also be used instead of agave flower stems.

# ECOTECHNIQUES

What are ecotechniques and how are they different from other techniques?

 Example: When an industry settles in a certain region, it has the potential to help improve the living conditions of the inhabitants, but this rarely happens. Usually industrial activity only benefits a few people and is more damaging than helpful. When an industry tries to improve the living conditions of everyone in the community, you can say that the industry is using ecotechniques.

The same happens in construction. When a house has a pleasant atmosphere, comfortable temperature, is well ventilated, receives sunlight, is not humid and has good acoustics, you can say that it is designed and built using ecotechniques.

## WHAT IS AN ECOTECHNIQUE

Heating water with a solar water heater instead of wood, gas or electricity ... this is an ecotechnique. Using waste to produce gas or making a pump to extract water with recycled bicycle parts ...these are also ecotechniques.

## WHY?

A solar water heater does not require a forest being cut down for firewood. Another characteristic of ecotechniques is that they help communities be independent and autonomous from industry of other regions. The production of adobe bricks from local clay is another ecotechnique because the material and the labor come from the same region.

Before designing or building a house, store or workshop, the members of a community must consider if they will use ecotechniques. To answer this question, consider the following:

**?** Will the new technique satisfy the basic necessities of the people, such as shelter, nourishment, health and education?

**?** Will the construction utilize local labor and materials?

**?** When applying the new technique, will the local people work on their own initiative and be directed by local people?

**?** Does the new technique take into consideration the traditional values of the community?

**?** Is the new technique simple to apply, and does it allow the creative participation of the people involved in the project?

**?** Does the technique contribute to the extinction of endangered resources or species, or pollute the environment?

**?** How does this new technique affect the buildings and the environment in the project's surroundings?

Here are a few examples of ecotechniques.

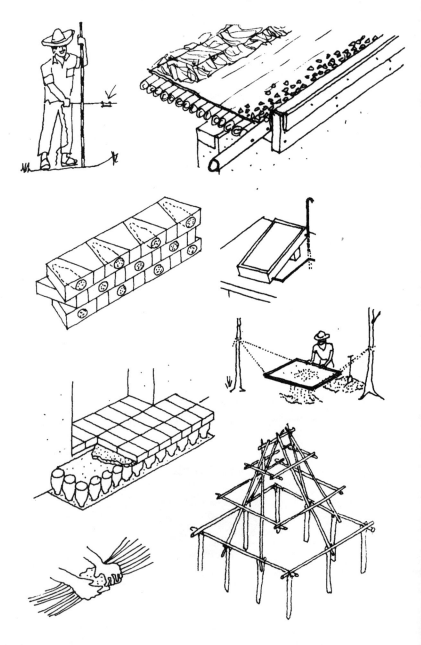

Do you recognize them?

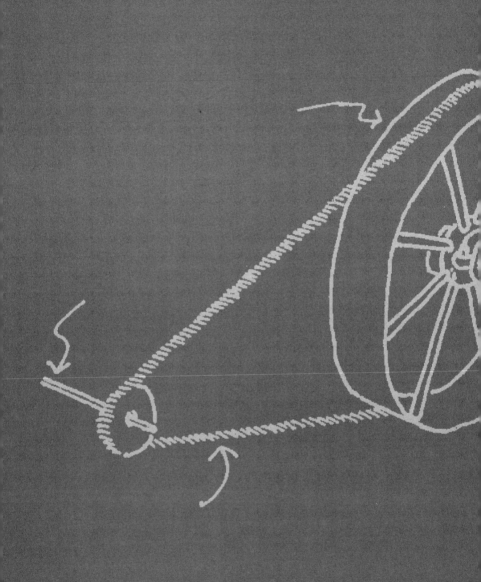

# ENERGY

**7**

# HEAT AND MOTION ENERGY

Energy is heat. Energy can also be motion.

Heat is used to cook or to heat houses in cold weather. Energy is also used to power equipment or tools such as water pumps and wood cutting tools.

Nature provides many forms of energy that generate heat. These natural sources of energy can be used in regions where other resources such as tree wood for burning are not available. And of course by using these alternative energies, forests are not destroyed, especially in regions where trees are not being replaced.

These other sources of energy are sun rays, wind power and water power. Water power is generated by the motion of rivers. Heat energy can also be generated from the decomposition of organic waste or burning the gas produced from this decomposition.

When considering using these types of energy, it is important to know that they will not always be available.

A water pump powered by a windmill does not work if there is no wind, and a solar heater does not function if it is raining. But when there is sun and wind, these energies are free gifts from the sky.

Always be prepared with a backup system. For example, install a cistern which can store water for the days when there is no wind, or a woodstove to heat water on a cloudy day.

## AN ANECDOTE

Once upon a time, there was a place where the electricity went out and failed to come back on. The inhabitants were very upset since they now were living in the dark at night.

The people of the community came together to try to find a solution to their problem. One person asked: "Since we do not have oil, or wood, or gas, how will we ever have energy or light again?"

Another person said: "Well, our fields are filled with flowers. We can use the beeswax to make an oil to power our machines and these machines will generate electricity to light our homes."

All seemed to agree this was a good idea. But yet another person said: "If we want light, why don't we just use the wax itself?"

Everyone laughed, declared this would be impossible to do and said: "How could this ever be done?"

Then the man who had made the suggestion pulled from his bag a piece of wax, and rolled it around a wick and lit the candle. And light appeared!

From then on, the people understood that it is always best to search for the simplest solution, using what you have on hand.

Always try to make the most out of the least!

## MONJOLO

The *monjolo,* a European innovation, used simple mechanics to replace the backbreaking work of pounding corn. Resembling an enormous seesaw, the *monjolo* consisted of a huge wooden beam, hollowed out at one end to form a trough, with a wooden head on the bottom of the beam at the other end. Balanced on a fulcrum, the head was heavier than the trough and rested in a bin of corn. But when water filled the trough, making that end heavier, the head rose until the trough hit the ground. Then the water spilled out and caused the head to crash down into the wooden bin filled with corn kernels. Over and over again, the head rose and fell as water filled the trough and spilled out on the ground. Creaking, groaning and thudding all the while, the *monjolo* eventually produced cornmeal with a minimum of human effort.

To build this grain mill, use a lever beam that is supported by a post freely in the center and install a container at one end and a weight at the other. The water falls into the container (a) causing it to move downward from the weight and then empties out, while the other end (b), now the heavier one, lands on the stand and grinds the grains (c).

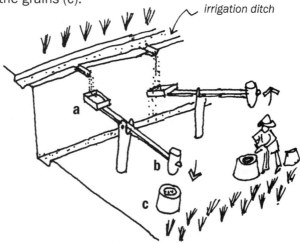

*irrigation ditch*

First test the length of the lever and the size of the containers to make sure they are the correct size for the quantity of water that is filtering through the fields.

## WINDMILLS

This mill is made with a 200-liter barrel which rotates slowly. It works with wind coming from any direction. Use a metal barrel installed on a wooden support.

Cut the barrel in half and then reunite the halves around a central axle rod, as illustrated below. The rod is welded to two circular plates at either end of the barrel. The plates connecting the halves are larger circles than the base of the barrel.

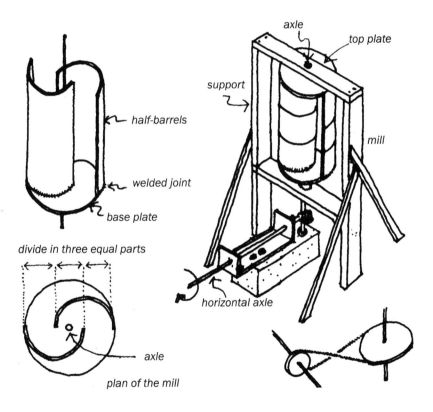

axle

top plate

support

half-barrels

mill

welded joint

base plate

divide in three equal parts

horizontal axle

axle

plan of the mill

There are many ways to use the axle movement of the mill. The large drawing shows a transfer to a horizontal motion, and the drawing in the bottom right corner, shows a similar way using a leather belt.

## CROSS-BARREL MILL

Two 200-liter barrels can be used to make a type of mill powered by light winds.

**1**    Cut the barrels in half and make a 1-inch-diameter hole in the top and bottom.

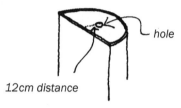

*12cm distance*                                        *hole*

**2**    Make a 10cm x 10cm lumber cross assembled with a 2cm-thick wood plate on the top and a 4mm steel plate on the bottom. Glue the cross to the wood plate and fasten the steel plate with bolts. Build a second identical cross with 5cm x 10cm lumber and two wood plates.

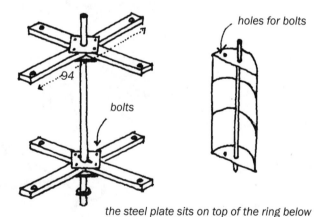

*holes for bolts*

*94*

*bolts*

*the steel plate sits on top of the ring below*

**3**    Now attach the half-barrels with bolts onto the cross with broomsticks so they do not loosen.

**4**   Make a 1cm hole in a 1.70m long and 3cm diameter tube.

**5**   The heaviest cross is mounted on a tube with a ring or bearing below and then installed on a horizontal member of the structure.

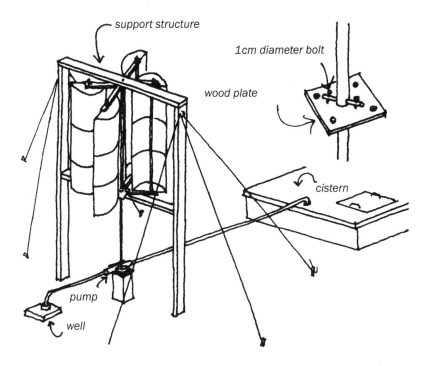

**6**   Install the other cross at the top of the half-barrels. The support structure is made with 8cm x 8cm lumber. Place the support structure on the highest point of the land so it receives the most wind possible. The mill must be well supported and the structure strengthened with stretched out wires tied to stakes in the ground.

In regions with strong winds, build a security system to close the
the half-barrels (helix) so the wind does not damage the pump.

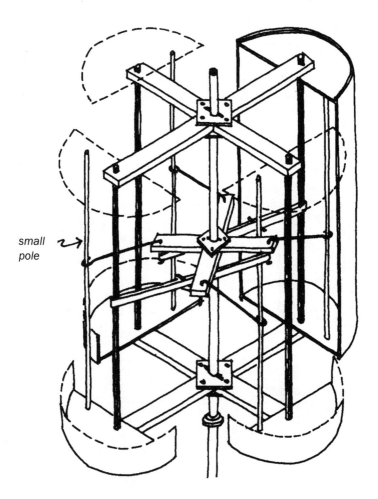

small
pole

Shown above is a partial view of the mill. Tie a third cross with
a rod and two bicycle inner tubes to the broomsticks of the half-
barrel helixes. Calibrate the tension in the inner tube with a bolt
fastened to the tube.

The third 5cm x 10cm wood cross is 26cm long.

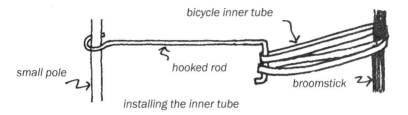

installing the inner tube

## GENERATING ELECTRICITY WITH A WATERWHEEL

In regions where there are a variety of materials and tools, a metal waterwheel can be built. The wheel is connected to an electrical generator and a pump or another type of device that rotates.

*The wheel is made of a series of tubes cut in half with a base that is connected to the axle wheel.*

*section and view of the scuppers*

The lower part of the wheel is submerged in the current of a stream. One end of the axle shaft is connected to the leather belt that moves the generator or pump.

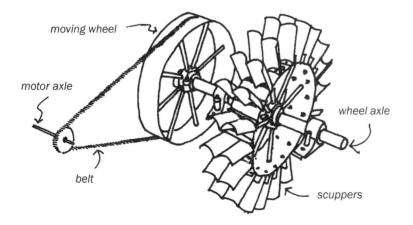

# SOLAR HEAT

## HOT WATER HEATERS

Described below is a way of building a water tank which is exposed to the sun and heats water.

But first, how does this work?

Try this experiment, using an empty beer can, a little black paint, pieces of white paper and a transparent plastic bag.

1   Paint the outside of the can matte black.

2   Fill the can with water and install it near the walls of the house. The wall absorbs the sun's heat during the whole day. If the wall is not painted white, place a white piece of paper between the can and the wall.

3   Place another piece of white paper underneath the can.

4   Cover the can loosely with a plastic bag which is well closed so that the hot air does not escape.

5   Leave this miniature heater a few hours in the sun. Then check how hot the water is.

The can should stay in the sun from the morning to the late afternoon without being shaded, by a balcony or tree for example.

transparent plastic bag

can painted matte black

small stones or sand
to hold down the plastic bag

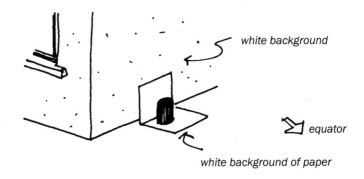

white background

equator

white background of paper

Before building a large water heater for a family, consider what will be needed:

→ The tank of the heater must be painted black to absorb the sun's heat.

→ The background (the wall or the ground) must be white to reflect the sun's rays onto the black tank.

→ The tank must be covered with transparent plastic or glass so the sun's heat does not escape. Also, without a cover the passing breeze will carry away the heat.

→ To prevent the day's heat from reducing the water's heat at night, the tank must be covered with an insulated lid made from materials such as straw or boards.

The heater also functions on overcast days. Only when it is raining will the heater not store heat.

## THE HEATER

To make a heater, the following materials are required:

 a 40- or 60-liter barrel (if we use larger barrels, the volume of cold water will be proportionally greater than the exterior surface of the reservoir and will take more time to heat up)

 matte black paint

 a transparent plastic sheet

First clean the interior of the reservoir so that there are no odors. Paint the inside with an anti-corrosive paint to prevent the metal from rusting. Pour the paint inside the barreland move it around, so that the paint covers the inside completely. Then paint the exterior in a matte black.

If there is no house plumbing, the reservoir can be placed on top of a table to facilitate access to it.

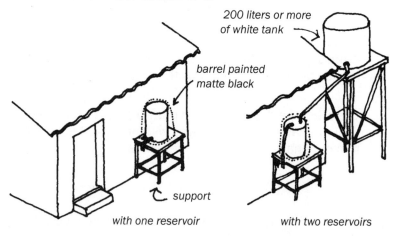

200 liters or more of white tank

barrel painted matte black

support

with one reservoir

with two reservoirs

The system works best with two reservoirs: a higher one to store cold water and a lower one to heat the water.

The inlet for cold water is at the bottom of the solar heater, and the outlet for the hot water is at the top of the solar heater.

 The reason for placing the pipes this way is simple: hot water is less dense than cold water and will always try to rise to the higher temperature level in a storage container.

As in the can test, the heater tank must be placed against a wall that receives a lot of sun which, in the Southern Hemisphere, is the north wall. The wall and the table are painted white.

Cover the entire tank with plastic. The hot air between the tank and the plastic must not escape.

Another way to conserve hot air is to build a box with a glass lid. The heater tank must be installed on its side. The rest of the box can be made with wood and the interior painted white.

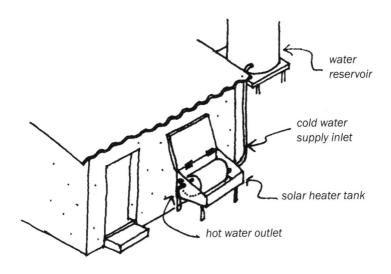

At night, cover the glass lid with a wooden top.

## INTEGRATED COLLECTORS

The previous examples were for heaters located outside the house. It is also possible to integrate collectors into the house. A good place for this type of installation is above the bathroom or kitchen where there is already plumbing.

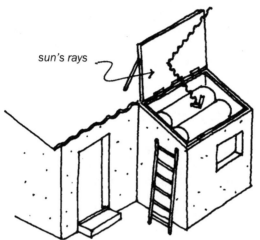

sun's rays

*Panel to cover the reservoir at night. The inner surfaces are painted white to reflect the sun's rays onto the tank.*

For large quantities of hot water, several small tanks work better than one large one.

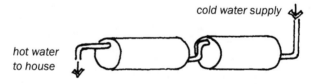

cold water supply

hot water to house

## ROOF COLLECTOR

Another way to build a collector is to integrate it into the roof. It should be installed as close as possible above a bathroom or kitchen to reduce the amount of piping.

Install a movable insulated cover below the glass top. This cover should be able to be closed and opened from inside the house.

Make an opening in the roof near the lowest edge. To prevent leaks the tiles protrude a few centimeters over the glass pane.

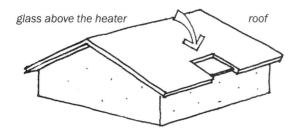

*glass above the heater*          *roof*

Install the cold water piping to the supply inlet. The end of this pipe is capped and the pipe is perforated along the bottom. The hot water outlet is, as usual, in the upper part of the tank.

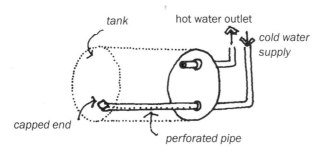

*tank*     hot water outlet

cold water
supply

*capped end*

*perforated pipe*

Illustrated below are some construction details:

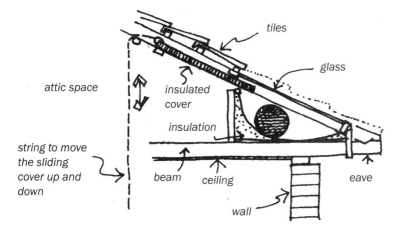

tiles

glass

*attic space*

*insulated
cover*

*insulation*

*string to move
the sliding
cover up and
down*

*beam*     *ceiling*          *eave*

*wall*

## SOLAR WATER HEATER PANELS

A car gasoline tank can be used to build an efficient solar heater. A panel box is made with the tank, a pane of glass and insulation. The pressure in the cold water tubing (c) pushes out the hot water (h). The cold water storage must be placed above the solar heater panel.

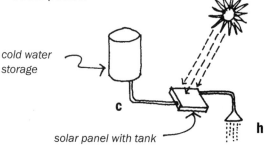

cold water storage

c

solar panel with tank

h

This type of heater does not require pressure valves or overflow tubes since as the pressure in the heater increases, the stored cold water is pushed out.

Build the panel with a 40-liter tank, which comes in various shapes.

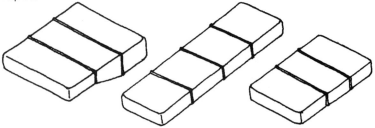

## CONSTRUCTION

1    Clean the inside and outside of the tank. Then prepare two pipes, one 12 cm long and the other longer than the tank. The part of the pipe inside the tank is capped at the end, and 2 mm holes are made every 3 cm along its lower surface.

**2**    Weld the piping and test the seal of the joint with water under pressure to make sure there are no leaks. Paint the outside part of the reservoir with matte black paint.

**3**    Install the panel and the insulation material. Then make a cover of the same shape and place a sheet of aluminum foil in the inside part of the cover.

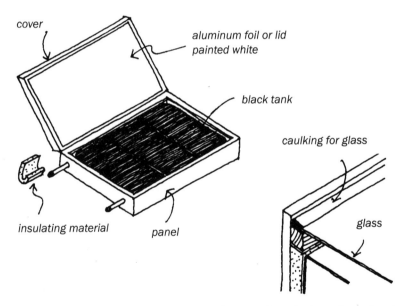

The panel has a 3cm x 3cm strip of wood 2cm below the edge to support the glass. The glass is sealed with silicon or another type of caulking.

Make sure there are no leaks around the edge of the glass or the pipe joints. At night close the panel so that the heat accumulated during the day does not escape.

The inside dimensions of the panel are the tank size plus the thickness of the insulation.

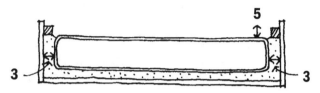

The cover can be loose or fastened to the panel with hinges. Be careful that the panel is well made so air does not escape. When the cover is open, the sun's rays reflect onto the tank.

The positioning of the heater depends on the type of roof, the orientation of the house and the location of the cold water storage.

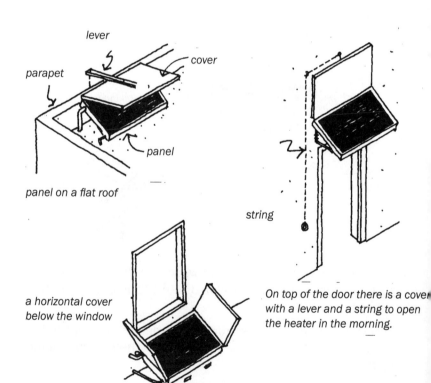

*panel on a flat roof*

*a horizontal cover below the window*

On top of the door there is a cover with a lever and a string to open the heater in the morning.

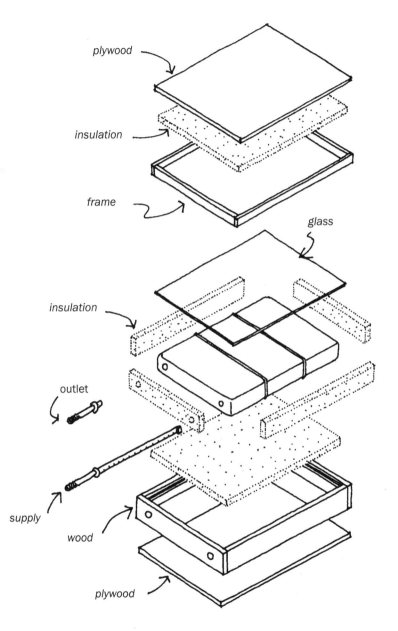

plywood

insulation

frame

glass

insulation

outlet

supply

wood

plywood

components of a 40-liter water heater

## THERMO-SYPHONING HEATER

The thermo-syphoning water heater is different from the previous ones described since the hot water storage tank is separate from the collector panel. With this system, there is no need to open and close the panel.

The tank can be made with a 120-liter barrel covered with insulation such as straw or newspaper so that heat does not escape.

The panel is a box made like the ones in the previous pages: with wood and insulation. Inside there is a grid of tubing on a thin metallic sheet. If sheet metal is not available, use thick aluminum foil. The tube grid is made with ½-inch copper tubing, elbow joints and T-joints. The panel box has a groove to support a sheet of glass.

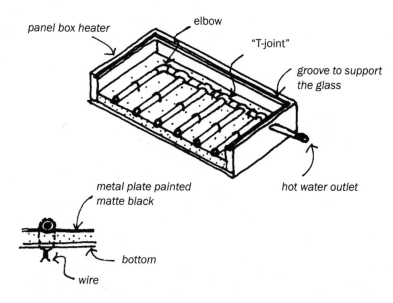

panel box heater

elbow

"T-joint"

groove to support the glass

metal plate painted matte black

hot water outlet

bottom

wire

The tubing must stay in contact with the metal plate. Pierce holes through the plate and the panel's plywood bottom. Tie a wire around the tubing and through the hole, so that the tube remains in contact with the plate.

Make a valve with a ball-float inside the controller can. This part can be used to control the entrance of cold water that comes from the cistern or reservoir.

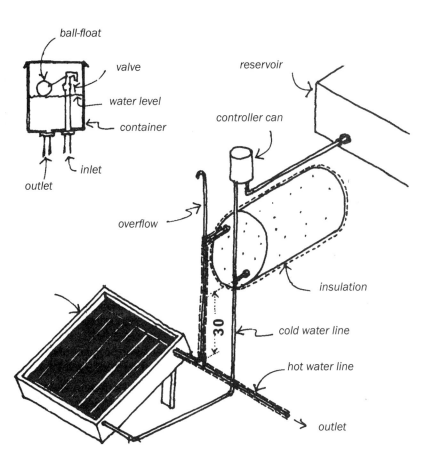

The hot water line and the piping supplying hot water to the kitchen and bathroom are wrapped in insulation.

The inlet from the cold water pipe to the reservoir should be at least 30 cms above the connection to the hot water pipe.

Since the water in the insulated storage tank is never as hot as the water in the collector panel, the water from the collector continuously rises into the tank as the cooler water from the tank falls into the collector panel. This natural separating effect is called thermo-syphoning.

The solar collector panel is installed outside the house, and the storage tank can be located in the house. The panel always must be at least 30cm lower than the storage tank.

## ORIENTATION

The heater is installed on a roof or a wall on the north* side of the building or house. Make sure that the chosen area receives sun all day long and that eaves or trees are not shading the area, especially during the hottest hours from 10 am to 4 pm.

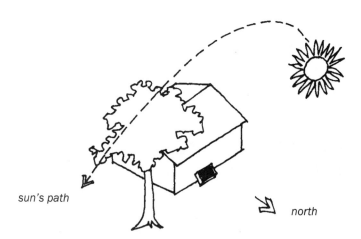

*sun's path*                                                    *north*

Take a close look at the drawing above. Is the solar water heater panel well located? In the winter, when the sun is low, this position works but in the summer the tree shades the panel after 1 pm. The panel must be relocated to the right and also be raised.

*This applies to the Southern Hemisphere; do the opposite in the Northern Hemisphere.

## PROBLEMS WITH THE PANELS

 Collectors that heat, cool or distill water must be well built and installed on the roof. With strong winds the supports can become loose, so build with nuts and bolts. Collectors must be positioned to absorb as much sun as possible and must be protected from wind with trees, walls or parapets that rise above the roofline.

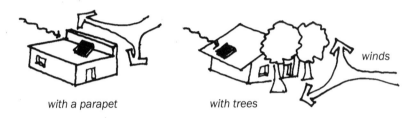

with a parapet          with trees

 In time corrosion can clog the tubing, so once in a while verify if the water is passing through the tubes smoothly and if any tube parts need to be replaced.

 The collector must never be empty. Without water to absorb the sun's heat, the temperature inside the collector panel becomes higher and the wooden box could break. Any plastic material used as insulation can melt and release toxic fumes.

Solar water heater panels can be purchased ready-made. Usually they are more efficient than the homemade kind. However, very hot water is not necessary for domestic uses such as bathing or washing dishes in hot tropical climates.

## HOSE WATER HEATER

Simple solar water heaters can be made with a black or dark green plastic hose:

1    Build a wood box of roughly 1m x 1m and 5cm high. Insulation materials such as straw matting, newspaper or sawdust will also be needed.

2    In the bottom install 1cm of the insulation. In the center of the bottom, make a hole of the same diameter as the hose and pass it through the box as illustrated below.

3    Connect the hose to the bottom with wire. The other end of the hose passes through a hole on the corner.

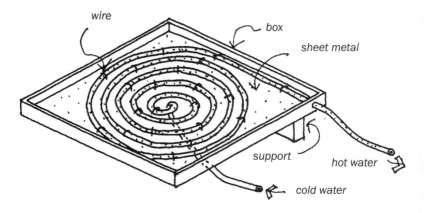

4    Cover the box with a pane of glass. The heater is installed on an angle with the hot water outlet placed at a higher level than the cold water inlet.

In the drawing above, the hose spiral is spaced wider than it should be so as to better understand how the heater is built.

Obviously to make these things work, we need sun, but we also do need water.

## HOW TO FIND SOURCES OF WATER

In a humid tropical climate, it is not difficult to find sources of water. The issue is the quality of the water, since often water is polluted with solid or liquid wastes.

In temperate climate zones, water is often found in the lower parts of a site, in areas with vegetation, or by excavating. The depth of excavation to find water depends on the type of plants.

In regions where there are heavy rains at certain times of the year, collect and store rainwater to use during the drier seasons.

In a dry tropical climate, the water table is deeper and more difficult to locate, so other solutions must be found. One way to know if there is water on a site is to lie on the ground before the sunrise, lift your head up and watch the surface of the land. As the first sun rays heat up the humid areas, a little vapor rises, signaling a water source deeper down.

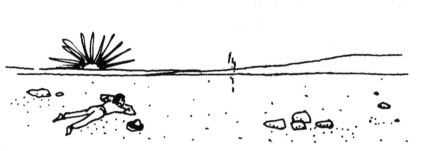

The sun's heat is also useful to dry food and even make ice.

## SOLAR DRYER

A solar dryer for fruit and vegetables can be made with wood and glass. The dryer is also a good place to store food and protect it from insects.

The dryer is oriented to the north and exposed to the sun. In the bottom of the box, place three drawers with metal mesh or wooden slat bottoms that allow air to circulate.

The box is made from boards or plywood with an insulated layer inside. Make holes on the sides and bottom for evaporation. The holes should be small so that insects do not enter.

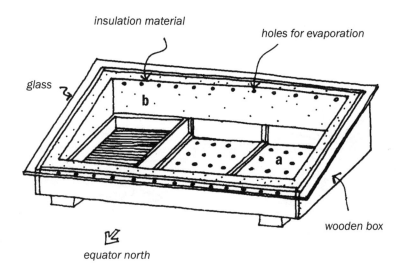

insulation material

holes for evaporation

glass

b

a

equator north

wooden box

**a)** base with holes
**b)** drawers with supporting slat bottoms for the fruit

Illustrated below is another type of dryer with a heater panel installed in front of the dryer.

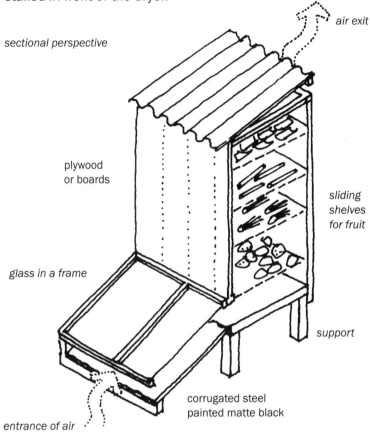

*sectional perspective*

*air exit*

plywood
or boards

*sliding
shelves
for fruit*

*glass in a frame*

*support*

corrugated steel
painted matte black

*entrance of air*

On a base of wooden legs, build a cabinet with sliding slat drawers which allow air to circulate around the food. Instead of sliding shelves, fixed shelves with different types of perforated or slat racks or trays can also be used.

The dryer is protected from rain with a metal or tile roof. Above the shelves and below the roof there is an opening for hot air to exit. Below there is another opening that connects to an air heater made with black sheet metal applied to the panels and covered with a glass pane.

## ICE MAKER

Ice can be made in hot arid regions with desert conditions where the night temperature is low.

The climatic conditions required are:

 a clear night without clouds

 no winds

 dry air

To know if conditions of a region are adequate for producing ice, try the following test:

**1** Excavate a hole in an open area close to a house or trees.

*excavate*

**2** Fill the hole with insulation such as straw or leaves.

**3** Install on the straw a couple of clay disks with water about 5cm below the ground level.

On a clear night without winds, the water in the disk turns into ice in the early hours of the morning. The disks must be removed before the ice melts with the rising sun. They can be placed in a box with an insulated lid or a jar. See the following chapter for more details.

In areas where there is wind at night, build a small wall with bricks and cement plaster around the side of the hole from which the wind is coming.

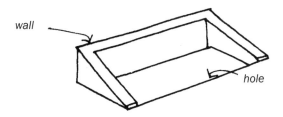

Another way to protect the hole from wind is to make a wooden structure covered with plastic.

The collector must be placed away from buildings that radiate heat at night as well as from trees.

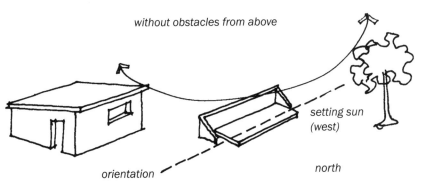

Two centimeters of water in a 50cm x 200cm collector produce 10 kilos of ice.

# STOVES

In many regions, wood is scarce. Stoves therefore should be built to conserve as much heat and energy as possible.

An example of heat efficiency is a rounded-bottom pot which heats water up much more quickly and keeps it evenly distributed compared to a flat-bottomed pot.

*The heat does not reach the sides, only the bottom.*

*Here the heat is more evenly distributed and the water heats up quickly.*

## CLAY STOVE

This type of clay and sand stove is efficient and saves on the quantity of wood used.

The type of the clay determines the proportion to use in the mixture. A stove may crack if the proportions are not correct, so it is always better to test mixtures first.

Start with a mixture of 2 parts clay for 1 part sand.

## CONSTRUCTION PHASES

**1**   Build the stove base with bricks, leaving an opening below
for the wood.

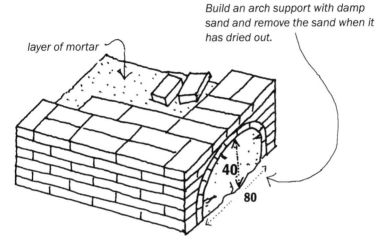

*layer of mortar*

*Build an arch support with damp
sand and remove the sand when it
has dried out.*

40

80

**2**   Build a formwork with four parts that can be reused. Fill the
form with the mixture and compact it down.

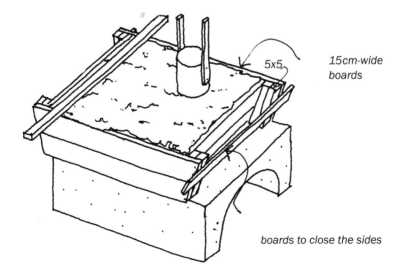

5x5

*15cm-wide
boards*

*boards to close the sides*

**3**    Wait two days and make three holes for pots and one smaller hole for the chimney. Shape the hole with a wet spade and then wet the bottom of a pot to mold the top of the opening to fit the pot.

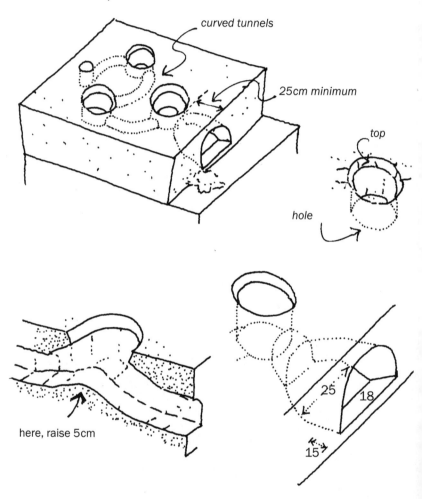

curved tunnels

25cm minimum

top

hole

here, raise 5cm

25  18

15

**4**    The openings are connected by 10cm-wide tunnels, made with wetted knives or blades. The tunnels must be curved. Raise the surface below the holes 5cm.

**5**   Wait two days for the mortar to dry, and then install the ventilation duct and the doors to control the air circulation in the chimney.

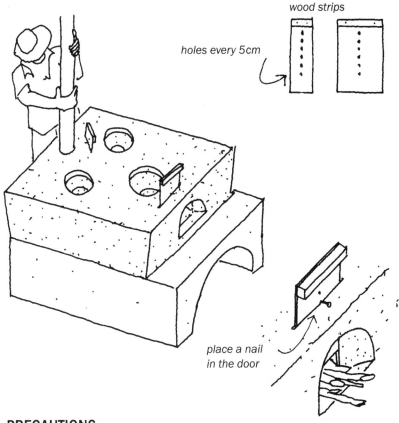

*wood strips*

*holes every 5cm*

*place a nail in the door*

## PRECAUTIONS

 After applying the finishing, wait two days before lighting a fire.

 The chimney duct must not be in contact with the woodwork of the roof.

 The chimney must be cleaned out every six months by removing ashes, to prevent fires.

## OTHER TYPES OF STOVES

In the model below, the third hole is replaced with a metal container to heat water:

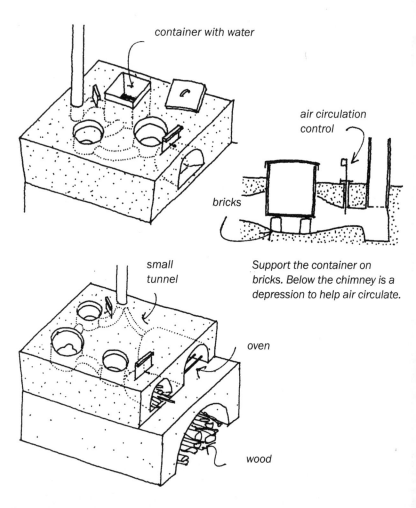

container with water

air circulation control

bricks

small tunnel

Support the container on bricks. Below the chimney is a depression to help air circulate.

oven

wood

To add an oven, change the position of the tunnels. The chimney duct is positioned on the side. Below the wood for the stove, place charcoal from the fire. The tunnel between the oven and chimney should be about 5cm in diameter.

## SOLAR STOVE

To make a simple stove to cook rice, beans and bananas, two boxes are needed, one larger than the other.

First cover the bottom of the larger box with 5cm of insulation such as paper, sawdust, or coconut fibers.

Then place the smaller box in the larger one and fill the spaces between the boxes with insulation.

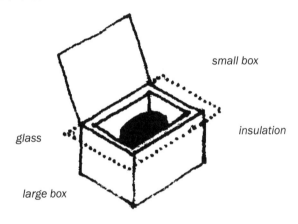

small box

glass

insulation

large box

In the bottom, install a black steel or clay panel. Place the food to cook in the box.

Cover the box with a small sheet of glass or transparent plastic. Make sure the joint between the glass and the box is well sealed so that heat does not escape.

To increase the temperature further, install a reflector made with aluminum foil, using the same technique as with the solar water heaters.

A more solid and durable solar oven can be made with sheet metal and bricks:

**1**    Make a stainless steel box with an angled opening. On the opposite side, make a small door flap.

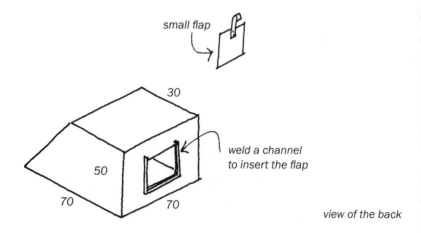

small flap

30

50

70          70

weld a channel
to insert the flap

view of the back

**2**    On the angle, weld four visors opening outwards like a head-dress. Paint the exterior surfaces black.

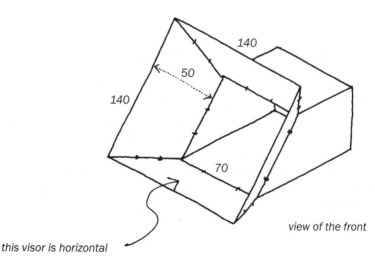

140

50

140

70

view of the front

this visor is horizontal

**3** Install on the box three or four caster wheels.

**4** Line the box with bricks.

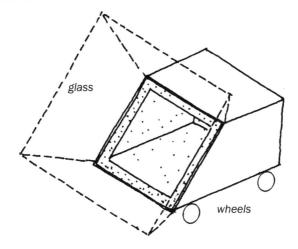

glass

wheels

**5** Install a glass pane sealed with silicon or caulking.

To heat up the oven, orient the opening towards the sun. Food to cook is placed in the oven through the small door.

Every half hour, turn the oven so that the opening always remains facing the sun.

## TECHNIQUES FOR REGIONS

In some regions, or during certain seasons, there are heavy rains and overcast skies making it difficult to heat water with solar energy. Described here are other ways to heat water.

**A**      Install a coil tube on the upper part of a traditional stove. The water is directed to a reservoir that is wrapped in insulation such as straw or paper.

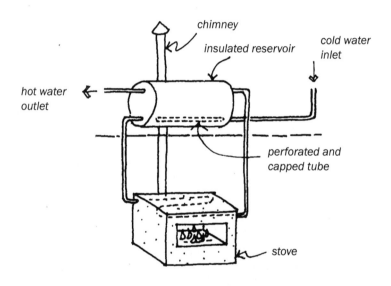

**B**      In forest regions, the water heater can be built with a barrel to use the least amount of wood possible.

Use a 200-liter reservoir. Weld a duct to the stove as a chimney and tubes for the water inlet and outlet. The water in the tank heats up when the fire is burning.

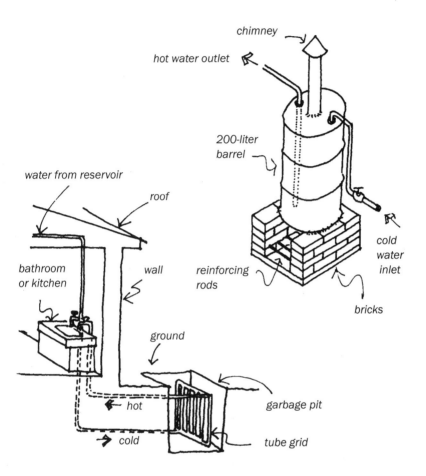

chimney

hot water outlet

200-liter barrel

water from reservoir

roof

bathroom or kitchen

wall

reinforcing rods

cold water inlet

bricks

ground

hot

cold

garbage pit

tube grid

**C**     Another method is to install a tube in a garbage pit that de-composes organic matter from the kitchen.

As decomposing matter generates heat, place a coil or recycled car or truck radiator in the garbage pit.

 Compost, the process of decomposition of organic waste, generates heat at a high-enough temperature to be collected and used. If this seems improbable, try this test. Place a few eggs in the compost and check if they have cooked a few hours later. Do clean them well, though, before eating them!

# WATER

8

## THE SOURCE OF WATER

The potable water faucet or public fountain must:

→ Be close to where the water is used to save on construction of infrastructure such as pipes and aqueducts.

→ Be easily accessible to the users; it should not be placed far away from the houses, or on steep land that is difficult to access.

→ Be close to land available for future construction. Local businesses may develop around this area.

→ Prevent wasting water by using excess water for plant irrigation.

→ Be located in a paved area to prevent the ground from becoming muddy. If clothes are being washed nearby, create shaded areas with trees or pergolas.

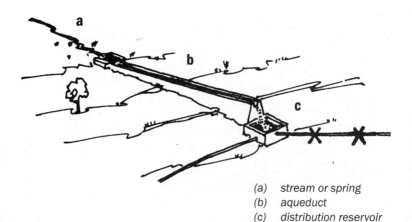

(a)   stream or spring
(b)   aqueduct
(c)   distribution reservoir

Other possibilities :

  Install a solar water heater for hot water.

  In dry regions, provide a solar distiller to recycle water.

Heaters and distillers can also be installed on the roof of a city market where a lot of water is used.

The local fountain loses its original function with the installation of plumbing. Therefore, place the fountain in an attractive and pleasant area that can be used as a leisure space in the future, since it is refreshing to be near water and plants.

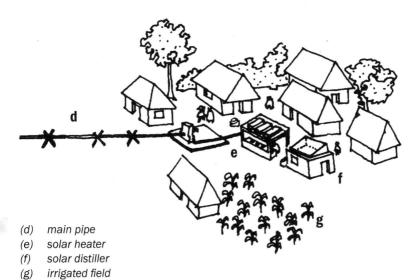

(d)   main pipe
(e)   solar heater
(f)   solar distiller
(g)   irrigated field

## WATER FROM A RIVER OR CREEK

A first step toward purifying river water can be made by burying a drum or a concrete box in the river bed. The upper part of the barrel is closed and the bottom, the mouth, is perforated. The river water passes through gravel and sand and then rises with a pump.

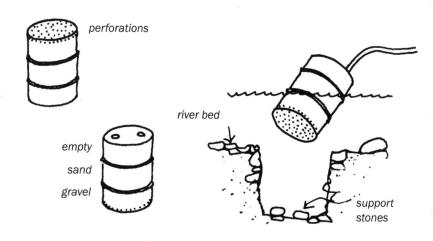

perforations

river bed

empty

sand

gravel

support stones

1    Perforate the bottom of the barrel and lower sides with a nail.
     *perforer le fond du baril et le bas des cotés avec un clou*

2    Fill the barrel with gravel and sand: ⅙ gravel, ⅘ sand, and leave the top ⅙ of the barrel empty.
     *remplir le baril avec du gravier et du sable et laisser le sommet du baril vide de 1/6 (1/6 gravier - 4/6 sable)*

3    Fasten a hose to the top cover.
     *fixer un tuyau sur le couvercle*

4    Excavate a hole in the river bed and install the barrel.
     *creuser un trou dans le lit de la rivière et installer le baril*

5    Cover the barrel with stones or other available river bed material.
     *couvrir le baril avec des pierres et autres matériaux disponibles dans le lit de la rivière*

6    Connect a pump to raise the water.
     *brancher une pompe pour élever l'eau.*

The next drawing shows how the river water filters through the river bed before entering the barrel.
*les dessins suivants montre comment l'eau de la rivière est filtrée dans le baril*

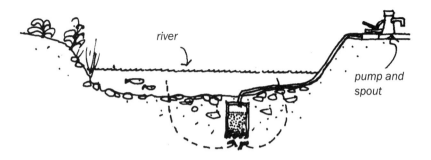

## WATER FROM A SPRING

To protect springs, do the following:

**1**    Remove the mud and earth in the riverbed down to the impermeable layer.

**2**    Build a masonry box with cement and sand finishing.

**3**    Install an outlet tube.

**4**    Cover the box with a lid.

**5**    Dig out a drainage canal above it to divert rainwater.

**6**    Bury the lid and the tube with earth. Build a support wall for the outlet tube.

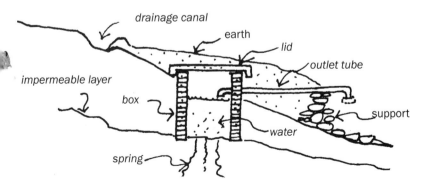

# PUMPS

## NARROW DIAMETER WELL

Dip a 2m-long and 4cm-diameter pipe in the water of a well. The water rises in the pipe up to level of water in the well. Cover the upper end of the pipe with one hand, and then raise the pipe; the water moves up along with the pipe. Lower the pipe quickly and uncover the end; momentum causes a larger quantity of the water to now fill the pipe. Continue this motion with the pipe until the water spouts out the end of the pipe.

This principle is used to build pumps. A 75mm-diameter, 4.5-meter-long pipe can be used to extract water from a 4-meter-deep narrow well.

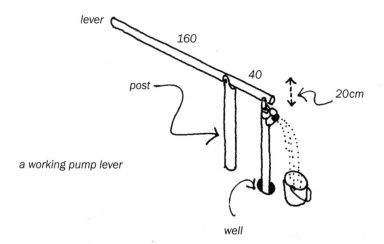

a working pump lever

The lever and post are made from wood. The lever is 2 meters long. Use short movements to pump the water – the pipe should not move more than 20cm.

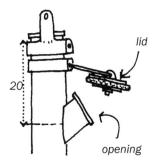

lid

20

opening

**1** The upper opening of the pipe is capped. Install a metal hinge to attach the lever.

**2** Twenty centimeters below the capped opening, weld a piece of tube of the same size at a 45-degree angle.

**3** The hinged lid is made out of two circular metal plates, with a rubber seal in between.

**4** File and polish the joint so as to make a tight air seal.

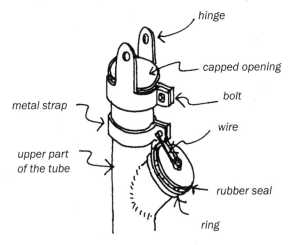

hinge

capped opening

bolt

metal strap

wire

upper part of the tube

rubber seal

ring

The lid is made with two metal rings and a rubber seal. There is a wire which connects the lid to the bolt of the metal strap. The lower ring is smaller so it can enter into the tube. The rubber seal closes the opening when the tube rises, as in the hand test.

Note: You can do most of this with plastic pipe, if it is available.

Another type of pump is described below:

This pump can be made from available materials, such as bamboo, steel or plastic pipes. The dimensions are variable; you should experiment to determine the best-sized pump for each condition.

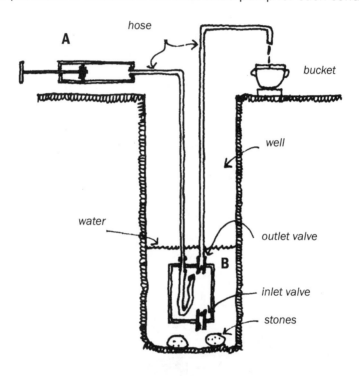

This device has two parts: a pump system (**A**), consisting of a pump and a sealed hose filled with water which inflates a capped inner tube inside a sealed container (**B**), which has two check valves and an outlet hose. The container should rest on stones at the bottom of the well to help prevent mud from fouling the inlet valve.

The pump pushes water down the hose which then expands the capped inner tube like a balloon. The expansion of the inner tube forces the well water in the container out through the upper check valve and up the outlet hose.

**1**     When the pump piston is pushed in, the inner tube fills with water and creates pressure in the container. Since the water cannot exit the lower check valve, it must rise through the upper valve.

**2**     When the pump piston is pulled out, the water is sucked up into the pump and the inner tube is emptied. This creates a negative pressure inside the container, and the well water is sucked into the container through the lower check valve.

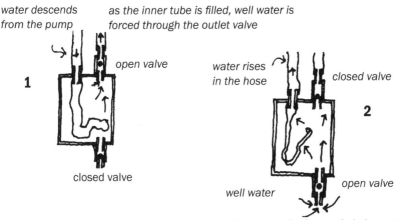

*water descends from the pump*

*as the inner tube is filled, well water is forced through the outlet valve*

*open valve*

**1**

*closed valve*

*water rises in the hose*

*closed valve*

**2**

*well water*

*open valve*

*as the inner tube is emptied, the water enters the container from below*

## CONSTRUCTION DETAILS

The pump is made from a 2-inch pipe with two drilled end-caps, and a plunger rod with a leather washer. Weld a small tube to the hole in one of the caps. Insert the rod through the hole in the other cap, attach a nut, a washer, the leather washer, a second washer, and the second nut to the rod. Then attach both caps to the pipe.

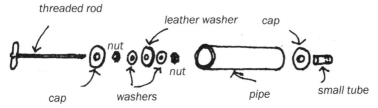

*threaded rod*

*leather washer*    *cap*

*nut*

*nut*

*cap*     *washers*     *pipe*     *small tube*

Weld the two valves and a ½-inch metal connecting tube to the metal container. Place the capped inner tube in the container through the tube, then fold the end of the inner tube over the metal tube (**a**).

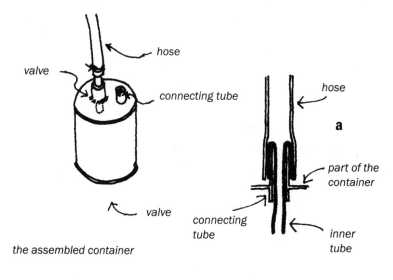

The valves are made with steel tubes containing a lightweight metal ball bearing; the ball must be light enough for the water to lift it, and it must be heavy enough to seal the opening when it falls.

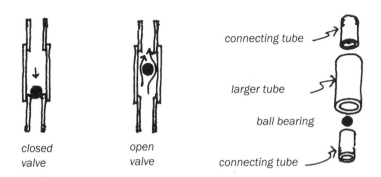

closed
valve

open
valve

connecting tube

larger tube

ball bearing

connecting tube

The ball bearing falls with its own weight into the lower tube, closing off the opening. When the water pressure from below increases, the bearing rises and water enters the container.

Another way to make valves is by using plastic tubes with a rounded rubber cap fastened to one side with a screw. The advantage of this type of valve is that it can be installed horizontally.

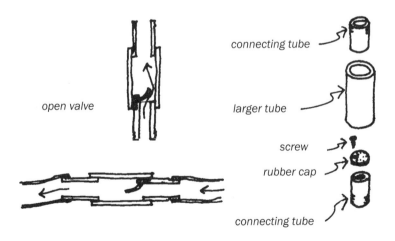

open valve

connecting tube

larger tube

screw

rubber cap

connecting tube

Verify that the check valve is only allowing water to pass in one direction.

A check valve can be made from one large tube, capped with two smaller tubes connected to the inlet and outlet hoses. One small tube extends past its cap into the large tube, is plugged, and has several holes drilled in its side. Before finally installing the caps to the large tube, slip a loosely snug rubber tube over the holes of the smaller tube.

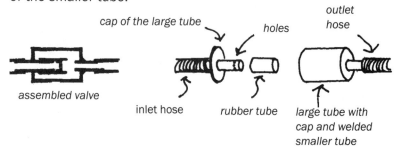

assembled valve

cap of the large tube    holes    outlet hose

inlet hose    rubber tube    large tube with cap and welded smaller tube

In areas with constant winds, connect a pump piston to a barrel mill. (See chapter 7.)

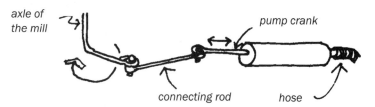

axle of the mill    pump crank

connecting rod    hose

Then connect the hose to a nearby cistern.

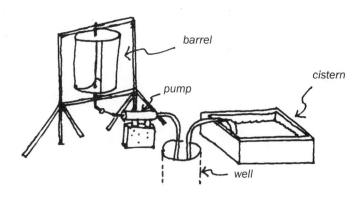

barrel

cistern

pump

well

## BUMP PUMP

Install a check valve on a supported rubber hose. Hit the hose with a hammer. Watch the water get pumped from one end to the other.

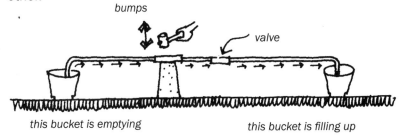

bumps

valve

*this bucket is emptying*     *this bucket is filling up*

At least 400 bumps per minute are needed for the water to move. The quicker the bumps, the more water will move. For example, you can pump 1000 liters of water per hour with 1600 bumps per minute on a 10cm-diameter hose,

How do you produce this many bumps? Use a wind-powered barrel mill with a metal chain welded around the outside base of a barrel.

Each link bumps a lever in a rapid rhythm that compresses the rubber tube against a metal backing plate. The lever is a rounded triangular shape, and is fastened to the plate with a screw. Lubricate as needed.

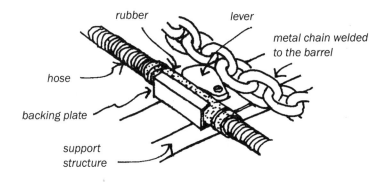

rubber     lever

metal chain welded to the barrel

hose

backing plate

support structure

Asssemble the structure with the barrel mill between the well and
the cistern:

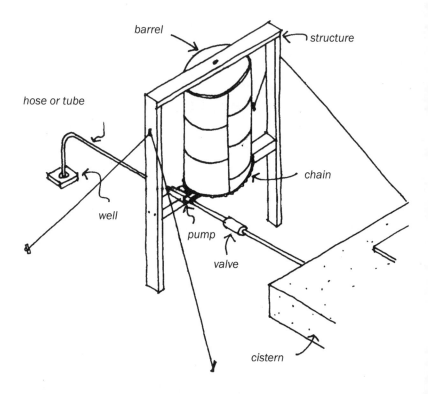

In a region with a constant breeze, the pump is always in motion,
and even a leaky cistern will remain filled.

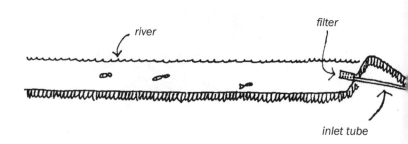

## HOW TO RAISE WATER WITH ITS OWN POWER

To raise river water up a sloped bank, a hydraulic ram-pump can be built to raise water with mechanical power, using as an energy source the difference in height between the water inlet and the level of the pump's location.

The drawing below shows an example of this system, with a 2-meter inlet-to-pump height difference and an 8-meter rise to the tank above. Using this difference, 200 liters of water per day can be pumped 20 meters uphill.

As the rise becomes greater, the quantity of pumped water decreases. For example, only 80 liters a day can be pumped up a 40-meter rise.

The water enters the pump through an inclined tube. The water rushing down the inlet pipe creates a rhythmic surge at the pump, forcing the water to rise to the tank above the pump.

The rhythm of the pumping must be adjusted so that the pump works slowly, and care must be taken that the level of the river always remains above the inlet pipe to prevent air from entering.

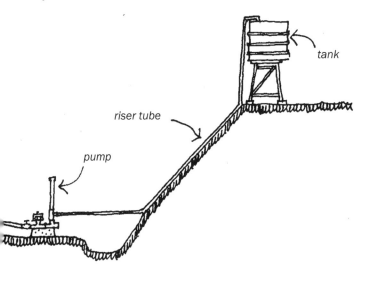

tank

riser tube

pump

## THE PARTS

The inlet tube has a 1:4 slope (15 degrees), and must not have any curves or joints. Place a filter or fine mesh over the inlet opening.

The pump is made from three 50mm T-fittings, 1 meter of tube of the same gauge, a few steel connection fittings, a 3mm steel plate, 2¾" reducer fittings, and several bolts with nuts. The pump must be solidly installed on a wood or concrete base to stabilize the motion of the moving water.

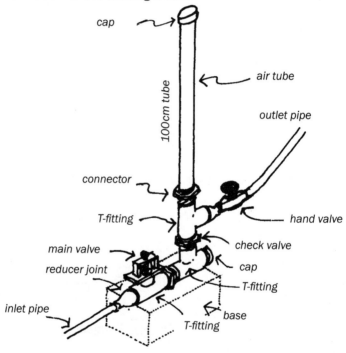

cap

100cm tube

air tube

outlet pipe

connector

T-fitting

hand valve

main valve

check valve

reducer joint

cap

T-fitting

inlet pipe

base

T-fitting

## CONSTRUCTION

**1** First assemble the main valve support structure using ¾-inch steel angle iron and a 50mm x 300mm steel plate. All parts must be welded solidly because the strong hammering action caused by the main valve may loosen the joints.

**2**     Next, assemble the main valve components. Add the 4 cm
        spring to the bolt, and insert the bolt into the support struc-
        ture, tightening the nuts so that the spring is compressed.

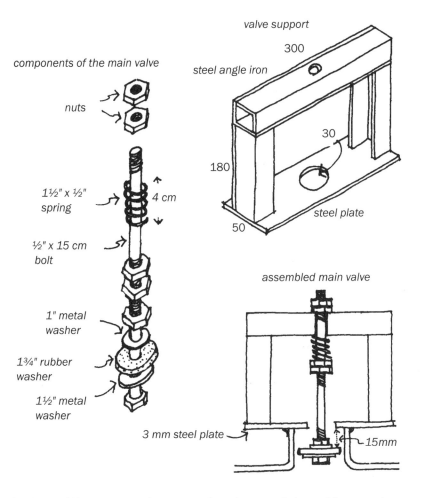

*components of the main valve*

*nuts*

*valve support*

300

*steel angle iron*

*1½" x ½" spring*

4 cm

180

30

*½" x 15 cm bolt*

50

*steel plate*

*1" metal washer*

*assembled main valve*

*1¾" rubber washer*

*1½" metal washer*

*3 mm steel plate*

15 mm

Leave a 15 mm space between the plate and the rubber washer.
The rhythm of the pumping action is regulated by adjusting the
compression of the spring.

**3** Now assemble the check valve that prevents water back-flow. It is made from a connector fitting, with a perforated steel disk welded inside. Fit a small cotter pin loosely into a 1mm hole in the side of the connector to act as a pressure-relief device.

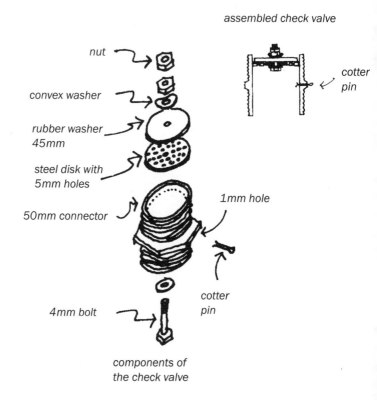

*assembled check valve*

nut

convex washer

rubber washer 45mm

steel disk with 5mm holes

50mm connector

1mm hole

cotter pin

4mm bolt

cotter pin

*components of the check valve*

**4** Bolt the rubber and metal washers to the top of the disk. The metal washer should be convex-shaped to ease the passage of water past the top edges of the rubber washer.

**5** Attach the capped 1-meter air chamber tube, and then connect the inlet and outlet pipes. Install a shut-off valve between the outlet pipe and the pump.

## OPERATING THE PUMP

Before operating, the outlet pipe is primed by filling it with water.

The pump operates as water descends the inclined inlet pipe and flows out to the ground through the open main valve. The velocity of the water forces the main valve to slam shut. The momentum surge of the water carries past the main valve and then pushes water through the check valve and into the outlet pipe. This releases the pressure back at the main valve, which is then pushed open by the spring. The process is then repeated as water once more flows down the inlet pipe.

The spring tension of the main valve controls the speed of this process. If there is too much spring tension, the valve does not close; if too little tension, the valve stays closed all the time. Proper tension allows the water flowing through the main valve to close the main valve forcefully, causing a surge of water past the check valve.

The pump must operate between 40 and 130 beats per minute. A greater quantity of water is pumped at slower speeds.

## PROBLEMS

 If the pump is not working after adjusting the main valve spring tension, check that the rubber washers are closing tightly.

 If air enters the outlet pipe, use a tighter-fitting cotter pin in the check valve hole.

 If the pump makes a lot of noise, use a looser cotter pin in the check valve hole.

This type of pump requires little maintenance. The filter mesh must be kept clean and the nuts tight, since they loosen in time. Also check the rubber washers and change them as needed.

# MOVING WATER

The next two pages show how two water sources are affected by the development of their neighboring communities.

Imagine a place with a hill and grove of trees...

→ A group of people build their houses in the grove where there is water. Trees are cut down. Without vegetation, the rainwater does not get absorbed and runs down to the base of the hill. Now the few remaining trees do not have water.

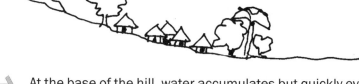

→ At the base of the hill, water accumulates but quickly evaporates. The people must now pipe the little water remaining uphill to their houses.

Meanwhile...

 Another group of people build their houses at the bottom of the hill, without removing any trees:

and when it rains,

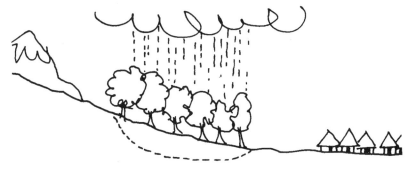

 the water remains in the grove and does not evaporate. The water is directed towards the settlement.

 It goes without saying that the beautiful grove is still there for walks and recreation...

## BAMBOO PIPING

Before making bamboo pipes, make a chisel to remove the knots from the bamboo:

*avant de fabriquer des tuyaux en bambou, faire un burin pour enlever les noeuds.*

**1** Use an end of a 12mm bolt or steel rod. Flatten one of the ends with a hammer.

*utiliser un bout de fer de 12mm diamètre ou du bois dur - aplatisser le bout avec un marteau*

$\updownarrow$ 12mm

*flatten one end*

**2** Sharpen the end with a file or rock.

*affûter le bout avec une lime ou un caillou*

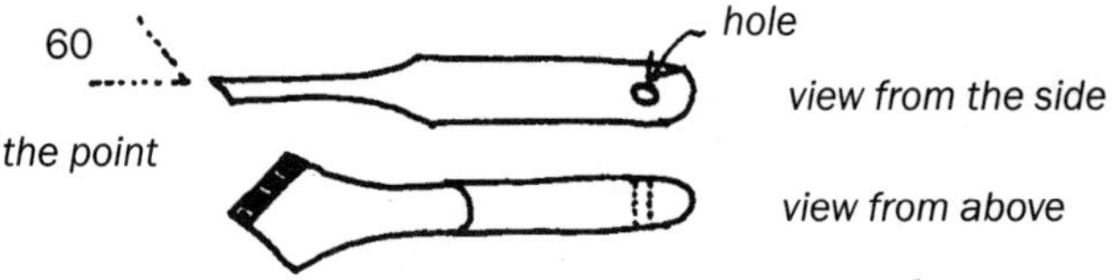

60

*hole*

*view from the side*

*the point*

*view from above*

**3** Insert the end into ½-inch-diameter and 6mm-long common water pipe. Make a 4mm hole and fasten them together with a nail or bolt, as shown below.

*insérer le bout dans un tuyau à eau sin 1/2 inch de long, fixer avec un clou ou une vis, l'ensemble*

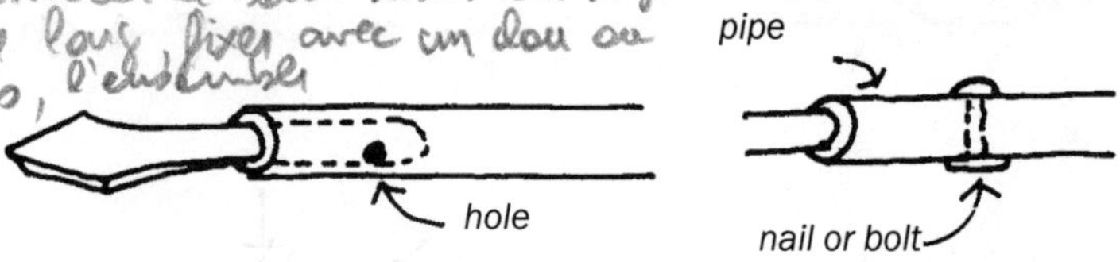

*pipe*

*hole*

*nail or bolt*

**4** On the other end of the pipe, install a bamboo rod capped by a knot to make a handle.

*à l'autre bout du tuyau, fixer un bambou fermé par un noeud pour faire une poignée*

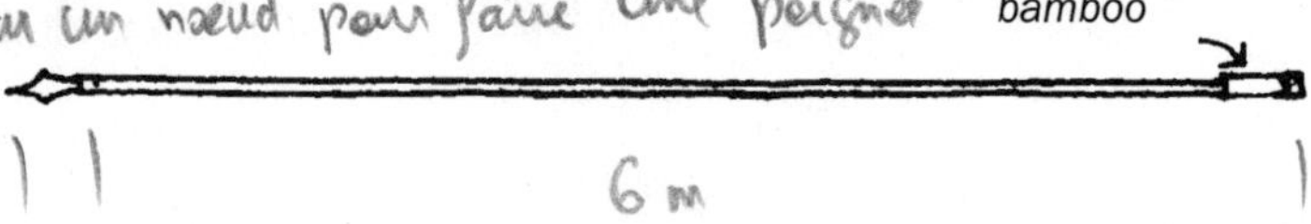

*bamboo*

6 m

The chisel is used in the following way:

*le burin est utilisé de la manière suivante*

One person holds the bamboo, while another inserts the chisel,
and a third rotates the tube using a plumber's wrench (with teeth
for gripping).

*une personne tient le bambeau pendant qu'une autre entre e burin et effectue des rotations, en utilisant une clé de plombier*

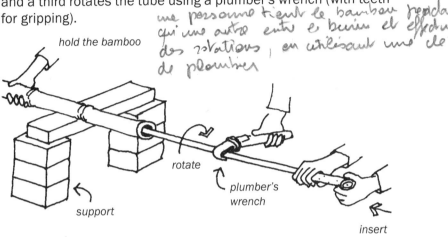

hold the bamboo

rotate

plumber's wrench

support

insert

*removing bamboo knots with a chisel*

If a wrench is not available, make a strap wrench with a strip of
leather and a wooden handle as illustrated below:

*Si il n'y a pas de clé disponible, fabriquez une clé à courroie avec une bande de cuir et une poignée en bois comme idessus ci-dessus*

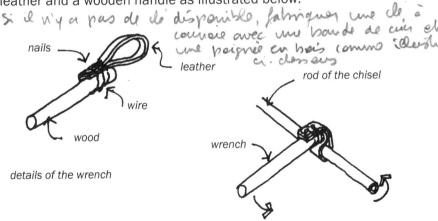

nails

leather

rod of the chisel

wire

wood

wrench

*details of the wrench*

*using the strap wrench*

## BAMBOO PIPES

Bamboo pipes can last between 4 and 6 years, depending on the quality of the bamboo and climate.

The best way to install the piping is underground on top of a layer of leaves and earth.

There are areas where the bamboo cannot be buried, such as on steep banks.

The joints between lengths of bamboo are made with leather or pieces of rubber from inner tubes.

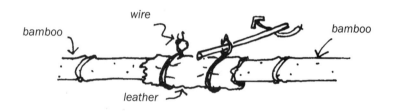

The leather must be soaked overnight and installed wet; as it dries, the leather shrinks tightly around the bamboo.

One advantage of this type of joint is that the bamboo pipes can be made to curve slightly.

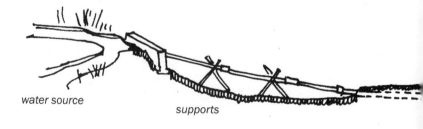

## OPEN PIPES

Some types of bamboo are not appropriate for piping but can be used to make open troughs.

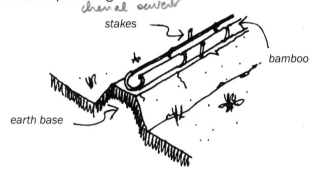

## BAMBOO GARDEN FAUCET

After installing the piping, make a bamboo faucet valve:

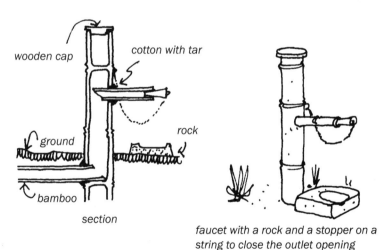

faucet with a rock and a stopper on a
string to close the outlet opening

buried bamboo piping

## EARTH-CEMENT DUCTS

*tuyau en plastique flexible*

Large ducts for drinking water distribution/main pipes can be made using an earth-cement mixture and a flexible, strong plastic hose. The hose is 20-30 meters long and has a 20cm diameter when full.

**1** Prepare the bottom of the trench with a thin layer of earth-cement.

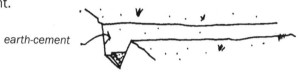

*earth-cement*

**2** Install the hose with one of its ends tightly closed and the other raised one meter above the ground and supported on a post.

**3** Fill the hose with water. The raised end creates pressure on the walls of the hose.

*tied end*        *fill the tube*

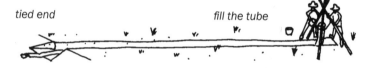

**4** Cover the pipe with an 8:1 mixture of earth-cement. Let it dry for a few days. When the cement is dry, fill the rest of the trench with earth.

*support posts*

*filler*

*plastic hose*

*trench*

*earth-cement duct*

**5** Finally, lower the raised end of the hose and let the water out. Pull the entire empty hose from the earth-cement duct and repeat the process until the duct reaches the required length.

## MILL TO RAISE WATER

A water mill can be built with bamboo tubes to raise water from a river having a strong current.

The ends of each tube are tied to the supports. One end is tied in front and the other in back of the blades. The closed end of each tube is farther away from the axle than the open end, so the water spills out of the raised tube.

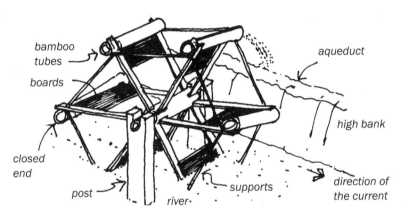

The support ends are connected with strips of bamboo or twine to reinforce the structure of the mill. Attached to the tube are blades made with boards fastened between two supports, so that the river's current makes the mill rotate.

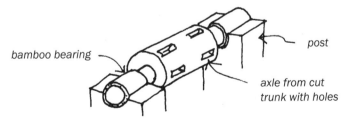

The axle is a large log with holes in which to insert the supports. At the ends of the tube, use pieces of bamboo as bearings. These bamboo pieces are supported on a notch in the posts so that the axle turns smoothly. Now build an aqueduct to carry the water to farm land or into cisterns.

# CISTERNS

In regions with long dry periods, it is convenient to have cisterns to store rainwater. The rain can be collected in roof gutters and directed to the cistern. Gutters can be made from metal, bamboo split in half or tree bark.

➡ The cistern must be close to the house and far from polluted areas such as toilets, stables or septic tanks.

➡ The size of the cistern depends on the length of the dry period and on the family's daily water use.

➡ At the beginning of the rainy season, discard the first few liters of rainwater because they are contaminated with dust and dirt from the roof.

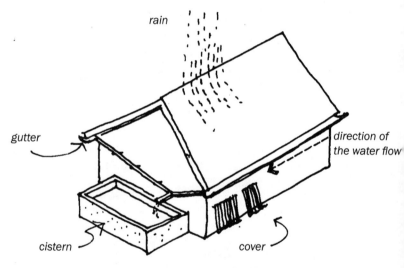

Water that runs off thatch roofs must be filtered before being used, because smoke from the chimney contaminates the thatch and makes the water taste unpleasant.

A good water storage system has three components:

**A** A cistern for the water.

**B** A gravel and sand filter.

**C** A sedimentation tank. This tank must be cleaned occasionally to remove the sludge from the bottom.

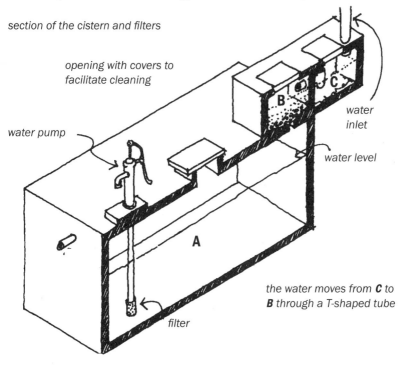

section of the cistern and filters

opening with covers to facilitate cleaning

water pump

water inlet

water level

the water moves from **C** to **B** through a T-shaped tube

**A**

filter

There are different ways to install the three parts, depending on
the space available.

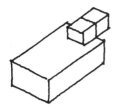 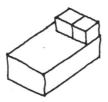 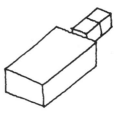

The walls are made with rocks, cement blocks or bricks.

**1**     First compact the floor and install rocks; let them settle for a few days.

**2**     Apply the earth-cement mixture and fill the rock joints.

**3**     To waterproof, apply cactus juice to the floor.

**4**     Make a smooth, hand-polished finish with a mixture of fine sand.

Repeat the process for the walls

## BARREL CISTERNS

In rainy areas where there are no dry seasons, large cisterns are not necessary. The cisterns can be integrated into the house.

The rainwater can be stored in tanks, reservoirs or linked drums.

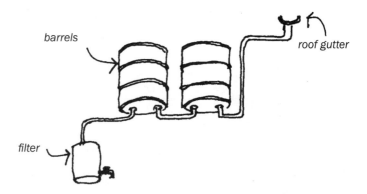

The barrels must be installed below the roof and above the areas where the water will be used, such as the kitchen and bathroom. A pump is not needed using this system. Entire or half-drums can be used. The tops are covered, but not sealed

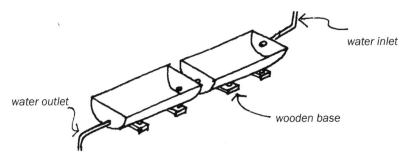

water inlet

water outlet

wooden base

Shown below are two examples of installation; the first one is for a house built on a slope, and the second is for a two-storey house on a flat site.

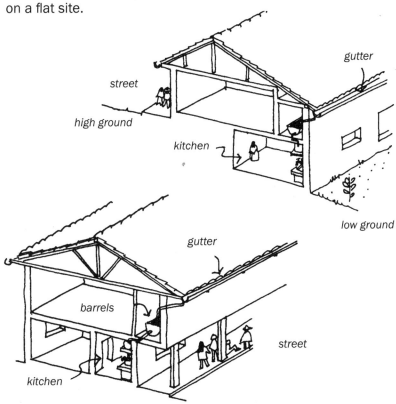

gutter

street

high ground

kitchen

low ground

gutter

barrels

kitchen

street

In urban zones where houses are built close together, courtyards or streets can be used to collect water.

## VENETIAN CISTERN

The water for a Venetian cistern can be collected from a courtyard. In the center or on one side of the cistern, install a pump to raise the filtered water.

The walls of the pump's well are impermeable and have holes in the lower part to allow water to enter.

Install spaced paving blocks at ground level to allow water to run through to the ground. A slight inclination slows down the filtration of water through the layers of sand on top of gravel.

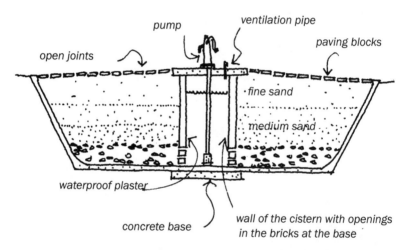

The cistern is made of bricks with a mortar finish. If the house does not have a courtyard, the cistern can be built in a garden.

## EXCAVATING A WELL

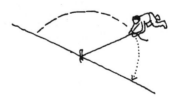

If the ground is very loose, a solid wall must be made.

**1** Construct a 2-meter-diameter flat wooden hoop from 10 cm x 20 cm boards held together with a metal band.

**2** Now make a circle on the ground which is a little larger than the hoop. Excavate a 50 cm trench and install a circular concrete foundation in the trench.

**3** Build up the wall above the hoop, leaving openings in the first four brick courses for water to enter.

**4** When the wall reaches a height of 1 meter high, excavate below the base of the hoop to allow the wall to gradually settle into the ground.

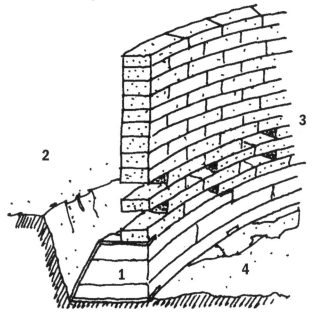

**5** After settling, build up another meter of wall.

**6** Repeat the process until the bottom of the well is far enough below the groundwater level to reliably produce sufficient water.

## A BAMBOO-CEMENT WATER RESERVOIR

Water reservoirs can be made using the construction technique for bamboo panels. (See chapter 6.)

Install a drainage tube in the lower part and apply mortar to a large bamboo basket. Apply 4 layers of mortar on both outside and inside, and let it cure for one week while covered with damp cloth. Then let it cure completely for three weeks.

Described below is the method for applying the layers of mortar:

**1**    Fill a box with 1½cm of mortar.

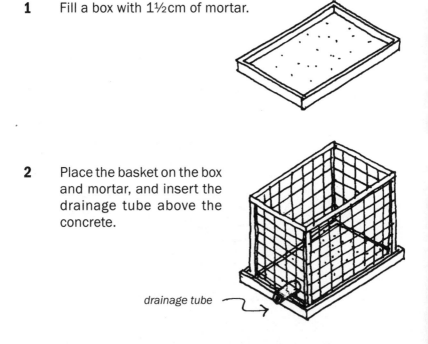

**2**    Place the basket on the box and mortar, and insert the drainage tube above the concrete.

*drainage tube*

The bamboo drainage tube should be soaked in water for three hours before applying the mortar around it.

**3**    Next apply a 1cm layer on
        the outside.

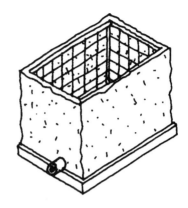

**4**    Two days later apply the
        inside layer.

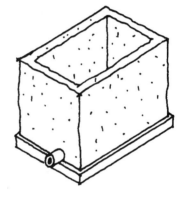

**5**    One day later, apply a sec-
        ond layer to both inside
        and outside.

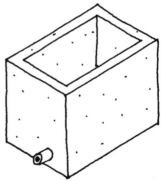

Polish the suface of the final layer with a rich mortar mixture.

# FILTERS

## WATER TREATMENT

A drum filter can be built to filter water. On the top, weld a funnel to make it easier to fill. Occasionally, clean the sand to remove sedimentation. When only half the quantity of sand remains, replace it with new sand and charcoal.

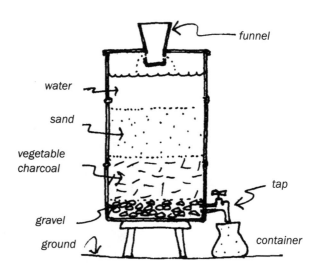

Polluted water must be disinfected beforehand by filtering it through a container with a layer of lime on top of a layer of sand. Place a plate under the filter to prevent the water from hollowing out the sand. Another better system is shown on page 636.

(a)  stones
(b)  sand with lime
(c)  stones
(d)  holes

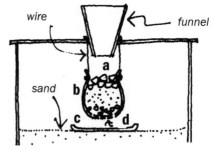

The water can also be boiled for 20 minutes and then poured from one container to another several times to oxiginate the water.

## AN EASY-MAINTENANCE FILTER

Described below is a drum filter where the water enters from below and exits from the top, making it a self-cleaning filter.

Construction:

**1**    Cut off one end of a drum and trim the end so it fits inside the drum. Drill 2mm to 3mm holes spaced 5cm from each other.

**2**    Drill and clean holes for the inlet and outlet pipes.

**3**    Paint the inside surface with non-toxic, anti-corrosive paint.

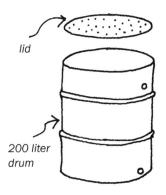

lid

200 liter drum

After the filter has been used for some time, the sedimentation in the sand must be removed. Close the inlet valve and remove the lid. Open the cleanout valve. The water discharged by the cleanout valve cleans the sand by flushing impurities. Close the cleanout valve, put the lid back on, and open the inlet valve.

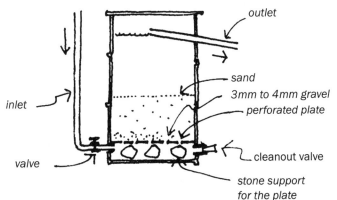

outlet

sand
3mm to 4mm gravel
perforated plate

inlet

valve

cleanout valve

stone support for the plate

Shown above is a section of the drum filter.

## BIOLOGICAL FILTER

A biological filter is a layer of organic matter, a type of slime layer, that gathers on the surface of the sand after two weeks of use. This fine layer is an efficient biological filter that retains and digests harmful microorganisms that might be in the water. Filter the water with a fine sieve beforehand, since the slime layer only filters microorganisms.

## BUILDING A FERROCONCRETE BIOLOGICAL FILTER

Build six 2m x 0.60m rectangular panels and two hexagonal panels with 0.60m sides, using the technique described on page 522.

**1**   Join the plates to make a hexagonal container. Install the container on a masonry base.

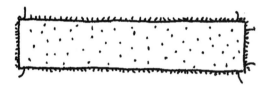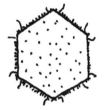

**2**   Install the inlet, outlet and cleaning pipes on the sides of the container. (See drawing next page.)

**3**   Apply an impermeable layer of cactus juice on the inside and outside surfaces. See page 332 for details.

**4**   Fill the container with water to check for leaks.

**5**   Place 50cm of gravel at the bottom of the filter and 50cm of sand on top of the gravel.

A 2m-high biofilter with a 60cm hexagonal base has approximately a 1m² filtering area and a capacity to filter 1600 liters of water a day.

## MAINTENANCE

In time, the slime layer becomes overgrown and the passage of water is reduced. To clean the filter, connect the inlet hose (**e**) to the outlet (**s**) to reverse the water flow. Plug the cleaning pipe (**t**) before opening the valve. The water rises and lifts the slime and the impurities. Once cleaned, place the hoses back to their original positions and wait two weeks for a new slime layer to form before drinking the water.

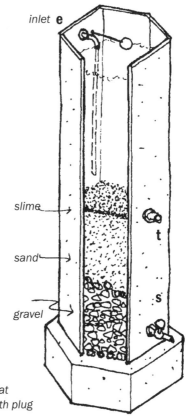

During this two-week wait, the water can be used for bathing, laundry or watering the garden.

Ideally, build two filters so that there is always one providing drinking water.

The sand in the filter must be fine and pre-cleaned. Add a hose spray attachment to the inlet tube to disperse the water and lessen the impact of the falling water to the top layer of sand.

The valve on the outlet is used to regulate the flow of the filtered water. The water must not run at a rate greater than one liter per minute for a 1m² filtering area.

*inlet* **e**

*slime*

*sand*

**t**

*gravel*

:**s**

(e)   *inlet with ball-float*
(t)   *cleaning tube with plug*
(s)   *outlet with valve*

In the illustration above, one of the vertical panels has been removed in order to display the interior layers of the filter.

## BASIN FILTER

A basin filter can be made that will prevent the earth near the house from becoming polluted by detergents and soaps.

**1**     In a common basin or sink, install a 25cm-long drainpipe.

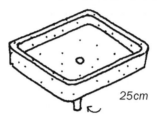

25cm

**2**     Construct a grease tank on a concrete base. (See page 614.) Cover the inside with an impermeable layer of cement. Dirty foam is kept from entering the filter by using two tubes of different diameters.

**3**     Insert one tube into the other and then attach both into one of the corners.

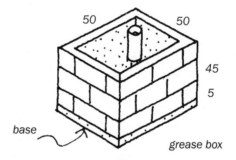

50          50

45

5

base

grease box

**4**     The brick filter box is built on a concrete pad. On the lower part of one side, install an outlet. On the upper inside part of another wall, install a projecting brick as a baffle to spread the force of the incoming water.

**5**    Fill the bottom of the box with coarse sand, add a layer of vegetable charcoal, and top with fine sand. Set the lid on and install the tank on top of the box. Occasionally, the filter will need to be disassembled to clean out the grease and replace the sand.

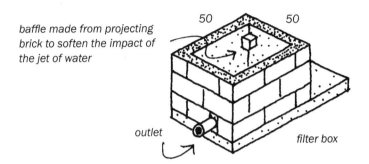

baffle made from projecting
brick to soften the impact of
the jet of water

50      50

outlet

filter box

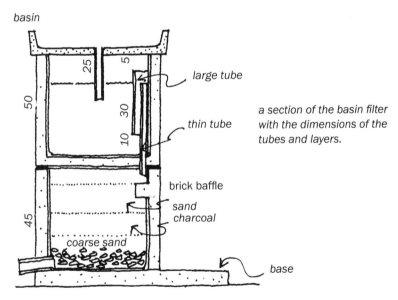

basin

25   5

50

30

10

45

large tube

thin tube

brick baffle

sand
charcoal

coarse sand

base

a section of the basin filter
with the dimensions of the
tubes and layers.

If the filter has been used for a while, remove the water from the grease box so it does not become foul.

The filtered water can be used to water plants.

# PURIFICATION

## PURIFYING WATER

A solar evaporator can be used to transform either salty or unclean water from sinks or showers into potable water. To understand how it works, try the following test:

**1**    Excavate a 60cm x 60cm x 60cm-deep hole in the ground.

**2**    Place a can in the bottom center of the hole.

**3**    Cover the hole with transparent plastic, holding down the edges with sand.

**4**    In the center place a small stone, so that the plastic is depressed slightly.

*the hole seen from above*

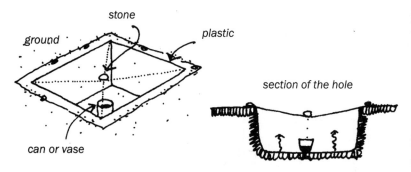

*After a clear day, the can will be full of water.*

In this test, water in the damp earth evaporates when the temperature rises under the plastic. When the vapor touches the plastic it transforms into drops in a process called condensation. The inclination of the plastic from the weight of the stone directs the drops to drip towards the center of the plastic, where they fall into the can.

A larger quantity of water can be produced by placing a few plants inside the hole.

## SOLAR DISTILLER

In regions with a lot of sun and scarce water, you can use a solar distiller to purify salt water or polluted water.

The distiller is made from a tray placed inside a wooden box that has a glass cover. One side of the box is higher than the other, creating a sloped cover to direct the water to a gutter. The box must be well sealed around the tray area.

Depending on the construction of the box and the climatic conditions, a distiller of this type with a one-meter-square tray can purify between four and nine liters of water per day.

## HOW THE DISTILLER WORKS

The sun's rays heat the water and it evaporates and rises (**1**). When the vapor hits the glass, it condenses into water drops (**2**) that run down the sloped glass cover into a gutter made from a half-tube (**3**); the drops flow through the sloped tube into a container.

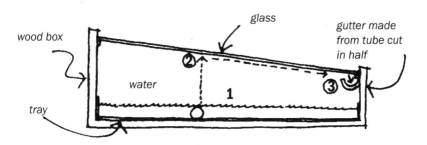

The gutter extends out from the box and is connected to a flexible tube linked to a container to collect the distilled water.

## HOW TO DISTILL LARGER QUANTITIES

➡ Install the sloped glass close to the top of the water's surface.

➡ Place a fine black cloth on top of the water. The fibers of the cloth help evaporation to occur.

➡ Install the distiller in such a way that wind passing over the glass cools it and increases condensation.

➡ Pre-heat the water before it enters the box with a small 10-liter solar heater. The connection pipe must be insulated.

➡ Vibration on the glass make the drops fall more quickly. You can produce vibrations on the boxes with a small windmill.

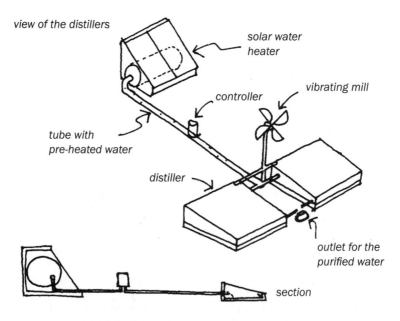

view of the distillers

solar water heater

controller

vibrating mill

tube with pre-heated water

distiller

outlet for the purified water

section

A contoller must be installed when using pre-heated water so that the water level in the trays remains consistent. See the discussion of thermo-syphoning heaters and their controllers (pp. 560-563 above).

## LOCATION

Locate the distiller on the sunny side of the house. To control the quantity of water in the tray and facilitate the cleaning of the glass, the distiller should be located in an accessible place. The distiller must not be shaded by roof eaves or trees.

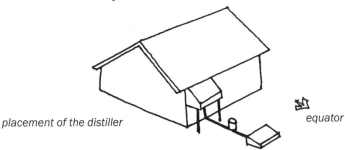

*placement of the distiller*

*equator*

## COMMON PROBLEMS

Shown below is an incorrectly built distiller:

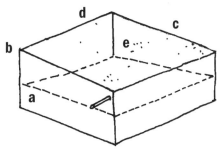

Why it is incorrect:

(**a**)    The water level is too high (more than 5 cm deep).

(**b**)    The air space between the water and the glass is too large: the glass is too high.

(**c**)    The glass is not sloped enough, so the drops do not fall towards the tube.

(**d**)    There is too much dust on the glass and water cannot heat up.

(**e**)    There is too much shade on the distiller.

## CONSTRUCTION OF LARGE DISTILLER

The tray is made from a 130cm x 90cm sheet of metal.

**1**    Fold up 5cm edges and spot-weld the corners together.

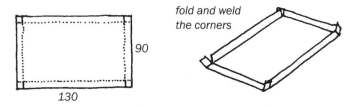

fold and weld
the corners

90

130

**2**    Paint the inside of the tray with matte black paint, and wrap it in insulating material such as 1-inch-thick styrofoam. If this is not locally available, use coconut fibers or sawdust.

**3**    Build a wooden box frame.

On the lower side of the box, install a tube cut in half lengthwise that projects out of both sides of the box. The tube is painted white on the inside. Now, install an inlet tube through which the non-potable water enters.

On top, install the glass pane in the frame using glass caulking or silicone.

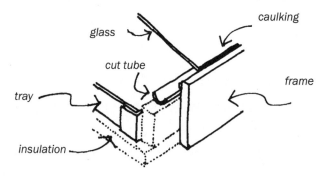

glass

caulking

cut tube

frame

tray

insulation

All the joints must be well sealed to keep hot air from escaping.

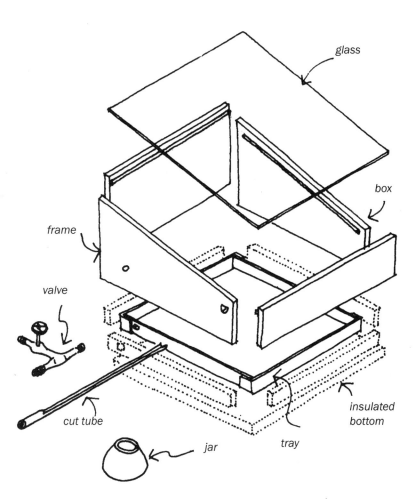

glass

box

frame

valve

cut tube

insulated
bottom

jar

tray

## MAINTENANCE

The glass must always be kept clean and dust-free. Check the sealed joints after a while to make sure no air is escaping between the wood frame and the glass pane.

When removing the potable water in the morning, refill the tray with non-potable water.

## OTHER TYPES OF DISTILLERS

An easy-to-maintain distiller can be made in regions where there is access to industrial products.

 Use a transparent plastic cover and an outlet tube cut lengthwise on one side of the box.

 The base is made from concrete, brick or metal, and is insulated. The area with the non-potable water is painted black, and the rest of the base is painted white.

The cover is embedded slightly into the ground, so that hot air does not escape, as shown below:

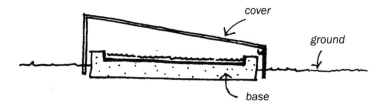

The jar is buried to keep the potable water cool.

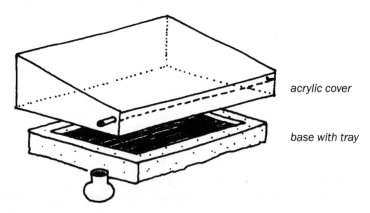

Another type of distiller that is easy and quick to build is made with a frame, a tube cut lengthwise or a piece of metal folded in a V-shape. The bottom can be made out of black plastic. The cover is a transparent plastic supported by a short pole.

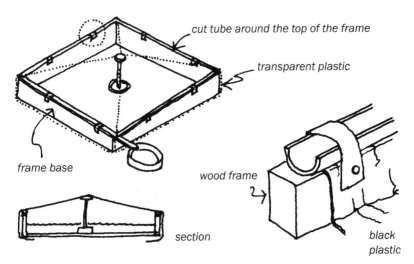

cut tube around the top of the frame

transparent plastic

frame base

wood frame

section

black plastic

Non-asbestos concrete tiles, or corrugated sheet metal made for roofing large spans, can also be used as a base for building distillers. The channels are covered with glass, as illustrated below.

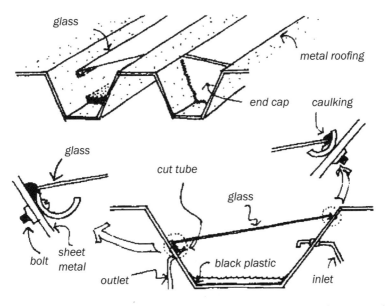

glass

metal roofing

end cap    caulking

glass

cut tube

glass

bolt    sheet metal

outlet

black plastic

inlet

section of a corrugated roofing channel

## COOLING PURIFIER

A purifier for salt water or used water (greywater) can also be used to cool water.

First build a box with a partition in the center. Cover the bottom and sides with black plastic.

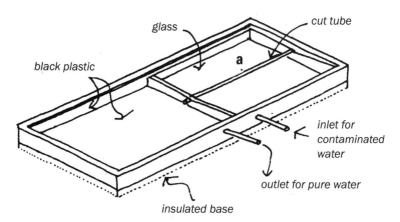

One of the sides of the box must have a tube cut lengthwise to collect the drops of water falling down the glass cover. Two pieces of glass are sloped towards the center and supported on an inverted steel T-section channel.

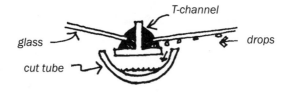

Shown below is a detail section of part (**a**) of the distiller.

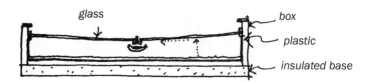

The purified water runs into another box to cool. The first box has an inlet for contaminated water. A wooden cover slides in tracks fastened to the top side above the glass sheets

At the end of the day, slide the glass cover over the wooden lid to expose the already distilled water to the night cold. During the day this position is reversed, and the cover acts as a thermal insulator for the water already distilled.

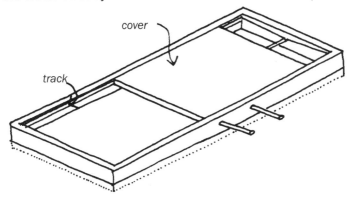

cover

track

At night uncover the holding area so that the water cools. During the day cover this area to keep the water cool.

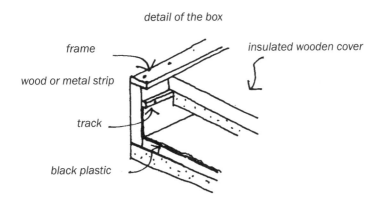

detail of the box

frame

insulated wooden cover

wood or metal strip

track

black plastic

The base and cover are insulated.

The distiller can be located on either the top or the side of a roof, depending on the roof's shape.

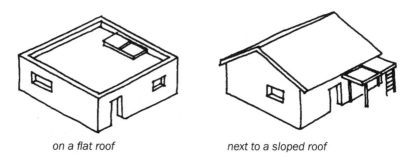

*on a flat roof*                    *next to a sloped roof*

In certain areas, the water could be exposed to insects or dust; cover the cold water box with glass or transparent plastic.

Move the cover with a string or use a ladder to reach the cover.

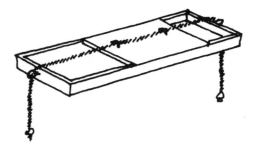

## COOL WATER

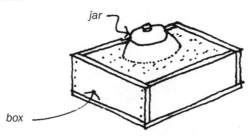

*jar*

*box*

To keep water cool, install a jar in a box of wet sand. The jar must be tightly closed.

Clay cooking pots can also be used:

 To cool air: Place a jar filled with water in windows or in other openings where air circulates. See chapter 3 for more details on this technique.

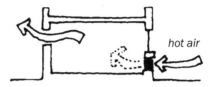

*section of the house with a cooling jar under the window*

*hot air*

 To preserve food: Place a glazed jar containing food inside an unglazed (porous) jar. Then add water between the two jars.

*lid*

*glazed jar*

*water*

*unglazed jar*

 To irrigate plants and trees: Use clay pots or vases with lids. Make small holes in the bottom of the containers. Bury the containers up to the necks. Fill them with water every 3 to 5 days. This technique uses much less water than surface irrigation.

*holes*

*water*

## DRIP IRRIGATION WITH CLAY POTS

Before embedding the jars in the garden beds, the ground must be prepared.

**1**   Making the garden beds.

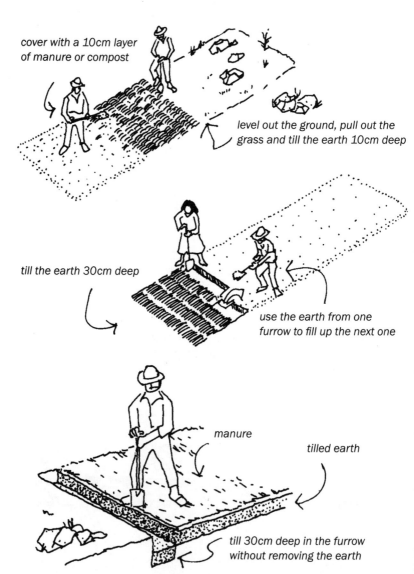

cover with a 10cm layer of manure or compost

level out the ground, pull out the grass and till the earth 10cm deep

till the earth 30cm deep

use the earth from one furrow to fill up the next one

manure

tilled earth

till 30cm deep in the furrow without removing the earth

**2**    After covering the beds with a new layer of manure, make
25cm-deep holes 40cm apart and insert the jars.

mouth of the jar must
be 5cm above ground

lids or stones
to cover the jars

**3**    Before planting seeds, fill the jars with water and cover the
opening with a lid or stone.

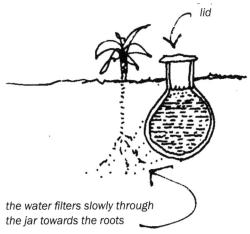

lid

the water filters slowly through
the jar towards the roots

Leave a 2-meter distance between jars in vegetable gardens with
trees or orchards.

Another way to irrigate is to place stones around tree trunks or bushes to gather moisture from the air.

## SOLAR FILTER

To purify a small quantity of impure water, pour it through a fine cloth placed over the opening of a transparent glass or plastic 2-liter bottle. Now shake the bottle. Plug the mouth of the bottle and let it sit facing the full sun — not in the shade — at a 45° angle for six hours.

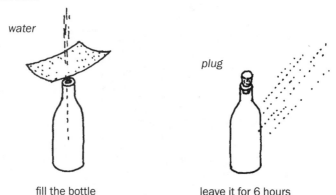

water

plug

fill the bottle              leave it for 6 hours

Water from this bottle must be used within the next six hours; bacteria can regroup and multiply if the water sits too long.

# COOLING & CONSERVATION

## FOOD STORAGE

Build a shelf unit with a tray at the top and standing in a larger tray at the bottom. Fill the top tray with water and cover the sides with a fine cloth with its lower ends touching the bottom tray. The water slowly wets the cloth, humidifying the shelf, and cooling the food.

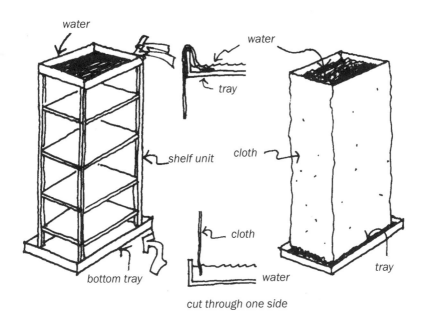

cut through one side

The cloth protects the food from insects and climbing creatures.

Another type of "refrigerator" is made with mosquito mesh and vegetable charcoal. Place a tray filled with water on top and a hanging cloth that is touching the charcoal.

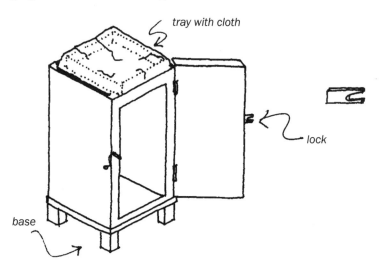

tray with cloth

lock

base

The lock is made with a piece of wood and a string with a big knot. The space between the cloths is filled with pieces of charcoal.

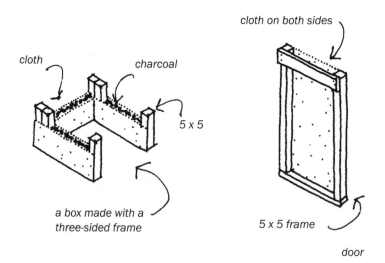

cloth on both sides

cloth            charcoal

5 x 5

a box made with a
three-sided frame

5 x 5 frame

door

In areas where water is scarce, use a vaporizer for bathing.

The vaporizer is a container with a pump that sprays vapor out like clouds of fine drops. These drops penetrate the surface of the skin. This cleans the skin very well and soap is not necessary.

Small or large vaporizers can be used to water plants as well.

*save on water with
a vaporizer or spray can*

## SAVING WATER

To use less water:

 Install a dry toilet to reduce daily use of water significantly. See chapter 9 for more details.

 Filter greywater (used water) and re-use it for irrigating or washing.

 Wash dishes and clothes with hot water from a solar heater. Hot water cleans more effectively and therefore uses less water.

 Bathe using a vaporizer that uses much less water.

The last two chapters showed ways to save energy and water.

The drawings below illustrate how these alternatives are used.

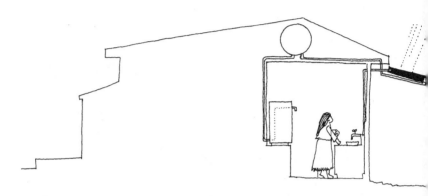

Here the kitchen water is heated with a solar collector.

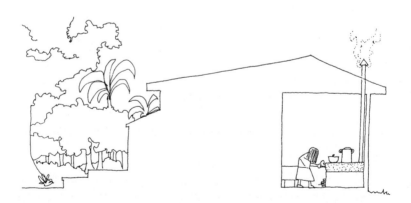

Here less wood is being used with a high-efficiency stove.

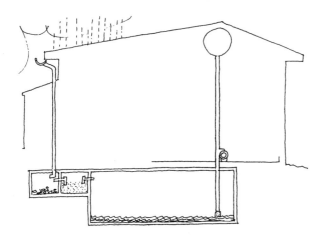

This rainwater is collected, filtered and stored in a cistern that feeds a reservoir.

A solar wall between a living room and a winter garden with the hot air rising to warm the living space.

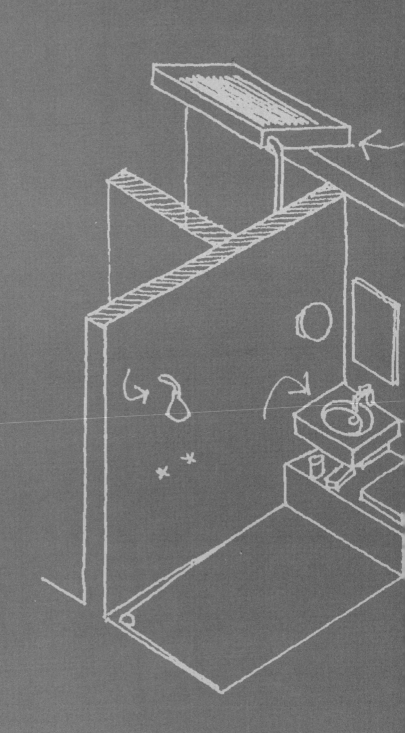

# SANITATION

9

# EQUIPMENT

Basically, there are two types of toilets: those that use water to flush out the human waste, and those that turn this waste into compost.

To choose which one to use, we must look at:

 The amount of water available. If there is only a limited amount, we should install a "dry" toilet.

 If we want to grow a vegetable garden and utilize the compost as a fertilizer.

 The environment, as a waterless toilet does not contaminate the subsoil nor the water table.

## FLUSH TOILETS

The used flush or black water from the outhouses should not pollute the drinking water source. Therefore the minimum distance between a water toilet and the well must be 15 meters and at least 5 meters from the house.

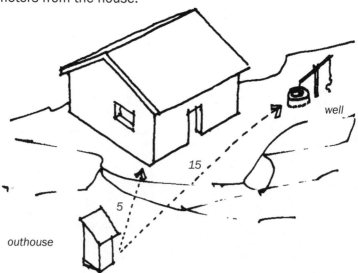

On sloping sites the outhouse must be located below the well or spring of drinking water.

## BUILDING AN OUTHOUSE

**1**    First make a solid border, with bricks or tree trunks, around
the edge of the pit.

**2**    Then build a concrete slab on top, with a bowl and a small
cabin.

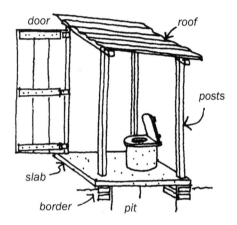

*View of an outhouse with the walls removed*

The reinforced border keeps the weight of the outhouse from destroying the edge of the pit. Moreover, it prevents rainwater from
running directly into the pit, which would make it collapse.

The bowl could be made out of wood or bricks with a wooden cover.
Shown below is a bowl made with bricks.

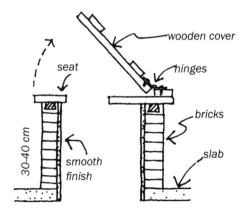

*section of bowl*

Instead of using a bowl, you could make a slab with a hole connected to a drainage pipe with a diameter of 10 or 15cm and a length of 30cm.

The slab is poured on the floor and covered with a piece of plastic, with a wooden frame which is removed after the concrete has set.

The drainpipe is set into the slab, with the rim slightly above the surface. In order not to dirty the feet, you make pads on both sides of the hole.

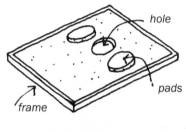

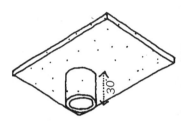

view from the top                    view from the bottom

## BUILDING THE PIT

Underneath the slab comes the pit, made with bricks or concrete blocks. This pit empties out via a pipe or draintiles into a trench.

Before using the system for the first time, you fill up the pit with water. There should always be sufficient water to make sure that the lower end of the pipe in the slab is submerged.

For this type of toilet, it isn't necessary to use clean water; you can use the water left over from washing clothes or dishes.

After a certain span of time, there will be a build-up of mud.

To ease the removal of the mud, make a sloped bottom floor; the cover slab is not fixed to the rim. With normal use, the pit needs to be cleaned once every two years. On the next page a section through the unit is shown.

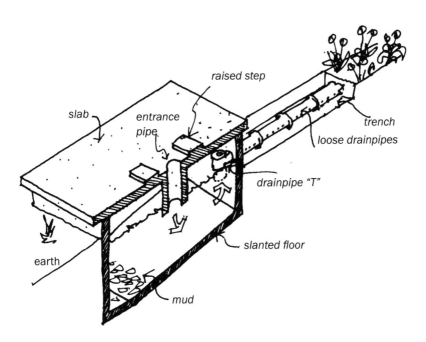

The exit drainpipes of 5 or 10cm are connected to the tank via a "T"-shaped pipe in order to keep the solids in the tank.

The plants in the trench help to purify the water; nevertheless this water is not fit for drinking and should be nowhere near a source of potable water.

## SEEPAGE TANK

On smaller-sized lots, instead of using a drainage trench like that illustrated above, you build a seepage or sump tank.

The wastewater which leaves the main tank goes to the seepage tank where it will leach into the surrounding soil. The dimensions and the amount of seepage will depend on the type of soil, which controls whether the water is drained slowly or rapidly.

The bottom floor and the walls are made with bricks or stones, leaving openings to let the water pass through.

The drawing below shows a section perspective:

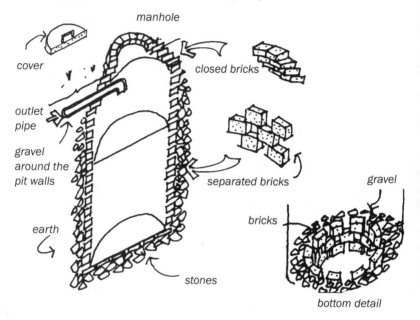

The rim above is made with joined bricks. The space between the walls and the excavation is filled with gravel or stones.

## COMPOSTING TOILETS

A waterless or composting toilet is appropriate when:

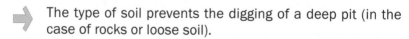 The type of soil prevents the digging of a deep pit (in the case of rocks or loose soil).

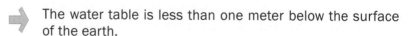 The water table is less than one meter below the surface of the earth.

Compost is needed to improve garden soil.

Sometimes people just make deep holes in the ground. When one is filled up, they cover the contents with earth and use the next hole.

Or the hole serves as a composting toilet, and after each use, the waste is covered with plants, turning the contents into fertilizer.

## TWO-COMPARTMENT COMPOST TOILET

**1** First you dig a hole with a depth of about 150 to 180 cm. The bottom will be the compartments' floor.

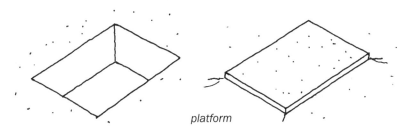

platform

In humid zones, use cement to strengthen the platform.

The compartments that receive the waste are made with bricks or blocks. The drawing below shows the use of 10 x 20 x 40 cm blocks.

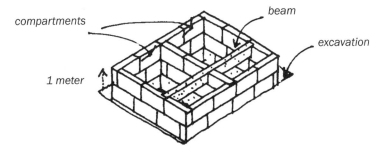

compartments

beam

excavation

1 meter

**2** The lower part of the compartments is raised to about one meter above the floor. To support the slab, use a small wooden or concrete beam.

**3**   Build the top part, leaving a double hole as a passageway
for the ventilation pipe.

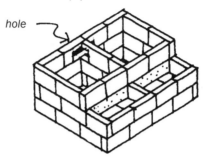

hole

**4**   Build the two covers out of concrete reinforced with chicken
wire. A block of wood is located at the spot where the waste
entrance pipe will be installed later.

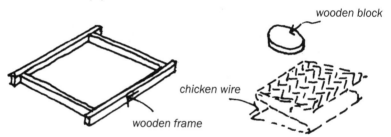

wooden block

chicken wire

wooden frame

**5**   To avoid entry of insects, seal the slabs and the vent pipe.
Then build two more covers for the lower part of the compartments.

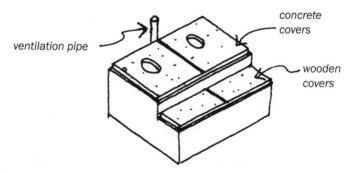

ventilation pipe

concrete
covers

wooden
covers

**6**   Next make two wooden covers for the compost-removal
openings.

**7**     The outhouse can be built using the same materials as were
        used for the house. The vent pipe could be bamboo, sheet-
        metal, or PVC; if hollow blocks are used for walls, you can
        leave a continuous opening like a built-in smokestack.

If the entrance of the outhouse faces south,* the covers should
be painted black.

Another way of reinforcing the edges of the excavation is by using
pieces of tree trunks in areas where cement is difficult to obtain.

**1**     Place 4 tree trunks
        over the hole.

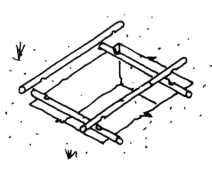

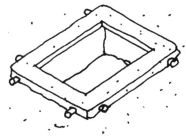

**2**     Make a mud frame to
        cover the tree trunks.

**3**     Using branches or bamboo
        as reinforcement, make a
        platform covered with mud
        as a base.

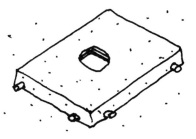

*This applies to the Southern Hemisphere; do the opposite in the Northern
Hemisphere.

Two important observations:

 To avoid leakage from rainwater, the compartments must be well sealed against infiltration.

 To prevent insects, which may carry diseases, from going inside the compartments, the joints between the covers and the slabs should be a tight fit.

## HOW TO USE THEM

Before using a composting toilet for the first time, fill the bottom part with humus, like dry leaves, straw or sawdust. This serves to absorb the liquids, is essential to the composting process and prevents the contents from getting solidified.

Only one compartment is used at a time. After it fills up, you cover the pile with cut grass and a thin layer of earth and then put a heavy weight, like a stone, on the cover and start using the other compartment.

Inside the outhouse, keep a small broom to clean the slab. Also have a small box with ashes, sawdust, or dry earth. After using the toilet, you throw a bit of the mix inside; the ashes serve to minimize smells.

When the second compartment is also full, it's time to clean out the first one, where the contents have turned into compost.

This compost is dry and odorless. Remove it with a shovel, and leave it exposed to the weather a while before using it in the garden as fertilizer.

However, the best way to get rid of waste is to build a "bason."

## THE BASON TOILET

Human waste (feces and urine) can be mixed with organic kitchen waste, and this mixture will slowly turn into an organic fertilizer in the shape of a loose, black earth.

Some of the advantages :

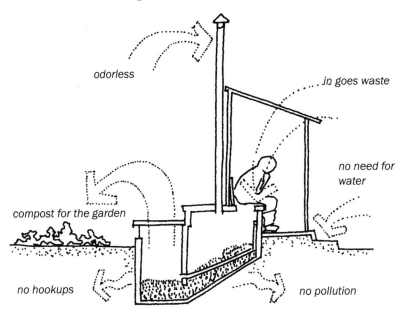

odorless

in goes waste

no need for water

compost for the garden

no hookups

no pollution

Thus, we can see that:

→ Human waste brought into contact with organic kitchen garbage will convert, in time (about six months), into an excellent fertilizer.

→ Incoming air ducts and a ventpipe make the operation odorless.

→ The bottom of the unit has a 30-degree slope to ease the downslide of the composting waste and leaves the material in a lower section, from which it can be removed yearly.

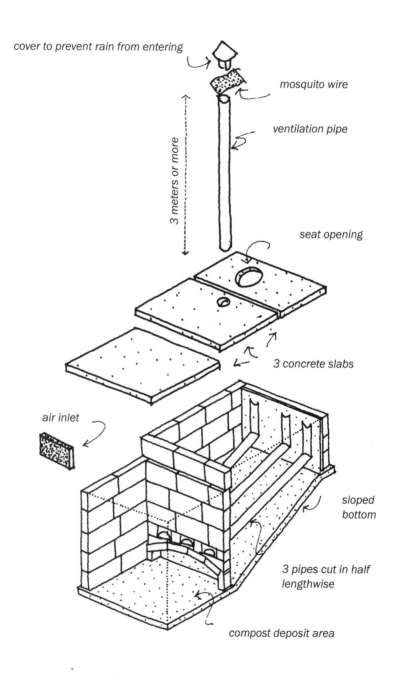

cover to prevent rain from entering

mosquito wire

3 meters or more

ventilation pipe

seat opening

3 concrete slabs

air inlet

sloped bottom

3 pipes cut in half lengthwise

compost deposit area

In addition to the bricks and cement, you will need wooden strips, 3cm wide; 1 metal pipe for ventilation; a PVC tube with a 10cm diameter; chicken wire; and some wooden boards for the seat and outside exit cover.

**1**     Make an excavation of about 2.50 x 1.25 meters; the lowest section, the compost area, stays at 1.20 meters below the bathroom floor; from there the bottom rises with a 30-degree slope.

**2**     Pour a 1.20 x 1.20 meter concrete floor as a base on the bottom area of the excavation.

**3**     Start the walls at the foundation, and as the height of the brick row gets to the sloped area, make the base with mortar.

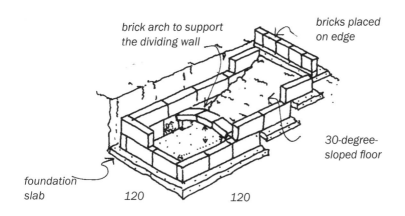

brick arch to support the dividing wall

bricks placed on edge

30-degree-sloped floor

foundation slab

120          120

To support the dividing wall, an arch is made at a 60cm distance from the end wall at a height of 30cm from the bottom. The top wall must be made with narrow bricks to make seat room.

**4**     Cover the sloped section with concrete; the thin wall above
          must have a very smooth finish.

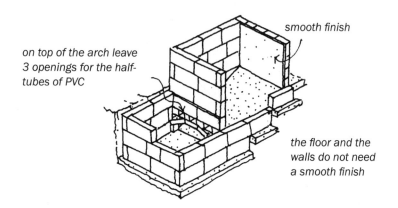

on top of the arch leave
3 openings for the half-
tubes of PVC

smooth finish

the floor and the
walls do not need
a smooth finish

Note: The blocks illustrated above have a dimension of 20 x 40
x 10cm.

**5**     The PVC pipes are cut in half to make rounded channels; for
          the inclined part, 3 pieces of 1.50 meters are needed and
          3 pieces of 50cm are nailed on the top wall.

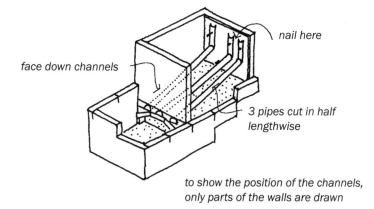

face down channels

nail here

3 pipes cut in half
lengthwise

to show the position of the channels,
only parts of the walls are drawn

The half-tube channels begin at the openings in the separation wall
and end about 10cm below the upper edge of the top wall.

First cut the pipes into 2 pieces of 150 cm and then cut them lengthwise in half.

If pipe is not available, then cut 20 cm-wide sheetmetal strips, bending them lengthwise in the middle and doubling the edges to strengthen them.

Make an elbow joint with the inclined and vertical sections; the points of the PVC pipes are bent using a small flame.

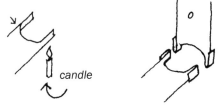

candle

**6**     A form is made with the wooden strips (see the drawings below) to make the openings for the ventpipe, and for the seat use a can and a pail; use ³⁄₁₆" rebar to make a 15 x 15 grid embedded in concrete.

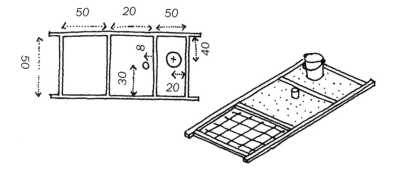

You can also use folded chicken wire instead of the rebar.

The dimensions shown above must be adjusted on the job, as the panels must have a close fit on top of the walls.

**7**   Two panels are set with mortar on the walls of the larger compartment; make certain that no cracks are left for insects to enter. The third panel has to be fixed on the walls using a weak mortar so you can remove the panel from time to time to remove the compost.

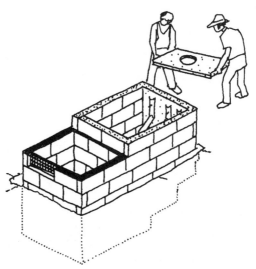

➡   Before covering the bason with the panels, put a 30cm layer of dry leaves, straw or hay on the bottom to receive the first waste.

**8**   The seat can also be made out of wooden boards; the opening is sealed with a piece of garden hose nailed to the cover.

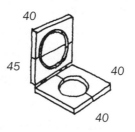

You can also get a plastic, factory-made seat and cover; however the cover has to fit tightly to keep out insects.

The small ventilation window is covered with window screen. The size of the window is the same as that of the concrete blocks used for the walls.

*opening is about 15cm above the ground*

 The ventpipe must be at least 3 meters long and start at the very top part of the upper compartment.

**9** The outer part of the ventpipe is painted matte black. This way the sun's rays will heat up the air inside and provide an updraft to force the compost odors away from the house.

*the top of the ventpipe is covered with mosquito wire to keep out the flies and with a cap to keep out rain*

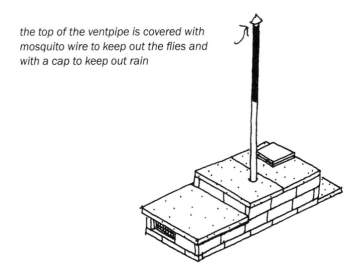

The overhanging edge of the lower panel keeps out the rain.

## THE PLACEMENT OF A BASON

On a sloped lot, the bason must be placed at the low side of the house in order to avoid rainwater building up at the foundation.

Moreover, the unit ought to be placed in such a way that the black-painted part of the ventpipe is exposed to the sun, free from the shade of the house or surrounding trees.

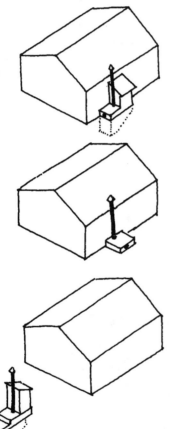

With existing houses, the bason is built against an outside wall.

With new construction, the bason is built inside the house and the compost compartment is part of the foundation.

A bason also could be built as a separate unit, but not close to a well, as the water could seep into the compartments and slow down the composting.

Note: It is recommended that the bason be built as shown in the drawings. Any deviation could hamper the operation inside the compartments.

In the case of a set of basons, as in a school, there could be one chamber below the floor panels with separate cubicles above. Since in public buildings there are proportionally more liquids, a narrow trench is made at the bottom of the lower compartment. The trench is open to the underside and filled with charcoal and gravel.

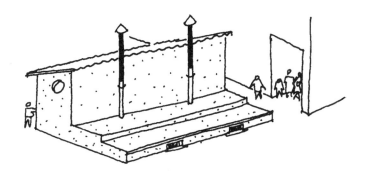

## WHAT ONE SHOULD KNOW ABOUT THE BASON

To facilitate the initial composting, you should cover the bottom with a layer of vegetable matter: leaves, hay, sawdust, and a bit of earth.

This layer will absorb the urine. No other liquid whatsoever should be poured into the compartments.

It could happen that during the first week flies will come out of the mixed waste; after that, the rising inside composting temperature should destroy insect larvae or eggs.

When the unit is not being used, the seat as well as the exit covers must be closed to maintain inside air circulation.

In addition to solid and liquid human waste, you can add organic kitchen garbage, and all kinds of vegetable waste, e.g., fruit peels or bones.

Never put cans, glass, plastics, wood, metals, soap, paints, medicines, detergents or cardboard in the bason.

## A PREFAB BASON

Using the thin-plate technique is a quicker and more economical way of making basons which could be produced in a neighborhood plant, thus also providing local jobs.

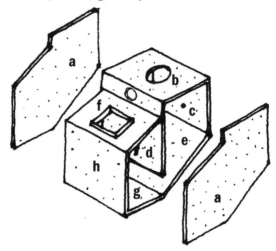

To assemble this type of bason, you will need nine panels of these dimensions:

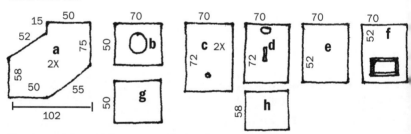

The type (c) panels carry a little piece of metal pipe to receive the end of the turning handle. In making panel type (b), which has the seat, use a plywood oval form for the opening. In the same way in panel (d), leave a circular space with a diameter of 10cm and a slot of 1 x 15cm. Panel (f) has an opening of 30 x 40 with an external rim of 2cm height.

To make the form for the panels use ½cm-thick strips, placed on a flat surface. With eight 8cm-wide strips, you can prefab all the panels.

Panel (a) fits in a square of 102cm. The size shown is for an average-sized family. You could enlarge the capacity, for example, by making the width of this unit 100cm instead of the 70 as indicated on the drawings.

**1** Lay out the pieces of wood on an even surface and secure the edges with small stakes.

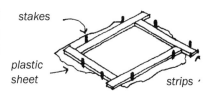

*stakes*
*plastic sheet*
*strips*

**2** Fill the area with a 1 to 2 mixture of cement and sand, making a layer of only ½ cm.

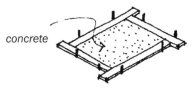

*concrete*

**3** Cover the first layer with a cement-soaked plastic net (using the weblike plastic bags you carry fruits or vegetables in). The web size must allow passage of the mixture. The net sticks out about 3cm on all sides to facilitate the joining of the panels. Put "U"-shaped wire on all corners.

*net*
*wire*

**4** On top of the first form, put more pieces of wood of equal thickness and fill up the center with another ½cm-thick layer of concrete mix. After 10 minutes, carefully remove the stakes and wooden strips.

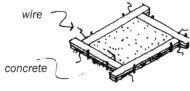

*wire*
*concrete*

Let dry for one week out of direct sun. During the first few days, keep the panel moist.

To make the other panels, use the same procedure, remembering to leave the required openings in panels (b), (c), (d) and (f).

With the side panel (a), cut and adjust the strip endings of the form to fit the shape of this panel.

## ASSEMBLING THE BASON

Start by placing an (a) panel flat on the ground, then the other panels are added, starting with panel (d). They are joined with the same concrete mix, after tying them together with the wires embedded in the panel corners.

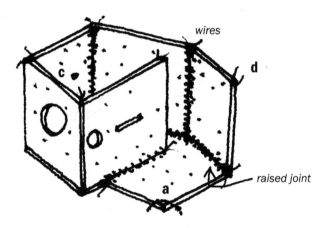

Fold the protruding edges of the plastic net and cover the joint with the concrete mix, leaving a slightly raised joining edge.

Note that panel (c) has the embedded pipe pointing towards the top and towards the bottom of the bason.

Close the bason by joining panel (a) on top and mortar the joints with concrete mix on the outside as well as the inside. Let the whole dry and harden for at least a week, and then put the bason in an upright position to reach and finish the remaining joints.

Instead of using channels to provide air to the waste mixture, use a handle made from ⅜" rebar to turn over the contents once a week, thus loosening up the compost and mixing in oxygen.

The handle is passed through the slot in panel (**d**) and pushed into the pipe ends of panel (**c**). In time, the handle will rust through, and you must insert another.

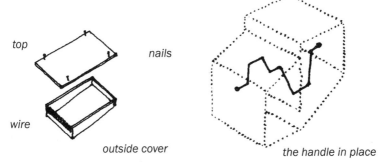

top

nails

wire

outside cover

the handle in place

The cover of the opening through which the finished compost is removed is made out of wood and should have the air entry slot protected with mosquito wire to keep insects out.

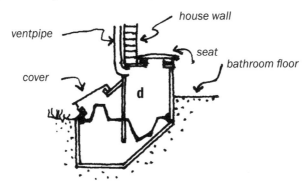

ventpipe

house wall

seat

bathroom floor

cover

d

The black-painted ventpipe is fixed to the bason at the opening in panel (**d**) using an elbow joint.

## BASON VARIETIES

The bason shown in the previous pages has dimensions suited for a small family. Units meant for larger families or for public facilities should have bigger volumes, simply by enlarging the lower part, like the one below with an additional 30cm to the height of the unit.

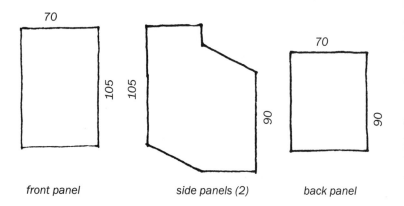

front panel                    side panels (2)                    back panel

Here, the interior panel, which divides the two chambers, should be 70 x 100 tall.

To make a bason, you do not need special skills, as the process is simple. When assembling the panels it may happen that the parts do not fit smoothly, in which case any excess edges can be snapped off with a pair of pliers; if there is a narrow gap, it can be filled with the same cement mix used for joining the panels.

## A RAISED SEAT

If the unit is placed in the basement or crawl space as part of the foundation (depending on soil condition), the top of the bason should be level with the floor. A cylinder made from plastic concrete is located on the top opening and is finished off with the usual wooden or plastic seat.

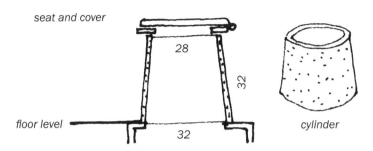

The cylinder is made with the same mix, using a plastic bucket as a form. The seat has to be fixed in such a way that insects cannot get inside.

## SEPARATING THE LIQUIDS

In humid climates, it is better to separate the urine from the other waste. This is done by adding a curved panel to the inside front of the cylinder. Using the same mix again, you form this panel in a half-funnel shape, with a hole at the bottom for attaching a hose.

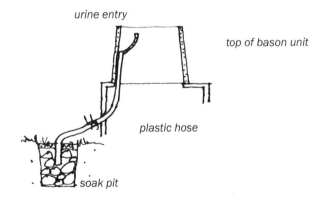

The hose passes through the inside of the bason, and at a lower point it passes through a side panel to the outside, where it empties into a soak pit.

## INSTALLING THE BASON

The bason box is located in such as way that the exterior wall is built on top of panel (**f**) and the adjoining panel (**d**).

The seat panel (**b**) must be 30 cm above the finished floor of the bathroom.

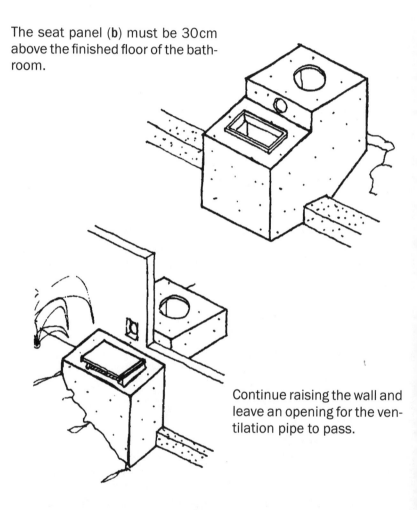

Continue raising the wall and leave an opening for the ventilation pipe to pass.

The wall foundations begin at both sides of the box.

To ventilate the bason, install a 100mm-diameter PVC pipe painted matte black where it is exposed to the sun.

The sun heats the tube and the interior heat rises, producing an air exhaust current outwards.

Finally, cover the opening of panel (f) (from which the compost is removed) with a wooden lid.

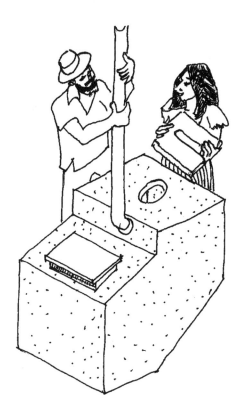

The edges of the lid overlap the opening to keep out rainwater.

Once the wall and floor finishings are applied, a normal toilet seat can be installed and adjusted to fit the opening.

## SAND FILTERS

A sand filter consists of a brick or concrete box filled with layers of sand and gravel. The water enters at one side and leaves at the opposite one. The sand has to be replaced from time to time whenever dirt has accumulated, in which case the water comes out discolored.

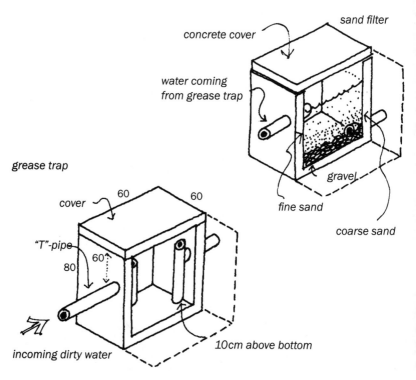

*isometric sections of grease trap and sand filter*

## GREASE TRAP

If you decide to use a sand filter to recycle the greywater (that is, water which comes from the sink, showers or laundry) a grease trap must be installed to separate the fatty substances from the wastewater.

Greywater contains impurities which should be removed; the grease trap and the filter are located in line. The insides should be water-proofed with mortar. The entry pipe is located directly above the water surface with an exit pipe made from a "T"-pipe section.

The trap has a concrete or wooden cover. Once in a while, the unit must be cleaned by removing the grease lumps which are floating on the water inside the trap.

## DWELLINGS WITHOUT SEWER CONNECTIONS

The drawing below shows a dwelling with an integrated water use system. Non-liquid waste coming from the kitchen and bathroom goes to a compost tank, the bason (**a**). Liquid waste goes first to the grease trap (**b**) and a sand filter (**c**), then is used to water the gardens. Rainwater is gathered from the roof and kept for drink-ing purposes in a storage tank (**d**), and when required it could be warmed in the solar water heater (**e**).

garden

Obviously more can be done. In very dry regions, you can recycle the wastewater for drinking, using a solar distiller.

# COBAN

To save piping materials in the construction of the bathroom and the kitchen, you can build them in such a way that a "service" wall is located between them. Moreover, if you filter the used water, install a grease trap and use a bason, then there is no need to have a septic tank.

This way, you can do without the municipal sewer network, which means that the city also saves on water distribution system expense by using less piping since the water demand will drop considerably.

This shared wall combination is called a "coban."

## DESIGN OF THE COMBINATIONS

The piping as well as the wiring are to be installed in an "H"-shaped wall that also incorporates the structure to support the watertank underneath the roof and above the ceiling.

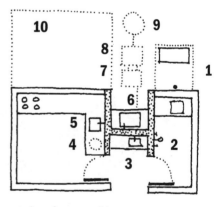

(1)   bason
(2)   shower
(3)   washbasin
(4)   water filter
(5)   sink
(6)   laundry
(7)   grease trap
(8)   sand filter
(9)   used water container
(10)  storage tank

*coban for a small house*

Rainwater goes straight to the tank. It can be pumped to the roof to a solar water-heating panel or tank. All piping is installed in an "H"-shaped wall where it is surface-mounted to make later repairs or changes easier.

By using larger spaces, the water circulation improves and the kitch-
en garbage can go directly into the bason via the outside (11):

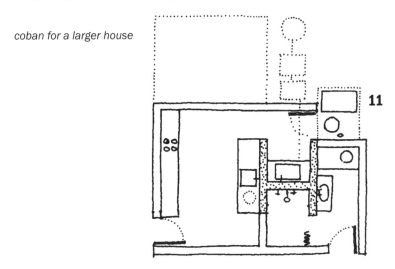

*coban for a larger house*

**11**

The kitchen is more spacious, while the shower is better located.

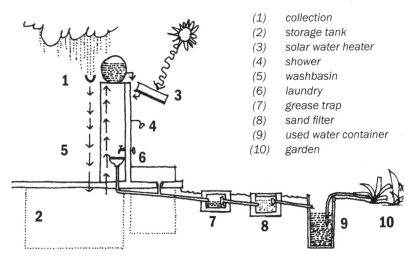

| | |
|---|---|
| (1) | collection |
| (2) | storage tank |
| (3) | solar water heater |
| (4) | shower |
| (5) | washbasin |
| (6) | laundry |
| (7) | grease trap |
| (8) | sand filter |
| (9) | used water container |
| (10) | garden |

The above section shows the water circulation, from rain clouds
to the vegetable gardens.

A perspective drawing of the coban components:

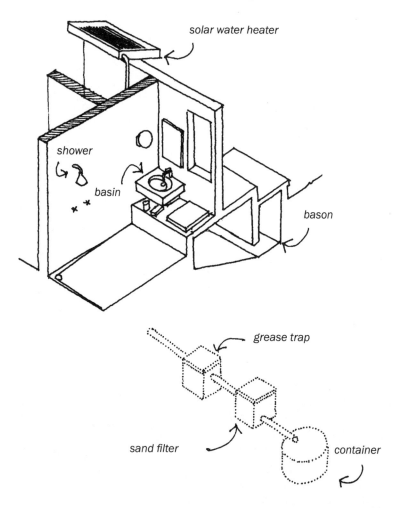

In those cases where flush toilets are going to be used, it's a good idea to separate the flush drain in such a way that the wastewater runs into the sewers. The other wastewater, that is, the greywater, may then pass through the filters and be recycled.

The foregoing perspective, now seen as a floorplan:

This could be the first phase of a building: to
start, make part of the "H"-wall.

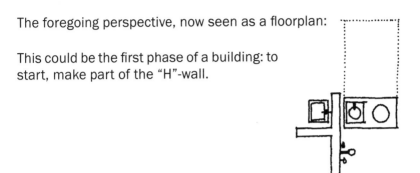

Some years later, when the house has been extended, add the
rest of the "H."

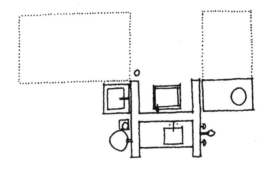

## RECYCLING WATER

In order to have piped water, the community has to invest heavily
in transportation, purification and distribution. Then, what happens
with that water? Typically almost half of it is used to remove human
waste from the house. This strongly contaminated water, or blackwater, is costly to purify in treatment plants. The remaining, water
or greywater, passes on to pollute streams and rivers.

Using a composting toilet, you immediately take care of blackwater
problem. By filtering the greywater, you are free to use it for watering the plants and trees, as the contaminating particles have been
removed. This water can also be used for washing and cleaning.

In choosing a location for a coban, you must consider:

**a** The area must be free of large rocks, so that you can excavate a place for the bason.

**b** The spot should be located on the high side of the lot, so that the rainwater runs towards the gardens, avoiding flooding of the foundations.

**c** The subsoil situation, whether there are rocks or water.

**d** The location of the remaining areas, with the bedroom facing east and the livingroom facing west.

**e** The location of the main access in relation to the street.

**f** The view, the wind directions, and the existing trees on the site.

**g** Site work spaces, the storage of building materials and access to the building area.

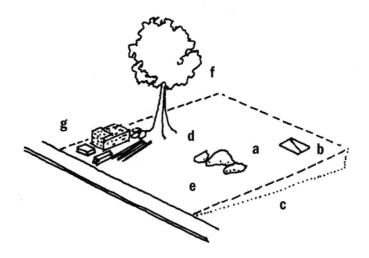

If possible, the house should be located at the high part of the terrain. When it's not, it's necessary to drain the ground around the house to prevent rainwater from running into the room.

The drainage is designed to assure that no puddles remain to turn the area into a place of mud. It also prevents the breeding of mosquitoes in standing water.

Drainage is effected with clay tiles or pipes, which run from the house to an area where the mud does not create a problem. The pipes are laid sloping slightly down to make the water run.

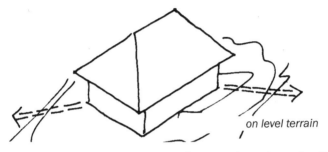

*on level terrain*

When a house is built on a sloping site, you do not want rainwater to accumulate at the upper foundation wall. The water must drain towards the side walls of the house and run down the slope.

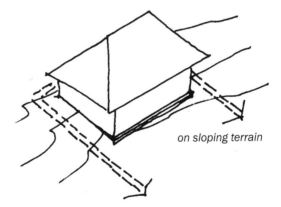

*on sloping terrain*

## LAYING PIPES

Most drain tiles have a 10 cm diameter and are laid inside a trench embedded in gravel. They are laid with a separation of 1 cm between them, and the open joint is covered with tarpaper.

Next, more gravel is put on top to cover the drain tiles. Then the trench is filled in with earth. This way the water can enter the tiles with ease and run away from the foundations.

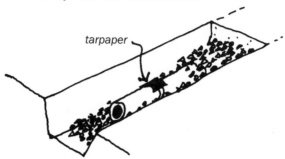

tarpaper

If tiles or pipes are not available, you can create drainage with gravel or crushed stones:

> Excavate the trenches and lay down a 15cm layer of gravel, stones, or even pieces of bricks or roof tiles. Level the trench with earth and compact well.

> On loose earth terrains, first lay down a sheet of tarpaper to prevent soil from below from clogging up the gravel.

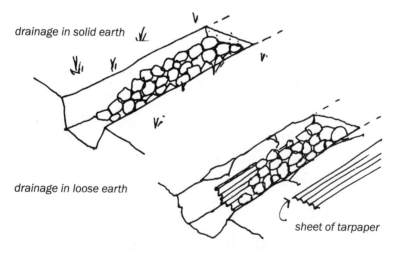

drainage in solid earth

drainage in loose earth

sheet of tarpaper

This method of making drains can also be used to let rainwater run underneath a road.

# MAPS & TABLES

10

# MATERIALS AND HEAT

Temperature inside a house is always different from the outside temperature.

Even without walls, the temperature underneath a roof will not be the same as the outside air, since the covered area is protected from sun and rain.

Comfort inside a house depends on the type of materials used in construction.

A house made with adobe walls and a straw roof is cooler during the summer and warmer in the winter than a house made with a concrete roof and walls.

A house having large windows has the opposite effect. Here the heat passes easily through the glass, making the house cold in the winter and hot in the summer.

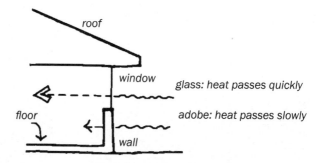

Some materials offer more resistance than others. It is obvious that the amount of material used is important, as the heat will pass more slowly through a thick wall, compared to a thin one made with the same materials.

## SOME MATERIALS AND THEIR RESISTANCES

The table on the opposite page shows a number of building materials and how their resistances to the passage of temperature vary.

We begin by assigning a factor of 1 to the resistance a sheet of glass 4mm thick offers. This value we shall use as a reference to compare with the values of the other materials.

To calculate these values for each material, we have assumed its most common thickness as a construction material.

For example, a 10cm-thick brick wall has ten times as much resistance as a glass curtain wall. A plaster finishing (3cm outside and 2cm inside) also has ten times as much resistance as glass.

Similarly, a brick wall finished with plaster has twenty times the resistance of glass.

|  | MATERIAL | VALUES |
|---|---|---|
| ROOFS | sheet metal | ½ |
|  | tarpaper | 4 |
|  | concrete | 4 |
|  | wood shingles | 24 |
|  | clay tiles | 28 |
| WALLS | glass: 4mm | 1 |
|  | wood: 25mm | 25 |
|  | plywood: 10mm | 12 |
|  | gypsum: 25mm | 40 |
|  | plaster: 50mm | 10 |
|  | earth: 200mm | 40 |
|  | brick: 100mm | 20 |
|  | stone: 200mm | 24 |
|  | pumice: 200mm | 42 |
|  | hollow cement block: 200mm | 32 |

# MEASUREMENTS

## UNITS OF LENGTH

| | | |
|---|---|---|
| km | 1 kilometer | 1000 meters |
| m | 1 meter | 100 centimeters |
| cm | 1 centimeter | 10 millimeters |
| inch | 1 inch | 2.54 cm |
| | ½ inch | 12.6 mm |
| | ¼ inch | 6.3 mm |

## UNITS OF SPACE

| | | |
|---|---|---|
| m² | 1 square meter | 1 meter x 1 meter |
| ha | 1 hectare | 100 meters x 100 meters |
| ha | 1 hectare | 10,000 square meters |

## UNITS OF WEIGHT

| | | |
|---|---|---|
| kg | 1 kilogram | 1,000 grams |
| tn | 1 metric ton | 1,000 kilograms |

Note: 1 liter of water has the weight of one kilogram.

## WOODEN BEAM DIMENSIONS

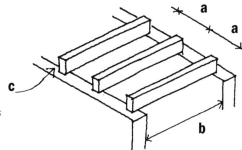

(a) separation in centimeters
(b) span in meters
(c) size in centimeters

| FLOOR JOISTS | | 30 | 40 | 60 | a |
|---|---|---|---|---|---|
| 5 x 15 | | 4.00 | 3.50 | 3.00 | |
| 5 x 20 | | 5.00 | 4.50 | 4.00 | |
| 5 x 25 | c | 6.00 | 5.50 | 4.50 | b |
| 8 x 15 | | 5.00 | 4.50 | 3.50 | |
| 8 x 20 | | 7.00 | 6.00 | 5.00 | |
| 8 x 30 | | 10.00 | 8.50 | 7.50 | |
| ROOF RAFTERS | | | | | a |
| 5 X 15 | | 5.00 | 4.50 | 3.00 | |
| 5 X 20 | | 7.00 | 6.00 | 5.00 | |
| 5 X 25 | c | 9.00 | 8.00 | 6.50 | b |
| 8 X 15 | | 6.50 | 5.50 | 4.50 | |
| 8 X 20 | | 8.50 | 8.00 | 6.50 | |
| 8 X 30 | | 11.00 | 10.50 | 9.50 | |

Suppose we want to lay a floor in a room of 5 meters width, that is, a span of 5 meters, using 8 x 20 beams, we must place them with a distance of 60cm between them. Using smaller beams, say of 5 x 20cm, this distance should be 30cm.

# MIXTURES

## MORTAR MIXTURES

| LIME | CEMENT | SAND* | SAND | APPLICATION |
|------|--------|-------|------|-------------|
| 0 | 1 | 2 | - | waterproofing |
| 4 | 1 | 12 | - | outside walls |
| 4 | 1 | 16 | - | inside walls |
| 2 | 1 | - | 6 | joining bricks |

* fine sand

Proportion by volume:
Lime 1, sand 5; which means, one bucket with lime and five with sand.

## CONCRETE MIXTURES

| CEMENT | SAND | SAND* | GRAVEL | APPLICATION |
|--------|------|-------|--------|-------------|
| 1 | 3 | - | 5 | shop floor |
| 1 | 2 | - | 4 | office floor |
| 1 | 2 | - | 3 | beams, columns |
| 4 | 5 | 1 | 10 | waterproofing |

## PLASTER MIXTURES

A good finish (being waterproof) to apply on adobe walls is:

| LIME | SAND | SAND* | GROUND BRICK | APPLICATION |
|------|------|-------|--------------|-------------|
| 1 | - | 6 | - | base layer |
| 1 | 5 | - | 1 | top layer |

Some other mixtures might show fine cracks over time.

| LIME | SAND * | SAND | APPLICATION |
|---|---|---|---|
| 2 | 5 | - | base layer |
| 1 | - | 5 | top layer |

Instead of lime, you can also use cement :

| CEMENT | SAND | APPLICATION |
|---|---|---|
| 1 | 10 | two layers |

| CEMENT | GYPSUM | APPLICATION |
|---|---|---|
| 1 | 20 | on walls and ceilings |

Besides these materials for mixtures, you can also use pumice, stone, straw, sawdust, shells, glass (bottles) and roofing tiles. You should always test bricks which are made with used ingredients in their mixtures for durability.

See chapter 5 for tests.

## WATERPROOFING ADDITIVES

| | |
|---|---|
| cactus juice | *cut up in pieces and and cover with water; after one week use the sticky liquid* |
| yellow soap | *dissolve in boiling water* |
| pumice stone | *boil and remove the foam* |
| used car oil | *collect at gas stations* |

 To improve the resistance of wood, you can paint it with a mix of leftover paints, adding some tar. This paint will be a dark brown color.

## WALL FINISHES FOR ADOBE

| | | |
|---|---|---|
| sand<br>lime<br>cement | 3<br>1<br>1 | easy to apply, but must be done periodically |
| two layers of tar; after each coat, cover with washed sand | | hard to apply, but will last a long time |
| application of hot linseed oil | | only in dry zones |

**1** Paint the wall using a wide sisal brush.

**2** On the dried wall, brush on a cement-water mix of one 50-kilo bag of cement mixed in 20 liters of water.

**3** Moisten the wall several times a day for 5 days.

**4** Apply a second cement-water mix; this time you can add pigments.

## HOW TO APPLY AN ADOBE FINISHING COAT

 For a rustic look on a wall made with concrete blocks, do the following:

**1** Apply a cement-paste mix with an added sealant to water-proof the block wall.

**2** Smooth out with the usual adobe mixture.

**3** When the surface has dried, smooth out the wall again, but now using a finer mixture.

**4** Keep the wall moist for three days.

The last mix is made with one 50kg bag of cement, two wheelbarrows of adobe, and 6 to 8 liters of waterproofing liquid.

# CLIMATE ZONES

Often we talk about a humid tropical climate to describe a jungle. Or we call desert a dry tropical climate. The temperate zone is either located in the mountains or outside the Tropics of Cancer or Capricorn.

However, we can often see all three climates in a mountainous region where the valleys are humid, higher up it will be dry, while at the top the climate is temperate.

To know in which zone we live, so that we can build our house in harmony with the natural world, we can look at the chart below:

|  | HUMID TROPICS △ |
|---|---|
| RAIN | almost all year |
| SKY | afternoon clouds |
| TEMPERATURE | hot during the day, less so at night |
| HUMIDITY | always quite high |
| VEGETATION | dense forest with many varieties of high trees and climbing vines |
| ANIMALS | jaguars, monkeys, colored birds, insects, anteaters, anacondas |
| SOIL | very wet earth, water table close to the surface |

| TEMPERATE ZONE ☐ | DRY TROPICS ○ |
|---|---|
| June to September, afternoons | sometimes during summer |
| darkens when it rains | almost always clear |
| very cold during winter, with frost at night | hot at day, cold at night |
| with rains | little humidity, very dry air |
| conifers, many types of fruit trees | cactus, a few small trees |
| mountain lions, eagles, snakes, insects | deer, scorpions, rattlers, emu, insects, armadillos |
| black earth with leaves, rocks in the higher parts | low water table, rocks, arid |

| | | | |
|---|---|---|---|
| CONSTRUCTION | WINDOWS | cross-ventilation | △ |
| | OPENINGS | remove heat and smoke | △ |
| | CEILING | traps warm air | ○ △ |
| | OVERHANG | shading walls and avoiding wetness | △ ☐ |
| | PÁTIO | to improve fresh air movement | ☐ |
| | CATCHER | to catch cooler air | ☐ |
| | ROOF | roof shape helps rainflow and inside air movement | △ ○ |
| | LOUVRES | to create shade and cool air | △ ☐ |
| | FIREPLACE | right location will help heating distribution | ○ |

| | | | |
|---|---|---|---|
| **NATURE** |  ORIENTATION | right layout of spaces inside | △ ○ □ |
| |  VEGETATION | to provide shade and evaporation | △ ○ □ |
| |  EARTH | to protect against extreme temperatures | ○ □ |
| |  SOIL | subsoil temperatures regulate comfort | □ |
| **MATERIALS** |  GLASS | to catch solar heat and distribute it inside | ○ |
| |  WALL | to slow down the heat transfer | ○ □ |
| |  POSTS | to facilitate ventilation in extreme heat | △ |
| |  CURVES | to raise wind velocity | △ ○ □ |
| |  FLOOR | to avoid humidity or cold rising | △ □ |

# ANGLES

## THE RELATIONSHIP BETWEEN DEGREES AND INCLINATIONS

Angles of solar heat collector inclination and roof slopes are given in degrees and through the proportion of the sides.

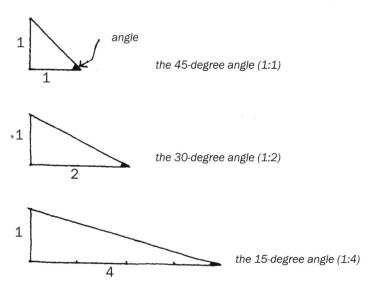

the 45-degree angle (1:1)

the 30-degree angle (1:2)

the 15-degree angle (1:4)

When deciding roof slopes you have to consider the climate, as well as the roofing materials.

Roof with:

| MATERIAL | ANGLE |
|---|---|
| grass fibers | between 45° and 60° |
| tiles | between 30° and 45° |
| shingles | between 15° and 30° |
| earth | less than 15° |
| concrete | less than 5° |

Usually in very humid, rainy areas made the slopes are steeper in order to improve water runoff.

## HOW TO CALCULATE ANGLES

You use a piece of paper with equal sides.

To get the proper angles, you can fold the paper in different ways:

*to get 45°*
*fold diagonally*

*for 60° make a two-thirds fold*

*for 30° make a one-third fold*

*for 15° fold a one-third fold in half*

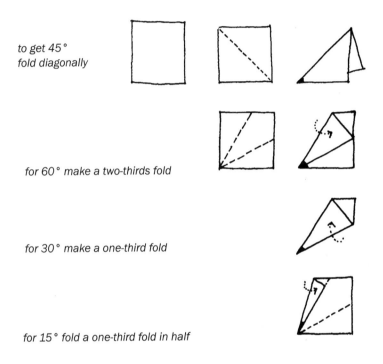

Another way to get 30° and 60° would be:

To get a 90° angle, draw a triangle with three sides in the proportion of 3, 4 and 5.

For example, the drawing below shows sides of 6, 8 and 10cm in order to get a 90° angle.

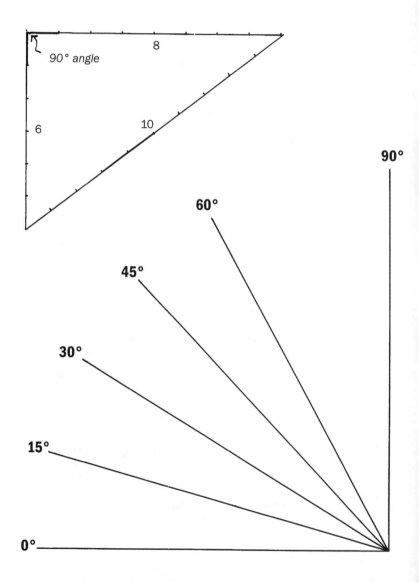

## PLANS OF TYPICAL HOUSES

The plans below all include a coban (kitchen/bathroom).

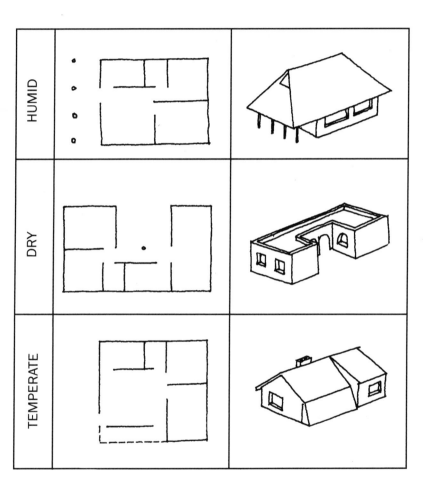

These plans are not final, the drawings only show some ideas. As we learned before, the final plan of a house depends on the size of the family, the slope of the site, the types of vegetation, and the positions of the sun.

## INCLINATIONS FOR SOLAR WATERHEATERS

To get the most out of a solar collector, it must be inclined towards the sun, depending on the local latitude. The map below shows the inclinations in degrees for the different regions of the world.

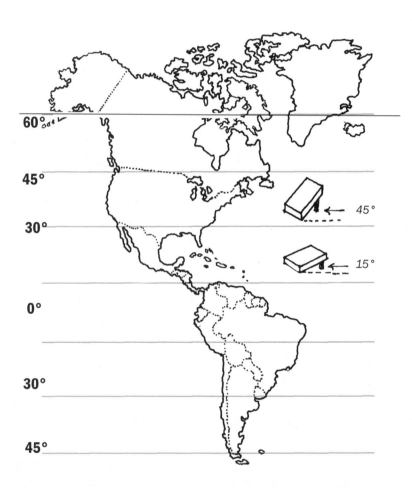

*Note: north of the equator, solar collectors must be inclined towards the south and vice versa.*

For example, in the countries far to the north of the equator, it would be necessary to incline the collector at 45 degrees.

# APPENDIX

11

# GLOSSARY

**Adobe:** Mixture of clay, sand and manure molded into sun-dried bricks. Sometimes cut straw or other vegetable fibers are added to make the bricks lighter.

**Balustrade:** Low brick or concrete wall, often with small openings, acting as a railing on terraces or balconies.

**Bason:** Waterless composting toilet which produces a rich garden fertilizer from human and organic kitchen waste.

**Cascaje:** Curved, thin concrete panel used for roofs or floor slabs.

**Coban:** Wall between bathroom and kitchen used to house water pipes.

**Column:** Vertical structural element supporting upper floor, slabs or roofs, made out of wood, bamboo, bricks, stones, concrete or steel.

**Eave:** Roof overhang which protects the walls below from heavy rains.

**Ferrocement:** Thin concrete panels, using chicken wire as reinforcment, used in many applications, such as roofs, walls, water tanks or even ship hulls.

**Forms:** Usually made from boards or plywood, acting as molds for concrete or rammed earth.

**Mezzanine:** An intermediate floor between main floors of a building with high ceilings.

**Ridge:** Uppermost part of a sloped roof.

**Shingle:** Rectangular, thin, tapered pieces of wood used to cover roofs or walls.

**Sill:** Bottom part of window or door frame.

**Sill plate:** Wooden board on top of a concrete or brick wall where the the roof rafters are attached.

**Tar:** Black petroleum-based substance, used to waterproof walls and floors.

**Tiles:** Roofing material usually made from baked clay, or metal and asphalt, mostly used for sheds or garages.

# BIBLIOGRAPHY

Accretion, Hilbertz, revista Hawaii Architect 6/82, USA

Arquitectura Autogobierno: Cuadernos de Material Didáctico, Vol. 2, México, DF.

Bamboo, Tool, Amsterdam, Netherlands

Bouwen in Indonesia, Gmelic, Uitgevery Stam. 1953, Haarlem, Netherlands

Cartilla de la vivienda, Colegio Nacional de Arquitectos, 1958, México, DF.

Desechos y Agua, Cornelio Hoogesteger, 1986, México, DF.

Ecotécnicas de la Vivienda: SEDUE. 1984. México, DF

Fiches Institute Tunisien de Technologie Apropriée, 1986, Tunísia.

Fiches Groupe de Recherce sur les Techniques Rurales, Paris, 1979, France.

Freedom to Build, Turner and Fichler, 1972, McMillan Co., New York, USA

Houses, How to Reduce Costs, Laurie Baker, Cosford, 1986, Trivandum, India

Indigenous Building and the Third World Development Workshop, Tehran, 1976, Iran

Inva-ram, Sjoerd Nienhuys, INVA, Tegucigalpa, Honduras, 1981

Manual on Hydraulic Ram, Watt, Intermediate Technology Publication, London, 1978, UK

Mejores Viviendas de Adobe, COBE, 1978, Lima, Peru

Manual de Construcción Rural, No. 2, Michmaker, Butters e Vallot, Gamma, Paris, 1979, France

Manual de Saneamiento, SSA, 1978, México, DF

Methane Digesters, Newsletter No. 3, New Alchemy Institute, MA., USA

Molino Tambo, Pascal Delcey, CEETEM, 1980, México, DF

Nuevas Técnicas de Construcción de Bambu, López, CIBAM, 1978 Bogotá, Colombia.

Oekologisches Bauen, Per Krusche, Umweltbundesamt, Bauverlag, 982, Berlin, Germany

Radical Technology, Boyle & Harper, Pantheon Books, 1974, USA.

Shelter, Shelter Publications, 1973, Bolinas, California, USA

Technical Research Bulletin, PWO, Papua Guinea, Vol 1

Ten Books on Architecture, Vitrivius, Dover Publications, New York, USA

The Ecol Operation, Alvaro Ortega et al, McGill University Press, 1972, Montreal, Canada

# INDEX

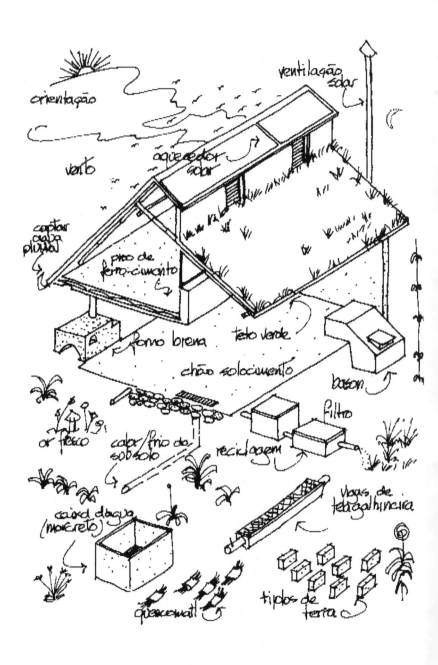

orientação

ventilação solar

verão

aquecedor solar

captar água pluvial

piso de ferro-cimento

teto verde

forno lenha

chão solocimento

bason

ar fresco

calor/frio do sobsolo

reciclagem

filtro

caixa d'água (morcreto)

vigas de tebagalhincira

quescowatl

tipos de terra

# TIBÁ WORKSHOPS

In Tupi, an indigenous language in Brazil, tibá means "a place where many people meet." TIBÁ is a center for bio-architecture and ecological building techniques in the Mata Atlantica (coastal jungle) of Brazil. Workshops are conducted in buildings surrounding a charming cobblestone square in the rainforest, with waterfalls, large ponds, orchards, and gardens. There are trails to explore, where one can observe the many birds and other animals of the jungle.

When TIBÁ started in 1987, its primary goal was to instruct people in the use of local materials, such as adobe or bamboo, combined with the use of passive heating, cooling and ventilation, in buildings. These days the use of natural materials has become rather well accepted, and TIBÁ has gone on to helping people change their mode of thinking: in brief, less logic and more intuition: workshops and volunteer programs geared to intuitive thinking and design, using the right side of the brain.

There are currently workshops on building with earth and bamboo, sustainable architecture, "permaculture," and more recently, classes in "agro-forestry" — gardens for food production, as well as utilization of fruits, roots, and medicinal herbs from the tropical forest.

*When a king dies, his people say:*
*"He did this; he did that..."*
*But when a great king dies, they say:*
*"We did everything ourselves."*
                              *–old Chinese saying*

For information on TIBÁ (Intuitive Technology & Bio-Architecture) and workshops by the author in Brazil, contact:

TIBÁ
Rua Inglés de Souza, 296
CEP 22460-110 Jardín Botánico
Rio de Janeiro - RJ - Brazil
Tel: (55-21) 2274-1762/Skype: tibarose
email: info@tibarose.com
Website: http://www.tibarose.com

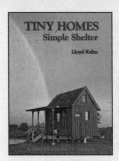

# Tiny Homes
## Simple Shelter
## by Lloyd Kahn

$28.95  9″ × 12″  224 pages
ISBN: 978-0-936070-52-0

*"Before McMansions, before the counterculture was granite and marble, there was Lloyd Kahn, champion of the hand-built house ... progenitor of the new do-it-yourself movement."* —The New York Times

**C**ome take a trip with us through the world of tiny houses. See firsthand the current trend in scaling back, reducing living expenses, and escaping bank mortgages or high rents.

There's a grassroots movement in building smaller homes these days. The real estate collapse, the economic downturn, and the growing scarcity of resources, have caused a sea change in thinking about shelter.

Here are some 150 builders who have created tiny homes (under 500 sq. ft.). Homes on land, homes on wheels, homes on the road, and homes on water, and homes in the trees. There are also studios, saunas, garden sheds, and greenhouses.

Here is a rich variety of small homemade shelters, with 1,300 photos, along with stories of people who have chosen to provide their own roofs overhead.

As you thumb through the pages, we hope you'll be as intrigued as we are with this new and growing trend in downsizing and self-sufficiency, and as excited as we are about the creativity and joy expressed in these little homes.

---

# Shelter
## Edited by Lloyd Kahn

$28.95
11″ × 14½″
176 pages
ISBN: 978-0-936070-11-7

**Over 250,000 copies sold**

**W**ith over 1,000 photographs, *Shelter* is a classic celebrating the imagination, resourcefulness, and exuberance of human habitat. First published in 1973, it is not only a record of the countercultural builders of the '60s, but also of buildings all over the world. It includes a history of shelter and the evolution of building types: tents, yurts, timber buildings, barns, small homes, domes, etc. There is a section on building materials, including heavy timber construction and stud framing, as well as stone, straw bale construction, adobe, plaster, and bamboo. There are interviews with builders and tips on recycled materials and wrecking. The spirit of the '60s counterculture is evident throughout the book, and the emphasis is on creating your own shelter (or space) with your own hands. A joyful, inspiring book.

*"How very fine it is to leaf through a 176-page book on architecture — and find no palaces, no pyramids or temples, no cathedrals, skyscrapers, Kremlins or Pentagons in sight ... instead, a book of homes, habitations for human beings in all their infinite variety."*

—Edward Abbey, *Natural History* magazine

---